History, on Proper Principles

HISTORY, ON PROPER PRINCIPLES

Essays in Honor of Forrest McDonald

edited by

Stephen M. Klugewicz and Lenore T. Ealy

Wilmington, Delaware

Library of Congress Cataloguing-in-Publication Data

History, on proper principles : essays in honor of Forrest McDonald /
Stephen M. Klugewicz [and] Lenore T. Ealy, editors.
    p. cm.
    Includes bibliographical references.
    ISBN 1-935191-68-3

    1. McDonald, Forrest. 2. Historians—United States. 3. Historiogra-
phy—United States—History—20th century. 4. United States—Historiography. I. Klugewicz, Stephen M. (Stephen Michael) II. Ealy, Lenore T.
III. McDonald, Forrest.

E175.5.M395H57 2010
907.2'02—dc22   2010006764

Published in the United States by:

ISI Books
Intercollegiate Studies Institute
3901 Centerville Road
Wilmington, Delaware 19807
www.isibooks.org

This volume is dedicated to the two people who inspired it,
whose standards of excellence in investigating, writing, and living America's story will
inspire generations of historians to come.

Forrest McDonald
and
Ellen Shapiro McDonald

Contents

Editors' Introduction

Forrest McDonald did not set out to be a historian. Had he been able to hit a curveball, he would likely have been a professional baseball player. "I believed, and believe to this day," McDonald wrote in 2004, "that as an outfielder I was of major league caliber."[1] Born in Orange, Texas, on January 7, 1927, McDonald decided upon graduation from high school to enter the University of Texas to play baseball. Soon realizing that he was a "good-field, no hit" type of player, McDonald gave up on baseball despite his love of the game, and in so doing displayed perhaps his most defining personal and professional trait—a clear-headed willingness to see things as they are, when looking at himself, at others, or at facts.

When McDonald returned to the University of Texas after a brief stint in the navy at the end of World War II, he thought his powers of clear-headed observation and his talent for writing were the right combination for a career as a novelist, so he enrolled as an English major. It was his encounter with a scholarly conflict between two of his history teachers that convinced him to pursue the field of history instead. "If learned scholars could disagree about as fundamental a subject as the formation of the United States Constitution," McDonald recalls thinking at the time, "the field of American history must be absolutely wide open."[2]

The scholarly disagreement that McDonald witnessed as an undergraduate centered on the influential thesis of Charles A. Beard. In his 1913 work, *An Economic Interpretation of the Constitution of the United States,* Beard had argued that the Constitution was written by wealthy landowners with a view toward securing their property against their less affluent countrymen. Beard dismissed the role of ideology in the founding and in history in general as the product of economic interest. Beard's thesis was both trendsetting and trendy, in that it appealed to and fueled the Progressive school of thought—with its emphasis on hidden motivations and conspiracies—that was on the ascendant in academia and throughout American society at the time.

As a graduate student, McDonald boldly decided to test the Beard thesis, a decision that led him to conduct research in every major historical archive on the East Coast, from Georgia to New Hampshire, over a seven-month period in 1951. Living on a meager budget and out of his automobile, McDonald spent every possible minute taking notes "of anything I could find pertaining to the political, economic, social, constitutional, and legal developments, state by state, from the Revolution to 1790."[3] By the end of 1951, he had compiled five thousand pages of notes that would provide the material for the books and articles he would write over the next five decades.

In 1958, the University of Chicago Press published *We the People: The Economic Origins of the Constitution,* the book that grew out of McDonald's graduate research. The heart of the book was a series of economic biographies of the delegates to the Philadelphia Convention of 1787–88 and of the delegates to the state ratifying conventions. McDonald shows that voting in these conventions did not reflect, as Beard had alleged, a divide between the wealthy (holders of public securities and owners of vast tracts of land) and the less well-off (debtors and small farmers). The case was much more complicated than that. "Some delegates, a dozen at the outside," McDonald concludes, "clearly acted according to the dictates of their personal economic interests, and about as many more to their philosophical convictions, even when these conflicted with their economic interests. But the conduct of most of the delegates, while partly a reflection of one or both of these personal considerations, was to a much greater extent a reflection of the interests and outlooks of the states and local areas they represented."[4]

McDonald's demolition of the Beard thesis led some observers to conclude that he had unjustifiably downplayed, if not dismissed, economic motives in the actions of men. This was far from the case, however. What McDonald rejected was Beard's reliance on economic motivations as the exclusive impulse in human action. "The very idea of economic man," McDonald explains, "is in truth simpleminded. It fails to take into account the complicated motivations that impel human beings to do what they do." Among these McDonald cites "the love of power" and patriotism, either of which "can override selfish considerations of economic gain."[5]

For McDonald, Beard's mistake lay not only in a faulty reductionist view of man but also in a faulty historical methodology. Beard had begun with a single, overarching thesis and then searched for facts that conformed to it. In *We the People,* McDonald warns that "no single system of interpretation can explain all historical phenomena; it is even unlikely that that a single system can adequately explain all aspects of a single historical event."[6] McDonald equates those historians—he means Beard and the Progressives—who look for a single, hidden explanation for a complex historical event with medieval alchemists. Such scholars failed to do the meticulous research necessary to draw conclusions the proper way—that is, from the evidence. In *We the People,* McDonald urged his peers to get their hands dirty by doing research in dusty state archives, where the records of the past held the only reliable evidence by which to draw a reliable historical interpretation. Ensuring that his students knew how to uncover and engage first-hand with the records of the past would become one of the hallmarks of his teaching career.

McDonald's contribution to American historiography has been great by any measure.[7] There is no doubt that his refutation of Charles Beard's Marxian interpretation of the founding and McDonald's subsequent writings on the Constitution—including *E Pluribus Unum: The Formation of the American Republic* (1965) and *Novus Ordo Seclorum: The Intellectual Origins of the Constitution* (1985)—have changed the nature of the debate among historians and better informed the educated public about the origins and workings of American constitutional government. His biography of Alexander Hamilton (1979) was groundbreaking, presenting an interpretation of this important founder that remains the standard to this day, despite the appearance of several subsequent biographies by others. His studies of the presidencies of George Washington (1974) and Thomas Jefferson (1976) and his book-length treatment of the presidency itself, *The American Presidency* (1994), are lasting contributions to the literature. His work on the Celtic Thesis, undertaken during the 1970s with his colleague Grady McWhiney, called into question the long-standing Frontier Thesis and caused historians to reexamine the idea of cultural persistence.[8] *States' Rights and the Union: Imperium in Imperio, 1776–1876,* published in 2000, remains the only full-length treatment of the history of states' rights, and as such fills an important gap in American historiography.

As an interpreter of American constitutional government, McDonald has achieved a national reputation among historians, statesmen, and the literary public that began with the publication of *We the People* in 1958. Respected historians David M. Potter and C. Vann Woodward praised *We the People* in the pages of the *Saturday Review* and the *New York Times,* and shortly after the book's publication McDonald appeared on NBC's *Continental Classroom* television show.[9] He delivered dozens of talks across the country during the bicentennial celebration of the Constitution, and in the 1980s *Novus Ordo Seclorum* was a Pulitzer Prize finalist. In 1987, the National Endowment for the Humanities (NEH) called upon McDonald to serve as the sixteenth Thomas Jefferson Lecturer in the Humanities. McDonald has met privately with at least three American presidents,[10] and has provided congressional testimony in two of the most significant episodes in modern history: the 1987 Robert Bork Supreme Court nomination hearings in the U.S. Senate and the impeachment proceedings held by the Judiciary Committee of the U.S. House of Representatives against President Bill Clinton in 1998, where he testified on the background and history of impeachment. During the presidency of George W. Bush, Deputy White House Chief of Staff Karl Rove invited McDonald to the White House on three occasions—to give a lecture on the presidency to some twenty-five senior White House staffers, again for dinner, and on the third occasion to talk history with the president as part of a small group of eminent historians.[11]

Despite the attention his work has received, McDonald has never been willing to compromise his intellectual integrity, as other historians routinely do, in return for plaudits or pecuniary rewards. The NEH honor included a $10,000 prize check, which McDonald, true to form, discreetly declined, since he believed that the very existence of the NEH offended constitutional principles. He did give the talk, however, on "The Intellectual World of the Founding Fathers." In 1991, during the bicentennial celebrations of the Bill of Rights, McDonald delivered a talk in Washington, D.C., titled "The Bill of Rights: Unnecessary and Pernicious," which reflected his view—held also by his hero Hamilton—that an enumerated list of rights actually works to restrict liberty. McDonald rightly predicted that he would not be invited again to give a talk on the sacred document.

Perhaps McDonald's most endearing moment of public honesty came in 1994, when he was Brian Lamb's guest on C-SPAN's *Booknotes* program to discuss *The American Presidency.* Lamb, seeking some insight into the historian's craft, asked, "If we could see you in your environment writing this book, what would we see?" McDonald replied, with a gleam in his eye quite familiar to those who know him, "You'd see me writing in the nude most of the time."

Those who know McDonald and his wife, Ellen Shapiro McDonald, speak fondly of the couple's eccentricities. The McDonalds detest having machinery in their home. They have resisted over the years, with varying degrees of success, among other modern conveniences: a microwave; a washing machine and dryer (Ellen washes the laundry with a washboard in the bathtub); a CD player (the first they owned came with a truck they bought); and, most successfully, a computer (McDonald writes not only sans clothing but also in longhand on legal yellow legal paper, and Ellen converts these drafts into printed manuscripts by way of an electric typewriter).

McDonald met Ellen while teaching summer school at Columbia University in the early '60s. He reports that he fell in love with "truly the best student I have ever had." Ellen would become his second wife, and professional partner. Over the years, many a student first sitting in a lecture course given by McDonald would spend a couple of days wondering who the woman was who would correct McDonald's slips and errors mid-sentence. Those who were fortunate enough to take the graduate-level research and writing course with the McDonalds endured and enjoyed rigorous training as Forrest sharpened their documentary and analytical skills and Ellen honed their writing with steely resolve. Since 1962, the couple has worked seamlessly as a team on every article, speech, and book, although Ellen has rarely consented to be formally credited for her efforts.[12] When McDonald accepted a job at the University of Alabama in 1976, he and Ellen bought a small farm in Coker, Alabama, some fifteen minutes from the main campus in Tuscaloosa, where the couple live and work to this day in splendid isolation.

Great scholars, like all great men, usually defy simple categorization. In McDonald's case, he would come to study some of American history's greatest men with an intensity that made him more intimate with these past statesmen than with most of his contemporaries. Examining McDonald's evaluations of these men and their careers may be the best way to shed light on McDonald's own character and career.

While on the faculty at Wayne State University, where he taught from 1967 to 1974, McDonald authored two entries in the University Press of Kansas's series on the presidency, *The Presidency of George Washington* and *The Presidency of Thomas Jefferson*. The nation's first president would become a subject of great interest to McDonald, and the nation's third president would become one of his favorite whipping boys.[13] It would be Alexander Hamilton, however, whom McDonald most came to admire among the founding generation. McDonald's work on these three great men deserves some commentary.

McDonald's unique contribution to the literature on Washington was to get at the very essence of the man, who was generally viewed by contemporaries and historians alike as distant, aloof, and unknowable at his core—a "marble man." McDonald, to the contrary, sees the great Virginian as very human in many respects; for example, he possessed a strong ambition and a violent temper. In explaining Washington's nearly flawless public persona, McDonald points to the early-eighteenth-century play *Cato,* by Joseph Addison, which depicts the life of the eponymous republican hero of the Roman Empire. Noting that General Washington staged the play numerous times for his troops during the Revolutionary War, McDonald suggests that Washington consciously decided to adopt as his own the persona of Cato. McDonald posits that the public Washington "was self-consciously playing a role" most of his life. In the eighteenth century, "one picked a role, like a part in a play, and contrived to act it unfailingly, ever to be in character. If one chose a character with which one was comfortable and if one played it long enough and consistently enough, by little and little it became a 'second nature' that in practice superseded the first. One became what one pretended to be."[14] Historians across the political spectrum—Garry Wills and Joseph J. Ellis among them—have echoed McDonald's characterization of Washington.[15]

While McDonald clearly admires Washington as one of the "giants" of the period, he has been highly critical of Thomas Jefferson, both as a man and as a statesman. McDonald views Jefferson as both a hypocrite (the man who praised those who labored in the earth "had never labored in the earth himself, having had slaves to do it for him") and as a "many-faceted man who was given to extreme and sometimes crackpot utterances."[16] Worse, Jefferson was a starry-eyed idealist. He was "backward-looking, determined to resist the emergence of the modern world." He and his followers were "reactionaries, swimming against the tide of history, for the world aborning was the depersonalized world of money, machines, cities, and big government."[17] McDonald deems Jefferson's second term as president a "shipwreck" and a "calamity," particularly because of the president's tyrannical enforcement of the disastrous Non-Importation Act of 1807, which made full use of the president's power as commander-in-chief to keep American commercial ships off the high seas and thus the United States out of war with France and England.[18]

If his antipathy toward Jefferson, the supposed champion of individual liberty, has surprised many of McDonald's conservative readers, his admiration for Jefferson's nemesis, Alexander Hamilton, has raised even more eyebrows. American proponents of limited government have often cast Hamilton as the godfather of big government. It was Hamilton, after all, who spoke in favor of a life term for the nation's new chief executive at the Constitutional Convention, who masterminded the creation of the First Bank of the United States, and who championed the public debt, paper money, protective tariffs, and publicly financed internal improvements. Modern liberals have been no warmer to Hamilton, seeing him, in McDonald's words, "as a champion of plutocracy" who was in large part responsible for creating a modern American society "composed of grubby, materialistic, self-seeking, acquisitive individualists."[19]

Alexander Hamilton: A Biography, penned in the 1970s, testifies to McDonald's determination to let the records of the past speak to the present. McDonald introduces a new paradigm by which to make sense of the momentous struggle in the early republic between Hamilton and Jefferson. McDonald's history has less to do with our modern political alignments and more to do with the circumstances that shaped those of the eighteenth century. To McDonald, Hamilton was the great egalitarian, the midwife of a new economic system that threatened to destroy the privilege and wealth of the old, landed aristocracy embodied by Jefferson.

McDonald describes how Hamilton's own personal history influenced his vision for America. Born in the West Indies as a bastard child, he worked himself out of poverty by means of his keen intellect and unrelenting hard work. As secretary of the treasury under Washington, he sought to create opportunity for all like himself who had talent and gumption. "Hamilton's audacious mission in life," McDonald writes, "was to remake American society in accordance with his own values. . . . To transform the established order, to make society more fluid and open to merit, to make industry both rewarding and necessary, all that was needed to be done was to monetize the whole—to rig the rules of the game so that money would become the universal measure of all things." Money, in Hamilton's view, was the great equalizer. "For money is oblivious to class, status, color, and inherited social position; money is the ultimate, neutral, impersonal arbiter."[20]

Though McDonald himself detests modern big government, he shares Hamilton's view that a government bigger—or at least stronger—than that created by the Articles of Confederation was a necessity for the nascent American nation, particularly through the first quarter of the nineteenth century.[21] McDonald shares with Hamilton the belief that by 1787 the Articles had proved to be a failure, yielding a central government far too weak to settle disputes between and among states. As a result, the Union was in peril a mere decade after American independence. In essays six through nine of *The Federalist Papers*, Hamilton painted a dire picture for his readers, contending that since the end of the Revolutionary War the states had engaged in petty bickering that retarded the economic and political development of the country and reduced "the national dignity and credit" to a "point of extreme depression." Anti-Federalist reassurances that a loose confederation would guarantee peace among the states better than would a federal system with a strengthened central government was a "deceitful dream of a golden age." Here is Hamilton the hard-headed realist, the type of historical figure that McDonald admires.[22]

If the Anti-Federalists and their intellectual successors, the Jeffersonians, had had their way, McDonald believes that the United States would likely have devolved ultimately into "a collection of banana republics." Hamilton's achievement was to create stability and credibility for the young nation through the strategic use of the inherent and "necessary and proper" powers of the national government. As a result, the conditions for the emergence of a market economy were created in America, ensuring "that the United States would become the richest, most powerful, freest country the world has ever known."[23] McDonald clearly sees Hamilton's achievement in light of its historical significance, not as a justification for modern policies of centralization. When pressed by modern critics of Hamilton who believe he paved the way for today's leviathan state, McDonald defends Hamilton's firm commitment to limited government: "He was the champion of liberty, of freedom under law, as opposed to those—the Jeffersonians—who defended privilege and authoritarianism."[24]

McDonald's affinity for Hamilton crosses the boundaries of mere affection into a deeper psychological identification. On at least one occasion in the classroom, McDonald stated—apparently at least half-seriously—that he himself was the reincarnation of Alexander Hamilton. McDonald seems to picture himself as bound together with Hamilton in eternal partnership. He concluded another classroom lecture by stating, "And that's why Jimmy Madison will be in Hell and Alex Hamilton and I will be in Heaven."[25]

McDonald's identification with Hamilton can be illustrated in terms of four traits the two men share:

(1) *A powerful intellect:* Like Hamilton, McDonald easily grasps the complexities of economics and financial matters. This ability, McDonald believes, is evidence of "superior intellect." In his preface to *Hamilton,* McDonald explains that Hamilton had previously been misunderstood even by his biographers because so few historians who wrote about him understood or liked economics: "It is as if study of Napoleon be done by people with no knowledge of military affairs, or of Bach by people with no interest in music."[26]

(2) *A strong ambition:* Hamilton began life as a bastard child in the West Indies. By means of his intellectual abilities and a tireless work ethic, he came to the attention of two businessmen who sent him to America for an education. From there, Hamilton made himself into one of the best lawyers in America, a distinguished officer in the Continental Army, and the right-hand man of the first United States president. McDonald's beginnings were not quite as humble as Hamilton's, but he too succeeded spectacularly in his chosen career path, becoming an accomplished and nationally known historian through his own self-described "boundless self-confidence and inexhaustible energy."[27] McDonald also benefited from the attention of mentors, such as Eugene Barker and Fulmer Mood at the University of Texas, who encouraged a talented and rather brash young man in his ambitions.

(3) *Physical courage:* Hamilton served in the Continental Army during the Revolution and led charges at Monmouth and Yorktown. During his lifetime, he challenged many men to duels, ultimately dying in one such contest, felled by a bullet from the pistol of Aaron Burr. McDonald has often ridiculed the likes of John Adams, Jefferson, and Madison for their lack of physical courage. As governor of Virginia, for example, Jefferson fled when the British invaded the commonwealth, and during his lectures McDonald loved to recount the story of the diminutive President Madison attempting to mount his horse at the approach of the British during the War of 1812, only to be urged by his wife, Dolly, to get down before he hurt himself.[28] McDonald, who was a navy volunteer during World War II, who had no fear of incoming fastballs in his years as an outfielder, and who has exerted much physical labor farming over the years, has little patience for such unmanly behavior.

(4) *Public virtue.* This is to be distinguished from private virtue. Hamilton certainly failed spectacularly in the latter, but McDonald, like the founders themselves, seems to put a higher emphasis on the importance of rectitude in public affairs than in private matters. As secretary of the treasury under Washington, Hamilton infamously became involved in an extramarital affair

with one Maria Reynolds, whose husband then blackmailed Hamilton. If Hamilton did not make secret payments, James Reynolds threatened to reveal all. Despite Hamilton's quiet cooperation with the blackmail scheme, rumors of the affair and the blackmail payments leaked out, and soon his Jeffersonian enemies were accusing Hamilton not only of the affair but of using public funds to pay the blackmail. It was here that Hamilton risked his own marriage and sacrificed his personal reputation—called "character" in the eighteenth century—so as not to bring discredit upon his public character, the government, and indeed his country. Hamilton confessed the affair and laid open his private financial accounts to prove that not one penny of public funds had been used to pay the blackmail. McDonald likewise puts a great emphasis on his professional integrity. Early on in his career, when composing a history of the Wisconsin utility companies, he found that the people he interviewed for the project—who would also be subjects in the manuscript—tried to sway his opinion of them for history by buying him drinks or meals. McDonald soon realized why they were treating him so nicely: "They saw my coming as the Day of Judgment, and thus to them my memory was the memory of History; it was the memory of mankind; perhaps it was even the memory of God. This is what everyone, in his own way, sought to buy." From the outset of his career, however, McDonald refused to compromise his principles of scholarship. "I am both fallible and corrupt," McDonald writes in recalling the experience, "but my memory, though fallible, is incorruptible."[29]

McDonald's rigorous allegiance to what he conceives as the proper principles of historical research has indeed been one of his most outstanding attributes. He never cuts corners. After completing the first five chapters of his biography of Alexander Hamilton, McDonald decided that his approach was all wrong and that he would have to start over. Most scholars, having already invested so much work in a project, would have forged ahead and settled for an imperfect product. At worst, they would have reworked what was already written. McDonald, however, threw the manuscript into the fireplace, and he and Ellen watched it burn.[30]

Once settled at the University of Alabama, McDonald penned the work that many consider to be his magnum opus, *Novus Ordo Seclorum: The Intellectual Origins of the Constitution,* published in 1985. The book was the last in McDonald's planned trilogy on the founding that began with *We the People* and *E Pluribus Unum.* Up to that time, McDonald had been wary of writing intellectual history per se, as it "tended to be the history of intellectuals, with but little relationship to real people."[31] In *Novus,* McDonald avoids this pitfall of intellectual history, while also avoiding the Beardian trap of seeking a single, overarching perspective or worldview by which to explain complex events.[32]

Novus is a strange intellectual history in some ways, for McDonald at many points downplays the role of ideas—or at least ideology—in tracing the history of the Revolution and the framing of the Constitution. Much of the book deals with the economic and power interests of the founders. "In the whole corpus of the ideological literature," McDonald complains in the preface to *Novus,* "there is scarcely a mention of what used to be called social, political, and economic 'reality,' or of such practical men of affairs as George Washington and Robert Morris, without whom, arguably, there might have been no founding."[33] McDonald's "intellectual" history of the founding, therefore, includes chapters titled "Systems of Political Economy," "The Lessons of Experience: 1776–1787," and "The Framers: Principles and Interests."

In declaring independence and in forming a government, McDonald argues in *Novus,* the founders adhered to no single intellectual theory or political theorist. Rather, they spoke a common political and legal language derived from the authors they all had read: Polybius, Cato, John Locke, William Blackstone, Montesquieu, John Trenchard, Thomas Gordon, James Harrington, David Hume. They drew selectively on these thinkers whenever convenient to buttress their arguments. Indeed, the framers of the Constitution, McDonald demonstrates, never let established political theory or intellectual consistency stand in the way of a good, practical solution to a thorny political/constitutional problem. An example is Hamilton's articulation of the idea of "divided sovereignty" to justify the Constitution's division of power between the state and the federal governments, each being supreme in its own sphere. Such an arrangement contradicted the great English legal scholar Blackstone's admonition that supreme lawmaking authority can rest only in one place.[34] McDonald sees the framers as ultimately practical men—that is, men like himself—who trusted historical experience above speculative theory.[35]

McDonald tried his hand at his brand of intellectual history again in 1994 with the publication of *The American Presidency: An Intellectual History.* McDonald was spurred to write the book because of his work on the presidencies of Washington and Jefferson and because of his conversations with Presidents Reagan and Nixon. "Though the caliber of people who have served as chief executive," McDonald concludes in the work's final chapter, "has declined erratically but persistently from the day George Washington left office, the presidency has been responsible for less harm and more good, in the nation and in the world, than perhaps any other secular institution in history."[36]

When McDonald realized that no one had ever written a history of states' rights, despite the significance of the subject in United States history, he wrote *States' Rights and the Union: Imperium in Imperio, 1776–1876* (2000). McDonald concludes that the doctrine of states' rights is historically justifiable, and he notes that it was often articulated by northerners despite its exclusive association with southerners in the contemporary mind.

In his 2004 memoir, *Recovering the Past,* McDonald reflects not merely on his own life and career as an historian but also comments on the practice of the profession itself. McDonald laments the fact that too many historians try to use the past to further their own "political or ideological agenda[s]."[37] The phenomenon of using the past to justify the present, called "presentism," is a serious transgression in McDonald's view, for it impedes the historian's ability to see the past objectively. "The best historians," McDonald writes, "are those who enjoy searching the record of the past for its own sake." Such an approach is "the purest motivation possible" for the study of history, and mitigates the danger of misreading history for one's own purposes: "Though it does not guarantee accuracy, it is proof against conscious or unconscious warping of the truth."[38]

McDonald does believe that interpretation is a legitimate aspect of the historian's task. In fact, he rejects the notion that the job of the historian simply is to relate history as it happened. Such an approach produces long, tedious, and unmemorable accounts of the past. "History is a mode of thinking that wrenches the past out of context and sequence," McDonald counters, "out of the way it really happened, and reorders it in an artificial way that facilitates understanding and remembering."[39] Imagination is a key skill of the historian.

Imagination, however, is best facilitated by immersing oneself in the historical sources themselves. McDonald believes that the historian has to be on guard against being influenced by what previous historians have written. Modern history departments are obsessed with ensuring that their faculty and graduate students master the "literature"—that is, with ensuring that they know what other scholars have said about a historical topic. A corollary of this obsession is the tendency for historians today to identify with a certain school of thought before they have even done research into the primary sources. From the beginning of his career as a historian, McDonald was fortunate to be spared, by mere chance of time and place, immersion into the intellectually confining paradigm of warring schools of thought: "I emerged from graduate school entirely ignorant of what had been happening in the profession over the course of the preceding three or four decades."[40] McDonald has consistently avoided being overly concerned with what other scholars have said on a subject. When contemplating writing a book or essay on a topic for the first time, his modus operandi is to ask Ellen to find the best three or four secondary works on the subject, to review them briefly, and to report to him on their central arguments. In this way, McDonald obtains a general idea of what has been written on a topic while preserving a clean-slate approach to his examination of the past.[41]

McDonald has thus stood as conspicuously apart in the world of academic politics as he has in the world of scholarship. In an era when academia is largely a tribal institution, with scholars dividing themselves into ideological camps and favoring their own philosophical allies, whether fellow professors or graduate students, McDonald has been that rare academic who has judged graduate students on their intellectual merits, not on their conformity to his own opinions. He has generously read manuscripts for junior scholars and welcomed friendships with colleagues from all political perspectives. The sole criterion he uses when judging the work of those in his field is intellectual prowess.

In the end, Forrest McDonald seems to be a bundle of contradictions: a southern agrarian who dislikes Thomas Jefferson; a proponent of states' rights who believes that the centralizing Federalist Party had the better policies; an advocate of limited government who adores Alexander Hamilton. The devotee of no particular school of historical thought, his work is underappreciated by those scholars who are obsessed with looking at history through various interpretative schools. The impossibility of neatly summarizing McDonald's thinking hints at his greatness.

By working from the particular to the general, McDonald has shown how simple explanations for the matrix of human actions, themselves the product of many and sometimes conflicting motivations, are always flawed or incomplete. He has demonstrated that the historian above all must be a pragmatist who looks at the reality of the past as it was, who gets his hands dirty by putting in long hours of research, who makes sense of vast quantities of data, and who then communicates what he has found in an understandable and interesting way to the general reader.

"History, on proper principles," McDonald told his audience in his address to the last class he taught as a regular faculty member at the University of Alabama, can help us "abandon our fragmented, problem-solving approach to knowledge and take up a holistic view of human affairs."[42] History, on proper principles, is that study which helps each of us both escape the provincialism of the present and receive the present with an attitude of gratitude and joy. It is with this attitude that Forrest McDonald has embraced life and love and learning, and it has been infectious. His legacy will surely be a dual one: his uncompromising method of "doing history" bequeathed to all who have benefited from his tutelage will stand alongside his magnificent oeuvre itself in inspiring future generations of historians.

The essays in this book were written by scholars who benefitted directly from the guidance of Forrest and Ellen McDonald. Some are former students, others are former peers.

C. Bradley Thompson argues that the American Revolution was at its heart a constitutional conflict. Eighteenth-century Americans, in order to oppose what they viewed as the tyranny of the British government, developed a radically new concept of constitutionalism. "For more than two centuries," Thompson concludes, "their heirs have continued to explore the theory and practice of constitutional government that emerged from the revolutionary crisis in eighteenth-century Anglo-American constitutional history."

McDonald believes that the American Revolution was at heart a conservative event, in that it was a step taken by the colonists to preserve their traditional rights as Englishmen. These rights were rooted in the common-law tradition. F. Thornton Miller examines this tradition in America. He finds that "in the aftermath of the American Revolution, the English common-law tradition was preserved in America primarily by southern jurists and lawyers, who found in it much to admire, particularly its assumption of the existence of unwritten rights and principles and its localism."

Steven D. Ealy challenges readers to reconsider the standing given to *The Federalist Papers* by historians, political scientists, and legal scholars as the sole authoritative interpretation of the American Constitution. Ealy suggests that we should see the *The Federalist* "not as the definitive interpretation of the Constitution, but . . . as one of the initial efforts at liquidating the meaning of the Constitution." Ealy thereby implicitly challenges the idea of original intent, championed by many conservatives, which holds that the founders' understanding should be given preeminence when deciphering the meaning of the document. Ealy's provocative and iconoclastic essay is just the kind of piece in which McDonald delights.

Melanie Randolph Miller writes on Gouverneur Morris, a high Federalist and one of McDonald's favorite founders, and his role as a speculator in the American war debt to France. Morris was accused both during his lifetime and by modern historians of pushing federal fiscal policies that would have benefited him personally, but Miller suggests that Morris's proposals were "reasonable and pragmatic" and "might well have done the United States greater credit (and France more good) than the route taken by Alexander Hamilton and Jefferson, in their respective posts as secretary of the treasury and secretary of state in Washington's first cabinet." In its examination of the interplay of fiscal policy, government power, and personal interest, Miller's essay reflects the spirit of *We the People*.

J. M. Bumsted examines the tour of Canada taken in 1803–4 by Thomas Douglas, the fifth Earl of Selkirk. The Scotsman had come to the conclusion that Canada might be an ideal land of opportunity for his impoverished countrymen. Somewhat surprisingly, Selkirk met resistance to his plan from the British government, and he "proceeded to wage a nearly solitary battle to secure for Scotsmen the right to emigrate from their native land, that they might embrace the challenges and opportunities that lay in Canada." Bumsted's portrait of the practical and determined Selkirk suggests a man of kindred spirit to McDonald, and in its close examination of extant documents exemplifies the work demanded of the historical biographer.

James Albritton examines the eighteenth-century clergyman John Witherspoon's philosophy of government. Witherspoon served as president of the College of New Jersey (later Princeton University) for most of the years from 1768 to 1794. There, scores of leading actors in the American Revolution and in the founding of the American government came under his influence. Albritton focuses in particular on Witherspoon's understanding of the relationship between church and state in America.

Richard K. Matthews has written previously on Thomas Jefferson, arguing that the Virginian stood outside of mainstream American thought in the founding era. Here, with Elric M. Kline, he builds on this idea, showing the similarities of thought between Jefferson and the French radical thinker Jean-Jacques Rousseau. Matthews and Kline do not go so far as to suggest that

Rousseau and Jefferson had any direct effect on each other's thinking, but the authors demonstrate how both men challenged in their own ways the political and social views of the influential English theorist John Locke.

The political conflict between Alexander Hamilton and Thomas Jefferson has been exhaustively studied by historians, but few have explored the two men's differing views on education. Karl Walling does just this, illustrating how contemporary Americans might benefit from examining Hamilton's emphasis on the importance of producing responsible statesmen and on Jefferson's concern for cultivating a vigilant citizenry.

Adam Tate examines the debate over the nature of republican government between John Adams and John Taylor of Caroline during their correspondence of 1813–15. Tate argues that Adams, "the secularized Yankee Puritan, and Taylor, the enlightened Virginia slaveholder," differed in their views of the relationship of state and society and thus in their vision of how liberty could be preserved in America. "For Adams and the nationalist strain of American political theory," Tate asserts, "politics was an art of balancing power and administering government in ways that could check the antisocial tendencies in human nature. For Taylor and the republican strain of American political theory, politics became the art of restraining government and keeping it out of social affairs."

McDonald made the case for the uniqueness of antebellum southern culture in his writings on the Celtic Thesis. Crawford King examines northern and southern cultural attitudes in the nineteenth century and finds two distinctly differing sets of attitudes toward economic development in particular. "Antebellum travelers and commentators," King writes, "have left a wealth of examples that point up the profound disparity between Northerners' drive for and Southerners' resistance to economic development." King concludes that the differences between the sections were so pronounced that there were indeed "two antebellum Americas that constituted the United States."

Some readers may not be aware of McDonald's interest in American history in the period between the twentieth century's world wars. McDonald in fact taught a class on this era for several years at the University of Alabama, the heart of the class being an examination of Franklin Roosevelt's New Deal. Burton W. Folsom Jr. focuses on a neglected corner of New Deal history— FDR's politicization of the Internal Revenue Service. Folsom argues that FDR used the IRS "as a means of attacking political enemies and generating more revenue for his New Deal programs."

Taking his cue from McDonald's memoirs, Bruce Frohnen makes the case that the study of history is itself a conservative endeavor, one that roots us not only in time and place but in our relationship to others. "Conservatism," Frohnen suggests, "should be used in reference primarily to a form of historical consciousness that appreciates tradition and seeks to sustain the tenuous threads that knit the past to the present and both to the future."

The final essay in this volume is a previously unpublished transcription of a speech Forrest McDonald delivered to the Economic Club of Indianapolis on April 19, 2006. Here McDonald revisits, in his last public lecture, a question that has occupied him across his long and productive career: What kind of economic order did the founding fathers contemplate when they established the constitutional order? McDonald's answer invites us to reflect not only on our own knowledge of the past, but on our distance from it and, of course, on the role of history, conducted on proper principles, in helping us build and travel the bridges that both divide and connect the present from the past.

The Revolutionary Origins of American Constitutionalism

C. BRADLEY THOMPSON

In 1763, at the successful conclusion to the Seven Years' War, American colonists were the freest and most prosperous people anywhere in the world. More Americans participated directly in the affairs of government than probably any other people in history. They were also, with good reason, voluntary and loyal subjects of the British Crown and proud members of the British Empire. Within a few years, however, the empire, at the peak of its glory and power, began to unravel. In 1764, 1765, and 1767, Parliament, with the consent of King George III passed the Sugar, Stamp and Townshend Acts, respectively, in order to begin the process of reforming the empire. The purpose of Britain's new colonial policy was to raise revenue, tighten the enforcement mechanisms of the Navigation Acts, and control the western territories with a large new continental army. American reaction to the Sugar, Stamp and Townshend Acts was immediate, swift, and ultimately violent. Up and down the Atlantic seaboard, American colonials rose in defiant opposition. They wrote pamphlets, drafted resolutions, petitioned Parliament, formed a continental Stamp Act Congress, boycotted the importation of British goods, rioted, assaulted the homes of stamp distributors, and eventually formed themselves into associations known as the "Sons of Liberty."

Genuinely surprised by the American reaction to its new colonial policy, Parliament quickly repealed the taxes associated with the Stamp and Townshend Acts. Parliament's show of good faith, however, was joined to a steely determination to protect its "right" to tax the colonists in the future. In fact, the single most important piece of parliamentary legislation passed during the

1

years of the imperial crisis imposed no tax at all. The Declaratory Act of 1766, passed in the wake of Parliament's repeal of the Stamp Act, was the lightning rod of the American Revolution. It embodied everything that imperial officials sought to defend and American colonials rejected. The Declaratory Act was a short piece of legislation that authorized Parliament to legislate for the colonies "in all cases whatsoever." In other words, the ultimate question that divided Anglo-Americans concerned Parliament's right to legislate for the colonies without their consent. Ultimately, the question was this: Was it possible to demarcate the lawmaking authority of two distinct but related political legislatures—Parliament and the various colonial assemblies?

In just a few short years, the relationship between Great Britain and her American colonies underwent a profound transformation. It was a critical moment and both sides knew it. From the American perspective, nothing less than freedom was at stake, and from the British perspective, the authority of Parliament was at issue. In the wake of the Stamp and Declaratory Acts, the English-speaking peoples began a ten-year transatlantic debate exploring the historical, legal, and philosophical dimensions of a constitutional, political and cultural relationship that had existed for more than 150 years. Having thus ventured into unknown territory, thoughtful Anglo-Americans began to survey the purposes and metes of government and to map out a new area of human freedom.

⟡

The American Revolution was first fought as a constitutional battle.[1] The outpouring of pamphlets and letters on both sides of the Atlantic from 1765 onward all speak to the constitutional nature of the contest. In 1768, for instance, Wills Hill, first Earl of Hillsborough and Britain's secretary of state for the colonies, identified the source of the controversy between Parliament and the colonial assemblies. Had the Americans petitioned Parliament "on the ground of expediency only," he wrote, "they would have succeeded; but while you call in question the right, we cannot hear you. It is essential to the constitution to preserve the supremacy of Parliament inviolate." Likewise, the Americans time and again announced that they were defending the "constitution" against the attempts of Parliament and British imperial officials to destroy it. In 1770, the Massachusetts Assembly told Governor Thomas Hutchinson that it was their "indispensable duty, as the guardians of the people's rights . . . to make a constitutional stand." Even General Thomas Gage, commander of British forces in America, understood, unlike Hillsborough, that the Americans were not reacting principally against the political imprudence of the Stamp Act. "The Question is not of the inexpediency of the Stamp Act, or of the inability of the Colonys to pay the Tax," Gage wrote, "but that it is unconstitutional, and contrary to their Rights." According to John Adams, the source of the dispute went to the very "foundations of the constitution." Several years later, Adams's cousin Samuel insisted that the American people were united in their "constitutional opposition to tyranny. You know there is a charm in the word 'constitutional.'"[2]

Back and forth they went like this for almost ten years, each side claiming fidelity to the "constitution." What is genuinely remarkable about this debate is the degree to which the antagonists were unwilling to compromise constitutionally in order to find a political solution. Both sides understood that if this constitutional issue could not be resolved constitutionally, they could all bid "Adieu to their pretended Darling the British Constitution in America." Defining the principles and institutions, rules and procedures, powers and boundaries of the "constitution" was the pivotal issue around which British imperial officials and American Whigs danced for ten years. In the end, a theoretical debate over the nature of the constitution led to revolution and war because there was no fixed standard or higher authority by which to settle the dispute, no "tribunal in the constitution, from whence redress could have been obtained."[3]

Complicating the debate was the very question of what constituted the British constitution itself. When American colonists declared the Stamp Act to be unconstitutional in 1765, what exactly did they mean? More to the point, to *what* exactly were they referring? The same can be asked of British parliamentarians who regarded the Stamp Act as perfectly constitutional. To say that the Stamp Act was constitutional or unconstitutional is to measure it against something; it is to judge it against a constitution. But to which constitution were Anglo-American statesmen referring? Which constitution were the two sides of the imperial crisis defending or claiming to be their ultimate guide and standard?

In 1765, an English writer observed, "There is scarce a word in the English language so frequently used, and so little understood as the word Constitution." A year later, John Adams conceded that there had recently been "great inquiry and some apparent puzzle among" colonial Americans about the precise "formal, logical, technical definition" of the British constitution.

Some equated the constitution with "the practice of parliament," some variously defined it as "the judgments and precedents of the king's courts" or as "custom," and still others equated it with the "whole body of the laws" or with the arrangement of "king, lords, and commons." Adams went on to note that there had also been much recent "inquiry and dispute" in the Anglo-American world "about the essentials and fundamentals of the constitution." To Adams, despite the "many definitions and descriptions" then popular in the eighteenth century, there seemed to be "nothing satisfactory to a rational mind in any of these definitions." By 1776, the term *constitution* had become so contested that Anglo-American Tories and Whigs lamented that it had become "absolutely necessary that we should have a new dictionary" to define it.[4] And there's the rub. In trying to sort out how eighteenth-century Anglo-Americans understood and then debated the idea of a constitution, we begin to plumb the depths of what the American Revolution was all about.

In the century and a half between the founding of Jamestown in 1607 and the outbreak of the Seven Years' War in 1756, there developed in the Anglo-American world a complicated understanding of what a constitution is and of the particular constitutional relationship between Great Britain and her North American colonies. It might even be said that the very idea of a constitution was invented by Anglo-Americans in the seventeenth and eighteenth centuries. Not since Ancient Rome had any nation in the world developed a constitutional system as sophisticated as that of the British. Of this we can be certain: virtually all subjects in the British Empire, on both sides of the Atlantic, were proud of their shared constitutional heritage. The British constitution was the pride and joy of Anglo-American poets, orators, lawyers, and statesmen, and it was the envy of all enlightened Europeans. Even French philosophes such as Voltaire and Montesquieu praised the British constitution as the best in the world. It was thought to be the source of all Anglo-American freedoms and prosperity. In 1761, an American advocate for the English constitution wrote for the *Boston Evening-Post* that, in England, "the law is both measure and bond of every subject's duty and allegiance; each man having a fixed fundamental right, born with him, as to freedom of his person, and property in his estate, which he cannot be deprived of, but either by his own consent, or some crime for which the law has impos'd such a penalty, or forfeiture." Three years later, James Otis, the first great intellectual of the American revolutionary movement, wrote that the British constitution in theory and administration "comes nearest the idea of perfection of any that has been reduced to practice."

Barely able to contain his pride, Otis declared: "This is government! This, is a constitution." He went on to describe it as the freest and best "now existing on earth." No less effusive, John Adams endorsed a common view that the English constitution was "the most perfect combination of human powers in society which finite wisdom has yet contrived and reduced to practice for the preservation of liberty and the production of happiness."[5]

It must be noted that prior to the last quarter of the eighteenth century in the Anglo-American world, the term *constitution* did not commonly refer to a written document. There was no musty parchment document under a glass case that politicians or judges could point to and say, "There it is, there's the constitution." How then did mid-eighteenth-century Anglo-Americans understand the very idea of a constitution?[6] Most Britons living at home or abroad would have accepted Lord Viscount Bolingbroke's well-known definition of a constitution, which he laid out in 1735: "By Constitution we mean, whenever we speak with propriety and exactness, that assemblage of laws, institutions, and customs, derived from certain *fixed* principles of reason . . . that compose the general system, according to which the community hath agree to be governed." Some fifty years later, William Paley, the great popularizer of eighteenth-century English moral and political philosophy, described the principles and institutions of the British constitution as growing out of the "acts of parliament, of decisions of courts of law, and of immemorial usages." It is from these sources, Paley continued, that the "nature and limitations" of the English system of jurisprudence are to be deduced, "and the authorities, to which all appeal ought to be made, and by which every constitutional doubt or question can alone be decided."[7] A constitution, according to Bolingbroke and Paley, was an inheritance, a compound of political and legal institutions, of written and unwritten laws past and present.

Most eighteenth-century Anglo-Americans would have understood *constitution* to mean the sum total of any given nation's common and statutory laws, its political customs, and its form of government. To speak of a particular nation's constitution was to refer to the way in which its government was constituted and functioned—what might be called its inherited forms and formalities. This is precisely how British Americans throughout the eighteenth century understood and defined *constitution*. In terms almost identical to their English cousins across the Atlantic, American colonials thought of the British constitution and the pseudo-constitutions that governed their separate colonies as the way in which political bodies were constituted—that is, the different ways in which the animating principles, institutions, laws, and customs of government were combined and brought to life. John Adams compared the British constitution to the "constitution of the human body," with its "contextures of the nerves, fibres, and muscles, or certain qualities of the blood and juices." Adams's anatomical analogy highlighted what he called the constitution's *"stamina vitae,* or essentials and fundamentals." Without these *stamina vitae,* Adams continued, the life of the constitution "cannot be preserved a moment." As late as 1776, the American Tory Charles Inglis was still defining the word constitution in Bolingbrokean terms. A constitution, he wrote, means "that assemblage of laws, customs and institutions which form the general system; according to which the several powers of the state are distributed, and their respective rights are secured to the different members of the community."[8]

When an eighteenth-century jurist, statesman, politician, or writer described a particular course of action by a government as constititutional (e.g., an act of Parliament or an act of a colonial assembly), what he meant to say was that the action had proceeded in conformity with common usages established by law, custom, and the extant political forms and formalities. This is precisely what Paley meant when he wrote that the "terms constitutional and unconstitutional, mean legal and illegal."

During the course of the imperial crisis, however, American colonials began a rapid retreat from this traditional definition of a constitution. By 1773, America's revolutionary statesmen openly challenged the conflation of the "legal" with the "constitutional." At the heart of the imperial crisis, Adams wrote, were the "different ideas" that Anglo-American statesmen associated with "the words legally and constitutionally."[9] This seemingly technical distinction cut to the core of what the American Revolution was all about.

We must first contrast the traditional eighteenth-century definition of a constitution with the radically new definition that developed out of the American Revolution. By seeing our beginning and end points at the outset, we can better understand the complicated historical *process* that led from one to the other. Consider, for instance, Thomas Paine's definition of a constitution in his 1790 work *Rights of Man:*

> A constitution is not a thing in name only, but in fact. It has not an
> ideal, but a real existence; and wherever it cannot be produced in a
> visible form, there is none. A constitution is a thing *antecedent* to a gov-

ernment, and a government is only the creature of a constitution. The constitution of a country is not the act of its government, but of the people constituting a government. . . . A constitution, therefore, is to a government, what the laws made afterwards by that government are to a court of judicature. The court of judicature does not make the laws, neither can it alter them; it only acts in conformity to the laws made; and the government is in like manner governed by the constitution.

Paine's view of a constitution was completely different from the common mid-eighteenth-century understanding. If the British did have a constitution, according to Paine, "it certainly could be referred to; and the debate on any constitutional point, would terminate by producing the Constitution." Of course, given the organic rather than exposited nature of the British constitution, that was impossible. In Parliament, mocked Paine, "One member says This is Constitution; another says, That is Constitution—To-day it is one thing; and tomorrow, it is something else—while the maintaining the debate proves there is none."[10] The problem with the British constitution from Paine's perspective is that it would not stand still; it was constantly changing, growing, and evolving. There was nothing permanently "fixed" about it; nothing to appeal to as a final standard. It was precisely the Americans' search for greater fixity that would come to distinguish their revolutionary constitutions from all others throughout history.

In the same year that *Rights of Man* was published, James Wilson began delivering a series of "Lectures on Law" at the College of Philadelphia. Wilson, a man whose politics had run in a very different direction from that of his former revolutionary colleague, nevertheless shared with Paine the new "American" understanding of a constitution. "No such thing as a constitution, properly so called, is known in Great Britain," Wilson told his students. In America the constitution is the "controller and the guide," while in Britain the constitution "is the creature and the dependent of the legislative power." Constitutionally speaking, America and Britain were the reverse images of each other: "Here, the people are masters of the government: there, the government is master of the people."[11]

For Paine, Wilson, and their fellow Americans, a constitution was something permanently fixed—an unmoved mover. A proper constitution is a cause and not an effect; it is a written document that defines and limits the powers of government. In postrevolutionary America, constitutions took on a meaning and an importance quite different from that of any other place in the world. To Americans, their constitutions had become "political bible[s]," according to Paine. Every family and every member of government possessed one, and "nothing was more common, when legislative debate arose on the principle of a bill, or on the extent of any species of authority, than for the members to take the printed constitution out of their pocket, and read the chapter with which such matter in debate was connected."[12] This uniquely American idea of a constitution was not, however, born phoenix-like, at one singular moment in time, or in the head of one man. It has a fascinating and complicated history that developed out of the polemical debates of the 1760s and 1770s. It is to that story that we must now turn.

When American revolutionaries denounced the Stamp Act as unconstitutional and when British imperial officials declared it to be constitutional, what exactly were they saying? By what standard were they measuring the constitutionality of the Stamp Act? More to the point, to which constitution were they referring?

A significant part of the problem—ours and theirs—is that eighteenth-century British and American statesmen recognized at least four different constitutions.[13] First, there was the traditional *English* constitution, by which was meant the pre-1688 constitution that culminated in the Glorious Revolution. This English constitution—which was also known as the ancient or Saxon constitution—was a constitution of restraint and defined limits that fixed, enshrined, and protected certain rights and liberties, fundamental laws and immutable customs, against their infringement by crown or Parliament. Second, there was the *British* constitution, or the post-1688 constitution, that came into existence after the unification of the English and Scottish parliaments under one crown in 1707. The defining characteristic of this eighteenth-century constitution was the principle that Parliament is not only sovereign but also absolutely, if not arbitrarily, supreme. In the minds of most but not all Englishmen in the eighteenth century, the British constitution had rendered the ancient constitution obsolete. Third, there were the *American* "constitutions," by which was meant the various colonial charters and political forms that governed the colonies. Finally, there was an informal, indeed, one might even call it a phantom *imperial* constitution that governed the political relationship between mother country and the rest of the empire in the seventeenth and eighteenth centuries. The imperial constitution consisted of the English, British, and American constitutions, as well as the direct and indirect legislation passed in the Old and New Worlds that had a bearing on the transatlantic relationship between Britain and her colonies.

There was considerable disagreement over the meaning, boundaries, and interpretation of the four Anglo-American constitutions. To compound matters, British and American statesmen often confused or conflated these constitutions. Sorting out how American revolutionaries and British imperial officials understood and used the various meanings of the term constitution is the first important step in understanding what the American Revolution was about.

British imperial officials and their Loyalist supporters in America defended the "right" of Parliament to legislate for the colonies and, more to the point, to tax them without their consent. Parliament's most thoughtful defenders in Britain included the statesman George Grenville and the two great eighteenth-century British jurists, Sir William Blackstone and Lord Mansfield. In America, Parliament's best defenders included Martin Howard of Rhode Island and Thomas Hutchinson and Daniel Leonard of Massachusetts.

The parliamentary position largely shunned philosophy, eschewing Lockean theory and its emphasis on reason, individual natural rights, and government by consent. The parliamentarians began with the idea that the British state—which included the North American colonies—was an organic whole that developed over the course of many centuries. Rather than beginning with individuals and their rights, they typically posited the priority of the "community" and the natural relations and associated duties that developed therein. Take the American Loyalist Martin Howard, for instance. In his pamphlet "A Letter from a Gentleman at Halifax," published in 1765, he wrote that he would "shun the walk of metaphysicks"—by which he meant the doctrine of natural rights—and would instead examine the "true natural relation . . . between colonies and their mother state." In his debate with William Pitt in the House of Commons, Grenville defined the relationship between the mother state and her colonies by reciprocal obligations: "Great Britain protects America: America is bound to yield obedience."[14]

According to eighteenth-century parliamentarians, when the colonists decided to leave the realm where they had been represented in Parliament for America, where it was virtually impossible to be represented, a new relationship developed. The colonists who left for America, they argued, forfeited some of their political rights. The home government, by contrast, did not forfeit its right to legislate for all Anglo-Americans. As Daniel Leonard put it in his debate with John Adams in 1774: "the constitutional authority of parliament extends to the colonies."[15]

Defenders of parliamentary sovereignty never wavered from this position. They argued that the colonies were first founded with this understanding well known and accepted on both sides of the Atlantic and, furthermore, that the colonists tacitly consented to parliamentary sovereignty throughout the seventeenth and eighteenth centuries. The fact that Parliament almost never exercised its sovereignty in full did not abrogate the right. As Thomas Hutchinson put it: "Indulgence showed in delaying to exercise the right ought not to be urged against the right itself."[16] What this meant in the context of 1765 was that Parliament was exercising its inherent right to tax the colonists for revenue.

In his debate with Lord Camden in the House of Lords in 1766, Lord Mansfield summarized the official British position in no uncertain terms: "That the British legislature, as to the power of making laws, represents the whole British Empire, and has authority to bind every part and every subject without the least distinction, whether such subjects have a right to vote or not, or whether the law binds places within the realm or without." From the parliamentarian position, how could it be otherwise? In his 1773 debate with the Massachusetts House of Representatives, Governor Thomas Hutchinson said that he knew of no line that could be "drawn between the supreme authority of Parliament and the total independence of the colonies." The Americans were either completely dependent on Parliament, or they were entirely independent. There was and could be "no possible medium between absolute independence and subjection to the authority of parliament."[17]

Here is the nub of the constitutional debate: American Whigs thought that a line could and should be drawn between Parliament and the colonial assemblies; British officialdom thought that no line could be drawn because, as Hutchinson said, it is impossible that "there should be two independent Legislatures in one and the same state." Such a situation the parliamentarians referred to as an *imperium in imperio*,—that is, a state within a state. According to Daniel Leonard, this was "the height of political absurdity."[18] All Britons, the parliamentarians held, were subject to the authority of Parliament, wherever they lived within the empire. Sovereignty, the essence of government, was indivisible, and Parliament's powers must be transcendent and absolutely supreme. The great jurist Sir William Blackstone put it this way in his famous *Commentaries on the Laws of England,* published in 1765. Parliament has, he said, "sovereign and uncontrolable [*sic*] authority in making, confirming, enlarging, restraining, abrogating, repealing, reviving, and expounding of laws, . . . this being the place where that absolute *despotic* power, which must in all governments reside somewhere, is entrusted by the constitution of these kingdoms."

Among Parliament's extraordinary powers, according to Blackstone, were the following:

1) It can regulate or new model the succession to the crown.

2) It can alter the established religion of the land.

3) It can change and create afresh even the constitution of the kingdom and of parliaments themselves.

4) It can, in short, do every thing that is not naturally impossible.[19]

To twenty-first-century Americans, Blackstone's account of Parliament's authority might seem rather ominous in its granting of unlimited power. Yet Blackstone and his fellow defenders of parliamentary sovereignty were enlightened Whigs of the classical-liberal variety who thought of themselves as genuine defenders of British common-law rights and liberties and of the British constitution. They commonly argued that to deny parliamentary sovereignty would be to subvert the fundamentals of government, to deprive Americans of their traditional British liberties, and to establish a foundation for absolute monarchy in America. Given that fact, how did British officials and American Loyalists think those rights and liberties would be protected if Parliament's powers were unlimited and omnipotent? And conversely, what did they think would happen if subjects of the realm or empire did not accept the doctrine of parliamentary sovereignty? Let us take up these two questions in turn.

Blackstone and the parliamentary Whigs began with a conceit—several actually. They believed that over the course of the previous thousand years, England had developed through its common law and balanced constitution the freest government in the world. More particularly, they believed—and with some historical justification—that British liberties were synonymous with the rise of Parliament's authority throughout the seventeenth and eighteenth centuries. It was Parliament that had traditionally been the bulwark of the people's liberties and rights against the crown's encroachments and occasional acts of tyranny. Parliament, after all, had enacted the Petition of Right, the

Act of Habeas Corpus, and the Bill of Rights of 1689. Most Britons believed that the High Court of Parliament would always attempt to make and interpret the law in light of the eternal principles of natural justice or natural law.

British parliamentarians also assumed that their unique legal and political culture produced a class of statesmen who were simply wiser and more just than those of other countries. Blackstone, for instance, believed that it was critically important that the members of Parliament be "most eminent for their probity, their fortitude, and their knowledge," and he shared the common view that it was England's glory to be possessed of a ruling aristocracy that was wise, just, and good.[20] Thus, parliamentary loyalists relied on the wisdom of British statesman and the genius of Britain's balanced constitution to protect the rights of all Englishmen, including those who were not actually represented in Parliament.[21]

Parliament's sovereign authority to tax American colonists was thought to derive in part from the unique understanding of political representation established by the eighteenth-century British constitution. Known as "virtual representation," this constitutional form presumed that all Anglo-Americans, within the realm and without, were virtually represented in the House of Commons and were therefore subject to parliamentary legislation. For parliamentarians, much rode on the integrity of the doctrine of virtual representation. At the time, just 17 percent of British men had the right to vote. Only landowners could exercise this right, with the result that some of London's wealthiest merchants could not vote because they owned no land. Additionally, Britain's electoral districts had not been updated in centuries, and some major cities—such as Manchester and Birmingham, each of which had hundreds of thousands of citizens—sent no representatives to Parliament. Contrariwise, some electoral districts had just a handful of voters, and the so-called "rotten boroughs," such as Old Sarum, were ghost towns.

The doctrine of virtual representation was based on and justified by certain assumptions, some fictional and some real. It was assumed, for instance, that British society was united by a common culture that was uniformly homogeneous. Members of the House of Commons were therefore said to represent the nation—indeed, the empire—as a whole, and not only the district that elected them. By this account, the American colonists were in fact represented in Parliament in the same way that the crown's nonvoting subjects in Manchester and Birmingham were. British imperial official Thomas Whately best summarized the doctrine of virtual representation during the debate about the

Stamp Act. The king's American subjects, he wrote in 1765, are in exactly the same situation as those who live in the realm: "all are virtually represented in Parliament; for every Member of Parliament sits in the House, not as Representative of his own Constituents, but as one of that august Assembly by which all the Commons of *Great Britain* are represented."[22] The doctrine of virtual representation was thus an important lynchpin in keeping parliamentary sovereignty intact.

The rising power, influence, and prestige of the colonists' representative bodies posed a serious challenge to the premise that sovereignty was indivisible, and British imperial officers feared that if the American colonists rejected or undermined the principle of parliamentary sovereignty the empire would collapse. Moral and political chaos would ensue. It was at this point in the debate that Anglo-American thinking leapfrogged over the constitutional issue of sovereignty and landed squarely in the philosophical territory first staked out by the seventeenth-century English philosopher John Locke. For many, this task began with a searching inquiry into the nature and meaning of Locke's theory of rights, consent, and government.

No parliamentarian more thoroughly scouted this unchartered philosophic terrain than did Thomas Hutchinson. To reject the doctrine of popular sovereignty was akin, he argued, to saying that "every individual has a right to judge when the acts of government are just and unjust and to submit or not submit accordingly." According to Hutchinson and the parliamentarians, the idea of popular sovereignty implied that laws could be disobeyed at will. Dividing sovereignty in this way was a form of political nihilism that could only result in the implosion of all government. Hutchinson worked out the full logic of the British position: "If I am at liberty to judge what is my natural right, which I have thus reserved, and what not, I may exempt myself from every act of government, for every act lays me under some restraint which I have a natural right to be free from. But pray tell me . . . which of our natural rights in a state of government must be supposed to be reserved?"[23] Hutchinson's answer was clear and simple: Once individuals consent to leave the state of nature and establish government in order to better protect their rights, they transfer to the government all their rights to hold in trust. And once they have consented to living under such a government, they owe it allegiance and full submission to all of its laws.

The parliamentarian position, whether they realized it or not, was a kind of democratized Hobbesianism. That is, they followed Thomas Hobbes in thinking that all political power had to be lodged somewhere. No government could last, they argued, if its laws were disobeyed at the whim of any individual or group of individuals. What would happen, Hutchinson asked, if judges or juries subjectively disregarded laws they did not like? The result, he answered, was that the nation would no longer be "governed by known, established laws," and instead the American colonies would be "subject to an arbitrary government by making the legislative and executive powers one and the same."[24]

Ultimately, the American Whig position, the parliamentarians said, blurred the distinction between a state of government and a state of nature. That being the case, the very purpose of government and the reason why men consent to live under it in the first place would be destroyed. In the end, the logic of the parliamentarians' argument led them to offer the Americans just two options: obey or rebel. There was and could be no middle ground. Otherwise, all government, Hutchinson wrote, "would be a mere rope of sand."[25]

As the parliamentarians worked out the logic of their concept of sovereignty, they were forced to revise simultaneously the traditional understanding of the British constitution and the nature of rights. Whereas the older understanding (including Bolingbroke's) posited that the British government was ultimately grounded in and guided by certain unchanging and absolute fundamental laws and rights, the new view that emerged as a result of the imperial crisis posited that the British constitution was simply synonymous with Parliament.[26] This exposition of the British constitution, advanced most clearly by Blackstone and Hutchinson, argued that constitutions and rights were historically relative to the needs of the times as determined by Parliament. As Hutchinson said:

> I readily admit it to be the happiness of the English constitution that there are certain fundamental principles, plain and intelligible, which in all judicatories are to be considered as the rule for construing law in all cases where there is room for doubt or uncertainty, but I should think it a great misfortune if when, in a long course of time and a total change of circumstances, the reason for establishing these principles ceases there should be no power subsisting to alter or repeal even these fundamentals. . . . I know of no principle in the English constitution more fundamental and which is more certain always to remain than this, viz., that no act can be made or passed in any Parliament which it shall not be in the power of a subsequent Parliament to alter and repeal.

For Hutchinson, the idea of natural rights was a noble myth. He believed instead that rights are historically and culturally conditioned. Hutchinson pointed out that there were no two cities where rights are similarly recognized, "and the rights of British subjects vary in every age and perhaps every session of Parliament." What this meant in the context of the 1760s was that there could be no absolute right to private property and no right to political representation. All were within the purview of Parliament's power. Not only did Hutchinson think he was *describing* the history of the English constitution and of English rights; he was also *prescribing* what the constitution and rights *ought* to be. For Hutchinson, there could be no absolute fundamental principles—including fundamental rights—that permanently delimit the powers and actions of government. Nor did he think that the ancient constitution was the product of anything like a Lockean social contract: Hutchinson then stated the Lockean problem that he and his fellow parliamentarians could not think their way out of by using Lockean principles, and he pointed toward their democratized Hobbesean solution—a solution that would guide and justify their actions against the recalcitrant Americans.

> You should consider how these fundamentals were settled at first. . . .
> [H]ave the people ever assembled together in one body so as that we
> may suppose these fundamentals to have been settled by the majority
> of individuals? If not, as no doubt you will allow, it must have been
> done by a less number either elected to represent the whole or assum-
> ing such representation without any election. Why has not the repre-
> sentative as good right at this day to alter fundamentals as it had at that
> day to establish them? . . . The same power may just as well alter them
> and in fact from time to time have been making continual alterations
> ever since we have any knowledge of the history of the constitution.[27]

Here, in a nutshell but at the deepest level, are the basic questions that would separate American Whigs from Anglo-American parliamentarians. How and by whom are fundamental principles first established in new governments? Can future generations, particularly their political representatives, alter fundamental rights and political forms?

For Hutchinson and the parliamentarians, the only unchanging fundamental principle was the doctrine of the absolute sovereignty of government. All rights and political forms are historicized—that is, they originate in the historical actions of a representative few and are subject to change over time only by the continuing representative sovereign. The Americans, as we shall see, attempted to complete the Lockean revolution in government by constitutionalizing certain fundamental moral principles, such as individual natural rights, and certain fundamental principles of limited government, such as separation of powers and federalism.

⁕⁂⁕

The Stamp Act crisis was a traumatic experience for the English-speaking world because it revealed in one explosive moment that the controversy between Parliament and the colonial assemblies could not be resolved through mutual acts of political expediency. A clash of principles held by principled men rarely lends itself to compromise. From the beginning, both sides understood that important constitutional, moral, and philosophical principles were at stake. The confrontation marks an extraordinary development in the history of political thought and action. It points to that singular moment in time when two radically different theories of government, both long present in a common culture but submerged just below political fault lines, pushed to the surface, forcing people to choose one or the other. Both sides in the controversy understood that the principles at stake would have profound consequences for the future. In one way or another, these two theories of constitutional authority have dominated our thinking about government ever since.

In responding to the Sugar, Stamp, Townshend, and Declaratory Acts and engaging the constitutional arguments of British imperial officials, the Americans embraced a much more philosophical form of argument than their opponents. They stood toe-to-toe with the British in their use of historical and constitutional arguments, but they also appealed to a moral tradition that the British accepted only partially in theory and rejected entirely in practice.[28]

From the Stamp Act to 1776 and beyond, American revolutionaries proved themselves to be committed and thoroughgoing Lockeans. They appealed constantly to philosophic concepts drawn from Locke's *Second Treatise of Government,* such as the laws of nature, natural rights, consent, and a social compact that were utterly absent from the British argument. Locke's theory of government was the foundation of the American position. It explained the world to them; it explained to them the nature of justice and the proper purposes and functions of government. In fact, the Americans applied Locke's theory directly to the issues of the imperial crisis—sometimes verbatim—and they extended the logic of the Englishman's ideas to the construction of new, revolutionary governments. In other words, they quite consciously completed the Lockean theory of government, and they put it into practice. They were Locke's truest and best progeny.

American pamphleteers of the period began with an assumption that the British rejected out of hand—that the Sugar and Stamp Acts were unconstitutional because they were unjust. The British, by contrast, argued that the Sugar and Stamp Acts might be unjust but they were nonetheless legal and therefore constitutional. This is a crucial distinction.

The American revolutionary position rested on the moral premise that the taxation of people without their consent is prohibited. This fundamental principle, they argued, is promised to all Englishmen by virtue of the British constitution. The British constitution referred to by the Americans was not the eighteenth-century constitution defended by the parliamentarians, however. Rather, it was the pre-1688 English constitution (also known as the "ancient" constitution) to which the Americans appealed. The traditional English constitution, at least as it was understood by American Whigs, was characterized by a rule of law designed to check and control arbitrary power on behalf of the people and their fundamental rights. The English constitution protected natural rights such as the rights to liberty and property by incorporating and enshrining common-law rights—such as the right to jury trial—that had developed from "time immemorial." American Whigs typically assumed that the famous "rights of Englishmen" were ultimately grounded in nature and nature's rights, both of which they attributed to divine provenance.

The American argument of 1776 did not emerge fully born in 1764. At first, the American position was a mélange of arguments that were simultaneously radical and conservative, forward and backward looking. The tensions and contradictions of the Americans' position in the mid-1760s as well as the germ of their most advanced ideas were most vividly illustrated in the argument presented by James Otis, the early intellectual leader of the patriot movement in Massachusetts. His 1764 pamphlet, "The Rights of the British Colonies Asserted and Proved," provides a remarkably revealing portrait of the American mind in the early years of the imperial crisis and points the way toward the development of a uniquely American form of constitutional government.

Otis's argument comprises three major components: first, that Parliament's recent attempt to tax the American colonies violates the principles of natural justice that underlie the British constitution; second, that the Americans are properly subject to Parliament's laws; and third, that the British constitution has the internal mechanisms to resolve this obvious contradiction.

All British subjects, according to Otis, whether they are born in the realm or in the dominions are, "by the law of God and nature, by the common law, and by act of parliament . . . entitled to all the natural, essential, inherent and inseparable rights of our fellow subjects in Great-Britain." They are "birth-rights guaranteed to all Englishmen," he wrote, and they cannot be taken away by any king or parliament; they are the foundation, the bedrock of the English constitution.[29] Otis consciously conflated the rights of Englishmen and the rights of men. This had an important implication: namely, that the rights of Englishmen were not the products of history as Thomas Hutchinson and the other parliamentarians assumed. Instead, Otis suggested, the rights of Englishmen are emanations from the natural rights of men. The common-law right to property, in other words, is grounded on the right to liberty, which in turn is grounded on the right to life, by which Otis meant the right to self-ownership and self-rule. Over the course of many centuries, these natural rights were thought to have become embedded in English common and statutory law, though no one really quite knew how that happened.

Otis argued that the rule of law and man's natural rights were built into the British constitution. They are, he said, "the first principles of law and justice, and the great barriers of a free state, and of the British constitution in particular." They establish the legitimate bounds that "God and nature" has "fixed" to government.[30] Beyond this, legitimate governments may not go. These principles could not be reconciled with the Sugar and Stamp Acts and with the parliamentarians' new and innovative interpretation of the British constitution.

At this point, however, Otis confronted a serious dilemma. Eighteenth-century parliamentarians argued that Parliament was absolutely sovereign in the empire and that it could tax the colonies without their consent. American Whigs, by contrast, argued that Parliament was supreme but that it must not pass laws that violated the natural and inherited common-law rights of Englishmen. How, then, could these two competing interpretations of the British constitution be resolved?

Surprisingly, following the lead of British parliamentarians, Otis recognized that the authority and power of Parliament were supreme and "uncontroulable" and that the colonists must therefore obey its laws. If Parliament were not supreme, he argued, echoing Thomas Hutchinson, political anarchy would result. How then could Parliament pass whatever laws it wanted without violating the rights enshrined in the constitution? Otis assumed the essential goodness of Parliament, which could only mean that Parliament had simply "erred," or been "misinformed," "deceived," and led astray. With time, Otis believed, Parliament would, in its "wisdom and justice," see the error of its ways and repeal the Sugar and Stamp Acts.[31]

Despite his hope that Parliament would act sensibly, Otis went on to draw an important distinction between what Parliament may and may not do: Parliament's powers, he argued, are "*jus dicere* only [which means 'to *declare* the law']"; they are not "*jus dare* [which means 'to *give* or to *make* the law']." *Jus dare* is a power, according to Otis, that belongs, strictly speaking, only to God. Otis was here tapping into a seventeenth-century natural- and common-law tradition, which held that Parliament's primary function was to discover the natural law and then promulgate it for society. This was precisely what prevented Parliament, though supreme, from becoming absolute, arbitrary, or omnipotent, according to Otis. It could not, he famously declared, "make 2 and 2, 5."[32]

Otis's intrinsicist jurisprudence provided American revolutionaries with three very important principles that would guide them over the course of the next ten years: first, that there are absolute laws of nature that must provide a permanent foundation for constitutions and governments; second, that the purpose of man-made law is to make laws that embody or reflect natural law; and third (for a few revolutionaries), that the laws of nature had their source in nature rather than in God's commands.

Ultimately, Otis said, there must be a "higher authority" than Parliament—namely, a constitution grounded on certain natural rights endowed by God: "Should an act of parliament be against any of *his* natural laws, which are *immutably* true, *their* declaration would be contrary to eternal truth, equity and justice, and consequently *void:* and so it would be adjudged by the parliament itself, when convinced of their mistake."[33]

Otis's first solution to the dilemma was therefore political rather than constitutional. In fact, it was very similar to Thomas Hutchinson's position. Otis expected a rational and just Parliament to correct its own mistakes, but surely this was a slender thread, a mere rope of sand on which to suspend American rights.

Ultimately, Otis offered a constitutional solution to the problem that was simultaneously conservative and radical. Paraphrasing the great seventeenth-century English jurist Sir Edward Coke, Otis wrote that if it can be plainly demonstrated that the law is against "*natural* equity [which in this context means natural justice], the executive courts will adjudge such acts void."[34] This extraordinarily important sentence points toward two crucial principles: first, that the constitution and the rights it enshrines are the fundamental law of the land and must not and cannot be violated by Parliament; and second, that there is a body, a neutral arbiter—namely, the king's courts—that has the authority to invalidate laws against the constitution. In other words, Otis seems to have pointed toward something like judicial review—a concept that was not recognized in eighteenth-century British constitutionalism.[35]

Grasping for some kind of fundamental, immutable, objectively observable standard by which to judge the constitutionality of the acts of crown or Parliament, Otis planted a seed in the American revolutionary mind that would grow and blossom over the course of the succeeding decades. He was searching for a constitution that "every man has a right to examine" in order to know the "origin, spring and foundation of every power and measure in a commonwealth." He wanted Anglo-Americans to have the right to examine their constitution in the same way that they might study a "piece of curious machinery, or a remarkable phenomenon in nature."[36] Whether he knew it or not, he was inching the American cause toward the idea of a written constitution as fundamental law.[37]

In addition to appealing to natural law and the ancient constitution, Americans also turned to the more recent history of the imperial constitution in defending their rights against Parliament. The passage of the Sugar and Stamp Acts in 1764 and 1765 forced American Whigs to differentiate and define, in the words of Daniel Dulany, the "nature of the dependence, and the degree of subordination" between Parliament and the colonial assemblies.[38] Americans found the constitutional sanction for their understanding of the imperial constitution in the form of their colonial charters. These charters permanently established, they argued, the constitutional boundaries between mother country and colonies. The various compacts between king and colonies had always been treated by the Americans as "permanent and perpetual, as unalterable as Magna Charta, or the primary principles of the English constitution."[39] In the eyes of many colonial Americans the charters took on the status of a transcendent, higher law that provided a bulwark against arbitrary power by restricting the ordinary actions of government at home and abroad.

The petition of the New York General Assembly in 1765 made clear the reasons why the Americans treated their charters as permanently binding contracts between the crown and colonists—as contracts that defined constitutionally the powers of the colonial governments in relationship to those of British government.

> The General Assembly of this Colony have no desire to derogate from the Power of the Parliament of *Great-Britain;* but they cannot avoid deprecating the Loss of such Rights as they have hitherto enjoyed, Rights established in the *first Dawn of our Constitution,* founded upon the most substantial Reasons, *confirmed by invariable Usage,* conducive to the best Ends; never abused to bad Purposes, and with the Loss, of which Liberty, Property, and all the Benefits of Life, tumble into Insecurity and Ruin.[40]

The American colonial charters were contracts between king and colonists that did not include Parliament. Most of the American charters were established during the reigns of James I and Charles I, when the king's prerogative powers were thought to include sole jurisdiction over the colonies. It is important to note that most of these charters were granted before Parliament consolidated its sovereignty in Britain in the early decades of the eighteenth century.

Over the course of the next 130 years, Parliament occasionally imposed duties on the external commerce of the colonies in order to regulate trade, but it never taxed the colonies for revenue. To the Americans, the absence of parliamentary taxation on the colonies established a precedent that became an important part of the evolving, unwritten, imperial constitution. By English legal standards, precedent, usage, and custom were powerful forces in establishing civil rights and constitutional principles. More importantly, American colonists assumed that Parliament's long-standing abstinence from taxing them for revenue was supported by those principles of the English constitution that recognized the existence of certain fundamental, unalterable rights. The English constitution to which American statesmen hearkened guaranteed basic natural and civil rights—including the right not to be taxed without representation—that could not be infringed by king or Parliament. The constitution was thought to put permanent limitations on the actions of government.

Daniel Dulany, in his important and influential 1765 pamphlet "Considerations on the Propriety of Imposing Taxes on the British Colonies," delineated Parliament's relationship to the colonies by attributing to the charters the status of constitutions:

In what the superior may *rightfully* controul, or compel, and in what the inferior ought to be at liberty to act without controul or compulsion, depends upon the nature of the dependence, and the degree of the subordination; and, these being ascertained, the measure of obedience, and submission, and the extent of the authority and superintendence will be settled. When powers, compatible with the relation between the superior and inferior, have, by *express compact,* been granted to, and accepted by, the latter, and have been, after that compact, repeatedly recognized by the former—. When they may be exercised effectually upon every occasion without any injury to that relation, the authority of the superior can't properly interpose; for, by the powers vested in the inferior, is the superior limited.[41]

Americans like Dulany considered their charters to be proto-constitutions. The charters defined the nature of the relationship between mother country and colony, limited the powers of Parliament over the colonies, guaranteed the colonists' traditional rights and privileges as loyal subjects of the crown, and defined the powers of the colonial governments. Americans claimed that it was their right as Englishmen to be exempted from parliamentary taxation without their consent, and that this was a right constitutionally protected by their charters.

The American argument based on the colonial charters was probably best expounded, certainly before 1773, by Virginian Richard Bland in his "An Inquiry Into the Rights of the British Colonies" (1766). The charters, according to Bland, were contracts between king and colonists that created distinct states, "independent, as to their *internal* government, of the original kingdom, but united with her, as to their *external* polity." To overturn these colonial constitutions by asserting a principle foreign to them was, Bland said, to "introduce principles of despotism unknown to a free constitution." As great as Parliament's powers might be, he warned, "it cannot, constitutionally, deprive the people of the natural rights; nor, in virtue of the same principle, can it deprive them of their civil rights, which are founded in compact, without their consent."[42] Here we see the sharpest divisions between the parliamentarians and the American constitutionalists. If Parliament were to usurp the Americans' individual rights, the colonists would be forced, according to Bland, to defend themselves with arms.

In his famous 1768 pamphlet "Letters from a Farmer in Pennsylvania," John Dickinson took the American argument one step further, defining with remarkable clarity the fundamental difference that was fast emerging in the trans-British world over the nature and meaning of constitutional government. A free people, Dickinson wrote in contradiction to the British parliamentarian position, is "not *those,* over whom government is reasonably and equitably exercised, but *those,* who live under a government so *constitutionally checked* and *controuled,* that proper provision is made against its being otherwise exercised." The conceit of British imperial officials was to think that the glory and equity of the British constitution was forever protected by equating it with a government "reasonably and equitably exercised." Dickinson, however, asserted that the distinction between the rule of law and the rule of men could not be blurred in this manner. It was not an adequate safeguard against tyranny to base government on the rule of good men; rather, liberty can only be secured by "a government so *constitutionally checked* and *controuled*" that it cannot become tyrannical.[43]

By the late 1760s, then, American constitutional theorists such as John Dickinson had clarified their understanding of the nature and jurisdictional boundaries of the British constitution—an understanding that was deeply conservative in its grounding in the ancient constitution and the colonial charters, yet radical in its appeal to Lockean theory and the idea of a written constitution. It was this innovative constitutional thinking that would lead Americans in a few short years ultimately to reject the English constitution entirely.

Over the course of the preceding 150 years, the colonists had become deeply attached to their charters, treating them as proto-constitutions that established, defined, and limited the powers of government. As a result, the American mind had become what we might call *constitutionalized.* During the imperial crisis American colonists were constantly searching for some kind of objective constitutional standard by which to measure and judge the actions of Parliament. The clearest and best statement of what the Americans were grasping for came in the "Massachusetts Circular Letter," composed in 1768 in response to the Townshend Acts. Written by Samuel Adams for the Massachusetts legislature, the Circular Letter looks back to the lost ancient constitution of England but in doing so it stands at the precipice of the future:

> That in all free States the Constitution is fixd; & as the supreme Legislative derives its Power & Authority *from* the Constitution, it cannot

overleap the Bounds of it without destroying its own foundation . . . That
it is an essential unalterable Right in nature, ingrafted into the British
Constitution, as a fundamental Law & ever held sacred & irrevocable by
the Subjects within the Realm, that what a man has honestly acquired is
absolutely his own, which he may freely give, but cannot be taken from
him without his consent.

The Circular Letter is remarkable in several respects. First, note the necessary relationship between a free state and a fixed constitution. The constitution of a free state must be cast in stone; it must be knowable to all citizens and it must permanently and clearly limit the boundaries of government
power. Second, constitutions are said to create legislatures and not the other
way around. This, of course, is a complete reversal of the eighteenth-century
British understanding of a constitution, and it is the first major innovative
step toward developing the idea of written constitution as fundamental law.
Third, it is important to note that Americans such as Sam Adams thought
that there are certain natural rights "ingrafted into the British Constitution,
as a fundamental Law & ever held sacred & irrevocable." This idea of natural rights being "ingrafted" into a constitution—any constitution—is critical
to the American attempt to create constitutions as fundamental law. Finally,
these natural rights, such as the right to property, are not held historically or
conditionally but unalterably, inalienably, and "absolutely." Once again, this
emerging American position contrasted sharply with Thomas Hutchinson's
view of the relationship between rights and constitutions.[44]

The Circular Letter was a turning point in the development of a uniquely
American conception of a constitution. Adams and his Massachusetts colleagues stepped over an intellectual and psychological barrier that hitherto had
confined the colonists to thinking strictly within the context of the traditional
English constitution. Finally liberated from their inherited forms and formalities, they were free to begin searching for a new constitutional foundation on
which to ground American rights and liberties.

A year after the publication of the Circular Letter, the Reverend John
Joachim Zubly of South Carolina addressed what was now emerging as the
central issue of the imperial crisis: the relationship of Parliament to the British
constitution. In "An Humble Inquiry Into the Nature of the Dependency of
the American Colonies Upon the Parliament of Great Britain," Zubly sought
to define the "very essence of the constitution." Like Otis, he acknowledged

Parliament to be the supreme legislature of the British empire, but Zubly dismissed the idea that Parliament was "absolutely" supreme. If it were, it could not be "bound by the constitution" and it could "alter" it at will. Zubly suggested instead that Parliament must be "agreeable to the constitution," by which he meant that "it can no more make laws, which are against the constitution, or the unalterable privileges of British subjects, than it can alter the constitution itself." Zubly extended Sam Adams's logic by arguing that the true "essence" of the British constitution clearly separated what constitutions do from what legislatures do. "Parliament," he wrote, "derives its authority and power from the constitution, and not the constitution from the Parliament."[45] In other words, a proper constitution, according to Zubly, is a permanent, fundamental law that creates and defines the powers of government and which cannot be altered by that same government. The South Carolinian's argument was yet another important step in the developing American idea of a constitution.

The Americans' final break with British constitutionalism came in 1776. After ten years of debating the nature of the British constitution, the most advanced revolutionary thinkers were now prepared to offer a radically new definition of a constitution that broke decisively with the entire tradition of Western constitutional thought and practice. The anonymous Philadelphia author of *Four Letters on Important Subjects* illuminated the issue as clearly as any American during the revolutionary era. Challenging the traditional eighteenth-century idea that a "Constitution, and a form of government" are "synonymous things," he argued that they were "not only different" but were actually "established for different purposes." Every nation has a government of one form or another, "but few, or perhaps none," he argued, "have truly a Constitution." In fact, the truth of the matter is, he announced, "the English have no *fixed* constitution."[46] The crown's prerogative, though limited in some ways, was nonetheless capable of changing the constitution in certain important respects, while Parliament's power was simply unlimited. Indeed, Parliament's power was so great that it could do anything "but make a man a woman." A proper constitution, by contrast, must be a "higher authority" that limited the powers of government through well-defined boundaries captured in a "written Charter." Finally, for the new American constitutions to become that "higher authority" or fundamental law, it was important that some thought be given to "the means of preserving it" against the grasping designs of the executive and legislative powers. The author of the *Four*

Letters approved of Machiavelli's maxim that constitutions be examined "at certain periods, according to its first principles" in order to "correct abuses, and supply defects."[47] Some mechanism, some device, was therefore necessary to identify the constitution's defects and provide the means by which to repair them. For the fundamental law to be truly fundamental, it must not be subject to the vicissitudes of time.

Ultimately, when it became clear that their research into the origins of these various constitutions made little difference to British imperial officials—in fact, when it became clear to them that the real problem lay in the extant constitutional structures, a few American colonists began to see the inadequacies not only of English constitutionalism but of their own as well. Psychologically as well as intellectually, it was the moment when the Americans finally gave up the idea of reforming their inherited constitutional structures and saw the possibilities of a brave new future.

In 1775, Moses Mather of Connecticut worked out the emerging logic of the American position in his remarkably daring and prescient *America's Appeal to the Impartial World*. Little known or read today, Mather's *Appeal* draws out the logic of James Otis's "Rights of the British Colonies Asserted and Proved" in a way that Otis himself was unable or unwilling to do. According to Mather, American Whigs simply could not accept a constitutional system that permitted the British Parliament to "alter the original principles of the constitution," thereby depriving the people of "liberties and properties" and allowing government to become "absolute and perpetual." In this moment of crisis, American colonials were now willing to say publicly that the British constitution did not have the necessary mechanisms to afford them constitutional "redress." The time had therefore come, Mather said, for Americans to reclaim "their native rights" and to know that they were "justified in making insurrection." Because the British constitution could offer no solution to violations of its provisions, American plaintiffs had "no other remedy" but to defend themselves with arms.[48]

By 1775, then, leading American Whig thinkers had explicated a revolutionary theory of constitutional government at odds with that of their British cousins. Building on James Otis's insights, American revolutionaries grounded their new constitutional theory on six principles: first, constitutions should be grounded on immutable, antecedent rights; second, constitutions should be defined by fixed principles and rules that control the operations of government; third, constitutions create governments and are paramount to them;

fourth, constitutions limit the powers and actions of government, particularly the lawmaking power; fifth, constitutions should be written; and sixth, constitutions must be distinguished from ordinary law and must be instituted as the permanent and fundamental law of the land. This new conception of a constitution would revolutionize American constitutional thought and practice. It was a daring leap forward, and no one on either side of the Atlantic in 1775 knew quite how this new understanding of a constitution would actually work in practice. They were about to find out. It took another dozen years for the Americans to experiment with various means of constitutionalizing their natural rights and liberties before they devised the nation's present constitutional foundations. For more than two centuries their heirs have continued to explore the theory and practice of constitutional government that emerged from the revolutionary crisis in eighteenth-century Anglo-American constitutional history.

The Common-Law Tradition, the Constitution, and Southern Jurisprudence

F. Thornton Miller

Many of the rights claimed by Americans in the eighteenth and nineteenth centuries were rooted in the English common law, an unwritten, slowly evolving law based on custom and usage that had existed, in the minds of Englishmen, since "time immemorial." Parliament incorporated some common-law rights in the English Bill of Rights. Beginning with George Mason's Virginia Declaration of Rights of 1776, the American states wrote common-law rights into their constitutions. During the ratification debates of 1787–88, Anti-Federalists argued that an explicit guarantee of common-law rights needed to be included in the Constitution. Indeed, much of the Bill of Rights reflected traditional common-law rights, such as the guarantee of local jury trial, the assurance that juries ought to rule on the facts of a case, and the notion that appellate courts should not reexamine facts.

In colonial America, the common law also served to strengthen local government at the expense of centralized power. According to the common law, each colony was a separate realm. No appellate court system operated within the British Empire to maintain uniformity in the law. Through modification by colonial court decisions and the statutes of the colonial legislatures, the common law came to differ from colony to colony. In addition, within each colony most litigation occurred at the local level. Though judges presided over trials and oversaw the admission of evidence, juries determined the guilt or innocence of defendants or, in civil suits, the damages to be paid. In general, judges saw to the law and juries saw to the facts. When the two were intermixed, however, juries determined both law and fact.

In the aftermath of the American Revolution, the English common-law tradition was preserved in America primarily by southern jurists and lawyers, who found in it much to admire, particularly its assumption of the existence of unwritten rights and principles and its localism. The career of Patrick Henry, the renowned Virginian lawyer, illustrates southerners' devotion to the local nature of the common law. The center of legal and political activity in Henry's Virginia was the county courthouse. Henry understood that, in practice, the common law was what juries believed it to be. Even if he lost arguments on points of law, Henry would often win the jury by emotional appeals and by avoiding wearying details and legal analyses. Henry's own lack of refinement and formal education endeared him to jurors. His kind of law appealed to small farmers suspicious of social change and to gentry who valued their independence and who sought to protect the interests of their state.[1]

After the ratification of the Constitution and the establishment of the federal judiciary, most litigation remained in local and state courts, and most suits were at common law. As in the colonial period, most nineteenth-century lawyers read law, apprenticed under a practicing lawyer, and were licensed to practice without having obtained a college degree, having attended a law school, or having passed a bar exam. Many of these country lawyers, often found at the county courthouse, needed a farm to supplement their income, or if they did have a sufficient income, they bought a plantation so as to attain the status of a country gentleman.[2]

By the nineteenth century, the volume of business before the courts was such that the various states set up appellate court systems, often with judges riding circuit through the counties. The expansion of the judiciary increased the need for lawyers. Camaraderie developed among judges and lawyers as they rode the circuit together and stayed at taverns and inns along the way. Although an appellate system allowed questions of law to be appealed above the local courts, at the trial-court level the local jury determined the most important questions for the litigants.

In the nineteenth century, southern jurists and lawyers fought to conserve the southern common-law tradition against legal reformers who sought to use the appellate court systems to attain uniformity in the law. Whereas country lawyers preferred to argue before local juries in county and state district and circuit courts, legal reformers preferred to argue before higher state and federal court judges. The reformers sought to overturn the common-law practice whereby juries determined not only fact but law. They favored a stronger role for judges, who would determine law and fact, instruct the juries, sum up the evidence, and call for new trials when they believed a jury went against the weight of the evidence.[3]

Legal reformers such as Joseph Story and Daniel Webster further aroused southern suspicions by seeking to strengthen the hand of the federal government. Reformers, for example, sought to expand the power of eminent domain so as to promote the development of the American economy. They also favored the creation of a strong federal judiciary. To this end, they embarked on a campaign to structure the new federal court system created in 1789 to their advantage. Under both the British imperial system and the Articles of Confederation, no appellate system existed above the provincial courts, and central government courts had no jurisdiction over individual citizens.[4] The Constitution for the first time created a national system in which federal courts possessed direct jurisdiction over individual citizens. Yet the Constitution's language about the structure of the federal court system was purposefully vague; Article III stipulated only that "the judicial Power of the United States, shall be vested in one supreme Court, and in such inferior Courts as the Congress may from time to time ordain and establish." To fill in the blanks, the First Congress of the United States passed the Judiciary Act of 1789.

The Judiciary Act was in many ways a compromise between Federalists, who favored a stronger national government, and Anti-Federalists, who had opposed the ratification of the Constitution on account of its concentration of power in a central authority. The Judiciary Act created an appellate system wherein questions of federal law could be appealed to the Supreme Court, and it also provided for a system of local justice. Each state was designated as a district in the federal court system, and judges were to reside in their districts. Juries were to see to questions of fact, and appeals would be on the record as it stood from the lower court. Anti-Federalists took comfort in the fact that local juries would be empowered under the Judiciary Act to issue verdicts and rule on damage amounts, no matter what a higher court ruled on a question of law.[5]

The Judiciary Act not only established a broad federal judicial system with courts in each state, it also drew upon the services of the state courts, decreeing that state courts had concurrent jurisdiction over federal and constitutional questions. Though Section 25 of the Judiciary Act allowed the Supreme Court to hear appeals from the state courts on questions concerning the Constitution, federal law, or treaties, there was no provision for appeals on any other grounds. In terms of state law—common law and statute—each state was, as in the colonial period, a separate realm. On state law, the state supreme court remained the highest court of law.

Federal courts had jurisdiction on questions of federal law, the Constitution, and treaties, and when the parties in a case were listed in Article III of the Constitution, such as suits between citizens of different states. For common-law suits in federal courts, Section 34 of the Judiciary Act stated "that the laws of the several states, except where the constitution, treaties or statutes of the United States shall otherwise require or provide, shall be regarded as rules of decision in trials at common law in the courts of the United States in cases where they apply." This meant that a federal court would follow the common-law rules of the state in which the district or circuit court resided.

<hr>

Two key cases in the 1790s, *Chisholm v. Georgia* and *Ware v. Hylton*, tested how well the new federal judiciary would work. *Chisholm* was a common-law suit initiated by citizens of South Carolina against the state of Georgia. Article III of the Constitution stipulated that suits between a state and citizens of another state fell under federal court jurisdiction. Though the language of the Constitution suggested that it was possible for a state to be a defendant as well as a plaintiff, debate in several state ratifying conventions had led to an understanding—and a proposed amendment to make it expressly clear—that a state could not be sued by a citizen of another state in federal court. The matter remained controversial in 1793, when in *Chisholm* the state of Georgia refused to appear in court, claiming that the Supreme Court had no jurisdiction to hear the case.[6]

Led by Chief Justice John Jay, a high Federalist, the Court ruled against Georgia in *Chisholm*. Justice James Iredell of North Carolina, however, gave the first great dissent in the history of the Court. He noted that the ruling opened a way to bring states before the Court in cases not authorized by the Judiciary Act of 1789. *Chisholm* did not involve a question regarding the Constitution, federal statute, or treaty, Iredell pointed out, but was instead a common-law suit. Citing Section 34 of the Judiciary Act, Iredell contended that the only law that applied in *Chisholm* was Georgia common law. Iredell further argued that under common law, an individual could not sue but only petition a sovereign for redress. Without Georgia's permission, Iredell concluded, the Supreme Court should not have heard the case.

Iredell and his sympathizers won a victory with the approval of the Eleventh Amendment in 1795, which excluded this kind of case from federal jurisdiction and forestalled the development of a highly centralized court system. But a new challenge to advocates of states' rights arose when the so-called British Debt Cases came to the attention of the Supreme Court in the 1796 case of *Ware v. Hylton*.

During the ratification debates, Anti-Federalists had raised the specter of American debtors being hauled before distant federal courts and placed at the mercy of British creditors. *Ware v. Hylton* began in the U.S. circuit court for the district of Virginia. Patrick Henry was the defense attorney, and he added to his fame as he once again condemned British tyranny and lauded American liberty in front of a packed courtroom. He argued that during the Revolution the bonds of Anglo-American society—including all legal and financial connections—had been broken. The court rejected this argument because the peace treaty of 1783 recognized the debts. However, Iredell, in the circuit court opinion, with Chief Justice Jay dissenting, stated that the treaty did not prevent Virginia, as a sovereign state, from confiscating the debts its citizens owed to the British. In the appeal to the Supreme Court, the majority of the court affirmed much of Iredell's lower court opinion but ruled that ratification of the Constitution retroactively nullified state laws contrary to the treaty. All debts owed to the British, therefore, were still valid.[7]

When *Ware* and similar debt suits were sent back to the circuit court for trial, juries subtracted from the awards interest earned during the war, despite Chief Justice Jay's instructions to the contrary. Jay was impotent to compel juries to follow his counsel because in debt cases law and fact were mixed, and therefore juries could determine both. Juries not only had discretion to decide the timing, method, and mode of repayment, but in the British Debt Cases they could even discharge the debts entirely on the grounds that the creditor was not in the state trying to collect the debt during the war and that the debtor was unable to pay interest.

The process in *Ware* and in the other debt cases reassured states' rights advocates that the federal judiciary could work as they had hoped. The appeal to the Supreme Court was on a point of law, and juries retained the right to determine law and fact, which in such debt cases allowed for local consideration of the debtors' circumstances. While states' rights advocates would have preferred for the Court completely to uphold Iredell's circuit court opinion, sympathetic juries had proven capable of tempering the law. The cases showed that under the Judiciary Act of 1789, the federal judicial branch could work similar to state judiciaries, where local juries played a significant role at the lower trial-court level.

Although the federal appellate court system was an innovation, Americans' experience with federalism per se had its origins in the colonial period. In the British Empire a de facto federal system had developed, with the central government in London seeing to such matters as foreign affairs, war and peace, treaties, the navy and army, and foreign trade, and the colonial governments seeing to local matters such as roads, ferries, bridges, police, public health, education, and religion. The delegates to the Philadelphia Convention of 1787 drew upon this political experience in crafting the new American Constitution. Article I, Section 8, which lists the powers of the United States Congress, retained a similar federal division of powers.[8]

The writings of Scottish Enlightenment philosophers, which influenced the framers of the Constitution, also supported the idea of the division of power.[9] Believing that private interests motivated people and politicians, the Scottish Enlightenment thinkers did not consider reliance on virtue sufficient to ensure the survival of republics. Instead, they relied on the structure of government, particularly on a division of powers and a system of checks and balances. Scottish Enlightenment thought expressed a preference for a federal system like the old, pre-1760s British Empire, where no absolute king or absolute central government ruled, no single court determined the law of the land, and most government and law remained at the local and provincial level. As in the economic system of competition advocated by Scotsman Adam Smith, under such an arrangement no part of the government held a monopoly on power; rather, there was competition among political power-holders. This federal system of divided powers resonated with the Americans.

Virginian James Madison best expounded the American theory of federalism in his *Federalist* essays, particularly numbers 10 and 51, and later in the pages of the *National Gazette,* particularly in his 1792 essay titled "Government of the United States." In America, Madison noted, power was divided first between the central government and the state governments, and second within each government—that is, among the legislative, executive, and judicial branches. Madison explained how self-interest would incline officeholders in each division of government to defend their power and check the expansion of power by other government divisions. Madison was careful to calibrate the division of power through a prudent assessment of current realities: In the 1780s he emphasized the need for a central government to check the states, and in the 1790s he emphasized the need for the states to check the central government. Madison added to his argument the need for political parties to check power.[10]

The ideology of the English Country Opposition provided another stream of influence on Americans in the eighteenth century. The Country Party in England arose in opposition to the Court Party of Robert Walpole, which, Country politicians feared, was centralizing political power in London. Believing that power corrupts, Country Party ideology advocated a healthy distrust of politicians. Americans drew on the rhetoric of the Country Opposition during the late eighteenth and early nineteenth centuries. During the Revolution, American patriots focused on London as the source of corruption; in opposing ratification of the Constitution in 1787 and 1788, Anti-Federalists warned of the dangers of the concentration of power; in the 1790s, the American inheritors of the English Country ideology focused their distrust on the new national government and specifically on the new Walpole—the first secretary of the treasury, Alexander Hamilton.

The opposition party, soon to be called the Republicans, coalesced around two Virginians: Thomas Jefferson, the secretary of state, and James Madison, famed as "The Father of the Constitution." Republicans contended that the federal government was limited in scope to the grant of powers explicitly given by the Constitution, a position strengthened by the ratification of the Tenth Amendment, which reserved "powers not delegated to the United States by the Constitution . . . to the States respectively, or to the people." The Federalist Party, which coalesced around Hamilton, argued that the list of Congress's enumerated powers in Article I, Section 8, was not exhaustive. They pointed to the "necessary and proper clause" at the end of Section 8, which stated that Congress had the power "to make all Laws which shall be necessary and proper for carrying into Execution the foregoing Powers." Republicans contended that the clause did not authorize Congress to add new powers.[11]

Much of the debate between Republicans and Federalists occurred in partisan newspapers. The Republican opposition in Congress was highly critical of the foreign policy of the George Washington and John Adams administrations, from the Jay Treaty of 1794, which Republicans saw as a sellout to Great Britain, to the Quasi War with France of 1798–1800, which Republicans viewed as a manifestation of Federalist partiality to Britain in its war against France's revolutionary government. Federalists, who held majorities in both houses of Congress, tried to quash Republican criticism—which they saw as a potential threat to the government—by passing in 1798 four laws that collectively became known as the Alien and Sedition Acts. Among other things, these acts made it a crime to publish "false, scandalous, and malicious writing" against the government or its officials. Republicans fought back through the state legislatures in which they held strong majorities. Most famously, the legislatures of Virginia and Kentucky issued statements condemning the Alien and Sedition Acts. These resolutions were authored secretly by James Madison (for Virginia) and Thomas Jefferson (for Kentucky). The Virginia legislature later issued a report, written mostly by Madison, which explained the resolutions.[12]

The Virginia and Kentucky Resolutions placed great importance on the ratifying conventions that approved the Constitution. In construing the Constitution, Madison and Jefferson argued, the understanding of the ratifiers in the state conventions was most important, not the intentions of the framers at the Philadelphia Convention. The people of the states granted specific, enumerated powers to the federal government and reserved other powers to the states. Enacting a sedition act, the Virginians concluded, was not one of the powers granted to Congress, and thus such an act violated the Tenth Amendment.

The Virginia and Kentucky Resolutions advanced the compact theory, which held that the sovereign people of the states, through the ratifying conventions, were parties of the compact that ratified the Constitution. It was not one sovereign American people that ratified the Constitution. Both the federal government and the states derived their power from the people of the states.[13] Although Jefferson used the words "void, and of no force" and "nullification" in the Kentucky Resolutions, Madison explained in Virginia's report that neither state was calling for actual nullification of a federal law; instead, they were asserting the doctrine of interposition, which asserted that states, being parties to the original constitutional compact, had the right to declare unconstitutional a federal law.[14]

In positing the states themselves, and not the federal courts, as the final arbiters of the constitutionality of federal law, the Virginia and Kentucky Resolutions reflected southern jurisprudence. From a traditional, conservative, and southern legal perspective, judges did not make law and courts did not actively check the other branches. However, southern jurists believed that the courts should inform the legislature if there was a clear conflict between a statute and fundamental law—in other words, a written constitution or a rule of law long practiced in the courts. That was the basis for judicial review, which developed in state courts after the War of Independence. In the case of judicial review, judges ruled on a conflict between a statute and the state constitution.

George Wythe, the first law professor in America at the College of William and Mary and a judge on the Virginia supreme court, took a judicial review position in his 1782 opinion in *Commonwealth v. Caton.* In *Caton,* the Virginia high court gave the state constitution standing in the law, treating it as more than a mere declaration of principles and accepting it as paramount over statute. Other state courts followed the Virginia example. Judicial review emerged, then, as a direct result of written constitutions and not by an effort of the courts to assert a dominant role in actively checking the other branches.[15]

At the federal level, the idea of judicial review—which was nowhere mentioned in the Constitution—was famously established in the opinion rendered by Chief Justice John Marshall in the 1803 case of *Marbury v. Madison.* Marshall, a Virginian and a Federalist, presided over the Supreme Court from 1801 until 1835, during which time he doubtlessly worked to expand judicial power. *Marbury,* however, was typical of early judicial review cases in that the Court expressed fidelity to a written constitution and did not directly seek to expand its own power. Indeed, *Marbury* served to restrain federal power. In ruling Section 13 of the Judiciary Act of 1789 unconstitutional, Chief Justice Marshall placed judicial review completely in the context of a conflict between a statute and the written constitution. "The powers of the legislature are defined and limited; and that those limits may not be mistaken or forgotten, the constitution is written. To what purpose are powers limited, and to what purpose is that limitation committed to writing, if these limits may, at any time, be passed by those intended to be restrained?" In resolving a conflict of law, Marshall asserted, the role of a court was clear: "It is emphatically the province and duty of the judicial department, to say what the law is." In a conflict between a statute and the Constitution, a court must side with the Constitution. *Marbury* did not subject statutes to the justices' opinions but rather to the written constitution. His opinion was not an attempt to expand federal power—the power of either the Congress or the judiciary—but rather to keep it "defined and limited."[16]

Though Marshall loosely interpreted the necessary and proper clause in order to keep the national bank in *McCulloch v. Maryland* (1819), he drew upon a historical understanding of the ratification of the Constitution in *Barron v. Baltimore* (1833). In *Barron,* the Supreme Court was given the opportunity to apply the federal Bill of Rights to the states. Litigant John Barron claimed that Baltimore, in city improvements that made his wharf useless, had violated the takings clause of the Fifth Amendment. The Marshall Court answered in the negative. "It is universally understood, it is a part of the history of the day," Marshall observed, that in the wake of the ratification debates, Congress proposed and the states ratified a bill of rights with safeguards against the new federal government, not the states. Marshall compared the Bill of Rights— which included the Fifth Amendment—to Section 9 of the Constitution, which he called a brief bill of rights limiting only the federal government. The sovereign people of the states, Marshall declared, through their state constitutions had empowered and restricted state governments and through the federal constitution had empowered and restricted the federal government. In *Barron,* then, the Marshall Court refrained from using the federal judiciary to strike down state legislation, instead bowing to the written constitution and the compact understanding of its ratification.[17]

Some judicial review cases did not deal with a conflict between a statute and a written constitution but, instead, with a conflict between a statute and a common-law principle. Southern jurists deemed such customary law equally important to written constitutions. Both were fundamental law. If a common-law right, for example, was not included in a written constitution— an example was the absence in the original constitution of a guarantee of jury trial in civil suits—it still continued to be a fundamental right in southern jurisprudence.

The case of *Crenshaw and Crenshaw v. Slate River Company* (1828) provides an excellent example of this way of thinking. In the 1820s, the Virginia state legislature chartered a company to open up for navigation the upper James River system. Such a project, however, endangered the interests of mills on the river; millers would be compelled to build and maintain locks if they wanted to avoid having their milldams destroyed as nuisances on a public waterway. The question in *Crenshaw and Crenshaw v. Slate River Company* was whether the state's actions required the process of eminent domain, which would involve paying the millers fair compensation. Attorneys for the company argued that rivers were public waterways, that the legislature could quash any county court grant to build a mill, and that because the millers were no longer legally protected they did not need to be compensated.[18]

In the nineteenth century, those who supported economic development, especially increased steamboat navigation, argued that rivers (far beyond the tidewater) were not private property and within the jurisdiction of local county courts but rather public property and within the jurisdiction of the states or federal government. A ruling in favor of the Slate River Company would have allowed Virginia to join a trend, prevalent especially in the Northeast, of putting commerce and economic development above local agricultural interests and property rights and of using the law as a means to transform the economy.[19]

The Virginia supreme court decided against the Slate River Company, ruling that though the legislature had the authority to take land for public use, including dams previously authorized by county courts, it had to proceed through common-law eminent domain and pay fair compensation. The same fundamental rules bound both county courts and the state legislature. The court, as in other judicial review cases, stated that it did not seek to check the legislature but simply to correct it on a common-law principle. Though this particular common-law right had not been included in the state bill of rights, it had passed the test of time, was therefore part of the "unwritten constitution," and was a property right that no government could properly take away.

In principle, then, the concept of judicial review, both at the federal and at the state levels, did not alarm states' rights supporters; cases such as *Barron* and *Crenshaw* even served to limit government. However, a series of rulings in the first half of the nineteenth century by John Marshall's Supreme Court worried states' rights advocates. Though Marshall was innately moderate, practical, and even conservative in terms of property rights and the sanctity of contracts, he often let his Federalist political agenda and nationalist instincts get the better of him. Especially in its review of state statutes, the Marshall Court displayed a nationalist bias. The Court often loosely construed the Constitution if necessary to uphold acts of Congress against the states—the case of *McCulloch v. Maryland* being a classic example. Because of this, defenders of states' rights viewed the judicial review of state acts by the Marshall Court as a threat to the states and the federal balance of power.

While chief justice, Marshall became enmeshed in contemporary political issues. He became involved in an exchange in the newspapers with Spencer Roane, a leading judge of the Virginia supreme court who had been an Anti-Federalist and was one of the leaders of the Republican Party. Marshall was on the defensive in a country moving in a states' rights and Jacksonian direction, and his sparring with Roane and rulings that angered many state politicians and Democrats in Congress compromised the prestige of the Supreme Court. Many of its pronouncements were simply ignored. Without consistent support from the president and Congress, the Court sometimes delivered rulings in a vacuum, the most famous of these concerning Georgia and the Cherokee Indians.[20]

Among the several acts of resistance by state courts to the centralization and nationalism of the Marshall Court, the most defiant was that of Marshall's own Virginia in the Fairfax litigation. These cases, which involved land that had been part of Lord Fairfax's proprietary domain, included legal challenges to the sale of Fairfax land confiscated during the Revolution and state actions against land the family still owned but hoped to sell to a syndicate headed by Marshall, an attorney for the Fairfax family. While a member of the state legislature, Marshall worked out a compromise act wherein the Fairfax family deeded to the state the confiscated land, which cleared the titles to all the Fairfax land the state had sold. In return, the state ceased the actions against the remaining Fairfax land, allowing the land sale to the Marshall syndicate to take place.[21]

One of the suits continued, however, which led Roane to criticize the Fairfax-Marshall side for agreeing to give up one half of the old proprietary domain (the confiscated land) in order to get the other half, and then hoping to throw out the compromise agreement to gain the whole. The state high court ruled against the Fairfax-Marshall side, but on appeal the Supreme Court reversed the decision in *Fairfax's Devisee v. Hunter's Lessee*. Due to his personal involvement, Marshall did not participate officially. Justice Story, in the opinion of the court, ignored the compromise, part of the record of the appeal, and ruled that the state high court erred in that the state should have gone through common-law proceedings instead of a general confiscation of the Fairfax land.[22]

Judge Roane led the state supreme court in actively defying the Marshall Court. He asked whether a revolution had been fought so that years later, through treaties and the Constitution, the Supreme Court could reestablish a feudal domain in republican Virginia. In *Hunter v. Martin, Devisee of Fairfax,* the state judges contended that Story violated the Judiciary Act of 1789 by discarding the compromise on the record of the appeal, and they further contended that the Court did not have jurisdiction to rule on state law. Nor did they intend on returning land to Fairfax that he had deeded to the state.

On appeal, Story and the Marshall Court again ruled for the Fairfax-Marshall side, in *Martin v. Hunter's Lessee.* Virginia ignored the ruling.[23]

The litigation exposed problems in the application of Section 25 of the Judiciary Act of 1789. Anti-Federalists and states' rights Republicans had not initially been critical of the act, especially since it drew upon the services of the state courts and allowed a concurrent jurisdiction for state courts on federal and constitutional questions. What finally alerted and alarmed Roane and other states' rights Republicans was the possible threat to state law and state courts from Section 25 appeals. Once a case was appealed from a state court to the Supreme Court on federal or constitutional questions, what was to stop the Court from ruling on matters in the case that were not directly related to federal or constitutional questions? The major problem with Section 25 was the interconnection of the federal and state governments in a way that violated divided sovereignty. The state court concluded that the two systems of government should be separate and that federal courts should try only federal questions.

Judge Roane and other states' rights jurists believed that federal jurisdiction over state courts was a real threat to the states and that, through Section 25 appeals, the Supreme Court could assert that it was the highest court of the common law of each state. State courts would then have a status similar to county courts. Roane was afraid that the result would be the emergence of just one American law, determined by the Supreme Court and binding on all other courts.

Southern jurists such as Roane contended that there was a connection between nationalism and the movement for uniformity in the law. Combining their traditional legal perspective with their defense of states' rights, they preferred diverse, local determination of common law and a decentralized court system to legal uniformity. They believed that legal reformers, seeking one law for one nation, were trying to break down the lines between the federal government and the states through appeals from state courts to federal courts and through federal judicial review of state actions. Their desire for a strong check on an expansion of jurisdiction through Section 25 appeals was realized in practice, to an extent, because state courts, such as Virginia's in the Fairfax litigation, followed the law of their state supreme court, rather than the rulings of federal courts. This made the appellate process more cumbersome and unreliable. In turn, lawyers seeking to bring cases under federal jurisdiction pursued other avenues, such as diversity of citizenship. This strategy presented another centralist threat, the development of a federal common law.

Several Federalist judges advanced the idea of a federal common law in the 1790s, but it remained controversial. Iredell in *Chisholm* had rejected the notion of a single federal common law that was separate from the common law in each state. The best argument against the idea came from Justice Samuel Chase in *U.S. v. Worral,* a case prosecuted at common law that did not involve the Constitution, federal statute, or treaty.[24] Chase had been a Maryland politician and judge and an Anti-Federalist during the ratification debate before joining the Federalist Party during the 1790s. His personality and manner in court during sedition trials and the trial of John Fries won him the hatred of Republicans, yet he wrote some well-reasoned opinions favorable to states' rights, as in *Ware* (discussed above).[25] During the Federalist era he continued to challenge the idea of a federal common law.

In *U.S. v. Worral,* Chase stated that the Constitution was the source of the jurisdiction of the federal government and that Congress could pass statutes making crimes and punishments as a necessary and proper part of carrying out its powers. He noted, however, a tendency "to supply the silence of the constitution, and statutes of the union, by resorting to the common law, for a definition and punishment of the offence which has been committed." He presented a concise historical overview of the common law in America and the problem with the idea of a federal common law:

> If [the U.S. has] a common law, it must, I presume, be that of England; and yet it is impossible to trace, when, or how, the system was adopted, or introduced. With respect to the individual states, the difficulty does not occur. When the American colonies were first settled by our ancestors, it was held, as well by the settlers, as by the judges and lawyers of England, that they brought hither as a birthright and inheritance, so much of the common law, as was applicable to their situation, and change of circumstances. But each colony judged for itself, what parts of the common law were applicable to its new condition; and in various modes, by legislative acts, by judicial decisions, or by constant usage, adopted some parts, and rejected others. Hence, he who shall travel through the different states, will soon discover, that the whole of the common law of England, has been no where introduced; that some states have rejected what others have adopted; and that there is, in short, a great and essential diversity, in the subjects to which the common law is applied, as well as in the extent of the appli-

cation. The common law, therefore, of one state, is not the common law of another; but the common law of England, is the law of each state, so far as each state has adopted it. . . . But the question recurs, when and how, have the courts of the United States acquired a common law jurisdiction in criminal cases? The United States must possess the common law themselves, before they can communicate it to their judicial agents: now the United States did not bring it with them from England; the constitution does not create it; and no act of congress has assumed it. Besides, what is the common law, to which we are referred? Is it the common law entire, as it exists in England; or modified as it exists in some of the states; and of the various modifications, which are we to select; the system of Georgia, or New-Hampshire, Pennsylvania or Connecticut?"[26]

He concluded that there was no federal common law.

Other Federalists, such as Chief Justice Oliver Ellsworth, justified the idea of a federal common law in terms of seditious libel and the Sedition Act. In the sedition trials, defense lawyers failed to persuade the Federalist judges, through judicial review, to strike down the Sedition Act as unconstitutional for violating the First Amendment. Federalists interpreted the First Amendment in a common-law context wherein the right to freedom of the press prevented prior constraint of publication by the government, or censorship, but not subsequent constraint of publication, or prosecution for seditious libel. Furthermore, they defended the Sedition Act as an improvement on the common law by accepting truth as a defense, considering the defendant's intent, and allowing juries to determine both law and fact.[27]

Republicans questioned defending the Sedition Act as an improvement on federal common law, since they did not agree that such a law existed. Madison, in the Virginia Report, explained why Republicans opposed the idea of a federal common law and believed that such a law would be unconstitutional. They were afraid that such a law would defeat the whole purpose of the Constitution in limiting the federal government, he wrote. Because of "the vast and multifarious jurisdiction involved in the common law; a law . . . overspreading the entire field of legislation . . . would sap the foundation of the Constitution as a system of limited and specified powers." If accepted it would vastly expand the jurisdiction of the federal judiciary and, because Congress would have the authority to modify the common law, it could be used to claim that Congress could legislate in all areas covered by the common law. "The authority of Congress would, therefore, be no longer under the limitations marked out in the Constitution," said Madison. "They would be authorized to legislate in all cases whatsoever." Again, there was the problem of states being reduced to the status of mere counties if there was "a law for the American people as one community." If federal courts heard appeals from the common-law rulings of the states, then the result would be one common law for all America.[28]

The Virginia report was followed by the publication of *Blackstone's Commentaries* by St. George Tucker, who served on Virginia's supreme court and had followed Wythe as law professor at the College of William and Mary. This first major American edition of the *Commentaries* became a standard addition to lawyers' and judges' libraries. The work included a history of the common law in America, including a section on Chase's opinion in *U.S. v. Worral.* Tucker showed that history, practice of the law, the Constitution, and federal statute did not support the view that there was a federal common law. In addition, the text included a commentary on the Constitution that defended a historical, original construction, as well as lengthy sections on law in America, specifically Virginia, and how and to what extent Blackstone was applicable to American courts. While Story at Harvard emphasized how the common law was the same in both England and America, Tucker stressed the diversity that existed among the various common-law realms.[29]

The issue of a federal common law appeared settled by the Supreme Court in 1812 in *U.S. v. Hudson and Goodwin,* a common-law seditious libel suit brought by Republicans against a Federalist newspaper after the Sedition Act had expired. Justice William Johnson gave the opinion of the Court. Jefferson had appointed Johnson, a former South Carolina politician and judge. For a while the lone Republican among Federalists, he became the Court's first major dissenter. His opinions foreshadowed the direction the Court would take as Federalists were replaced by Republican and Democrat appointments.[30]

In *U.S. v. Hudson and Goodwin,* Johnson stated, as Iredell and Chase had noted in prior cases, that Congress needed to pass statutes to establish crimes and punishments. He took the opportunity both to discuss the limited nature of the federal government and to note the problems with a federal common law:

> The powers of the general Government are made up of concessions
> from the several states—whatever is not expressly given to the former,
> the latter expressly reserve. The judicial power of the United States is a

constituent part of those concessions. . . . When a Court is created, and
its operations confined to certain specific objects, with what propriety
can it assume to itself a jurisdiction—much more extended—in its
nature very indefinite—applicable to a great variety of subjects—varying in every state in the Union. . . .

The Court concluded that the federal judiciary did not have a common-law
criminal jurisdiction.

Justice Story disagreed. *U.S. v. Hudson and Goodwin* had dealt only with
criminal law. Story had long asserted that a federal common law could at
least be established in commercial law, where there was much agreement
among the many countries engaged in international trade and where there
was also agreement in the U.S. among the federal and state courts. Marshall
remained unconvinced by Story's theory and led the Court in refusing to
accept the concept of a federal common law. Marshall shared with Johnson an
unwillingness to seek judicial authority beyond the Constitution and federal
statute. After Johnson and Marshall had departed, however, Story prevailed.
Story never thought that Section 34 of the Judiciary Act of 1789 should have
restrained the federal courts. Writing the opinion of the Taney Court in *Swift
v. Tyson,* Story reinterpreted "laws of the several states" in Section 34 to mean
not common law but only statute law. In common-law suits, federal courts
would no longer have to follow state common law, except where a legislature
passed a statute to make an exception to the commercial law. This meant that
at least in commercial law there now *was* a federal common law.[31]

Soon, in *Lane v. Vick,* the Court applied the *Swift* rule on Section 34
beyond commercial law. This case, which came under federal jurisdiction
via diversity of citizenship, was an appeal from the U.S. circuit court for the
southern district of Mississippi. It did not involve the Constitution, federal
statute, treaty, or commercial law. The question involved the construction of
a will—the will of Newit Vick, founder of Vicksburg, Mississippi. The Mississippi supreme court had already determined the question. Under the earlier
interpretation of Section 34 of the Judiciary Act of 1789, the Supreme Court
would have followed the ruling of the Mississippi high court. In this case,
however, the *Swift* precedent allowed a majority of the Supreme Court to rule
differently.[32]

Justice John McKinley wrote the first dissent to the developing *Swift* doctrine. McKinley, a Van Buren appointee, had been a Democratic senator from

Alabama. His circuit included Alabama, Mississippi, Louisiana, and Arkansas. Throughout his service on the Court, he tried to preserve the federal balance and keep the federal courts in their proper jurisdictional bounds. In his dissenting opinion, McKinley asked on what basis the Court could rule against a state supreme court's interpretation of that state's common law when no federal question was raised and no commercial law was involved. He asserted that, in delineating the powers of the federal courts in the Judiciary Act of 1789, Congress had "directed, that the laws of the several states should be regarded as the rules of decision in suits at common law, in cases where they apply." "And upon these principles," he continued, "has this court acted from the commencement of the government down to the present term of this court. That they should continue so to act, is of great importance to the peace and harmony of the people of the United States." If the Court ruled on state law contrary to the rulings of the state supreme courts, then the result would be a conflict between federal and state law and a contest between federal and state courts. As McKinley predicted, the *Swift* doctrine created discord, with two common-law systems operating in each state. Authorized by neither the Constitution nor federal statute, the Supreme Court was now essentially promulgating judge-made law.[33]

Justice McKinley also played a prominent role in the Alabama Bank Cases. In the U.S. circuit court for the southern district of Alabama, McKinley ruled in favor of Alabama's power to prohibit out-of-state banks from buying and selling bills of exchange in the state. The cases were appealed to the Supreme Court, where Chief Justice Roger Taney, writing for the majority, stated that the bank corporations were similar to citizens of one nation who did business in other nations through a kind of international law known as the comity of nations. The Court declared that the law of comity applied to the American states, and therefore out-of-state banks could buy and sell bills of exchange in Alabama just as they could elsewhere. (As was typical of the Taney Court, a compromise provision for states' rights was offered. This compromise allowed a legislature to make an exception to the law of comity.) In his dissent, McKinley stated that international law did not apply to these cases since states were not nations. Most importantly, echoing his dissent in *Lane,* he criticized the majority for trying to justify the Court's jurisdiction in international law. The Court, chided McKinley, was exceeding its bounds beyond the limits of federal statute and the Constitution.[34]

During the early republic, southern jurists defended the common-law tradition and the written constitution, and those of a less Federalist persuasion opposed centralist legal reform and uniformity. Southern jurists tended to accept diversity in the law and to prefer a judicially segmented society, wherein protection could be provided by walls of separation and differing lines of jurisdiction.

These southern jurists used judicial review to maintain the limits on government provided by written constitutions (as in *Commonwealth v. Caton* and *Marbury*); insisted on the importance of the history of constitutional ratification (as in *Barron*); wrote Supreme Court opinions that attempted to circumscribe the Court's jurisdictional bounds and to slow its progression toward judge-made law (as with Iredell in *Chisholm,* or with Johnson of South Carolina and McKinley of Alabama); opposed the concept of a federal common law (as with Johnson's opinion in *U.S. v. Hudson and Goodwin*) or else opposed its further development (as with McKinley in *Lane*); resisted changes in eminent domain that prioritized economic development over provincial agricultural interests and older common-law rules and procedures (as in *Crenshaw*); defended common-law diversity and preserved a historical construction of the Constitution through their writing on the law (as with Tucker's *Blackstone*); dragged out at the trial court level, with local juries, the rulings of higher courts (as in *Ware*); used the cumbersome machinery of separate jurisdictions for state courts to frustrate the federal courts (as in *Martin*); tried to build walls of separation, as in the Alabama Bank Cases; and, at times, outright defied the Supreme Court (as with Roane and the Virginia high court in *Hunter*).

During this time, judicial review generally served, in the state and federal courts, to uphold the importance of written constitutions. Especially for the generation that wrote them, there was a reverence for these documents. Madison and Marshall largely shared in the other southerners' defense of constitutional limitations on the scope of federal law and argued for the importance of the historical understanding of the Constitution at its ratification. Nevertheless, Madison, Marshall, Tucker, and the more moderate southern jurists, while they sought to maintain a federal balance of power, could not go to the decentralizing lengths of a Roane or, indeed, a John Calhoun.

In the early years of the nineteenth century, many Old Republicans and states' rights Democrats continued to uphold the southerners' view of the federal system. They looked back to the historical context of the ratification of the Constitution and tried to maintain the proper line between the federal government and the states. Whereas centralist legal reformers tried to justify their goals through new interpretations of the Constitution, conceptions of the natural law or progress, or appeals to the will of the people, southern jurists looked to history, experience, and the common-law rules and principles that had passed the test of time. As the century aged, southern jurists did not soften in their resistance to the central government's efforts to cross lines of jurisdiction and achieve a uniform law. The more resolute among them were ready to present the plea for preservation of the states as distinct realms and to resist the movement toward one people, one nation, and one law.

Publius on "Liquidation" and the Meaning of the Constitution

STEVEN D. EALY

Years ago, when I was teaching political science at a state college in Savannah, Georgia, I assigned *The Federalist Papers* in a class on modern political thought, along with works by Thomas Hobbes, John Locke, and Karl Marx. Rather than requiring my students to write a term paper, I had them write a short critique on each of the books read for the class. I had assumed that writing on *The Federalist* would be the easiest of the four assignments, but it in fact proved to be the most difficult.

The students' problem was not that *The Federalist* was the most difficult of the texts we read, but rather that it was the most familiar. Reading *The Federalist* took them into a world with which they were already familiar, and they could find no ground from which to criticize Publius or his arguments. The critical concepts they had at their disposal—limited government, checks and balances, separation of powers, the danger of majority tyranny—*came* from *The Federalist*. It was at this point that I began to understand that in key ways our real constitution—the one under which we Americans actually operate—was not the document written in Philadelphia in the summer of 1787, but was instead *The Federalist Papers*. The document written in Philadelphia was the constitution on paper, but for my students the argument of *The Federalist* was the constitution written on their hearts. This is not to claim, of course, that these students had previously studied or even ever heard of *The Federalist Papers*—rather, it is to suggest that the intellectual framework of *The Federalist* was the air they had been breathing their entire lives. Its arguments were for them the common sense of political life.[1]

This story can cut two ways, I think. If my students were representative of contemporary Americans, then an understanding of *The Federalist Papers* perhaps takes us a long way in understanding the dynamics of American politics and the operation of the American political system. On the other hand, the preeminence given to *The Federalist Papers* may short-circuit the process of self-government by distorting our perceptions and dampening what should be an ongoing debate about the basic concerns of American politics.

The claim that *The Federalist Papers* is the constitution written on the hearts of the American people is perhaps a reflection on the nature of the Constitution itself. According to Willmoore Kendall, "The Philadelphia Constitution, the Constitution submitted by the Convention for ratification by the American people, is, to put the matter in its simplest terms, not one but many constitutions—a crossroads, from which, once having situated itself there, the people of America might have moved in any of several directions, might have moved . . . to this or that one of many alternative political systems under which we might have governed ourselves."[2]

If Kendall is correct, the Constitution does not embody a substantive political philosophy, regardless of what philosophy or philosophies may have been held by its authors and ratifiers. Rather, the Constitution provides structures and procedures that can be used to pursue a wide variety of ends. In another essay Kendall speaks of the "implicit constitutional morality" of *The Federalist*'s model of democracy and of the competing "populistic model of democracy."[3] This raises the following interesting question: is there an "implicit constitutional morality" in the Constitution itself? If the Constitution is truly a "crossroads" containing multiple potentialities, the answer to the question appears to be "no"—many models, each containing an "implicit constitutional morality," can legitimately attempt to attach themselves to the Constitution, with very different policy outcomes. Kendall concludes that one must understand *The Federalist* as an attempt "to impose upon that constitution a particular meaning that is present in it *only* potentially."[4]

As preface to a consideration of what *The Federalist* has to say on the national and/or federal foundations of the Constitution, I want to examine Publius's notion of "liquidation of meaning."[5] I think a consideration of this curious expression can help in placing *The Federalist*'s understanding of the Constitution in the appropriate framework.

"All new laws, though penned with the greatest technical skill and passed on the fullest and most mature deliberation," writes Publius in *Federalist* 37, "are considered as more or less obscure and equivocal, until their meaning be liquidated and ascertained by a series of particular discussions and adjudications" (37:229).[6] In *Federalist* 82, Publius returns to this notion:

> The erection of a new government, whatever care or wisdom may distinguish the work, cannot fail to originate questions of intricacy and nicety; and these may, in a particular manner, be expected to flow from the establishment of a constitution founded upon the total or partial incorporation of a number of distinct sovereignties. 'Tis time only that can mature and perfect so compound a system, can liquidate the meaning of all the parts, and can adjust them to each other in a harmonious and consistent WHOLE.[7] (82:491)

If this view is correct, it would be impossible to know exactly what specific provisions of the Constitution then under consideration actually meant and how the government it established would function until after the Constitution was adopted and the newly established government had begun operations. It is crucial to remember that the detailed analyses and discussions contained in *The Federalist Papers* are prospective and suggestive in nature when dealing with the meaning of the proposed constitution and the operation of the new government.

In addition to these theoretical discussions of the necessity and importance of liquidating the meaning of new laws, Publius's third use of the term provides a specific example of how liquidation will occur, and perhaps illustrates how far-reaching the implications of this notion are. In *Federalist* 78, Publius writes that when two statutes clash, "it is the province of the courts to liquidate and fix their meaning and operation" (78:468). From this premise concerning clashing statutes, Publius builds his argument for the judicial power to invalidate laws contrary to the Constitution. We need not follow his argument in detail, but we do need to reflect on his claim that the power of judicial review rests not on the language of the Constitution but on the general theory of judicial interpretation. In *Federalist* 81, Publius writes that the doctrine of invalidating laws contrary to the Constitution "is not deducible from any circumstance peculiar to the plan of the convention; but from the general theory of a limited constitution" (81:482). Thus, arguably the most important power the courts hold is based not on the clear language of the Constitution but on a particular reading of its meaning—that is, on the "liquidation of meaning" of its obscure and imprecise language.

Martin Diamond argues that "*The Federalist* deals largely with factual matters."[8] But given the prospective nature of *The Federalist,* at least in terms of the operation of the new government, this claim cannot stand. Publius may be prophetic and accurately predictive, or he may be trying to shape the future through the force of his argument, but he is not being "factual" when he describes what the relations between the national government and the states, or between the various branches of the national government, will be like once the new system is set in motion. Whether one maintains that what Publius writes represents his best guess at how the system will work, or (along with Kendall) that Publius's arguments are designed to send readers down one of the potential roads the Constitution itself holds open, one may also conclude that Publius's arguments are designed as much to allay fears and secure ratification of the Constitution as they are to provide an unbiased and authoritative interpretation of the meaning of the Constitution and the intentions of its framers.

That Publius is providing a "best guess"—or an intentionally optimistic or politically skewed reading—rather than a definitive reading of the Constitution is not surprising, given what he says about the obscurity of some of the topics he covers and the difficulties involved in articulating complicated matters. Publius offers a long discussion of the "sources of vague and incorrect definitions" in *Federalist* 37, and it is during this discussion that he first introduces the importance of liquidation of meaning in the first quotation above.

According to Publius, there are three primary causes for vague definitions: "indistinctness of the object," "imperfection of the organ of conception," or "inadequateness of the vehicle of ideas." In the first case, "sense, perception, judgment, desire, volition, memory, imagination" may have not been clearly distinguished (37:227). In the second, he uses as an example the inability of naturalists to clearly demarcate the line between vegetable and animal. It is the third cause of imprecision, the very limits of language itself, however, that is most relevant to his subject (37:229).

Publius's discussion of language is worth lingering over for a moment, because he points to a crucial difficulty. He begins simply: "The use of words is to express ideas." Clarity "requires not only that the ideas should be distinctly formed, but that they should be expressed by words distinctly and exclusively appropriate to them." At this point a problem arises, however, because "no language is so copious as to supply words and phrases for every complex idea, or so correct as not to include many equivocally denoting different ideas." That is, we must use imprecise and equivocal language to speak about precise objects. (As Robert Frost would have it, metaphor is at the heart of all thought.)[9] This "unavoidable inaccuracy" will vary "according to the complexity and novelty of the objects defined" (37:229).[10] Many of the objects defined and discussed in *The Federalist* are novel, and almost all are complex.

This whole discussion of "vague definitions" is entered into by Publius in an effort to explain the convention's difficulties in "marking the proper line of partition between the authority of the general and that of the State governments" (37:227). Thus, to foreshadow the next section of my argument, what in other passages Publius attempts to portray as clearcut and unproblematic is here confessed to be obscure and speculative. He concludes, "The convention, in delineating the boundary between the federal and State jurisdictions, must have experienced the full effect" of indistinctness, imperfection, and linguistic inadequacy (37:229).[11]

The issue of the partition of authority between the states and the general government lies at the heart of the tightly reasoned argument Publius offers in *Federalist* 39, but this issue cannot be settled in advance, as Publius strives to do. Rather, resolution of this issue will require time and "a particular series of discussions and adjudications." That is, liquidation of meaning is crucial for all of the issues Publius examines in *Federalist* 39.

Much has been made of the "split personality" of Publius. Some have sought to use individual papers as evidence for or against a particular position they want to connect with Hamilton, Madison, or Jay; some have used the notion of "split personality" as a way to undermine the authority of *The Federalist Papers*.[12] But on the question of "liquidation of meaning" there is no split personality—James Madison was the author of the passage from *Federalist* 37 and Alexander Hamilton the author of *Federalist* 82.

I tend to agree with those who say that we should understand the author of *The Federalist Papers* to be one "Publius," not three separate authors writing independently and at times in conflict with each other.[13] But this does not mean that there is perfect consistency within the series of papers penned by Publius. Rather, I think Publius was working through a series of difficult issues, and at the time of writing he was of two minds on many of the topics he addressed.

<hr/>

Before turning to a discussion of the set of issues revolving around the federal/national distinction in *The Federalist,* I will set the scene by recounting a part of the debate that took place in the Philadelphia Convention that drafted the Constitution. On May 30, 1787, Edmund Randolph, one of Virginia's delegates, moved the consideration of three propositions:

1. that a Union of the States merely federal will not accomplish the objects proposed by the articles of Confederation, namely common defense, security of liberty, & general welfare.

2. that no treaty or treaties among the whole or part of the State, as individual Sovereignties, would be sufficient.

3. that a national Government ought to be established consisting of a supreme Legislative, Executive & Judiciary.[14]

The attention of the delegates quickly turned to the third proposition. Two delegates from South Carolina expressed their concerns. Charles Pinckney "wished to know of Mr. Randolph whether he meant to abolish the State Governments altogether."[15] General Charles Cotesworth Pinckney "expressed a doubt whether the act of Congress recommending the Convention, or the Commissions of the Deputies to it, could authorize a discussion of a System founded on different principles from the federal Constitution."[16] Elbridge Gerry of Massachusetts shared General Pinckney's doubt. Both of these concerns would be raised during the ratification debates in the states and addressed by Publius in *The Federalist Papers*.[17]

Gouverneur Morris of Pennsylvania then defined the terms under consideration by the convention. He "explained the distinction between a *federal* and *national, supreme,* Government; the former being a mere compact resting on the good faith of the parties; the latter having a compleat and *compulsive* operation. He contended that in all Communities there must be one supreme power, and one only."[18]

This brief glance at the Philadelphia Convention helps to establish the framework for my remarks. What is it exactly that the Constitution proposes: a federal system, retaining state sovereignty and equality, or a national system in which the states are reduced in authority and the general government is the primary locus of political power? The center of my reflections will be *Federalist* 39, in which Publius makes the celebrated claim that "the proposed Constitution . . . is, in strictness, neither a national nor a federal Constitution, but a composition of both" (39:246). Publius thus claims that the proposed Constitution offers something new under the sun in two regards: it is a system that is neither national nor federal, and it is a system with two supreme powers.[19]

In *Federalist* 39, Publius considers the charge that rather than preserving the federal form of government, "which regards the Union as a Confederacy of sovereign states," the Constitution establishes a national government, "which regards the Union as a consolidation of the States" (39:243). Publius then outlines "the real character of the government" proposed under the Constitution by considering it in relation to five concerns: its foundation, the source of its power, the operation of its powers, the extent of its powers, and the authority to amend the Constitution in the future.

Publius holds that the foundation of the Constitution is a federal rather than a national act, in that its ratification requires action on the part of each of the several states acting independently. Furthermore, Publius argues, this action is based not on the principle of majority rule, but on the "unanimous assent of the several States that are parties to it" (39:243–44).

Next Publius argues that in regard to the source of its powers, the government established by the Constitution is mixed. Seats in the House of Representatives will be allocated proportionally based on state population and will be filled by popular election. The House thus represents the national principle. The Senate, on the other hand, represents the states equally, regardless of size, and senators will be selected by the states rather than by the people through direct popular election. The Senate, then, embodies the federal principle. Election of the president is a compound process that is itself a mixture of these competing principles.

As for Publius's third concern—the operation of government—in a federal system "the powers operate on the political bodies composing the Confederacy in their political capacities" (39:245)—that is, on the states—while in a national system these powers operate directly "on the individual citizens composing the nation in their individual capacities." The requirement that the central government act through the states constitutes one of Publius's major criticisms of the Articles of Confederation.[20] The operation of government under the proposed Constitution, Publius concludes, is national in nature.

While Publius maintains that in the operation of its powers the new government will be national, this is not the case in regard to the extent of its powers, his fourth point of concern. "The idea of a national government," writes Publius, "involves in it not only an authority over the individual citizens, but an indefinite supremacy over all persons and things, so far as they are objects of lawful government. Among a people consolidated into one nation, this supremacy is completely vested in the national legislature" (39:245). In a federal system, on the other hand, sovereign power "is vested partly in the general and partly in the municipal legislatures." In addition, in a national system local authorities are subordinate to the national government, "and may be controlled, directed, or abolished by it at pleasure." In a federal system, local authorities "form distinct and independent portions of the supremacy." As long as all governments stay within their own spheres, the general government cannot control the states, and the states cannot control the general government. After his analysis, Publius provides a slightly tentative conclusion: "In this relation, then, the proposed government cannot be deemed a national one; since its jurisdiction extends to certain enumerated objects only, and leaves to the several States a residuary and inviolable sovereignty over all other objects" (39:245). Note that in his summary at the conclusion of this paper Publius is not tentative at all; he clearly says that, in regard to the extent of its powers, the Constitution is federal rather than national (39:246).[21]

On his final point of concern, the amendment process, Publius finds that the proposed Constitution is neither wholly national nor wholly federal. Both houses of Congress, as well as the legislatures of the states, are involved in amending the Constitution. The amendment process is therefore mixed.

Publius concludes, therefore, that the proposed Constitution is, "in strictness, neither a national nor a federal Constitution, but a composition of both" (39:246). By his accounting, in fact, the Constitution tilts slightly toward the federal rather than the national side of the controversy. In terms of its foundations (only states adopting the new constitution are bound by it, thus operating on the basis of unanimity) and extent of powers (with the general government limited to enumerated powers only) the new system is federal. In terms of its operation (directly on the citizens rather than through the state governments) it is national. Finally, in terms of the sources of power (the House is national and the Senate federal) and the amendment process (which requires support in both legislative branches and within the states) the new constitution is mixed. By this tally, we have a constitution that is federal on two issues of concern, national on one, and mixed on the other two.

Before accepting this accounting at face value we should review some of the other things Publius says in regard to the foundations of government, the source and extent of its powers, and the operations of the national government under the Constitution.

In *Federalist* 9, Publius seems to take a more cavalier attitude toward the distinction between federal and national systems than he does in *Federalist* 39. This number is worth quoting at some length. "The definition of a *confederate republic* seems simply to be 'an assemblage of societies,' or an association of two or more states into one state," writes Publius (9:76). He then makes the following claim: "The extent, modification, and objects of the federal authority are mere matters of discretion." As I read it, this suggests that the powers of the states ("federal authority") are matters of discretion rather than matters of principle—matters of detail rather than of serious import. This interpretation is reinforced as Publius continues: "So long as the separate organization of the members be not abolished; so long as it exists, by a constitutional necessity, for local purposes; though it should be in perfect subordination to the general authority of the union, it would still be, in fact and in theory, an association of states, or a confederacy." Publius concludes this discussion by arguing, "The proposed Constitution, so far from implying an abolition of the State governments, makes them constituent parts of the national sovereignty, by allowing them a direct representation in the Senate, and leaves in their possession certain exclusive and very important portions of sovereign power." Those "portions of sovereign power" left to the states, I presume, involve primarily "local purposes" but also include the Senate's power to approve treaties.

Returning to *Federalist* 39, we can now consider each of the five aspects of national-state relations discussed there. First, Publius concluded that the foundation of the proposed constitution was federal because it was to be ratified by the states and requires the unanimous consent of the states that will be party to the new government. This argument is made as if the convention and the states that would consider ratification were starting from scratch in an effort to establish some sort of union, but this was not the case. As its preamble instructs us, the Constitution is established "in Order to form a more perfect Union"—thus recognizing that a union among the states already existed, a union established by the Articles of Confederation. In thinking about the foundation of the new constitution, one must also take into account the impact of this founding on the already existing union. This is acknowledged by Publius, who writes in *Federalist* 40: "The truth is that the great principles of the Constitution proposed by the convention may be considered less as absolutely new than as the expansion of principles which are found in the Articles of Confederation" (40:251). In *Federalist* 40, Publius also acknowledges that the proposed ratification process departs from the requirements of the then existing legal framework of the union—the Articles—which require unanimity among the states. While Publius provides a prudential and contextual argument for this diversion from legal requirements, he does not provide an argument from principle (see 40:251, 43:279).[22] As Publius writes near the end of *Federalist* 39, "Were it wholly federal, the concurrence of each State in the Union would be essential to every alteration that would be binding on all" (39:246). In a crucial way, the foundation of the new ("more perfect") union is the destruction of the old (less perfect) union, and since the destruction of the old constitution does not accord with a key principle of a federal system—unanimity—neither does the foundation of the new constitution.[23]

Where does sovereign power reside in this new system? If in the states, we seem to have a federal system; if in the central government, we have a national system. What type of system do we have if that ultimate power resides in neither, but in "the people"? In *Federalist* 39, Publius is careful to argue that the ratification process is federal: "It is to be the assent and ratification of the several States, derived from the supreme authority in each State—the authority of the people themselves" (39:243). Even here, however, it must be emphasized that Publius points beyond the states "to the people themselves."

In other papers, Publius is not so careful to recognize the states' position of preeminence. In reflecting on what participants in the Philadelphia Convention thought, he writes in *Federalist* 40 that "they must have borne in mind that as a plan to be framed and proposed was to be submitted to *the people themselves,* the disapprobation of this supreme authority would destroy it forever; its approbation blot out antecedent errors and irregularities" (40:253; italics in original). No mention here of the states as the foundation of the Constitution, nor in *Federalist* 84 in the argument against a bill of rights. Bills of rights "have no application to constitutions, professedly founded upon the power of the people and executed by their immediate representatives and servants" (84:513). Immediately thereafter, Publius quotes the Preamble to the Constitution, which begins, "We the people of the United States. . . ."[24] Based on the arguments of Publius himself, there are grounds to question his designation of the foundation of the proposed constitution as clearly federal in nature. The thrust of Publius's argument is twofold: away from state unanimity and toward "the people." One could conclude, therefore, that the foundation of the proposed constitution is national, not federal.

On his second point, the sources from which the powers of government are drawn, Publius in *Federalist* 39 finds that the system proposed is "partly federal and partly national." The House is national, with representatives tied closely to the people; the Senate is federal, with senators tied closely to the states; the presidency is mixed. In thinking this matter through, one should consider the following: Each house of Congress is the sole judge of its own membership; the salaries paid to these legislators come from the national treasury; there are no provisions for recall of legislators; and nothing binds them to follow the instructions of either the people of their districts or the states that appointed them. As for the president, he is subject to impeachment and trial by the branches of the national legislature, but not the states. Thus, in crucial matters officials in the national government are at least temporarily free from local control (as long as they can stand the political pressure). In considering the sources of power, we need to move beyond elective offices and note that appointment to seats in the judicial branch is controlled entirely within the general government and for a period of good behavior. The powers of government are drawn from the Constitution, rather than from the people or the states. Thus, one could conclude that the source of the ordinary powers of the national government is national, rather than mixed, as Publius asserts.

In terms of its operation, Publius argues, the national government acts directly on the people and is not dependent on the states to enforce national laws. Publius is consistent throughout *The Federalist Papers* on this point. One of his major criticisms of the weaknesses of the Articles of Confederation is that the central government is dependent on state enforcement. Thus, in its operation, the Constitution is national in nature.

In regard to his fourth concern, the extent of powers under the proposed constitution, Publius concludes in *Federalist* 39 that the proposed system is federal in that the jurisdiction of the national government "extends to certain enumerated objects only" (39:245).[25] Thus, according to Publius, there is a sphere in which "local or municipal authorities" remain supreme, and a sphere in which the "general authority" is supreme. Immediately after this claim, however, Publius raises a difficulty: who resolves controversies over exactly where the boundary between these spheres is located? The answer Publius gives is the Supreme Court—"the tribunal which is ultimately to decide is to be established under the general government" (39:245).[26] He then attempts to downplay the significance of this admission by arguing that such decisions will be "impartially made" (39:245–46). An impartial accounting might hold, as a minimum, that the placement of this arbiter within the general government means that the proposed system is at best mixed in regard to the extent of powers.

But one must consider another crucial dimension of the enumeration of powers in the Constitution. The last item in the list of powers granted to Congress—Article I, Section 8, Paragraph 18—reads as follows: Congress shall have power "To make all Laws which shall be necessary and proper for carrying into Execution the foregoing Powers, and all other Powers vested by this Constitution in the Government of the United States, or in any Department or Officer thereof." What does the "necessary and proper clause" do to the notion of enumerated powers? In *Federalist* 44, Publius argues that such a grant of power is absolutely essential: "Without the *substance* of this power, the whole Constitution would be a dead letter" (44:284). Publius argues that for powers under the Articles of Confederation to be exercised, the doctrine of construction or implication was crucial. The Articles restricted Congress to those powers "expressly delegated." A rigorous enforcement of this provision would "disarm the government of all real authority whatever." He enunciates a general rule of law: "No axiom is more clearly established in law, or in reason, than that wherever the end is required, the means are authorized; wherever a general power to do a thing is given, every particular power necessary for doing it is included" (44:285).[27]

In *Federalist* 45, Publius compares the powers delegated to the national government with those retained by the states. National powers "will be exercised principally on external objects, as war, peace, negotiation, and foreign commerce" (45:292). State powers, on the other hand, "will extend to all the objects which, in the ordinary course of affairs, concern the lives, liberties, and properties of the people, and the internal order, improvement, and prosperity of the State" (45:293). Since periods of war and danger will be rare, the states will thus enjoy an advantage over the national government, Publius concludes. He does recognize, however, that "the operations of the federal government will be most extensive and important in times of war and danger" (45:293). If we should ever enter a time of perpetual war and danger,[28] we would then be faced with the possibility of the perpetual superiority of the national over the state governments.[29]

While Publius argues in *Federalist* 39 that the enumeration of powers in the proposed constitution is a limitation on the general government, his description of "a limited Constitution" in *Federalist* 78 is considerably different. There Publius writes, "By a limited Constitution, I understand one which contains certain specified exceptions to the legislative authority; such, for instance, as that it shall pass no bills of attainder, no *ex post facto* laws, and the like" (78:466). To put it bluntly, it appears that Publius offers two competing views of the extent of legislative power: in *Federalist* 39, legislative power is limited by the enumeration of certain specific powers, while in *Federalist* 78, legislative power is limited by the existence of exceptions to legislative authority. The view expressed in *Federalist* 39 strikes me as being much more forceful as a control on Congress, but even there Publius admits the final arbiter of the extent of this power will reside in the general government. All of these items—the role of the national judiciary in policing the division of powers between states and national government, the existence of implied powers through the necessary and proper clause, the various national powers that would come to the fore during times of danger and war, and the expansive reading of "a limited Constitution" in *Federalist* 78—allow one to conclude that in regard to the extent of power granted the general government under the Constitution, we have a national rather than a federal system.

Publius argues that the amendment process is mixed, involving both the states and the general government. I concur with this analysis.[30]

According to Publius in *Federalist* 39, the Constitution is truly a mixture of national and federal features. But my alternative account of the five areas of concern Publius investigates leads to the conclusion that the Constitution is national in its foundation, in the source of its power, in its operation, and in the extent of its authority. According to my alternative account, only in the area of amendment is the Constitution mixed.

If the above analysis is correct, and Publius actually captures the ambiguity of the relationship between the national and state governments, what does this show about *The Federalist Papers,* or the Constitution, or the American political system generally? Let me return momentarily to my teaching days. After using *The Federalist Papers* over a period of years in my American thought courses, I replaced it on the syllabus with James Madison's *Notes of Debates in the Federal Convention of 1787.* I made this change because *The Federalist* seemed to settle matters once and for all; it seemed to make the Constitution and the American political system appear to be a done deal. This reduced the responsibility of my students merely to learning the lessons of their elders and betters and acting appropriately. Madison's "Notes," on the other hand, captured the vitality of political debate and encouraged my students to participate in that debate. This text helped them understand that they could be part of the ongoing debate about the nature of our constitutional order that has been taking place in America since the eighteenth century.

How can we fit *The Federalist Papers* into the framework of that debate? I have suggested that the Constitution itself does not embody a substantive political philosophy—rather, it provides structures and procedures that can be used to pursue a variety of ends. The preamble outlines certain purposes to be achieved but does not define the meaning of those purposes, nor does it substantively tie the institutions of government to them in more than a general way. The framers may have shared, in broad terms, a substantive political or social philosophy that they assumed as the foundation for the Constitution. Nevertheless, that philosophy is not a part of the constitutional framework. That philosophy, to use a term that Tocqueville uses in his *Democracy in America* a few generations later, might be designated as the mores of the people. If the Constitution is a neutral set of procedures and mechanisms grounded in a set of mores that emphasize suspicion of power, individual and collective self-restraint, and commitment to a clear-cut and relatively stable set of moral beliefs, those mechanisms and procedures will lead to fairly minimal intrusion into the private lives of citizens and will provide material benefits for them. Change the mores of the people, and those same neutral mechanisms may produce very different results. Such a change in outcomes does not necessarily signal a "derailment" of the American system.[31]

The way to integrate *The Federalist Papers* into the ongoing political debate in America is to understand them not as the definitive interpretation of the Constitution but rather as one of the initial efforts at liquidating the meaning of the Constitution. As an effort aimed at the liquidation of meaning, *The Federalist* takes its place alongside the newspaper and pamphlet literature from the same period. This would include Anti-Federalist writers such as Brutus and the Federal Farmer, as well as proponents of the Constitution such as John Dickinson.[32] If *The Federalist Papers* are to be regarded as authoritative, that authority should be understood, as Albert Furtwangler has suggested, in terms of their "power to influence other minds, to draw on such wide experience and deep knowledge that others come to rely on [their] judgment."[33]

If Publius is correct, and the meaning of the Constitution requires the liquidation that comes through time, argument, experience, adjudication, and war, how much time should be allotted for such liquidation to take place:

the term of the first chief executive? the first Congress? the chief justiceship of John Marshall? the period that runs through the administration of Jefferson? Madison? Lincoln? Wilson? Roosevelt? Johnson? Reagan? In "American Conservatism and the 'Prayer' Decisions," Willmoore Kendall implies that he thought the period of "liquidation of meaning" was open-ended: "We judge, and with good reason, that judicial review is the chief institutional barrier that ultimately protects us against (as I like to call it) the *plebiscitary potential* in our Constitution, that is, its potential for transforming itself into something very like the British Constitution."[34]

James Madison apparently had a shorter timeframe in mind as the appropriate period of liquidation. In a letter of September 2, 1819, to Judge Roane, Madison was critical of the Supreme Court's decision in *McCulloch v. Maryland*. He wrote, "It could not but happen, and was foreseen at the birth of the Constitution, that difficulties and differences of opinion might occasionally arise in expounding terms and phrases necessarily used in such a charter; more especially those which divide legislation between the general and local governments; and that it might require regular course of practice to liquidate and settle the meaning of some of them. But it was anticipated, I believe, by few, if any, of the friends of the Constitution, that a rule of construction would be introduced as broad and pliant as what has occurred."[35] I take Madison's critique of the Marshall Court's decision—a battle of political titans—as evidence that the Constitution is, as Kendall argues, "a crossroads" not easily liquidated and only rarely settled.

Ours is a history of decisions and reversals. Of precedents and precedents overturned. The poet Fred Turner puts it this way: "Separation of powers makes politics into a drama, not a treatise. Perhaps the true hidden presence behind the Constitution is William Shakespeare. All the world's a stage. We are all actors, in both senses of the word."[36]

Perhaps rather than looking for the substantive truth captured by the giants of the founding era, we should understand that self-government was at the heart of the revolutionary and constitutional enterprise. Willmoore Kendall again offers a provocative perspective on this issue. He writes:

> as disciples of Publius, what we should want above all is that the relevant questions shall be decided by the "deliberate sense of the community"—and the deliberate sense of the community not about the intent of the Founders (it was, above all, that we should govern our-

selves, and so prove to mankind that self-government is possible); and not, Talmudically, about the meaning of verbal formulae penned by the dead hand of the past, but about the merits of the competing policy alternatives amongst which we, as a self-governing people, are obliged to choose. Which is to say: about the appropriateness of competing policies to our conception of ourselves as a people, to our historic destiny as we understand it, to our settled views as to the nature of the good society.[37]

The founders, including Publius, can serve as exemplars in self-government. As such, they can strengthen and encourage us as we take our chances at liquidating the meaning of the Constitution. If, on the other hand, we treat them as demigods whose wisdom utterly transcends our own and who have already spoken the final word on the nature of America and its Constitution, the always difficult task of self-government becomes impossible.[38]

Gouverneur Morris and Speculation in the American Debt to France: A Reconsideration

MELANIE RANDOLPH MILLER

> The honest Nation is that which like the honest Man "hath to its plighted Faith and vow forever firmly stood, and tho it promise to its Loss yet makes that Promise good."[1]
> —Gouverneur Morris to Thomas Jefferson, December 21, 1792

Gouverneur Morris, significant contributor to the American Constitution and controversial successor to Thomas Jefferson as minister to France during the French Revolution, remains one of our least studied founding fathers.[2] Yet Morris is engaging to examine from a number of angles: not only did he possess a vivid personality—one that attracted many, though it repelled not a few—he was also politically and financially sophisticated and a writer of wit and eloquence. His experiences in France (1789–94) as a businessman, as a self-appointed political counselor to the dying monarchy, and, thereafter, as an American minister to the royal court and the revolutionary regime that overthrew it make an extraordinary story and yield new insight into the American domestic and foreign policy issues of the time.

In his own day, many people disliked Morris. In January 1792, when Morris's nomination as minister was debated in the Senate, James Monroe concluded his denunciation of Morris's "not conciliatory" manners and "indiscreet" character by adding, as the clincher, "He went to Europe to sell lands and Certificates." William Short, Jefferson's secretary in Paris, who desperately hoped to obtain the nomination himself, repeatedly suggested to Jefferson the unsuitability of appointing a man such as Morris, who was disliked by all the French (according to Short) and "in commerce." Morris also has been subjected to considerable disparagement in recent times by diplomatic historians, such as Alexander DeConde and Frank Reuter, and by American historians of the early national period, such as Julian Boyd, erudite editor of the Jefferson papers. Their disapproval is broad-based, covering nearly every aspect of Morris's activities in Europe.[3] In this essay, I will address Morris's involvement in debt speculation.

The American war debts to France, Spain, and Holland were a matter of considerable concern to the American government and American business-men during the Confederation period and the early years of the new national government, and figure in much of the diplomatic correspondence of the era. Americans were anxious about repayment of these loans as an essential step toward establishing national creditworthiness, the sine qua non of commercial prosperity. The loans also offered the prospect of speculation, one of the most glittering avenues to easy profit made possible by the anticipated ratification of the new federal constitution. Understanding the debt speculation and its context is not a dry exercise. In the early years of the new republic, a man's fortune could rise spectacularly. His fall might be equally dramatic, and debtor's prison eventu-ally snapped up many high rollers, including the financier Robert Morris (no relation to Gouverneur Morris) and Alexander Hamilton's friend the devious William Duer, whom Jefferson called the "King of the Alley."

Here I want to suggest that Morris's debt proposals can be understood as neither inappropriate nor as a discredit to his country, but instead as both rea-sonable and pragmatic. More than that, I argue that adoption of his plan might well have done the United States greater credit (and France more good) than the route taken by Alexander Hamilton and Jefferson in their respective posts as secretary of the treasury and secretary of state in Washington's first cabinet.

⁓

Gouverneur Morris was born in 1752 at Morrisania in the Bronx. His family was of the New York aristocracy. His grandfather had been a supreme court justice in New York and governor of New Jersey, and his father, Lewis Mor-ris Jr., was an admiralty judge. Gouverneur was the only son of Lewis's sec-ond marriage. Although he died when Gouverneur was only ten, Lewis had already recognized his youngest son's remarkable abilities and provided in his will for Morris to receive an excellent education. Gouverneur entered King's College (now Columbia University) at the unusually young age of twelve and after graduating studied law. He later returned to King's College for a master's degree, which he received at the age of nineteen.

Morris demonstrated a gift for understanding finance at an early age and made a name for himself in 1770 when he published a number of sophisticated essays criticizing a bill before the New York Assembly that provided for the issue of loan certificates. When the Revolution came, Morris joined two of his half-brothers in choosing the American side, and his talents were soon put to work on behalf of the Continental Congress, for whom Morris performed a multitude of tasks, including chairing numerous critically important committees and drafting their reports, and writing, as he would boastfully but accurately describe, "almost if not all of the publications of Congress of any importance."[4] In that capacity he met George Washington and became one of his many devoted young protégés. Washington liked Morris, was impressed by him, and would remain his loyal friend. Robert Morris, superintendent of finance during the war, also recognized Morris's skills, and hired him as his assistant. In 1782, the Morrises submitted a report to Congress on the public credit that is still considered a remarkable work and has been identified as the basis for Alexander Hamilton's more famous "Report on the Public Credit," which shaped American fiscal policy throughout the 1790s and helped set the young country on its feet financially. Morris and Hamilton were good friends, and they often discussed the financial issues facing the new nation.

In 1787, Gouverneur reluctantly agreed to accept an appointment as a delegate for Pennsylvania at the Constitutional Convention, where he played a significant role in the debates and wrote the final, compiled draft of the Constitution. After the convention was over, he refused Hamilton's request to contribute to the *Federalist* and returned to his business partnership with Robert, which they had formed in 1784. It was on Robert's behalf that Gouverneur went to France at the end of 1788. Robert was having difficulties with the French Farmers-General concerning a tobacco contract, and Gouverneur, who spoke French fluently, was sent to sort things out. He was also to look into deals for sales of American lands and American securities.

Morris got to know Jefferson in Paris and was soon introduced into the inner circle of revolutionary aristocrats. Many of them were fascinated by the humorous one-legged American (Morris had lost a leg in a carriage accident in 1780) whose conversational skills rivaled those of his French hosts. They were also eager to learn about republicanism from someone who had helped write the American Constitution. However, Morris's consistently disapproving advice and bleak predictions about the likely course of the French Revolution, which the French today regard as remarkably prescient, led to his eventual estrangement from some of these reformers, including Lafayette. Other more conservative reformers, including close counselors to King Louis XVI, such as the French foreign minister the Comte de Montmorin, trusted Morris's judgment and sought his advice for themselves and on behalf of the king and queen.

In January 1792, at President Washington's behest and after a bitter Senate battle, Morris was named American minister to France. Even after his appointment, he continued to counsel the court and assisted in abortive attempts to help the royal family escape. After the defeat of efforts to save Louis XVI, his energies were dedicated to the often nearly impossible task of assisting Americans caught up in the revolutionary chaos. In 1794, in response to complaints from the French Committee of Public Safety, which believed Morris was sending damning reports about France back to the United States, the American government recalled Morris, who was replaced by James Monroe.

Morris's arrival in France coincided with rising tensions between the two nations over America's war debt to France. A 1783 *memoire* signed by Franklin itemized the American debt, which stood as follows:

1. 1 million livres in 1777.

2. 18 million livres given in specie; repayments of principal and interest to begin the third year after the peace and completed in twelve years.

3. 5 million Dutch florins (approximately equal to 10 million livres tournois), from Dutch loans to the King in 1781, to be repaid in Holland in ten payments with 4 percent interest per year.

4. 6 million livres in 1783.

Total: 35 million livres tournois [at that time equal to about $6,352,000]

America's substantial debt to a cash-poor France was more than a financial transaction; it was also a debt of honor, representing an infusion of one nation's lifeblood into another. French support had been vital to America's victory, but it had also sapped the already weakened French economy and by every account accelerated the arrival of the French Revolution. The debt was also, to the commercial eye, an opportunity not to be missed, for it presented the possibility of purchasing the debt from France at a discount and eventually receiving full value from the United States.

The attractiveness of speculation grew as the American government proved unable to keep up with the repayment schedules. The U.S. suspended loan payments after 1785. By 1786 two years' interest on the 1783 loan of six million livres was overdue, and the government defaulted on the principal installments due in 1787. That year, commissioners of the U.S. Treasury told the bankers in Amsterdam there would be no more interest payments until the new American government was installed.[5]

America's failure to make timely repayments was an embarrassment to many American leaders. As America's minister to France under the Confederation Congress, Jefferson had the distressing task of facing French frustration about overdue payments. With John Adams's encouragement, he wrote more than once to Jay, Madison, and Washington, urging that the U.S. pay off the debt to France by raising new loans through banks in Holland.[6] However, Jefferson and Adams may not have appreciated the practical difficulty that entering into new loans presented to the lame-duck Confederation Congress. The real need, as it had been throughout the 1780s, was for a more robust form of national government, which would come into being under the new Constitution. The new government could promulgate reliable revenue measures to restore American creditworthiness and give the United States bargaining power in negotiating terms for loans. These steps would take time.

Addressing the war debt was among the first orders of business for the new government, however. Hamilton only had been secretary of the treasury for two days when he called on the French ambassador, the Comte de Moustier, on September 13, 1789. Hamilton informed Moustier that he would request Congress to authorize loans sufficient to liquidate all of America's domestic and foreign debt. Mere passage of the legislation, however, would not repay the French; loans would have to be raised and payment schedules established. In the meantime, Hamilton suggested, America would appreciate having principal payments delayed for a few years, during which it would pay interest. He sent the same information to William Short, who was acting as chargé d'affaires in Paris.[7]

Hamilton's request was consistent with Moustier's own desire to obtain interest payments in kind as a means of promoting Franco-American commerce, while preserving the principal as political leverage for France. However, Moustier, who had not been in France for two years, may not have realized the crisis state of his country's finances. It was this critical situation that drove French finance minister Jacques Necker to negotiate with speculators who offered, in the face of American delays, to buy the full French debt at a discount and provide immediate relief.

There appears to have been differing opinions among the Americans about the legitimacy of commercial speculation on the war debt. According to Julian Boyd, Jefferson consistently resisted such private schemes as venal.[8] If so, this was a debatable characterization. The proposals to buy the French debt came from some of the most financially knowledgeable men of the time, and Hamilton gave these proposals serious consideration. While speculation—and its French equivalent, *agiotage*—had a negative connotation, many believed the proposals were an honest means of assisting France in its immediate need without strapping the United States. This was Morris's analysis of the situation. He wrote to Washington in 1791 that since the United States was

> not in Condition to pay our Debt to France, a Bargain by which the Period can be prolonged without Loss to either Party is desirable. I say without Loss, because the Conduct of this Nation has been so generous that it would be very ungrateful indeed to take Advantage of those Necessities which the Succor afforded to America has occasioned. Such Bargain must be either with the Government or with Individuals. But after the repeated Delays on our Part, to ask longer Time now would not look well. . . . A Bargain with Individuals has the Advantage of bringing in the Aid of private Interest to the Support of our Credit, and what is of very great Consequence, it would leave us at Liberty to make use of that Credit for the Arrangement of our domestic Affairs.[9]

As we shall see shortly, Morris's letter to Washington concealed his personal stake in the matter, but it nevertheless stated a persuasive case for the role of speculation in preserving America's international reputation.

The possibilities presented by domestic and foreign debt securities intrigued American and foreign investors alike, and there was no shortage of prospective speculators. As early as 1786, America's bankers in Holland offered to buy $4.4 million of the French debt for $3.7 million (this was a 16 percent discount, a bargain for the Dutch), but Congress, concerned about undermining what was then shaky American credit, refused.[10] By late 1788, the situation had changed. With ratification of the new Constitution—and therefore eventual American repayment—seemingly certain, and with France in increasing difficulties, would-be speculators perceived that they might now have a role to play.

Gouverneur and Robert had discussed purchasing the debt before Gouverneur left for Paris that fall; once in Europe, Morris joined forces with Daniel Parker, an American businessman with a dubious past. He would prove a nettlesome associate, and Gouverneur spent much time in Europe bailing him out of difficulties. (John Adams called Parker "the great Speculator in American Paper, who, though I love him very well, is too ingenious for me.") Their plan, as originally proposed to the French in May 1789, would have postponed receipt of principal payments from the U.S. for five to six years in exchange for receiving the arrearages of interest.[11]

Another group of speculators included Brissot de Warville, who later played a key role in the Girondin period of the French Revolution. Brissot, who had traveled in America in 1788, was the agent of the Swiss banker and entrepreneur Etienne Clavière. Clavière, whose dishonesty has been established by historians, would be appointed the Girondist finance minister and, like Brissot, would become a bitter enemy of Morris while he was minister to France.[12] Parker had been involved with Brissot and Clavière before joining the Morrises and had introduced Brissot to William Duer and Andrew Craigie (another American entrepreneur). In October 1788, Duer, Craigie, Brissot, and Clavière agreed to work for ratification by the American government of the transfer of the debt to themselves. If they encountered difficulties, they thought that placement of an American minister in Holland might provide the necessary influence.[13]

There is no evidence in Morris's papers that he joined this association, although various historians assume that he did,[14] basing this conclusion on a memorandum written by Morris's friend Rufus King on December 21, 1788. The memo concerned a conversation in which Duer invited King to join the Brissot group. Duer, quite at ease in making private use of information and influence derived from his official position as assistant secretary of the Treasury Board (the predecessor to the Treasury Department), told King that both Morrises had proposed joining with Duer and would try to influence Henry Knox to push Gouverneur's appointment to Holland. Duer, who disliked Gouverneur, opposed the appointment.[15]

In any event, the discussions between the Morrises and Duer's group led to nothing. Gouverneur talked to Clavière in France in early 1789 on the subject but found him and Brissot to be "very different Beings from what [Duer] supposes," who could do them "no Good."[16] Clavière and Brissot remained unfriendly competitors of Gouverneur, and that hostility may have had much to do with Brissot's political denunciations of Morris in 1792 and Clavière's eventual advocacy of Morris's recall from France.

In mid-August 1789, while Morris was on a short business trip to London, Jefferson received a letter from the Amsterdam bankers suggesting that he obtain authorization to negotiate Dutch loans to pay the French debt in full.[17] Two weeks later, still in London, Morris received from Parker "Intelligence which affects deeply our Plan about a purchase of the American Debt to France." Julian Boyd reasonably suggests that this "Intelligence" was of the Dutch proposal. Since this transfer of debt would have dashed the hopes of all the speculators, Boyd concludes that the information led to Morris's departure from London the next day. Gouverneur's September diary recounts that he called on Jefferson on returning to Paris and "cast about to know if any Thing has been done respecting the Debt to France but cannot perceive that there has. Avoid mentioning it to Mr. Jefferson for the present."[18] This reticence about showing his hand to Jefferson is hard to interpret, particularly since he discussed his proposals with Short after Jefferson's departure to join Washington's cabinet and obtained Short's approval as well as that of Lafayette. An explanation may be found, however, in his injunction to Necker in late October 1789: "That it is necessary to keep the Transaction secret, because whether we bargain or not if my Name be mentioned it will destroy the Utility of my Friends in America, who have been and will continue to be firm Advocates for doing Justice to every Body."[19]

This appears to mean that if Morris were known in America to be associated with the proposal, his partners, such as Robert Morris, would be much less effective in advocating its adoption by Hamilton and Washington because of their obvious conflict of interest. Another possible reason for Morris's reserve could have been his interest in obtaining a post as minister to Holland. In any event, it is unlikely that Jefferson was ignorant of Morris's project, since he was well acquainted with most of the French and American parties concerned in all of the various debt schemes.[20] When Jefferson was later specifically informed of Morris's involvement by Short, his response, though he opposed *all* private speculation proposals, expressed neither surprise nor disapprobation.[21]

In late September 1789, just prior to departing for America, Jefferson showed Morris his instructions from Jay. Based on a resolution of the Confederation Congress, these instructions ruled out transfers of the American debt. Morris urged Jefferson nevertheless to go to Holland and accept the Dutch offer. He argued that the instructions were obsolete since they predated the new federal government, and moreover that they concerned only a 1786 purchase proposal by the Dutch bankers. He noted privately that Jefferson's real objection was probably "to a Journey which would postpone his return to America."[22] Events were to prove Morris's assessment correct. The new government would undoubtedly have endorsed Jefferson if he had authorized the loans. If Jefferson had taken Morris's advice, the move would have extinguished a significant part of the profit from Morris's own speculation scheme, but Morris wrote more than once to his partners that his recommendations would always put the interests of the United States first "even tho' it militate with my personal interests."[23]

By the late fall of 1789, Necker, who had been casting about for ways to ease the worsening crisis, was leaning towards Morris's proposal. This success can be attributed to Morris's powers of persuasion as well as to his deepening friendship with foreign minister Montmorin. However, both ministers' chronic indecision made Morris's task extremely demanding. Among Necker's anxieties was a lack of security backing Morris's proposal. When he told this to Morris, in the salon of his daughter, Mme de Staël, Morris was taken aback. "[N]o house in Europe is sufficient for so large a Sum," he told Necker, "and therefore that Security as such is Nonsense but that he shall run no Risk for he shall not part with the Effects till he receives the Payment." Necker persisted, however, and the argument grew heated, with voices raised, until Mme de Staël directed Morris to send her father to sit by her. Morris, probably embarrassed, defused the situation with a flash of wit: "I tell her smiling that it is a dangerous Task to send away Monsr. Necker and those who tried it once [referring to the King's exile of Necker in 1787] had sufficient Cause to repent of it. This little Observation brings back good humor. . . ."[24]

Morris's diary records his unceasing efforts to reassure Necker and Montmorin, to maintain Short's support, and to inculcate Jean-Baptiste Ternant—who was preparing to leave for America as the new French minister—with enthusiasm for the scheme. He did not bribe these gentlemen but he did suspect that the rascally Parker had promised Ternant a small share.[25] The plan called for a purchase of the full loan in livres (not *assignats,* a significant detail, as we shall see), including arrearages and future payments in 1790 and 1791. Morris and his associates would apply to the United States government for payment in 5 percent obligations for Dutch guilders, with the first installment to be paid in 1795. The United States would thus obtain a five-year delay before more payments would be due, giving the new nation time to address its domestic debt.[26]

The possibility of Morris's success alarmed the Dutch bankers, since it meant that they might lose their grip on meeting America's credit needs. Having failed to divert Necker with an offer to buy six million livres of the debt at an 11 2/3 percent discount (which, again, would be no mean profit for the Dutch),[27] they toyed with joining Morris, which he encouraged as a means of allaying Necker's concerns about security. When they asked for a three-quarters share, Morris indignantly refused. Nonetheless, these seasoned European men of finance seemed eager to deal, and by early January 1790 Morris believed they had a firm agreement. It was not to last: when the bankers' representatives in Paris, including Jacob Van Staphorst, reported the news back to Amsterdam, the bankers apparently recoiled. They kept Morris and Van Staphorst at bay for several weeks, then unexpectedly issued an unauthorized loan for three million florins on behalf of the United States. This action was communicated in a letter to Hamilton along with a remarkable memorandum pressing Hamilton to reject Morris's proposal.[28]

The memo is full of purported concern for the United States. The bankers indicated that they had held aloof from any private proposals to purchase the debt until they saw that Necker was considering Morris's scheme, at which time they decided to make their own six-million-livre proposition mentioned above. Necker had refused this as too small; he counteroffered to treat for the whole debt. The bankers told Hamilton that they would have been happy to accept this proposal or let matters lie dormant until a response came from America, "but we have had the chagrin to learn that some Gentlemen have formed, and presented to the Minister a Plan for the Purchase of the whole Claim of France against the united States . . . which afford[s] the Prospect of a most enormous profit to the Speculators, and we have but too much reason to apprehend there are Persons concerned in the affair, capable of influencing its acceptance by the French Ministry."

The bankers admitted that they had been offered a share, but, "[d]eeming ourselves the natural Guardians of the Honor and credit of the united States" they had instead issued the unauthorized loan, for "we stood in need of no other Consideration to induce us to forego Any personal advantages." They warned that if Morris's scheme had been adopted, the French National Assembly would have learned "that the french ministry at a huge profit to speculators had abandoned it to the speculators' mercy." They added that Short would advise the French ministry against such agreements, an assertion that made Short indignant.[29]

Presumably the "personal advantage" the bankers were foregoing was on the difference in the exchange with France and the 11 percent discount they would have received if Necker had accepted their six-million-livre offer; the advantage they would receive instead was the 4 to 6 percent commission on the loans. Such commissions were not exactly minimal for the enormous sums of money involved, particularly if they succeeded in obtaining directions from the United States to pay for the entire debt via Dutch loans, a mechanism that resulted, Morris observed, in no "Shadow of Risque" to them. As Morris noted with savage irony, the bankers' objection to his scheme was essentially that it would provide too great a profit to its actors; a profit they preferred to make themselves.[30]

Morris viewed the unauthorized Dutch loan as a breach of their agreement. The day after he learned of it, in the heat of anger, he wrote Hamilton denouncing the bankers. The letter reflects Morris's comments to his diary and confirms his genuine outrage; but it also contains a troubling paragraph: "Mr. Necker, pressed for Money, had listened to Overtures for selling the Debt of the United States, and mentioned the Matter to some Members of the national Assembly, by which Means it became known to the principal Americans and Friends of America here. I own that upon the first Mention of the Matter it appeared to me a Matter of Indifference and so I expressed myself. Our Duty is to pay to such Creditors as may possess the Demand."[31] Morris went on to say that the bankers' earlier six-million-livre proposal would only have paid part of the debt and thereby would have hurt American credit, and that under these circumstances, Morris decided to make his own proposal for the whole. Of course, this was not true: Morris had gone to France to pursue debt speculation, yet he implied that he got involved only when he learned of another proposal he considered dishonorable to the United States.

Hamilton had long been aware that various speculation schemes were afoot and very likely knew of Morris's efforts, so Morris's protestations must have been suspect to him.[32] Morris's motives for presenting this version of events to Hamilton may have arisen from his recent receipt of a request from

Washington to go to London to talk with the British about completion of the 1783 peace treaty terms. He perceived, probably rightly, that his association with debt speculation was not consistent with the role of a diplomat. Regardless, this part of his letter to Hamilton seems an artificial attempt by Morris to disassociate himself from the business.

For his part, Hamilton promptly wrote to Holland to endorse the unexpected loan, although he had to reserve official approval until Congress passed the enabling acts in August 1790. He also indicated that he expected to instruct them to raise additional loans. Hamilton used florid language to commend the bankers, but it is worth noting that he did *not* tell them that he would not consider future speculation proposals. In fact, he told Short to stay open to such approaches.[33]

Hamilton did not reply to Morris. Boyd suggests that Hamilton was motivated to favor the bankers because of his hopes of obtaining Dutch financing support for his Society for Establishing Useful Manufactures, a project close to Hamilton's heart. Regardless, there seems no reason to impute impropriety to Hamilton for his decision, for the United States had a secure relationship with its Dutch bankers, one worth protecting. Once the initial disappointment ebbed, Morris apparently recognized this. His papers show that he did not blame Hamilton for failing to respond to his angry letter, and he continued to view him as a good friend. He did not write Hamilton again about his speculation proposals, however.[34]

Although the bankers' action, as they had hoped, put an end to Morris's scheme, it also exacerbated French frustration, because it now put a quick recovery of the full debt out of reach. They were determined to obtain what they could, however, and began to pressure Short to remit the three million florins (worth about 7.2 million livres, approximately 20 percent of the principal America owed France), even though the loan had not yet been sanctioned by the United States. However, as Morris had predicted, the United States did *not* apply the full amount of the loan towards the French debt, but only half. In addition, the first payment out of the loan was not made to France until nearly a year later, and it would be five years before the French were fully paid, a long delay Morris's plan would have avoided. Under these circumstances, it can be argued that Morris's proposal would have done more to help the French and establish American international creditworthiness than the piecemeal raising of Dutch loans, an approach Morris strongly criticized. In his view, payment "in the Lump" (full payment) would have been best for the United States and for France, since it would allow the United States to apply Dutch loans to redeeming its domestic debt, to the benefit of American credit.[35]

Hamilton's determination that only half of the new Dutch loan should actually go to the desperate French was further modified by Jefferson, who, exhibiting little concern for the French crisis, instructed Short in August 1790 to "find excuses" to pay *none* of it until he obtained in exchange French concessions regarding trade with the French West Indies. Short followed Hamilton's instructions instead and in November 1790 made a payment of 2,171,637 livres at the French treasury for sums due in 1786. A December payment of 1,440,362 livres was made on account of upcoming sums due.[36]

There are other important issues in the debt episode to be explored besides the payment dates, including the reduction in principal to be accepted by the French and the currency to be used. A common objection to the speculators—and thus to Gouverneur Morris—lay in the fact that France, were she to agree to the proposals, would collect less than she had been promised by the United States. The difference between the two amounts would derive either from the fall in the exchange of the livre against the Dutch florin, or simply from the French agreeing to accept a lesser amount in full payment in order to get the money sooner and with certainty. In this connection, Morris has been criticized for suggesting that while it would not look good if the United States took such a "profit," there would be no problem if the profit went to the speculators.[37]

Such criticism is naïve. The United States was in the ignominious position of being unable to meet current payments and of being in arrears. The French were in immediate need of money. "[T]hey have no doubt of receiving Payment from the United States," Montmorin told Morris in late 1789, but "they want now to receive Money." The only rational motive for private speculators to assist either party lay in profit; the profit lay at first in buying the debt at a discount, but as the livre began to fall the discount was no longer necessary because the debt contracts called for payment in livres rather than Dutch florins and the profit would be made on the difference. This drop in the exchange rate had already begun at the time of Morris's proposal in the fall of 1789, and it continued through the spring of 1791 (by then France was using paper *assignats,* which suffered their own depreciation against face value).[38]

The correspondence concerning the proposals indicates that French reservations about the various private speculators' proposals did *not* include an objection to loss on the exchange if the speculators were to buy the debt. However, with respect to an exchange loss France would suffer on payments by the United States, through Dutch loans, it appears they *did* object—understandably, since they were dealing directly with the debtor itself, which had received the full benefit of the loan. Thus, they asked Short at the time of his first payments in 1790 to pay part of it in florins, because the payments were to go against the 1781 French loan from Holland, a debt in florins contracted by France for the benefit of the United States. He agreed, but he also insisted on credit against the American debt in livres, which meant that the exchange benefit remained with the United States. According to Morris, the loss caused a "good Deal of murmuring" in France.[39]

Furthermore, in assessing the speculators' potential "private" profits, one must consider the sizable commissions obtained by the Dutch banks for raising the loans needed by the United States to pay off the interest and principal. These commissions prompted the numerous proposals made by the houses, including their proposal to Jefferson in August 1789, discussed above. It is difficult to see a moral distinction between the motives of these bankers and other speculators; neither of them were governments, but rather businessmen offering something that had to be paid for.

According to Boyd, a central point of disagreement between Hamilton and Jefferson on the debt matter was the propriety of taking advantage of the depreciation of French money. He asserts that Jefferson, unlike Hamilton, was opposed to taking advantage of *any* devaluation, and also that he was opposed from the outset. Neither assertion is substantiated. Moreover, Boyd's analysis fails to distinguish between the change in the rate of exchange between France and Holland, due to France's worsening fiscal situation, and the depreciation of the paper *assignats,* which was an internal phenomenon. The distinction is critical to understanding the positions of Hamilton, Jefferson, Short, and Morris.

The livre (in currency) had begun to fall against the Dutch florin by 1789, and although there were fluctuations, by the late spring of 1791 it had dropped about 20 percent from its consistent value in the 1780s. Hamilton assumed, as did Short, that the United States would be entitled to benefit from the drop in the livre in the exchange with Holland since its agreement with France called for payments in livres. The issue was complicated by the introduction of *assignats. Assignats* were originally conceived of as bonds secured by nationalized church lands and were first issued as such in April 1790. Morris instantly termed them "paper money," noting to Robert that they did not "bear that Name but we have lived long enough to consider Things rather than Names." Morris's insight was astute. Within months, *assignats* were indeed paper money with face values of livres. As France ran out of money, it printed *assignats* in ever-increasing amounts; the second major issue came in the fall of 1790 (Necker resigned in protest). The inevitable result was inflation and devaluation of the *assignats,* which were down to 82 percent of face value by November 1791, 63 percent in January 1792, and 48 percent by December 1793. This was just as Morris predicted to Short in a letter of September 1790. Noting that cautious men should not make economic predictions, he commented, "But I am not a cautious man. I therefore give it as my opinion, that they [the French] will issue the paper currency, and substitute thereby depreciation in the place of bankruptcy, or rather suspension." This is precisely what happened.[40]

Because both hard currency (e.g., the *louis, écu, liard*) and the *assignats* had face values of livres, the distinction becomes confusing. The livre (*tournois*) was an "accounting unit" and established the price of commodities and contractual matters (e.g., leases and debts). Hard currency, on the other hand, was used for transactions. The relation between the two had been fixed by the king more than eighty years before; the *louis,* for example, had a value of twenty-four livres *tournois.* With the appearance of *assignats* and their associated deflation in comparison to specie, hard currency naturally began to disappear.[41]

France was thus suffering a loss in the exchange with Amsterdam *and* a loss due to depreciation of *assignats.* These were two distinct trends, but—because hard currency was disappearing—if florins were borrowed in Amsterdam and changed there to *assignats* for payments on the American loans, the French loss represented a combination of the two. This was made crystal clear in a letter from Short to Hamilton regarding one of the loans he had raised. Short explained that the solution for making up the *assignat* depreciation to the French, while also allowing the United States to take advantage of the exchange drop, was to have payments made to the French at Antwerp. Otherwise, he told the secretary, it was uncertain whether "between the day of purchasing the bills at Antwerp & that of receiving them at Paris there would not be such a fall to be a loss to the U.S. who were to find their indemnity in the course of exchange for that they intend allowing France for depreciation on assignats"[42]

Jefferson would have known before he left France in 1789 that the livre was falling against the florin. He also was specifically advised, in April 1791, that part of the first payments made by Short in late 1790 were credited in livres, giving the U.S. the benefit of the exchange loss (about 10 percent in November 1790, or around twice the interest rates specified in the loan agreements). However, when he gave Short instructions in August 1790 and April 1791 with respect to delaying payments from the three-million-florin loan of 1790, he said *nothing* about the matter. Boyd places heavy reliance on Jefferson's statement in April 1791 to the French chargé d'affaires, Louis-Guillaume Otto, telling him that payment would be made "in specie." Use of specie would have nothing to do with benefiting from the rate of exchange. Moreover, as Morris later wrote to Washington, payments in specie were not a proper means of remedying the drop in the exchange rate because its use would cost the U.S. an additional 5 percent unrelated to the exchange or depreciation of the *assignat,* something Hamilton and Jefferson apparently did not realize. Short explained the same thing to them.[43]

Since Jefferson must have known of the drop in the exchange rate, it seems fair to conclude that when he received a memo in April 1791 from Hamilton that referred to the United States taking advantage of the exchange drop he made no objection because he had none. When he wrote to Otto on the subject a month later, he did not repeat the assurance of payment in specie, and he did not address the question of loss on the exchange—probably because he agreed with Hamilton. This conclusion is unaffected by his letter of April 25, 1791, directing Short to reject all proposals by private speculators because the United States would not want to be subjected to "the chicaneries and vexations of private avarice," and because America reserved the right to make its payments "no where but into the Treasury of France, according to their contract." The letter made no mention of not taking advantage of the exchange (indeed, no mention of devaluation at all). The concern Jefferson expressed was for protection of the *United States,* not France, a point further illustrated by the fact that Jefferson told Otto he was concerned about having "such a large mass of American obligations in the hands of individuals"—that is, private speculators. Knowledgeable businessmen such as Morris did not share this concern; there were already enormous numbers of American domestic securities in European hands.[44]

It was not until the new French minister, Ternant, arrived in Jefferson's office in Philadelphia in August 1791 and presented a protest that Jefferson acted. It is not entirely certain whether Ternant was complaining about a loss on the exchange, a loss due to depreciation of *assignats,* or both; Jefferson described it in his response to Ternant only as a protest regarding payment of loans using *assignats.* It most likely concerned both, for both losses would have seemed unfair to France. Although small variations in the exchange were certainly normal, the drop in the livre by the time of Short's first payments was quite significant and certainly unanticipated when the loans were made. In June 1791 Short reported to Hamilton that the exchange had "undergone a precipitous fall which had astonished everybody, the more so as it far exceeded the progressive depreciation of assignats."[45]

Boyd, though he speaks of "depreciated currency," blurs the two types of devaluation and suggests that taking advantage of either would have been dishonorable. Yet the two secretaries, faced with Ternant's protest, agreed that there should be compensation to France, just not *for the exchange.* Jefferson drafted a letter to Ternant saying that the United States would not pay in a depreciated medium and that it would make payments "in their just value" and avoid "all benefit from depreciation," desiring only to be "guarded against any unjust loss from the circumstances of mere exchange." Hamilton asked Jefferson to change the note by eliminating the reference to the exchange and providing that allowance for depreciation would be made at final reckoning rather than at the time of each payment. Jefferson agreed.[46]

Boyd apparently read the letter to mean that the United States was renouncing *all* benefit due to France's financial crisis, which had caused the drop in the exchange and depreciation of *assignats:* "[Hamilton] eliminated the assurance that payments would be made in their just value and also deferred settlement of the question of depreciation and the rate of exchange to the time of final liquidation of the debt. But what remained was unequivocal. Speaking for the president, Jefferson gave the pledge of the government that it would entertain 'no idea of paying their debt in a depreciated medium.'"[47] This is described by Boyd as a "victory for the Secretary of State" (and, by inference, a defeat for Hamilton and the speculators) "in his defense of a settlement of the debt that would be just and honorable." Yet the language proposed by Jefferson was not really different from Hamilton's: both versions indicate (Jefferson's directly, Hamilton's by omission) that the United States intended to continue to get the benefit of the exchange, a very significant benefit indeed. The promise not to pay in "a depreciated medium" was clearly a promise not to pay in paper *assignats,* as opposed to livres in hard currency or in bills of exchange for florins calculated as equivalent to the face value of livre-*assignats* at the current rate of exchange. The most that might be said for this promise is that Jefferson did not realize that France was suffering on *both* accounts. This interpretation may flatter the secretary's sense of fairness but not his intelligence.

That the United States intended to retain the benefit of the exchange was laid out in a letter from Hamilton to Short that discussed how the "equitable allowance" ceded to Ternant could be calculated. Hamilton pointed out that "mere depreciation" had to be distinguished from the rate of exchange and, referring to a letter from Short giving the two different devaluation rates, he suggested that the appropriate adjustment would compensate for the depreciation but take advantage of the exchange rate, and would perhaps be determined as the mean between the two.[48]

Thus, Jefferson and Hamilton were agreed that France would have to accept the exchange loss. In this, they ignored the comments made by Morris in his May 1791 letter to Washington, in which he pointed out that Short's 1790 payment, which had taken advantage of the exchange rate, had angered the French. By using Dutch loans to pay off the debt, thereby accruing the exchange benefit, Morris suggested, the reputation of the United States would be hurt. For

> about one third of our Debt to France arose from a Loan made on our Account in Holland of five Millions of florins, for which the King paid us here ten Million of Livres without any Deduction for Charges of any Sort. The Nation is now obliged to pay these ten Millions in Holland, and for us to borrow that Amount there and then squeeze them in an exchange which distresses both their Commerce and Finances, looks hard. . . . [I]t is not possible for a Nation to make the Advantage which Individuals do in such Things because they must employ Individuals, each of whom will be too apt to look a little to his own Advantage.[49]

Boyd views this letter as damaging to Morris's integrity: "The phrasing was more elegant [than that used by other speculators] . . . but in essence this was the same argument. . . . [T]he United States could not honorably profit from the necessities of France, but it could permit private speculators to do this."[50] Boyd, however, seems to want it both ways, having previously criticized Hamilton and Short's assumption that the United States should "profit from the necessities of France" on the exchange. In fact, that criticism—a criticism that we have established must be extended to Jefferson—is more justifiable than censure of Morris's proposal. To the extent that the secretaries were simply doing what was in America's best interests as a financial matter, and what the debt contract specified, they were justified. Yet, as Morris had perceived, it was an advantage that "look[ed] hard" to the French, an observation suggesting that Morris was more attuned to the diplomatic nuances of the affair than was either Hamilton or Jefferson.

Hamilton wrote Washington's response to Morris. He again distinguished between the exchange drop and the depreciation of *assignats* and stated clearly that the United States should get the benefit of the exchange, not the speculators.[51]

Morris's proposals were fiscally feasible and probably diplomatically sound, and thus it would seem that his promotion of them was equally legitimate. However, his diary entries concerning a second scheme under French consideration from the fall of 1790 to the summer of 1791 reveal that Morris was willing to go to questionable lengths to try and influence his government.

In late January 1790, Morris received instructions from Washington to meet with the British government. He told Necker, who was still hoping for a new proposal from Morris, that it was "possible the United States may employ me," and that he would "from Motives of Delicacy decline all farther Dealing with him, but in such case I will cause the Thing to be done by others." He tried one last time, unsuccessfully, to convince the bankers in Amsterdam to accept his original proposal, and in the next year he joined no debt-purchase projects.[52]

He was still well aware of the efforts of other speculators, however, including a proposal put forward by the Paris bankers Schweitzer, Jeanneret & Cie. in late 1790. They were joined by another business associate of Morris, James Swan, and claimed to represent Genoese capitalists. Even though Swan told Jefferson (whom he had known in France) and Henry Knox, in letters of October 3, 1790, that Morris was a partner in the deal, he was not—not *yet*. This is established by a diary entry of November 8, 1790, two days after Morris's return to Paris. In a conversation with Swan, Morris told him that there were "Reasons" (Washington's assignment) preventing him from joining, but that he thought it "a good Thing" and would support a share for Robert Morris. He also advised Short that he had "declined an Interest" in the proposal. Short, who was desperately hoping to be appointed minister to France, opposed the Schweitzer proposal because it might be "suspected that he [Short] holds an interest in it," another indication that diplomatic service and speculation were not considered appropriate bedfellows. In mid-December, Swan also told Short that Morris was a partner. However, Morris's diary entries say nothing of the matter and it appears that Swan was trying to pressure Short, who looked to Morris for financial advice. This was typical of Swan, and Morris would later warn Short that Swan was "in the Habit of using both of our Names for his particular Purposes."[53]

In late November 1790, Montmorin told Morris that the French would not accept *any* debt proposal without consulting Morris. Thereafter, Morris reviewed successive drafts of the Schweitzer plan and finally agreed it was acceptable.[54] In late December, Morris received a letter from Jefferson approving his handling of the mission to London and advising him to proceed no further, thereby releasing Morris from his self-imposed disqualification from debt speculation. Thus, on April 4, 1791, when Morris was approached by Swan's associates, he was receptive: "They have employed a person in America designated by Mr. Swan, who is empowered to distribute Douceurs [bribes] to the Amount of 16,000 pounds sterling. They have given 200000# [livres] to Rayneval and the same Sum to [unidentified.] I promise to read the Papers and consider the Subject. Swan is to receive Something for his Trouble."[55] Morris did not know that the person "employed" in America was to be Henry Knox. The previous December, Swan had written Knox and claimed (falsely) that the French ministry had already agreed to the plan. He offered Knox a commission of 1 percent. Knox passed the letter on to Hamilton.[56]

On April 5, 1791, Morris, convinced that the bankers had access to the necessary resources, agreed to a one-quarter share (presumably of the commission, although that is not clear, but it appears the capital was coming only from the bankers). On April 9, Morris told Short that the proposal was a "good one for the United States, provided they abate the Commission. This is my sincere Belief." Morris thought he had convinced Short, but he was wrong.[57]

In view of his decision to join the project, it is at first confusing that, a little over a month later, on May 26, Morris told Swan of "my Surprize at hearing that I am considered in America as speculating in the Debt to France." Swan assured him, falsely, "that he has never said or done any Thing to raise such Idea and that he will exert himself to remove it." Swan wrote promptly to

Knox that Morris "positively declined any share or portion, & has uniformly since held to the same principle." Of course, Swan and Morris knew this was not true.[58]

The reason for Morris's secrecy is apparent in his May 27 letter to Washington, which included a copy of the proposal. Morris wrote to Washington that "altho I did by no Means consider that [mission] in the Light of an Appointment to Office, yet from Motives of Delicacy I determined to extricate myself from the Affair of the Debt as speedily as I could with Propriety." He then explained his support for a private purchase of the French debt, giving cogent reasons, although Hamilton would reject them. Morris explained his support for a lump-sum payment by which the American debt to France could be entirely satisfied. Such a loan would be difficult to obtain from the Dutch, he urged, or at least to obtain speedily; in the meantime, domestic security speculation was running rampant, with many millions of these securities already in Europe. Acceptance of the speculators' arrangement would permit the United States to use Dutch loans against domestic securities instead—specifically, it would allow the U.S. to borrow from the Dutch at 5 percent and to redeem all of America's 6 percent domestic debt at par, thereby saving one-fifth of the interest, a sizeable amount and "much more than ever we shall get by any Management of our Debts on this Side of the Water."[59]

Morris's sincerity in these arguments is clear from his diary entries. However, he made no mention of his own involvement, and, as such, the letter cannot be described as anything but a bald attempt to influence Washington to approve the Schweitzer proposal. Admitting his involvement would have greatly undermined the letter's impact, but Morris did not simply sin by omission; the letter was actively misleading. He told Washington not only of his withdrawal from the 1789 debt proposal but, more important, of his recusal from sharing in any debt speculations after being sent to London. The implication was that, although the mission was over, he was *still* not a participant, which was false. He then described the approach by the Schweitzer group asking him for his "good Offices." Morris had in fact accepted a share in exchange for those good offices, that is, for trying to influence the president, but he told Washington that he had simply referred them to "Short, or to their own Ministry, whose Support would be much more efficacious than the Sentiments of any private Individual." He did *not* say that he had *recommended* it to Short. He concluded by asking Washington to attribute his recommendations "I pray you, to the true Cause."

This letter, by any yardstick, was not honest. However, in analyzing its reflection on Morris's character, the situation must be divided into two aspects: the merit of the proposal, and the merit of Morris's method of promoting it. We have seen that a purchase of the American debt by private speculators might have been the best way to address the debt for both countries. It is evident, nevertheless, that once Morris had determined that the financial scheme was respectable on its merits and decided to join it, he was willing to use crass means to secure it, including offering shares to important people in the French ministry (a common but scarcely admirable practice), countenancing the paying of *douceurs* to others, and using his American contacts in an indirect and thus not commendable fashion. He did believe his financial judgments were right and in the public interest, and it is difficult to dispute his claim to superior financial understanding. Morris was far and away the most financially knowledgeable and experienced American in France at the time, with inside knowledge of both countries' circumstances.

Yet Morris misled Washington, who he knew was no fiscal expert, doubtless because he thought that a recommendation based on his supposedly disinterested word would be the best way to obtain the president's endorsement. The reasons for his deceit are apparent: Morris was very worried about money during this period, for he had come close to disaster in December 1790, thanks to Daniel Parker, and he was still trying to cover the shortfall the following June. In addition, while he was not ashamed of being a businessman, something southern gentlemen like Short and others vilified him for, Morris knew that it might disqualify him for a diplomatic position, and he had some hope of being appointed to either Britain or France. Swan told Knox that Morris was unhappy about being characterized as a speculator in the foreign debt because it constituted "an objection against his being a diplomatique man."[60]

A related but not identical point is Morris's conviction that appointment to a public post would require him to stay out of business because of the potential for conflicts of interest. He had done so during his mission to Britain, and later, after his appointment as minister to France, he "quitted business" (other than American land sales). In May 1793, during the great upheavals in France, at a time when "Communication with England, and indeed with all foreign countries was never in the Memory of Man so difficult and uncertain," he would not use the diplomatic pouch for his commercial correspondence, because "I do not chuse even in Matters of indifference to make my public Character subservient to private Purposes for I have observ'd that Men slide easily into a Practice of that sort and seldom stop at the Point which on cooler thought they might wish."[61]

Morris was not, in short, faultless. Yet the debt proposal is the only instance in the papers examined for this essay, covering the entirety of Morris's stay in France, in which Morris appears to have tried to influence his American friends in an official position on a matter relating to his personal gain. Whether or not posterity judges Morris harshly for his actions in this case, a frank consideration should be made of the fiscal and diplomatic merits of what he was proposing.

The Schweitzer plan originally called for paying the French off through supplying salt provisions, paid for by the American government, to the French marine. The bankers modified the proposal in view of Short's new instructions to raise loans for the debt, and eventually they offered a loan to cover the entire debt at terms comparable to those offered by the Dutch. There is no indication as to whether payment would have been in *assignats* or livres, although Hamilton assumed it would have been in *assignats*. The benefit to the speculators due to depreciation of the *assignat* would have been considerable. However, this benefit in itself cannot be a basis for criticism, for it will be recalled that at the time the proposal was planned the United States was itself still intending to take advantage of the *assignat* depreciation.[62]

Short was suspicious of the group and unwilling to recommend their proposal because it would mean the United States would lose the advantage of the exchange and the *assignat* depreciation (the determination of Jefferson and Hamilton *not* to take the *assignat* advantage was still months away).[63]

Hamilton and Jefferson learned of the Schweitzer proposal around the beginning of April 1791, before Morris wrote to Washington. Both secretaries opposed the proposal for different reasons. Hamilton objected to a delay on principal payments which could entail loss of the exchange advantage, but he instructed Short that other private proposals might be acceptable. Jefferson, as discussed above, objected to private speculation as a risk to the United States, and told Short to "dissuade the government as far as you can prudently from listening to any overtures of that kind."[64]

On June 11, 1791, while Morris was on a trip to London, Short received these letters, which he would surely have communicated to the Schweitzer group (although, oddly, a letter of June 12 to Morris makes no mention of it). Regardless, Morris must have learned of the rejection, but he did not immediately give up. After he returned to Paris on July 1, he obtained, through

Montmorin, copies of French dispatches and Jefferson's letters about the debt. Morris then briefed the Schweitzer agents and sent them again to try to win over Short.[65]

Short continued to resist and pursued instead his instructions to raise new loans. The matter thereafter disappears from Morris's papers, indicating that he probably accepted by the end of the summer that the scheme was dead. He helped Short negotiate a loan for the United States with a Belgian banker named DeWolf, with whom Morris had numerous business dealings. His papers and account books contain no indication that he received a commission on this loan.

Later that year, when Morris learned that the United States had agreed to compensate France for *assignat* depreciation, he wrote to Washington of his approval: "In the proposition of S.J. and Co. I saw the means of saving Somewhat to the United States, without incurring the Odium of a Payment in depreciated Paper; but since a Determination to pay in Value is adopted, I heartily and entirely approve of the Rejection of their Offer."[66] It is very likely that Morris, though disappointed in his private hopes, was honest in this sentiment.

Whether there are any laurels to be handed out in the episode of the French debt rests on what is to be considered "honorable" and "dishonorable." To some the debt speculation proposals may seem "dishonorable." This analysis would benefit from the salt of reality: France needed money immediately and the United States could not (and later would not) pay immediately; the resulting impasse and delay were most "dishonorable" to America. If speculators had bought the debt as early as 1789, as Morris urged, or even in 1791, France would have gotten assistance much sooner. Whether prompt repayment might have helped check the bloody revolutionary tide that was rising can be nothing but conjecture; it should not prevent us from noting the indifference of the American government to the distress of its wartime ally.

Jefferson's concern about private speculation had to do with American creditworthiness, not with treating France fairly. Until the French objected, *all* American officials involved in this matter—including Jefferson—considered the United States entitled to the exchange advantage *and* to the enormous *assignat*-depreciation advantage. The French, though they may have "muttered," as Morris reported, apparently did not insist on compensation for the exchange, yet the loss of the exchange alone was quite significant and benefited the United States considerably at French expense. Again, this does not appear to be a worthy demonstration of what Jefferson called America's "spirit of sincere friendship and attachment" to France in her hour of need.[67]

The debt remained a contentious issue for the two countries. In the first half of 1792, Short and Morris worked in vain to have the French Legislative Assembly agree to remittance of debt payments in the form of supplies to the French affected by the slave revolt in Santo Domingo (Hamilton worked out something similar with Ternant in America). When the king fell in August, the new revolutionary leaders demanded that Morris, now minister to France, pay the full remaining debt in advance, though he had no such authority from his government. When he refused but offered to request such authority, the outraged Girondin ministers made the first of several demands for his recall. He was indeed recalled, but not for two more years, and for other reasons. Still, the issue tainted him in the eyes of subsequent revolutionary regimes.[68]

In the end, while Morris's speculation on the American war debt to France failed, other bankers and private speculators prevailed. Although the bulk of the French debt was paid through Dutch loans by 1794, the remainder was snapped up by the persistent and resourceful James Swan. In 1796 the United States Treasury agreed with Swan, who was acting as a purchasing agent for the embattled French Directory, to convert the loan into United States domestic bonds of 5 1/2 percent interest; Swan received the bonds, assumed the debt, and paid it to France in the form of supplies.[69]

Thus, Jefferson's objections to the role of speculators was neither as effective nor as diplomatically honorable as historians have assumed. At the same time, a fair assessment of Morris's speculation effort suggests that it was based on sound reasoning and a sincere conviction that it would benefit France. Despite his disingenuous letter to Washington, it appears that Morris's conscience was clear. In the summer of 1792, he wrote his brother-in-law that he could "fairly stand forth and challenge the world to produce against me a single instance of mean or cruel or dishonest or dishonorable conduct."[70] His proposals, had they been accepted, might well have been the best means of assisting the ally who had made America's independence possible.

Lord Selkirk's Tour of North America, 1803–4

J. M. BUMSTED

During the summer of 2003, the town of Belfast, Prince Edward Island, held a celebration honoring the town's benefactor, Thomas Douglas, Fifth Earl of Selkirk (1771–1820). Selkirk had visited the Scottish highlands in 1792, the year when the "Highland Clearances" began in earnest, and had been deeply affected by the plight of families who were callously, sometimes violently, turned out from their homes in order that their (largely English) landowners might enjoy greater profit by raising sheep. Selkirk knew that although the displaced Highlanders might find better-paying work in the Lowlands, their hearts lay in the Highlands and in farming.

When he made these observations, Selkirk was a young man of twenty-one, and it must have seemed impossible to him that he would ever be in a position to do anything to help them. Nonetheless, he felt driven to try. He studied Scots history and culture, even learning Scots Gaelic. He came to the conclusion that emigration to Canada might offer displaced Highlanders an opportunity to earn more money than was likely in the Highlands, and that they once again might become the farmers they still longed to be. One might reasonably have expected, as Selkirk did, that the government would be happy to be free of this surplus population, especially the many Catholics among them. Yet initially the government—perhaps reluctant to lose a supply of inexpensive labor—opposed the emigration. Then in 1799, Selkirk unexpectedly inherited the means to put his theories about emigration and resettlement into action. His four elder brothers predeceased their father, and upon the death of the fourth Earl of Selkirk in 1799, Thomas found himself elevated to that position and in control of a large fortune. Selkirk proceeded to wage a nearly solitary battle to secure for Scotsmen the right to emigrate from their native land, that they might embrace the challenges and opportunities that lay in Canada.

Though Selkirk's mission was rooted in a sincere concern for the Scots, it is difficult to calculate with certainty how much of him was altruistic philanthropist, and how much was calculating land developer—that is, how much personal gain served as a motive for his plans. The best evidence we have as to what kind of man Selkirk was lies in his North American diary of 1803–4, which he kept during his travels through Canada and the United States.

Selkirk covered a vast amount of territory in his journey. During the summer of 1803 he sailed from Scotland to British North America aboard a three-ship flotilla carrying more than eight hundred Highlanders. These Scotsmen were participants in Selkirk's attempt to demonstrate that redundant Highlanders could be made useful to the British Empire by becoming settlers in Britain's American colonies. The ships stopped first at Prince Edward Island, an island colony off the coast of New Brunswick that had stagnated since its founding in the 1770s.[1] Lord Selkirk spent a little more than a month there organizing his settlement before heading south, towards Halifax. From the Nova Scotia capital he sailed for Boston, traveling by carriage across Massachusetts to Albany, New York, then to Upper Canada (today's southern Ontario), where he searched for land that would be suitable for a sheep farm and a second settlement.

Selkirk had many reasons for visiting North America, especially the United States. His family had acquired from the Colden family some upstate New York property that needed inspecting. Selkirk was also eager to observe the social and economic consequences of the American Revolution, which his family had supported in part because of the prospects an American victory would create for large-scale land investment. A product of the Scottish Enlightenment, the earl saw himself as part of a new breed of political economists.[2] For more than a year, he traveled across the northeastern part of the continent, talking to and absorbing information from everyone he encountered and keeping careful notes of his observations.

<hr />

Selkirk's travel diary, which begins on August 3 upon his arrival at Prince Edward Island, offers a detailed account of his journey.[3] As with almost all Selkirk's papers, the original of this diary was lost in a fire at St. Mary's Isle. What survives are handwritten transcripts made by volunteers hired by the (then) Public Archives of Canada. Apparently, these people were instructed to copy only material of interest to Canadians. The evidence suggests that Selkirk kept more diaries, but this is the only one that survives even in transcribed form. It is impossible to tell from the transcript whether the original diary actually began on August 3, or whether only the transcript begins on that date.[4] Because this is his travel diary, not a personal diary, few of Selkirk's private thoughts are included. The diary tells us a good deal about what he did and what he observed, but precious little about the inner workings of the man himself. Nonetheless, this diary provides our most sustained, autobiographical record of Selkirk's life, and from it we can glean considerable insight into the man.

Selkirk's diary entries have some curious omissions. He was, for example, apparently accompanied for more than a year by a manservant named Jilks, yet Jilks is never mentioned in the diary. Selkirk may also have been accompanied on his journey in North America by a "Dr. Shaw," a medical attendant who sailed on one of the vessels that voyaged to Prince Edward Island. It is equally likely that Shaw was a companion for only a portion of the journey; certainly he was part of the group that arrived at Baldoonin early June 1804. In any event, the invisibility of those who accompanied Selkirk in the capacity of servants does not necessarily indicate any grave flaw in Selkirk's character; most aristocrats kept something of a distance between themselves and their servants. Still, the earl clearly did not humanize those who looked after him, in contrast to his late elder brother, Lord Daer, whose ease and familiarity towards those who tended to his needs had favorably impressed Robert Burns so many years before.[5]

Selkirk's journey across North America began in mid-September 1803, when, accompanied by a number of local officials, he left Prince Edward Island and traveled from Charlottetown to Point Prim, then across the Northumberland Strait to Nova Scotia. This north shore of Nova Scotia had been settled by Highlanders since the early 1770s, and Selkirk was anxious to investigate their progress. As usual, he interrogated everyone he met. Outside Pictou, he learned from two newcomers building a stone house that, "if my Gaelic did not deceive me," they had purchased one hundred acres of land for a total of one hundred guineas.[6] This aside is one of the few times in this diary that Selkirk alludes to his competence in Gaelic, a language in which he seems not entirely at ease.[7]

Selkirk's observations around Pictou confirmed the impression he had formed on Prince Edward Island that all settlers, including Highlanders, preferred lots with water frontage. "The general appearance of the Settlement," Selkirk wrote, "strongly recalled some Scenes in Swisserland."[8] He was impressed by the settlement at Truro, which had been established by Scots-Irishmen from New Hampshire before the American Revolution. The area had become prosperous, he noted, through raising beef cattle for the Halifax market. Selkirk arrived in Halifax on September 23 and remained in the Nova Scotia capital until October 7, enjoying during this stay "a continual succession of dinner parties."[9] When not socializing, he continued questioning everyone, learning all he could about areas unfamiliar to most Englishmen. He spent much time with Father Edmund Burke, a Roman Catholic priest who had spent some years in Upper Canada before moving to Halifax.[10] In 1801, Burke had been appointed vicar general of Quebec; an influential political as well as religious figure, he would become the first vicar apostolic of Nova Scotia. Burke shared Selkirk's passion for shaping the settlement of Canada, and they spent hours together poring over maps of Upper Canada and discussing where the best place to locate a settlement might be.

On October 7, the earl set sail from Halifax for Boston, where upon his arrival a few days later he was whisked off to the theatre. This was housed in a building larger than the King's Theatre in Edinburgh. The earl found "the acting tolerable—music detestable."[11] Selkirk commented how few ladies were present and seems to have not been much smitten with matters theatrical. Unsurprisingly, he found, at least in the upper circles of society where he was entertained, strong support for Federalism and friendship for Great Britain. Boston seemed like "an English country town," but with better gardens.

On October 19, Selkirk left Boston, setting out across Massachusetts in "my own carriage"[12]—a carriage Selkirk had apparently arranged to have shipped across the Atlantic to Boston. Selkirk's carriage was considerably heavier than the local standard; six months later, he would marvel at how American carriages were "ingeniously constructed for lightness and cheapness."[13] As Selkirk's carriage rumbled across the state of Massachusetts, he paid particular attention to the geological features of the landscape and to agricultural practices, especially regarding the raising of livestock, including a lengthy entry on sheep he composed while staying at Williams's Tavern in Marlborough.

Like most aristocratic travelers of the time, Selkirk was a tolerable artist who worked in pencil and in watercolors. He apparently astonished the

"Country people" at Belchertown "when I sat down to take a sketch of Country."[14] His few surviving sketches—none, unfortunately, from this journey—indicate that he was capable of producing a decent likeness of the landscape. Selkirk recorded all sorts of curious bits of information as he crossed Massachusetts—how, for example, the citizens of Cheshire had produced a huge, 1200-pound cheese, which they had sent as a gift to Thomas Jefferson. Ever the developer, the earl kept notes about building construction, how a house "2 Stories & garret 40 by 28" could be built for about one thousand dollars.[15] Selkirk's carriage meandered on through western Massachusetts and into eastern New York on a turnpike that was a privately owned, for-profit toll road. Selkirk learned that more than five hundred families traveled each autumn via this route into the west. As he pointed out in his diary, the presence of a decent road was advantageous not only for carrying produce to market, but for bringing purchasers to the farmer's door. It was, perhaps, this toll road that inspired Selkirk's later interest in road building. Certainly, Selkirk's comments about the countryside increasingly related to good and bad settlement practices.

Selkirk arrived in the evening at his Albany hotel to find "a party of wild young aristocrats worthy of London or Edr [Edinburgh]." He eagerly joined them, later reporting that the resultant merrymaking "made us very thick."[16] Selkirk did not drink to excess, but as this entry suggests he was not averse to the odd evening of heavy conviviality. Like most occasional drinkers, he probably felt quite proud of himself for getting "thick." This was the first occasion in the United States on which Selkirk indicated that he had fallen among congenial spirits from his own social class. He was impressed by the Albany aristocracy, whose position was based—as in Britain—upon large landholdings. The young bucks he had met were connected to the great landholding families of the region, and Selkirk quickly found himself invited to dinner with the Van Rensselaers, arguably the richest and most aristocratic of their set.

It was at this time that, using a letter of introduction from a London Huguenot merchant, Selkirk met one of the most influential leaders in American history, Alexander Hamilton.[17] By the time Selkirk met Hamilton in 1803, the statesman no longer held public office and was living in semi-retirement in upstate New York. He was also using the title of "general," a rank he had attained in the 1790s during his service during the Quasi War with France.[18]

Selkirk was dazzled by Hamilton, who was thirteen years his senior. The earl wrote in the diary that he had seldom "met with a man of whom I formed a higher opinion—the clearness of his ideas, & the readiness with which he brings forward a solid reason for every opinion he advances combine with his very extensive information in giving an uncommon zest to his conversation—and to this he joins a degree of candour in discussion very rarely to be met with."[19] As Selkirk had met and conversed with a good many leading figures of the day, including Thomas Paine, philosophers involved in the French Revolution, and the leaders of the Scottish Enlightenment, this reaction indicates in what very high esteem he held Hamilton.[20] The day after he arrived in Albany, Selkirk had sent Hamilton his letter of introduction.[21] Hamilton called on Selkirk at his hotel the following day, then invited the earl to spend an entire day at the home of his father-in-law, General Philip Schuyler. Selkirk's diary reports little of his conversations with these men, but the discussions that day would form the basis for Selkirk's analysis of the polity of the United States.

At Buffalo Creek, New York, Selkirk penned an essay that reflected his Hamiltonian view of the American polity. Selkirk opens his essay by commenting on the "great feebleness" of the American government in enforcing laws opposed by local interests.[22] The military establishment, he believed, was too weak to support the constituted authorities. Selkirk dismissed the American Constitution as a "patched work" full of "a jumble of contradictory principles." The presidency was such a political prize that it served as the basis for partisan party politics, which he deemed "the bane of America." Partisan politics, concluded Selkirk, had resulted in government by patronage, which extended even into the military.[23] The Federalists had sought to correct this problem by proposing that presidents and senators serve lifetime terms, thus reintroducing into government the hereditary principle, but Hamilton and others in Albany thought the idea too unpopular to advocate openly.

In his essay, Selkirk reported on Hamilton's musings during their discussions in Albany. Hamilton insisted that the political division between the Federalists and the Anti-Federalists was based on a conflict between commercial and agricultural interests. Thomas Jefferson, argued Hamilton, considered capitalism incompatible with a Republican government. The Republicans had not so much won in 1800 as the Federalists had lost, because their measures were so unpopular.[24]

Hamilton also claimed that the rivalry between Virginia and Massachusetts had developed in such a way as to isolate New England, and that New England might "thro' disgust incline for a total separation." Hamilton was opposed to permitting any such separation; he insisted that, after any such division, new parties that were equally contentious would appear. The preservation of the unity of the American Empire, Selkirk thought, seemed to be Hamilton's primary object. "The Evils of democracy," Selkirk wrote, "are less in proportion to the extent of Empire, as the division of different districts prevents the mob uniting & their contradictory prejudices & sentiments prevents the precipitate measures that would be likely in a smaller state." Whether Selkirk borrowed this generalization from Hamilton or whether it was his own creation is not entirely clear. Selkirk reported how, unlike most Federalists, Hamilton wholeheartedly supported the Louisiana Purchase, his only complaint being the administration's failure to act more quickly. The purchase contributed to the popularity of the Jefferson government. Hamilton admitted, recorded Selkirk, "that as *Territory* Louisiana is of no value to the U.S. & thinks they ought to exchange the Western bank of Mississippi for the Floridas."[25]

Selkirk shared with the Federalists a fear for the future of large property holders in America. The earl thought that the problem, at least in New York, was less a "disregard of property" than the presence of several great landed proprietors. Yet he seemed to accept that "except as an article of speculation in which the capital value only is thought of . . . no rich man would think of vesting money in the purchase of Land as in Europe to produce an annual revenue." This realization led to another: that the "almost total want of a Landed Aristocracy" in America was perhaps responsible for Americans' "sordid attention to money." Selkirk believed that the Americans had compounded their problems by copying England overmuch, rather than by striking out on their own or by copying from other aspects of their legal and governmental heritage, including that of Scotland. He gave as examples the "servil" replication of the English Poor Laws and the English common law, neither of which exists in Scots law.

Selkirk commented little on "the manners of the people," other than to note that they probably had little to do with the American government. He reported that every gentleman whom he consulted spoke disparagingly about the moral character of the backcountry people, who exhibited "litigious cunning" and a propensity for drink. Selkirk blamed the litigiousness on the universal diffusion of education, which was sufficient to destroy the "simplicity of ignorance" yet insufficient to substitute "the correctness of principle." He reported that Hamilton even maintained that universal education made the people presumptuous about their own judgments and "therefore more liable to be misled by demagogues." Selkirk's diary reveals no evidence of the deep-seated anti-Americanism he would subsequently demonstrate. He found neither surliness, nor incivility, nor disrespect among the Americans he met on his travels, providing he addressed them "as an equal."

The essay makes other, broader observations concerning whether the United States had a government that would prove capable of providing social order and protection for investment. These were issues of considerable interest to Selkirk, as he was trying to decide where to locate his sheep farm. In describing a dispute between New York settlers and a Pennsylvania land company, Selkirk noted how the courts were unable to protect land titles against squatters.

Selkirk was at this time heading westward toward his Genesee lands. These properties were connected to landholdings acquired earlier by Sir William Pulteney and other Scottish speculators in the region.[26] When he reached Geneva, New York, Selkirk tried but failed to find Pulteney's agent. From others at the local land office with whom he spoke, he was able to get a clearer picture of what had happened in Genesee, where, through the agency of one Charles Williamson, British investors had invested hundreds of thousands of pounds in land speculation. There had been some suggestion in Great Britain that fraud had been involved. Selkirk believed this was not the case. Pulteney had paid too much for the initial land purchase, then was encouraged to buy even more land, given Williamson's willingness to make sales on credit. Williamson, meanwhile, had spent profligately to develop the land, building hotels, theatres, and race tracks, but he did not particularly benefit Pulteney's investment. The locals spoke highly of Williamson and did not think his motives dishonest. Selkirk did not offer a final judgment in his diary, but he did record that while the deal was as bad as had been reported, the problems did not include fraud. As he traveled west, Selkirk commented on other large-scale land speculations and concluded that most would eventually be successful, so long as they did not have to compete with land west of the Mississippi.

Had Selkirk entertained any notions of developing his Genesee holdings, he was doubtless disabused of them by what he was told in Albany and by what he discovered at the scene. The United States was not a particularly good place for a Scottish nobleman to attempt to build an estate. He hoped that British America would be more welcoming.

By mid-November 1803, Selkirk, traveling on horseback, had crossed the Niagara River, entered Upper Canada, and encountered Niagara Falls. Like most early visitors to Niagara Falls, Selkirk was bowled over by its splendor: "The great falls goes indeed beyond imagination, & exceeded every idea I had formed of its grandeur." In Niagara he visited with Thomas Clark, a native of Drumfriesshire who had come to Canada in 1791 to work for his cousin Robert Hamilton.[27] Hamilton was the major military supplier at Niagara, and Clark followed in his footsteps. He had built a wharf and storehouse at Queenston in 1799, subsequently founding, in 1800, a firm with several other Scots arrivals who traded mainly in flour. By 1803, Clark, Hamilton, and John Forsyth controlled local commerce, their position based on a government contract. Selkirk was much impressed with Robert Hamilton, whom he described as a "very respectable & intelligent man, & of very liberal ideas."

From Thomas Clark and Robert Hamilton, Selkirk received his first glimpse of the western fur trade. They told Selkirk about fur trading at the confluence of Lakes Huron and Michigan, an area known as Michilimakinac, and about fur trading conducted by independent traders who were not employees of the North West Company. Selkirk's extensive notes emphasize the vigor with which independent traders, who were mainly Lowland Scots, competed for western furs with the Highlanders employed by the North West Company. But the earl seemed even more interested in Sandy Brown's reports about his sheep. Brown was the shepherd who had brought Selkirk's flock west from Albany the previous year. Selkirk's agent, William Burn had sheared the sheep and sold much of the wool. Selkirk was told that the flock, while mixed, would serve as the basis of a "good breed." He also learned that sheep could be profitably driven to Upper Canada, where both wool and sheep would bring a good price.

While near Niagara, Selkirk encountered an American who had recently settled in Canada, yet had retained his American citizenship. Asked how he reconciled swearing allegiance to two different governments, the settler "answered that the Oath to each only applied while resident within their territories—he could never take an Oath to be otherwise understood." Selkirk observed that everything he had heard about the Americans who moved to Canada indicated "that they are merely induced by the facility of getting land, and that loyalty [to Britain] is a mere pretext."

Historians have often linked Selkirk with another early developer of Upper Canada, Colonel Thomas Talbot, who by 1803 had begun developing a private estate on the western frontier. Although Selkirk and Talbot were both noncorporate, individual landholders, they approached land development from distinctly different philosophical positions.[28] Talbot intended to be the squire of his estates in traditional English aristocratic fashion, living in residence and interacting with those who settled on his lands, many as tenants. Selkirk, on the other hand, was more interested in philanthropy and investment than in securing feudal standing in the New World, and he planned to be an absentee developer. Unlike Talbot, Selkirk already had an estate back in Scotland, while Talbot had nothing comparable in Britain. As early as 1803, Talbot was promoting his intentions to favor British over American settlers, in order to control "the growing tendency to insubordination and revolt" in Upper Canada.[29] Selkirk never mentions discussing this subject with Talbot, but he may have been influenced by his political opinions. When they met, the Irish-born Talbot was returning from York to his land near Dunwich. Selkirk's Scottish hosts told him that they expected Talbot's plan—which was to offer small, fifty-acre allotments to settlers—to fail, as the plots were not of sufficient size to make farming profitable.

Selkirk had hoped to make direct contact at Queenston with William Burn, who had left White Creek, New York, for Queenston in Upper Canada in early September 1803, but he was forced to sail on the last vessel bound for York (later renamed Toronto) on November 20 without having done so.[30] The schooner on which Selkirk took passage had to be towed to port in York by rowboats manned by voyageurs heading for Montreal as passengers. York was then an unprepossessing community of sixty or seventy houses erected on lots still "very ragged from the Stumps" and ranging from only a quarter-acre to a single acre in size. A single, two-room structure housed all the available agencies of the government and sat on marshy ground that bred fever and ague. Selkirk describes Governor Simcoe's decision to change the capital of Upper Canada from Niagara to York in 1794 as "slap dash." It forced government officials to abandon comfortable homes and communities for "an absolute wood where people were sometimes losing themselves between one hut & another."[31] Simcoe had made this change partly because of York's harbor and partly because the surrounding land was unclaimed. It thus could be taken over by his "friends." Selkirk thought little of Simcoe's contribution to the development of Upper Canada. He quoted the Mohawk leader Joseph Brant as saying, "Gen S. has done great deal for this province, he has changed the name of every place in it."[32] Selkirk added that Simcoe's general system was to ape England "without regard to the circumstances of the country." This was particularly true in his decision to adopt English law in its entirety, despite the fact that its intricacy was totally unsuitable to an infant country without professionals to implement the law. This inability to staff all the courts actually thwarted justice.

Selkirk was equally unimpressed with Upper Canada's current officialdom and, especially, with the venal public culture of the colony. In York he met Sheriff Alexander Macdonell, who would become his Upper Canadian advisor and agent. This was the beginning of a protracted and somewhat unsatisfactory relationship with the Macdonell family in North America. Macdonell was politically ambitious.[33] He had acquired some military experience in the American Revolution, had been a client of John Graves Simcoe, and was fluent in French, English, Gaelic, and several aboriginal languages. In 1803 the sheriff was a prominent member of the small bachelor elite in the tiny capital, dining in the mess, drinking tea and wine in great quantities, and playing whist in the evening. Lieutenant Governor Peter Hunter tried to warn Selkirk of Macdonell's weaknesses, but his advice was not heeded.[34] Perhaps this was because Macdonell was a Highland Catholic, a group to whom Selkirk was always partial.

The earl's careful investigation of land-granting procedures in Upper Canada soon led him to conclude that the system had many difficulties and was subject to much abuse. Many confusions remained from the earlier granting of land to both Loyalists and soldiers, and the surveyor general had enormous power to assist or hinder those seeking land. Nevertheless, Selkirk felt that he had established a good relationship with Lieutenant Governor Hunter, and he was sufficiently confident about land grants to write in late December to an American acquaintance about his plans to bring a "settlement of Highlanders to a Township near Lake Erie." He also mentioned his desire for a "few of their countrymen who have long been in America" to "instruct the newcomers in the methods of the country."[35]

At York, Selkirk finally caught up with his agent, William Burn, and decided where he wanted to locate his next settlement. It would not be a fortuitous choice. With additional input from Burn, who had spent the autumn scouting for land in western Upper Canada, the earl decided on the Chenail Ecarté on the north shore of Lake St. Clair, not far from Detroit, as the site of his future settlement. The land there was marshy and would not require much clearing to be suitable for sheep. Unfortunately, having not attended medical lectures at Edinburgh, Selkirk failed to realize that marshy land was apt to be malarial. After drafting detailed instructions for William Burn about the exact locations for his lands, Selkirk set off on January 4, 1804, for Montreal, traveling by horse along the north shore of Lake Ontario.[36] Burn, meanwhile, headed west to the northeast corner of Lake St. Clair. Unable to procure enough land in a single township, he instead laid claim to two adjoining, unoccupied half-townships. Selkirk eventually petitioned for, and received, 1,200 acres personally and another two hundred acres for each of fifteen heads of families coming from St. Mary's Isle to the new settlement, which Selkirk named Baldoon.[37] He then proceeded to give fifty of the two hundred acres to each of the heads of families, keeping one hundred fifty acres for himself.

As he journeyed to Montreal, Selkirk continued to make detailed observations of the settlements and their populations, paying particular attention to the occasional pockets of ethnic communities he found along the way. At Presqu'isle he found a settlement established by American New Englanders who had been attracted by Governor Simcoe's proclamation of free land in 1796. The earl admitted that the appearance of this settlement seemed to confirm the superiority of New Englanders as settlers, since the relatively new community was materially as far advanced as the far older Niagara River settlements. Selkirk found Kingston much superior to York. He then moved on to Glengarry, in southeastern Upper Canada, calling at the Osnabrook farm of Captain Miles Macdonell, who was Sheriff Alexander's brother-in-law. Selkirk approved of what he saw and heard regarding Miles, who was "much of a gentleman in manners & sentiment" and was "so popular that he could get work done when nobody else could." These qualities Selkirk regarded as important, and he filed Miles away for future reference. For his part, Miles was equally impressed with Selkirk and later commented about the visit at length in a letter to his brother.[38] In this letter, Miles observed, "Mere farming will hardly support my family in the manner I could wish," a sentiment that he had probably shared with Selkirk and that indicated he might be receptive to Selkirk's subsequent offers of employment. In Glengarry, Selkirk found a thriving Highland community. The houses, while poor by American or English standards, were "a wonderful advance from the Hovels of Glengarry [in Scotland]" and equal to those of "farmers of 100 or 150£ a year in Galloway."[39] The Highlanders of Glengarry had adjusted well to North American conditions while maintaining their own traditions. Selkirk was suitably impressed.

Selkirk was also favorably impressed by French Canada, especially "the appearance of old settlement & thick population" that made it seem quite European. In Montreal he was royally entertained by the "grandees, nabobs of the N.W.Co. etc," most of whom were Highland Scots. He learned a good deal more about the economics and politics of the fur trade, recording in detail in his journal the information that was shared with him. He noted that Simon McTavish was the leading force behind the old Northwest Company, and he recorded how coercion was used in managing French Canadian employees. Selkirk thought that this disciplined approach would enable the Canadians to easily triumph over the Americans in the west. McTavish was quite open about his plan to challenge the validity of the charter of the Hudson's Bay Company, in order "to force the H. Bay Co. to a compromise."[40]

Later, the Nor'westers would accuse the earl of abusing their hospitality by accepting their confidences without indicating his direct interest in their affairs. Such charges were only half true. Selkirk did allow himself to be wined and dined at the Beaver Club, the private lair of Montreal's fur barons. He did indeed listen to their boasting about their plans and to their summations of their business activity. He undoubtedly did not feel obliged to reveal his previous attempt to interest the British government in settlements in Red River or at the Falls of St. Mary, sites of pivotal concern to the Northwest Company, as they were crucial to their extended transportation and supply system. There is no evidence, however, that at this time Selkirk had any special interest in the Hudson's Bay Company or the fur trade. He recorded careful observations in Montreal, as he did everywhere else during his journey across North America. Fascinated by everything he saw and heard, Selkirk was receptive to information from any source; conversely, most people in North America, including Montreal fur traders, were eager to impress a visiting British lord with their accomplishments.

In Quebec City for the opening of the legislature, Selkirk's Scottish experience enabled him to grasp the problems of French Canada quite easily, although his expression of them was a bit awkward: "The English at Quebec & Montreal cry out in the true John Bull style against their [the French's] obstinate aversion to institutions which they [the English] have never taken any pains to make them understand—& are surprised at the natural & universally experienced dislike of a conquered people to their conquerors & to every thing which puts them in mind of their subjection." Selkirk had earlier recorded, with some astonishment, the efforts of the Lower Canadian legislature to force the universal adoption of American sleighs, which were wider and longer than the French variety, noting that "the Canadians [were] prejudiced against everything English & as much wedded to old habits as the people of an old country, were obstinate, & evaded every attempt to enforce the law."[41] He was struck by the English absence of "system in dealing with Canada," observing that "the only chance of reconciling the people would have been either to use every effort to change them entirely in language & Institutions & make them forget that they were not English—or keeping them as French to give a Government adapted to them as such, & keep every thing English out of sight—neither of these plans has been followed, & the policy of Govt. has been a kind of vibration between them."[42] The result, thought the earl, was confusion and contradiction. Fluent in a French polished during years in the drawing rooms of revolutionary Paris, Selkirk observed that "even in private society . . . the English & Canadians draw asunder."[43] He clearly did not approve.

On February 21, Lord Selkirk left Montreal in a hired American sleigh, with a second for his "Servants."[44] He did not record who was in the second sleigh, although presumably it included the redoubtable Jilks and perhaps Dr. Shaw. He traveled through Burlington, Vermont, to Albany, where he again met General Hamilton. At Albany a Colonel Troup blamed the failure of the Genesee speculation on Charles Williamson's overextension, claiming that Williamson had been infected with land mania and had not kept regular accounts. "Probably too coming from a narrow situation to the command of a very heavy purse his head was a little turned," Selkirk added.[45] He did not yet have enough experience with North American agents to know how common this syndrome was, nor did he learn anything useful from this particular debacle. The earl did get to hear Alexander Hamilton make several speeches on legal matters, which impressed him greatly. The New York legislature was in session, giving Selkirk an opportunity to see American democracy in action.

Selkirk found every political issue in New York influenced by the state's forthcoming gubernatorial election, which was "the universal subject of discussion." Most Federalists, Selkirk learned, considered the leading candidate for the post, Aaron Burr, "a man of no principle." After a personal interview with Burr, Selkirk came away convinced that he was "one of the most guarded & reserved men I ever conversed with," capable of talking for hours without revealing his opinions. From Hamilton, Selkirk heard once more the speculation that New England was on the verge of separating from the Union. "He thinks Burr if at the Head of New York may come into the measure as more easy to acquire an entire ascendancy in the divided than in the entire field."[46] Hamilton also feared the prospect of anarchy, given the escalating virulence of the parties. He insisted that the military would be useless in the event of a war between the North and the South. Selkirk himself suspected that a separatist movement would not extend beyond New England without the support of Burr. These, in any event, were the rumors floating around New York City in March 1804. Neither Selkirk nor his New York acquaintances anticipated that, within a few months, Hamilton would be dead, shot by Burr during a duel.[47]

On April 24, 1804, Selkirk left New York in a sloop heading north along the Hudson River, ending the last ten miles of his journey to Albany on foot, his thoughts turning now to the settlement he proposed to found in Upper Canada.

During Selkirk's first stay in Albany, he had ordered William Burn to proceed immediately from Queenston to Baldoon, where he was to clear land and sow Indian corn, potatoes, and timothy in anticipation of the earl's arrival in early May. With ten oxen, Burn departed Lake Erie on April 4 and arrived at Baldoon on May 9. He hired local labor and began to clear and plant. Meanwhile, Selkirk determined through local enquiry that the best way to get settlers and sheep to Canada was by boat. Along the way he agreed with a Colonel Walker to take charge of his New York lands, which were to be sold on credit. Walker would receive a percentage of the proceeds, which meant that he would have an incentive to keep close watch over the settlers—to make sure that they were progressing. With this arrangement in place, Selkirk was freed from the need to make any additional investment in these properties. By May 20, 1804, he reached Queenston, where he checked on his sheep. He paid Richard Savage the traveling expenses awarded him by Messrs. Hamilton and Clark—there obviously had been a disagreement over the amount—and noted that the settlement was "final."[48] Sandy Brown reported twenty dead sheep. Selkirk ordered the flock sheared and arranged to turn over management to one Lionel Johnson for the summer. He then set off to go around the lake to York, riding "thro' horrible roads" into mainly unsettled territory.

Although the diary does not explicitly indicate why Selkirk went to York, the purpose of this journey appears to have been to offer Sheriff Macdonell the management of his Baldoon settlement, which he did on May 27. Selkirk's notation in a supplementary diary (apparently brief notes for further elaboration in the full diary) is sketchy: "Salary 200£—Sheep—Distillery—Settlement etc. (Burn, Brown, Wright)—he did not answer positively but seemed inclined—quere if could keep Shirriffdom wd. marry at S[andwich]—comes journey, notwithstanding Election." Selkirk thus offered Macdonell a princely salary of two hundred pounds per year in return for the supervision of all aspects of the new settlement, including subordinate personnel. The "Wright" to whom Selkirk alludes was Archibald Wright, whom Selkirk had promised a place in Upper Canada. Burn was receiving eighty pounds per annum, eight pounds of which was to be deducted from his wages and forwarded to his mother in Scotland. Alexander ("Sandy") Brown was to receive thirty pounds per annum.[49] From the beginning, however, Macdonell himself introduced the problems that would bedevil his agency: first, the question of residing at the settlement; second, the question of holding onto the sheriff's appointment, which would require his absence; and finally, the question of his continued political involvement, which again would militate against residency on the Chenail Ecarté.

Selkirk left York on May 29 by boat, accompanied by Sheriff Macdonell and apparently also by Dr. Shaw. Journeying westward, he was soon at the head of the lake, the site of what is now Hamilton, where he was joined by his prospective agent, Joseph Brant. They would arrive at Baldoon on June 8. In his journal, William Burn recorded that Selkirk arrived with "2 Gentlemen or sumthing like Gentlemen," a reference apparently to Alexander Macdonell and Dr. Shaw that suggests he was not much impressed by Selkirk's two companions. It is difficult to determine whether Burn was more upset that the size of the party put a strain on the settlement's limited sleeping facilities, or by the earl's failure to order a day's drinking to celebrate his arrival. It was becoming clear that Burn would have to work under Macdonell's supervision, for the earl and the sheriff had discussed his appointment continually on their way to Baldoon. At the settlement, Selkirk made it clear to Macdonell that he would be required to reside at Sandwich, if not at the settlement, and to give up the sheriffdom. Selkirk offered to try to get another appointment for Macdonell to replace that which he would have to surrender. Macdonell "understood that in accepting my agency he would take to it as his personal employment & that he relinquished every idea of applying personally or by friends for Govt. promotion, & if offered would not accept it till I be acquainted & had time to provide another in his place."[50] By July 2, Macdonell spoke of the appointment as settled and desired to return to York to sort out his affairs.

Selkirk's notes while at Baldoon reflect his usual flurry of activity, organizing construction materials for the settlement and arranging for supplies of food to be imported for the incoming settlers. He planned construction of a barn and fourteen houses. On paper, the preparations are impressive. The execution of his plans, however, was considerably less so. After Selkirk left Baldoon at the end of July, on the eve of the expected arrival of the major party of 101 Highlanders who were to settle there, sickness struck. Most of these settlers had been recruited in the Hebrides in late 1802; they had been housed at St. Mary's Isle during 1803, and finally transported to Quebec aboard the *Oughton* in 1804. A few of this party had left St. Mary's Isle later in 1803, but had been turned around by wartime conditions on the Atlantic. The list of passengers, labeled "Passengers, Labourers for the Earl of Selkirk's Settlement in North America," survives in the Selkirk papers.[51] Not all of these people were indentured laborers; in fact, most had prepaid their passage. These settlers, many of whom were already ill, appeared on September 5 only to find themselves in the midst of an epidemic and in a place that lacked the necessary, and promised, supplies.

Burn had not proved a good manager. During the late summer of 1804, large quantities of grain whiskey had been shipped to Baldoon. This was promptly consumed by Selkirk's hired workmen, including William Burn. Eight barrels, each of which held thirty-nine gallons of whiskey on July 1, were by early September entirely empty.[52] The small party of Baldoon workmen was ravaged by fever, probably malarial, beginning in late August. Many settlers arrived already ill from their long journey and quickly succumbed to the added insult of conditions at Baldoon. William Burn himself died of fever on September 15 after two weeks of suffering. Alexander Macdonell would later attribute Burn's demise as much to the "effects of excessive intemperance" as to the "prevailing fever." Moreover, the settlement lacked winter provisions. The housing Selkirk had ordered to be constructed wasn't completed. Burn's books and papers were in such disarray that Selkirk was never able to determine whether Burn's aged mother in Scotland was entitled to any back pay. As years of expenditure and correspondence with his estate managers would demonstrate, Baldoon would continue to pose problems for Selkirk. Developing settlements on paper was just not the same as developing settlements under real-life conditions.

When Selkirk returned to York, he attempted to make a deal with the government of the province. He wrote General Hunter on August 30, offering to build a road fifty feet wide, at his own expense, in the western region. He guaranteed that the road would be free of stumps and roots for twelve feet of its width and that it would have bridges and a firm surface. In return, Selkirk wanted a grant of six hundred thousand acres along either side of the road. According to the earl's calculations, based on American figures he had gathered, roads in Upper Canada would cost between $600 and $1,000 per mile. The road from Grand River to Chatham would cost at least $100,000, while the road from York to Amherstburgh would cost a minimum of $200,000. This land was presently without much value because of the absence of transportation.[53] On September 18, the Upper Canada executive council rejected this proposal, believing Selkirk had considerably overestimated the cost of building the road and had overpriced the value of his services.[54] Both Selkirk's offer and the council's refusal were defensible positions. Like most developers, Selkirk valued the land at its pre-improvement price, as would the developers who later built most of Canada's railroads. The Canadians, however, based their assessment of value on post-improvement values. While at York, Selkirk also tried to secure another government appointment for Sheriff Macdonell, as he had promised Macdonell he would do, but here, too, he was unsuccessful.[55]

How could Selkirk's plans for Baldoon have gone so thoroughly wrong?[56] Selkirk had named Baldoon after the family estates that had been sold off in Scotland; perhaps the name suggests an attempt to create in the New World something lost in the Old. He spent much time writing careful and detailed instructions for its management.[57] Unlike Prince Edward Island, with which he had become involved to fulfill his commitments, Baldoon seemed to represent on paper both a public and a personal vision for Selkirk. On the public side, he intended for Baldoon to demonstrate the efficacy of the planned resettlement of Highlanders and to provide a living example of his dream of "National Settlements" constituted of people who, though non-English in culture and language, could nonetheless help preserve the heartland of British North America from the pernicious influence of American culture. With regard to his private interests, Selkirk also would be carving out a major North American estate for himself and his heirs, based upon scientific techniques of agriculture and careful settlement planning, approaches not commonly practiced in North America. He sought to utilize the same improvement techniques in Upper Canada that had worked for his family in Kirkcudbright. The problem was that Upper Canada was not the South of Scotland. Finding loyal agents would be much more difficult in North America than in Galloway, and more to the point, Selkirk would be thousands of miles away and unable to supervise them.

Having transferred his management responsibilities to Sheriff Macdonell's supposedly competent hands, Selkirk felt that he could leave Baldoon. Yet one wonders why, given all the effort he had thus far invested in Baldoon, the earl did not wait for his settlers to arrive in order to make certain that all was well. Selkirk may have felt less of a sense of personal obligation to these than to other settlers, as many of these settlers had earlier refused to shift destination to Prince Edward Island in 1803, and had even threatened court action against Selkirk. Thus, he may have been fulfilling his obligations to them without feeling any real sense of responsibility for them.

Whatever the reasons for his fairly precipitous departure, not only from Baldoon but from North America, it seems clear that Selkirk had no intention of remaining in the New World longer than was absolutely necessary. Selkirk's diary offers no hint that might explain the haste with which he retuned to Prince Edward Island via York and Montreal. He arrived on October 2, late in the year for travel to and from Prince Edward Island. In a whirlwind of activity he attempted to resolve problems that had arisen in his absence, particularly a conflict between James Williams and Angus MacAulay that would continue to simmer for many years. A number of disputes with Selkirk had emerged among the settlers as well. Dr. MacAulay insisted that Selkirk's terms for settlers had been so favorable to the emigrants "as to give rise to suspicion of more distant views—on Fur Trade—or Copper Mines." McAulay wanted matters settled to the settlers' satisfaction. The earl recorded in his diary that "these ideas are probably the result of his own imagination rather than what he has heard from others—but attend."[58] There is no evidence that Selkirk ever did understand McAulay's point, although the ` also consulted with a number of individuals in the region regarding future emigration to the Gulf of St. Lawrence, for he intended to send more settlers to the island. By November 20, Selkirk was back in New York and awaiting passage to England. The last entry he made while in North America was a highly favorable character reference for Miles Macdonell.

After his return to Britain, Selkirk's only entry in this diary was a sketch of his brother Daer's shrine at Exeter Cathedral, at which he had obviously stopped.[59] The visit to Daer's final resting place probably reflected Selkirk's desire to exorcise ghosts. Daer, his memory, and the family traditions had hovered over him for many years, but now he was finally free. He had established his own career path, one distinct and apart from Daer and the family. He had also begun to define better his own political views. Within a few years, Selkirk would publicly repudiate any sympathy with parliamentary reform, basing his rejection of long-standing family principles on "the observations which I had occasion to make in the United States of America," where "universal suffrage and frequency of election prove no bar to the misconduct of representatives; and as a political adventurer, raised to power by popular favour, is fully as likely to abuse that power, as is the purchaser of a rotten borough."[60] Selkirk's tour of North America, and his discussions with Alexander Hamilton, had obviously played some part in his political conversion.

In the annals of Canadian history, Selkirk has long been acknowledged to have exercised considerable influence on the nation's development, yet the man himself has remained, for over two hundred years, something of a mystery, and his actions have inspired diametrically opposed opinions about his motives and achievements. Selkirk's diary of his North American tour suggests that he was very much a man of the Enlightenment, always asking questions, collecting information, and relying on detailed advance planning. He tended to be a man more of reason than of action. Whatever its limitations— as an incomplete transcription and in the relatively impersonal nature of its content—Selkirk's North American diary helps us understand more fully the true nature of this unquestionably important figure in Canadian history.

John Witherspoon's Philosophy of Moral Government

James M. Albritton

> There is not a single instance in history in which civil government
> was lost, and religious liberty preserved entire. If therefore we yield
> up our temporal property, we at the same time deliver the conscience
> into bondage.
>
> —John Witherspoon, "The Dominion of Providence over the Pas-
> sions of Men," May 17, 1776

Throughout the history of western Christianity, the relationship between
church and state has been a source of tension and sometimes of violence.
During the Reformation, the French Reformer John Calvin argued for a partial separation of the sacred and secular realms, as a way to mitigate conflict
between the two. The Scottish-American churchman John Witherspoon formulated his understanding of the relationship between church and state on
the basis of Calvin's, but Witherspoon's view was tempered by his experience
in the Church of Scotland. In that church, the connection between church
and state had led to the loss of virtue and the sacrifice of liberties. Political
appointments to the establishment universities of Scotland resulted in generations of church and political leaders trained in man-centered moral philosophy. At the same time, patronage led to the placement of pastors lacking piety
and virtue, who in turn cultivated generations of gentry devoid of Christian
character. These self-interested elites felt no compunction about depriving
the people of their liberties. Witherspoon, therefore, went further than Calvin and advocated for America a more complete separation between church
and state. Nevertheless, formal separation for Witherspoon did not imply that

republican government could do without the church and its inculcation of Christian piety.

John Witherspoon's words and deeds during the American Revolution reflected his belief that both church and state ought to have virtue and liberty as their foundation and end.[1] The church, Witherspoon believed, has a responsibility to the state and to its members. Likewise, the state has a responsibility to the church and to its citizens. Each has a responsibility to use its God-given authority within its respective realm, but Witherspoon believed that it was solely the church that had the responsibility of producing virtuous leaders and citizens, and this was to be accomplished by the teaching of true religion—which meant, in his view, orthodox Christianity.

Witherspoon addressed the need for true religion many times during the Revolution. The first opportunity came in *A Pastoral Letter from the Synod of New York and Philadelphia*. In response to the open aggression at Concord and Lexington, the synod asked Witherspoon to draft a letter to its congregations "to be read from the Pulpits on Thursday, June 29, 1775, being the Day of the general Fast," called for by the Continental Congress. In the face of this violence and the certainty of more to come, Witherspoon encouraged those Presbyterians who would risk their lives for the sake of liberty to be prepared for death. He expanded this call to all who would take part in the conflict, realizing that soldiers were not the only ones exposed to harm. "Let therefore every one, who from generosity of spirit, or benevolence of heart, offers himself as a champion in his country's cause, be persuaded to reverence the name, and walk in the fear of the *Prince of the kings of the earth,* and then he may, with the most unshaken firmness, expect the issue either in victory or death." Witherspoon considered the conflict with Great Britain important, but even more important was the state of men's souls.[2]

On the campus of the College of New Jersey, where he served as president, Witherspoon used every opportunity to evangelize his students. In *An Address to the Students in the Senior Class,* given "On the Lord's Day preceding Commencement, September 23, 1775," which followed the baccalaureate sermon entitled *Christian Magnanimity,* Witherspoon made a personal plea to those graduating into a turbulent and uncertain world. "The care of your souls is the one thing needful," Witherspoon admonished his students. "All mankind, of every rank, denomination and profession, are sinners by nature." Virtue and morality, he warned, are not enough. Quoting Jesus' words to the Pharisee Nicodemus, Witherspoon challenged his students: "Except a man be born again, he cannot enter into the kingdom of God." For this reason, "true religion must arise from a clear and deep conviction of your lost state by nature and practice, and an unfeigned reliance on the pardoning mercy and sanctifying grace of God." He knew that many of his listeners would play important roles in the Revolution, and that some would lose their lives in the conflict.[3]

Almost a year after he wrote the *Pastoral Letter*, Witherspoon preached his most widely published sermon, *The Dominion of Providence over the Passions of Men*, in which he again pleaded for the salvation of men's souls. He preached this sermon to the congregation at Princeton on May 17, 1776, "being the General Fast appointed by the congress through the United Colonies." He began with a plea for true religion, which must come from a real sense of sin. "Nothing can be more absolutely necessary to true religion, than a clear and full conviction of the sinfulness of our nature and state. Without this there can be neither repentance in the sinner, nor humility in the believer." With this reality in mind, he again compared the situation in the American colonies, with its hopes and fears, to eternity. "I do not blame your ardor in preparing for the resolute defense of your temporal rights. But consider I beseech you, the truly infinite importance of the salvation of your souls." Witherspoon agreed with most of his congregation on the politics surrounding the conflict with England, but he would not have them neglect a matter of eternal importance as they struggled for a temporal prize that would fade into oblivion at their deaths.[4]

As the Revolutionary War came to a close, Witherspoon challenged Americans to consider not only the state of their souls but also the responsibility entailed in victory. On November 28, 1782, a public day of thanksgiving proclaimed by the Confederation Congress, Witherspoon reminded his congregation that the American triumph was an open display of God's temporal salvation. "All temporal comforts," Witherspoon proclaimed, "derive their value from their being the fruits of divine goodness, the evidence of covenant love, and the earnest of everlasting mercy. It is therefore our indispensable duty to endeavor to obtain the sanctified improvement of every blessing, whether public or personal." In Witherspoon's view, only a Christian can truly appreciate the blessings of God, and only a Christian can respond to those blessings so as to make the most beneficial use of them.[5]

In addition to presenting the need for true religion, Witherspoon used every opportunity to demonstrate the dependence of true virtue on true religion. He affirmed this belief in his lectures on moral philosophy, in his sermons, and in pamphlets. In September 1775, for instance, President Witherspoon preached a baccalaureate sermon, titled *Christian Magnanimity,* defending the proposition that all real virtues are Christian virtues. Worried that the world had come to believe, and had influenced young Christians to believe, that magnanimity is not a Christian virtue, Witherspoon pointed to the example of pious Christians and Christian martyrs: "Can any person, think you, who hath gone to the field of battle in quest of glory, or who hath braved the danger of the seas in quest of wealth or power, be once compared with those who have cheerfully given up the precious life, or submitted their bodies to the torture, to keep their consciences undefiled?"[6]

Witherspoon intended the sermon to reinforce everything the seniors had learned regarding virtue and its foundation in true religion. In addition, he used this sermon to fortify the leaders and sons of liberty who would leave the College of New Jersey and enter a world where false virtue masqueraded as true. He fought the same battle he had waged in Scotland against a virtue of etiquette and approbation, an anthropocentric morality. Witherspoon warned that "if there is such a thing as a *worldly virtue,* a system of principles and duty, dictated by the spirit of the world . . . and if this is at bottom, essentially different from, and sometimes directly opposed to the spirit of the gospel, it must be of all others, the most dangerous temptation, to persons of a liberal education and an ingenious turn of mind."[7]

Witherspoon offered the example of the military conflict between Great Britain and the American colonies as proof of man's sinfulness and need of true religion. In *The Dominion of Providence over the Passions of Men,* he suggested that worldly virtue had come to predominate in Great Britain and had led directly to the disintegration of its American empire. "A good form of government may hold the rotten materials together for some time, but beyond a certain pitch, even the best constitution will be ineffectual." True religion and the true virtue that flows from it, Witherspoon asserted, are responsible for keeping a nation from destruction. "When true religion and internal principles maintain their vigour, the attempts of the most powerful enemies to oppress them are commonly baffled and disappointed."[8]

In addition to urging a devotion to true religion, Witherspoon also exhorted his students and parishioners to do their virtuous duties. In his *Pastoral Letter* of 1775, Witherspoon reminded his flock that the Christian must rise to his duty in arms. He called on the ministers and officers of Presbyterian churches "to watch over the morals of their several members." He encouraged his Presbyterian brethren that "a spirit of candor, charity and mutual esteem be preserved, and promoted toward those of different religious denominations." Lastly, he called those who would serve in combat to show mercy and humanity. He reminded men that they should not be eager to fight, but neither should they avoid combat when the time came. "That man will fight most bravely, who never fights till it is necessary, and who ceases to fight as soon as the necessity is over."[9]

A few months after his *Pastoral Letter,* Witherspoon preached the baccalaureate sermon to his seniors, proclaiming that the duty of virtuous leaders to themselves and their posterity is to apply the magnanimity of their Christian hearts to the American cause. He admonished those who would enlist in the service of their country to do so with proper motives. The man who accomplishes the most illustrious task with the greatest courage for the sole purpose of attaining fame and fortune has become "hateful and contemptible" rather than great. Only virtuous magnanimity is honorable.[10]

In *The Dominion of Providence over the Passions of Men*, Witherspoon declared that "the cause [of liberty] is sacred, and the champions for it ought to be holy." Witherspoon exhorted military commanders to banish all profanity and blasphemy from their ranks, and he urged the citizenry to practice industry and frugality. "It is in the man of piety and inward principle," Witherspoon asserted, "that we may expect to find the uncorrupted patriot, the useful citizen, and the invincible soldier." Virtue and liberty are both the foundation and the end of church and state. "God grant that in America true religion and civil liberty may be inseparable, and that the unjust attempts to destroy the one, may in the issue tend to the support and establishment of both."[11]

As the war drew to an end and peace seemed imminent, Witherspoon suggested in a Thanksgiving Day sermon that the church must provide virtuous leaders for the state because the laws and constitution can only go so far. The morality of the people, not the law of the land, provides the security of society. And Witherspoon believed that this morality is based in true religion, orthodox Christianity. Therefore, he pleaded with "the teachers and rulers of every religious denomination . . . to watch over the manners of their several members." The church owed this to the state for the liberty it provided. "The return that is expected from [the church] to the community, is that by the influence of [its] religious government, [its] people may be the more regular citizens, and the more useful members of society."[12]

During the course of the 1770s, Witherspoon moved from a position of peaceful protest against the injustices of British policies to open opposition to British rule. Witherspoon came to believe that the church had an obligation to itself and to its members to stand against an oppressive state. Witherspoon formulated much of his view on opposition to civil authority in light of the Calvinist tradition in Scotland and the principles enunciated in Calvin's *Institutes of the Christian Religion.* In the first edition of this work, Calvin wrote in opposition to the practice of Francis I of France, who was persecuting Protestants. Calvin argued that Protestants are orthodox Christians, deserving freedom to worship as they choose. Calvin taught that spiritual and civil governments differ in that the former deals with the inner morality of the soul, while the latter deals with outer morality and civic justice. Yet he believed that the two should not be completely separated. The civil government must protect religion and piety as well as society and peace, though it had no business making laws concerning worship. Calvin summarized his understanding of civil government's responsibility to religion and the church: "In short, it provides that a public manifestation of religion may exist among Christians, and that humanity be maintained among men." The civil government may not mandate how Christians should worship, but it is bound to protect the right of Christians to worship and the Christian religion itself from public sacrilege and blasphemy.[13]

Calvin also believed that God ordains magistrates, and even if they are oppressive, "Scripture expressly affirms that it is the providence of God's wisdom that kings reign." Calvin believed as a general maxim that those who cast off kings cast off the providence of God. He did qualify this belief, however, in light of the value he accorded political liberty. "Nothing is more desirable than liberty," Calvin asserted, deeming it "an inestimable good," and "more than the half of life." With this in mind, Calvin suggested two ways in which men could justly challenge civil authority. First, God sometimes calls men to be his instruments against wicked kings, and these men do not violate the design of providence because they are called by God to do his work. Second, Calvin urged the "magistrates of the people"—elected or appointed representatives—to recognize that their obligation to protect freedom dictates their opposition to and removal of oppressive authority.[14]

In the *Pastoral Letter,* written after the violence at Lexington and Concord,

Witherspoon echoed Calvin's instruction to submit to authority. Witherspoon urged Presbyterians to "let every opportunity be taken to express your attachment and respect to our sovereign king George." He reminded his fellow Presbyterians that God, in his providence, had made George III their king. At the same time, he called for a devotion "to the revolution principles, by which his august family was seated on the British throne." The instrument God had used to place George on that throne was the English Parliament, the "magistrates of the people," who had ousted an oppressive Stewart king in the Glorious Revolution and placed William and Mary on the throne. Likewise, the Long Parliament had ousted a previous Stewart king on the basis of the same principles, but with a much more violent outcome. Though Witherspoon recommended reconciliation in the present crisis between America and Britain, he did not dismiss a more violent option.[15]

In *The Dominion of Providence over the Passions of Men,* Witherspoon went further and suggested that the church must stand against the oppressive authority of the state. In this sermon, he argued that Great Britain had abandoned true religion and thereby unchained the passions of men's hearts and minds. Nevertheless, these developments worked to glorify God, no matter what men intended: "The ambition of mistaken princes, the cunning and cruelty of oppressive and corrupt ministers, and even the inhumanity of brutal soldiers, however dreadful, shall finally promote the glory of God, and in the mean time, while the storm continues, his mercy and kindness shall appear in prescribing bounds to their rage and fury." Assuming an intimate connection between civil and religious liberty, Witherspoon urged the church to become involved in political affairs: "There is not a single instance in history in which civil liberty was lost, and religious liberty preserved entire. If therefore we yield up our temporal property, we at the same time deliver the conscience into bondage."[16]

Witherspoon believed that individual Christians must participate in government, and he lived out this belief. He was involved in politics on campus, wrote articles on political topics, served in local and national assemblies, and encouraged other Christians to act in similar fashion. His induction into politics at the College of New Jersey came almost immediately after his installation as president. On September 28, 1768, not two months after his arrival in North America, Witherspoon opened his first commencement ceremony at the college with an inaugural address on the connection between piety and learning. Yet the political environment had stirred students with heady notions of liberty. The British Parliament had passed the Townshend Acts the previous year, and many colonies had turned to non-importation to protest the unconstitutional nature of the acts. John Dickinson, from neighboring Pennsylvania, had written his letters outlining the unconstitutionality of the Townshend Acts. At the commencement ceremony, Witherspoon gave his students free reign on the subject of liberty.

Sitting on the commencement stage, Witherspoon heard the salutatorian give a rousing Latin oration on civil liberty. Other senior orations included defenses of the propositions "It is to the interest of any nation to have the trade of its new countries as free from embarrassment as possible" and "It is lawful for every man, and in many cases his indisputable duty, to hazard his life in defence of his civil liberty." Finally, the valedictorian spoke on patriotism. Though he himself did not speak on liberty, Witherspoon's toleration of the open expression of such sentiments by others was indicative of his own opinions. Presiding over his second commencement in September 1769, Witherspoon shared the stage with three noted champions of American liberties: John Dickinson; Joseph Galloway, speaker of the Pennsylvania Assembly; and John Hancock, owner of the well-known sloop *Liberty*. The College of New Jersey honored Dickinson and Galloway with the first honorary doctorates from an American institution and Hancock with an honorary master's degree. In later years, the commencement proceedings at the college focused more and more on American liberties. When the class of 1771 dressed in American-manufactured cloth, one attendee observed, "What too sanguine Hope can we have of those Gentlemen, and such Principles so early instilled in them?" At the same commencement, James Witherspoon, eldest son of the president, defended the thesis "Subjects were bounden to resist their king and defend their liberties if he ignored the laws of the State or treated his subjects cruelly," while the king's appointed governor, William Franklin, sat a few feet away.[17]

Witherspoon allowed activities on campus that would have been forbidden had he not been sympathetic to American liberty. Just prior to his arrival on campus, the faculty had suspended the Well Meaning and the Plain Dealing clubs, because the rivalry between the two had grown so intense. Witherspoon supervised the reorganization of the societies as the Cliosophic Society and the American Whig Society, and he structured their activities to complement the academic goals and political sentiments of the college. These societies became an essential part of campus life and served as the training ground for such American leaders as James Madison, Oliver Ellsworth, and William

Paterson. Witherspoon made the societies part of commencement and other special occasions, showcasing young talent such as Philip Freneau, whose 1772 commencement poem, "The Rising Glory of America," advocated American independence long before it became a popular sentiment. The societies served as an impetus to words and deeds. In July 1770, a letter from New York merchants to Philadelphia merchants encouraging a breach of the non-importation agreement passed through Princeton. A group of students seized the document and burnt it in a bell-tolling ceremony. Witherspoon did nothing. Similarly, in January 1774, just one month after the Boston Tea Party, the students decided to show their patriotism by seizing the steward's winter supply of tea (about a dozen pounds) and burning it in another bell-tolling ceremony in the center of campus. They also placed an effigy of Massachusetts's Governor Hutchinson in the middle of the bonfire with a tea canister around its neck. Again, Dr. Witherspoon and the faculty took no action against the students.[18]

Equally important as his encouragement of politics on campus, Witherspoon participated in local government, thereby setting an example for his students of how to put piety into practice. Calvin had recommended service in government as a calling ordained by God. He called the office of civil authority "the most sacred and by far the most honorable of all callings in the whole life of mortal men." Witherspoon agreed with Calvin's view, and when Somerset County, New Jersey, organized its committee of correspondence, he allowed himself to be elected to the committee and agreed to serve for one year. The people of Somerset County formed their committee on July 4, 1774. On July 21, Witherspoon traveled to New Brunswick to meet with representatives from all the New Jersey committees of correspondence for the purpose of selecting the New Jersey delegation to the First Continental Congress. Just as Witherspoon had shown leadership in the Somerset County committee by drafting resolutions and instructions for the delegation, he demonstrated the same leadership in the New Jersey meeting. Witherspoon made a habit of writing out the ideas he thought he might have an opportunity to deliver extempore in open assemblies. During this period he drafted an essay titled "Thoughts on American Liberty," which he never published. The essay reflects his views on the American situation and probably the content of the resolutions he drafted in both the Somerset County and New Jersey meetings. In the essay he defined the Continental Congress as "the representative of the great body of the people of North America," implicitly giving it legitimacy as the body that could justly confront oppressive authority—the role Calvin had assigned to the "magistrates of the people." Witherspoon encouraged the congress "to unite the colonies, and make them as one body, in any measure of self-defence, to assure the people of Great-Britain that we will not submit voluntarily, and convince them that it would be either impossible or unprofitable for them to compel us by open violence." In addition, he made eight recommendations that ranged from professing loyalty to the king to making preparations for war. In July 1775, the people of Somerset County reelected Witherspoon to the committee of correspondence, and the committee selected him as its chairman.[19]

As chairman of the Somerset County committee of correspondence, Witherspoon pushed both the county and the state toward independence. On March 27, 1776, Witherspoon and the Somerset County committee issued a call for a meeting of all the New Jersey committees to be held on April 18, 1776, prior to the election of delegates to the New Jersey provincial congress. On the morning of that meeting Witherspoon announced that its purpose was to "consider the peculiar situation of the Province, and the propriety of declaring a separation from Great Britain and forming an independent Constitution." Witherspoon's action preceded John Adams's resolution urging the colonies to take such measures. He then suggested that the meeting adjourn until afternoon, at which time he would present his arguments. When the meeting reconvened, Witherspoon spoke for an hour and a half on the uselessness "of professing full allegiance to Great Britain and support of her courts of justice."

In the spring of 1776 he had drafted another essay, "On the Controversy about Independence," in which he argued that submission to England would result in "the total and absolute ruin of the colonies" and that slavery would be "riveted on us and our posterity." He concluded that the colonies struggled not only against the king and parliament, but also against the prejudice of the whole British people, who, by their desires, direct the king and parliament: "Nothing is more manifest, than that the people of Great-Britain, and even the king and ministry, have been hitherto exceedingly ignorant of the state of things in America. For this reason, their measures have been ridiculous in the highest degree, and the issue disgraceful." Witherspoon did not believe that anything could change the minds of the British people; therefore, independence was preferable. Nevertheless, Elias Boudinot, a Presbyterian and trustee of the college, questioned the wisdom and prudence of this measure, since the Continental Congress had been elected to deal with such matters and the province should not act separately. Of the thirty-six votes cast, only a few supported Witherspoon's motion.[20]

Despite this legislative defeat, the people of Somerset County elected Witherspoon to be part of the delegation to the provincial congress of New Jersey. Three alumni of the college joined Witherspoon in this delegation: James Linn, Frederick Frelinghusen, and William Paterson. Soon afterward, the provincial congress selected Witherspoon to a committee charged with arresting Governor Franklin. Franklin had tried to maintain colonial government and authority in opposition to the Continental Congress's directive to abandon the government of the crown because it had become unsupportable. Witherspoon participated in Franklin's deposition and reportedly became so angry that he reverted to his native Scotch tongue during "the torrent of his invective." After the provincial congress reestablished provincial government on its terms, it turned to selecting a new delegation to the Continental Congress. On June 21, 1776, the provincial congress of New Jersey appointed Witherspoon as part of a five-man delegation to the congress. The delegation reported to the meeting in Philadelphia on June 28, 1776, and from there Witherspoon made his mark on national government.[21]

<hr />

Witherspoon moved from local politics to national politics at an important time, and he served on this larger stage with honor and distinction. During the period leading up to his selection as a delegate to the Continental Congress, Witherspoon had extensively used his pen to persuade and educate the public. In the published edition of his sermon *The Dominion of Providence,* Witherspoon added an *Address to the Natives of Scotland Residing in America.* Upon his arrival in America, Witherspoon had joined the St. Andrews Society, which helped emigrants from Scotland settle in America. In 1774, he preached a sermon in New York to raise money for the society. As a result of his efforts, Scots knew Witherspoon and, to some degree, trusted him. Many of the recent emigrants maintained strong ties to their homeland and believed all the information contained in letters from home regarding the conflict between Britain and her American colonies. Witherspoon wrote to rekindle their confidence in their new home, to correct misinformation, and to enlist their support in the cause. He argued that the conflict had moved beyond the point of reconciliation, and that both America and Britain would prosper from America's independence. Furthermore, he corrected the views of those who believed that the Wilkites in Britain's Parliament were somehow associated with the American desire for independence. Lastly, he encouraged them, as nonnatives, to learn from the native colonials and to support the cause of liberty and free government.[22]

In another article, known only by the "Aristides" pseudonym under which it was published in the spring of 1776, Witherspoon publicly opposed the tactics used by those who still favored reconciliation over independence. He singled out for attack two documents: *Plain Truth* and "Cato's Letters," both attributed to William Smith, provost of the College of Philadelphia. Smith had published *Plain Truth* as a reponse to Thomas Paine's pamphlet *Common Sense*. As pamphlets they were both sold in the open market for about the same price. Yet no one bought *Plain Truth,* so Smith resorted to publishing the same arguments in the form of eight letters from "Cato" in the *Pennsylvania Gazette* between March 13 and April 24, 1776. As "Aristides," Witherspoon objected to both *Plain Truth* and "Cato's Letters." He disliked *Plain Truth* because it embodied many of the things he so despised about the Moderate Party of Scotland. It was written in bad taste, it was unclear, it was overly polished, "covered over, from head to foot, with a detestable and stinking varnish," and it did not engage the arguments of *Common Sense* but simply insisted that America could not resist the power of Great Britain. He objected to "Cato's Letters" primarily because the content failed to address the pertinent issues in the debate between those who favored reconciliation and those who advocated independence.[23]

In a further effort to educate the general public, Witherspoon wrote a series of seven articles for the *Pennsylvania Magazine,* the first three appearing in May, June, and July of 1776. Witherspoon titled the articles "The Druid," evoking the wooded surroundings of his home where he wrote them. In the first installment, he argued that it would be a mistake for Americans to prepare to be soldiers and not scholars in their troubled times. He believed that in times of controversy, the public mind is fully engaged and receptive to a discussion of important issues. Furthermore, he anticipated that Americans would soon need a full grasp of political and moral philosophy as they formed an independent government. He concluded with his familiar theme—that a virtuous nation is an invincible nation.

The June installment attempted to answer important questions about the nature of war. Witherspoon used material directly from his lectures on moral philosophy that covered the laws of nature and nations. He argued that wars fought to protect just and natural rights may be fought with open violence in accordance with a sense of conscience and the sanctions of the Supreme Judge. In the July installment, he discussed the nature of civil and foreign wars. He admitted that society considered civil wars to be instigated by disorderly citizens against the general principles of law and order. He claimed that the civil wars of England and France to determine the succession of the crown were wrong and illegitimate. On the other hand, civil wars fought to relieve government oppression were legitimate and were called revolutions if successful and rebellions if failures. He concluded this article by arguing that civil wars fought on legitimate claims ought to be fought as foreign wars—with a sense of duty on both sides.[24]

When he and the New Jersey delegation arrived in Philadelphia, the congress, in committee of the whole, was discussing a resolution on independence. John Adams recapitulated the arguments given by both sides for the benefit of the New Jersey delegation. Afterwards, the delegation signified that its members were ready to vote, and on July 2, 1776, John Witherspoon voted with the Continental Congress to approve the resolution for independence from Great Britain. The congress then went into committee of the whole to discuss a draft of a declaration of this independence. Again, Witherspoon voted with the congress to approve the Declaration of Independence on July 4, 1776, two years after he had been chosen to serve on the Somerset County committee of correspondence.

The congress spent much of July debating the Articles of Confederation that would organize the newly declared independent states. Witherspoon took an active role in this debate. The ideas contained in "Part of a Speech in Congress upon the Confederation" reflect his concepts of human nature, moral and political philosophy, and virtue. Witherspoon argued for a perpetual union among the states, not just a union for the duration of the war effort. He feared that the weakness of a temporary union would weaken the war effort, as each state would act in its own self-interest and neglect the needs of its fellow states. Also, he feared civil wars in and among the states after the war for independence had been won. As individual states, they would resolve conflicts by violence in the absence of an overarching authority. He urged the congress to enact the confederation as soon as possible, as doing so later would be more problematic. Witherspoon believed that the union of the states would be a blessing to later generations.

In addition to his participation in the debates of the congress, Witherspoon also served on many committees when his wisdom and experience were needed. For example, he guided those committees that handled "the capture of Henry Laurens by the British, the New Hampshire Grants controversy, and the mutiny of the Pennsylvania Line." Likewise, Congress utilized his experience on three standing committees: the Board of War, the Foreign Affairs Committee, and the Committee for Clothing for the Army. On both the Board of War and on the Foreign Affairs Committee he pushed for the centralization of power behind George Washington and Benjamin Franklin, respectively. In later years he also served on committees dealing with financial matters. Witherspoon's moral philosophy continually found expression in his service to the nation in Congress.[25]

As the sole clergyman in the Continental Congress, Witherspoon was assigned to committees dealing with national piety. In November 1776, he chaired a committee "to prepare an address, to the inhabitants of America, and a recommendation to the states for a day of fasting, humiliation, and prayer." The congress felt the need for such action as the British army approached Philadelphia and it was forced to leave the city. Similarly, in the fall of 1781, Congress considered the situation of the country so fortunate that on September 15, it selected Witherspoon as chairman of a committee to draft a proclamation of thanksgiving for the United States. For whatever reason, Witherspoon did not report his proclamation until October 26, which allowed him to include thanksgiving for Washington's victory at Yorktown on October 19 of that year. Again in the fall of 1782, as peace seemed imminent, Congress turned to Witherspoon, and he responded with another thanksgiving day proclamation.[26]

In giving thanks to the Almighty for American successes, Witherspoon often exhorted Christians to their virtuous duty to the state. In the "Sermon Delivered at a Public Thanksgiving after Peace," he recalled the role that national piety had played in the American victories at Trenton and Princeton, and he called on Christians to play an active role in the government of their new nation. The people of a republic, Witherspoon, asserted, play a vital role in preserving virtue, not only as individuals, but as the body politic. "Those who wish well to the state ought to chuse to places of trust, men of inward principle, justified by exemplary conversation." Furthermore, he chastised those who make unwise choices: "Those therefore who pay no regard to religion and sobriety, in the persons whom they send to the legislature of any state, are guilty of the greatest absurdity, and will soon pay dear for their folly." Elected representatives of the people, in turn, must fulfill their duty. They must "promote religion, sobriety, industry, and every social virtue among those who are committed to their care." Additionally, they must attend to the "impartial support and faithful guardianship of the rights of conscience." Witherspoon expected that the personal example of elected representatives served as one of the best methods of promoting these values and accomplishing the goal of protecting conscience. He outlined their good example as consisting in "reverence for the name of God, a punctual attendance on the public and private duties of religion, as well as sobriety and purity of conversation." These "are especially incumbent on those who are honored with places of power and trust." Witherspoon envisioned a relationship in which liberty for the church to practice virtue produced morality in the state, which in turn encouraged freedom of conscience. A republic, Witherspoon concluded, "must either preserve its virtue or lose its liberty."[27]

In outlining the proper relationship between church and state, Witherspoon believed that the state must fulfill two obligations. Government must encourage Christian piety, and it must protect liberty of conscience. The Continental Congress fulfilled the first obligation of encouraging Christian piety by proclaiming public fast days. Witherspoon participated in three of these fast days, the first two as an official of the church, the third as an official of the state. Witherspoon drafted the *Pastoral Letter* for the Synod of New York and Philadelphia in response to Lexington and Concord, but the synod asked that the letter be read from the pulpits on June 29, 1775, which Congress had appointed as a day of fasting. Thus, the state encouraged the practice of Christian piety throughout the colonies, and the church responded. Similarly, on May 17, 1776, Witherspoon preached his famous sermon *The Dominion of Providence* on the day Congress had recommended as a day of public fasting and prayer. The Continental Congress had drafted and passed both of these proclamations before Witherspoon had joined its ranks. Therefore, a general consensus existed among the delegates to the Continental Congress regarding the state's role in encouraging Christian piety. In addition, on December 11, 1776, the Continental Congress passed a fast day proclamation that Witherspoon had written at the members' request. In the document, the congress claimed that it made the proclamation in order "to reverence the Providence of God, and look up to him as the supreme disposer of all events, and the arbiter of the fate of nations." With this in view, the congress asked the states and the people of the states "to implore of Almighty God the forgiveness of the many sins prevailing among all ranks," and then to request his assistance in the "Just and necessary war." Moreover, Congress "recommend[ed] to all the members of the United States . . . the exercise of repentance and reformation." Lastly, the Congress required of its officers and soldiers strict observation of that part of the articles of war "which forbids profane swearing, and all immorality." Using Witherspoon's words, the Congress encouraged the practice of piety in repentance, supplication, reformation, and morality by the American people.[28]

Similarly, after the Articles of Confederation had been passed, the Confederation Congress exercised its obligation to encourage Christian piety and to promote liberty of conscience. It protected liberty of conscience by simply refusing to establish any one Christian religion or denomination for the United States. Likewise, it encouraged piety by proclaiming public days of thanksgiving. Witherspoon wrote two of the resolutions passed by Congress. On October 26, 1781, Congress passed a resolution recommending that December 13 "be religiously observed as a Day of Thanksgiving and Prayer." In this proclamation Congress acknowledged that "it hath pleased Almighty God, the father of all mercies, remarkably to assist and support the United States of America." For this reason, Congress felt compelled to lead the people in remembering the good providence of God in many wonderful events, but especially in the establishment of the Confederation and in the victory over Cornwallis. It therefore recommended a day of thanksgiving and prayer "to celebrate the praise of our gracious Benefactor." In addition, Congress encouraged confession of sins and the grace of pardon as well as supplication for the public inclination to obey all God's laws.

On October 11, 1782, Congress passed another proclamation recommending a day of thanksgiving to be held on Thursday, November 28, 1782. Though the content of this proclamation resembled that of the first proclamation, Congress adopted a more official and authoritative tone in the second proclamation. First, Congress established itself as a national body by calling itself "the United States in Congress assembled." Likewise, it requested the states to use its authority "in appointing and commanding" the observation of the thanksgiving day. Like the first, the proclamation of 1782 documented God's providence and mercy, acknowledged the nation's duty to pray for God's mercy and to thank him for the mercy he had already shown, recognized the obligation of the people to show their gratitude by obedience to God's commands, and recommended that the people do so. New to the second proclamation, Congress added a secondary reason for such piety—"the practice of true and undefiled religion, which is the great foundation of public prosperity and national happiness."[29]

Witherspoon used the power of his pen to persuade civil authorities to protect the liberty of conscience. In an article about the state constitution of Georgia, he opposed that state's designs to remove clergymen from the free exercise of their right to participate in the political process as officeholders. Witherspoon reported that the Georgia constitution contained a resolution that "no clergyman of any denomination shall be a member of the General Assembly." Though he had no authority, Witherspoon questioned the resolution, and his Socratic attack on the state of Georgia reeked with sarcasm. "Before any man among us was ordained a minister, was he not a citizen of the United States, and if being in Georgia, a citizen of the state of Georgia?" He continued, "Is it a sin against the public to become a minister? Does it merit that the person who is guilty of it should be immediately deprived of one of his most important rights as a citizen?" Witherspoon joked that he could not understand why such a resolution existed except that Georgia wanted to make sure ministers were not distracted from their spiritual functions. He concluded with another sardonic jab: What if the clergyman is defrocked "for cursing and swearing, drunkenness or uncleanness"? Shall he be "fully restored to all the privileges of a free citizen," shall his offense be forgotten, and shall he be elected to the Senate or the House of Representatives?[30]

Witherspoon believed that Georgia's prohibition against clergymen serving in its legislature misconstrued the idea of separation of church and state. Far from protecting the two spheres, the restriction did harm to the church by violating the rights of conscience and to the state by diminishing the number of pious people serving in office. The oppression of conscience, Witherspoon feared, would lead to a decrease in public virtue, which would then lead to further oppression of conscience.

⌐⌐⌐⌐⌐⌐

Witherspoon's experience in governance soon found application directly in ecclesiastical issues. In 1787, as delegates from the states formed a new government for the United States in Philadelphia, Witherspoon and other leading Presbyterians began the reorganization of the American Presbyterian Church in the same city. In this setting, Witherspoon departed from traditional Cal vinism and Presbyterianism by advocating a stricter separation between church and state than he had heretofore advocated. In so doing, Witherspoon simply built on the American Presbyterian tradition, which had always been more liberal than the Scottish church regarding the connection between church and state. For example, in 1729, when the Synod of North America adopted the documents of the Westminster Assembly, the synod did not receive those passages that gave the civil magistrates power over the exercise of ministerial authority. It was this American version of the *Westminster Confession of Faith* that Witherspoon sought to codify in the 1780s.

In 1785, the Synod of New York and Philadelphia appointed Witherspoon chairman of a special committee "to consider the constitution of the Church of Scotland and other Protestant churches and, agreeably to the procedure for Presbyterian government, to compile a system of general rules for the government of the Synod, the presbyteries under its inspection, and the people of its communion." In addition, the synod made Witherspoon chairman of another committee tasked with the responsibility of preparing a book of discipline and government. Through this committee, Witherspoon influenced changes in the Confession of Faith. At the synod meeting of 1787, the synod discussed Witherspoon's plan of government. A single presbytery offered comments for discussion, after which the plan was printed for broader distribution. The following year the synod approved and adopted the work of both of Witherspoon's committees and called for the first meeting of the General Assembly of the Presbyterian Church in the United States of America to convene in May 1789 at the Second Presbyterian Church of Philadelphia. The synod asked Witherspoon to preach the opening sermon and to preside over the meeting until the election of a moderator. Witherspoon was the leading Presbyterian in the new nation, and as such he hoped to establish a new church that was not manipulated by the affairs of politics, but instead attended to the spiritual needs of its congregations.[31]

The American version of the *Westminster Confession of Faith* contained three changes from the original. The first change dealt with the magistrate's power to censure spiritual offenses. In his *Institutes of the Christian Religion*, Calvin had written that civil government has as its end "to cherish and protect the outward worship of God, to defend sound doctrine of piety and the position of the church." Reflecting this position, the divines of the Westminster Assembly gave authority to the civil magistrate to punish those who practice or publish ideas contrary to "lawful power." The final phrase of chapter 20, Section 4 reads, "They may be proceeded against by the censures of the

Church, and by the power of the civil magistrate." Thus, the Westminster Assembly authorized the use of civil authority and power to prosecute those who conscientiously opposed civil or ecclesiastical authority. Witherspoon and the American Presbyterian church departed from Calvin and the Westminster divines. The last phrase of the American version of the *Confession* reads, "They may lawfully be called to account, and proceeded against by the censures of the Church." Although Section 4 mentions opposition to civil authority, it primarily treats opposition to ecclesiastical authority. For this reason, Witherspoon, his committee, and the synod removed the phraseology that permitted the civil magistrate authority over an ecclesiastical matter. Witherspoon's concept of government encouragement of Christian piety did not include what Calvin perceived as the civil authority's obligation to defend sound doctrine. Witherspoon agreed with Calvin that the two governments, civil and ecclesiastical, are not "antithetical," yet he believed that one ought not to exercise authority in the realm of the other.[32]

Similarly, Witherspoon and his committee revised Chapter 23, Section 3 of the *Westminster Confession of Faith* so as to eliminate any hint of civil authority over ecclesiastical affairs. As with Section 4 of Chapter 20, the Westminster divines followed Calvin's lead. Calvin believed the civil government "prevents the public idolatry, sacrilege against God's name, blasphemies against his truth, and other public offenses against religion from arising and spreading among the people." Calvin allowed the civil authority to correct the spiritual sins of the people. Nevertheless, Calvin forbade civil magistrates to make "laws according to their own decision concerning religion and the worship of God." The Westminster divines tried to achieve the same delicate balance between a magistrate who protects the church and prosecutes blasphemies without favoring one denomination or overstepping his own piety. Section 3 of chapter 23 begins, "The civil magistrate may not assume to himself the administration of the Word and sacraments, or the power of the keys of the kingdom of heaven." Nevertheless, Section 3 continues by claiming that the civil magistrate "hath authority, and it is his duty, to take order, that unity and peace be preserved in the Church, that the truth of God be kept pure and entire, that all blasphemies and heresies be suppressed, all corruptions and abuses in worship and discipline prevented and reformed, and all the ordinances of God duly settled, administered, and observed." Furthermore, the Westminster divines gave civil magistrates "power to call synods, to present at them, and to provide that whatsoever is transacted in them be according to the mind of God."[33]

Witherspoon had learned from his experience in the Church of Scotland that civil authority over the church for the purpose of protecting the purity of the church resulted in the institutionalization of impiety and unorthodoxy. Civil authority should have no power over spiritual matters, Witherspoon held. For this reason, the American version of Chapter 23, Section 3 of the *Confession* begins: "Civil magistrates may not assume to themselves the administration of the Word and sacraments, or the power of the keys of the kingdom of heaven, or in the least interfere in matters of faith." Witherspoon and his committee defined civil magistrates as having authority "to protect the Church of our common Lord, without giving the preference to any denomination of Christians above the rest; in such a manner that all ecclesiastical persons whatever shall enjoy the full, free, and unquestioned liberty of discharging every part of their sacred functions, without violence or danger." Moreover, the American version prevents magistrates from hindering the "regular government and discipline" of the church "as Jesus Christ hath appointed," and it encourages magistrates to their duty to protect individuals from religious and moral slander. The American version concludes that the civil magistrate must "take order, that all religious and ecclesiastical assemblies be held without molestation or disturbance." Thus, whereas Calvin and the Westminster divines had allowed the magistrates' power to enter into the ecclesiastical realm, Witherspoon and his committee reaffirmed that the church ought to remain free from political interference.[34]

In addition to delineating the boundaries between church and state, Witherspoon demonstrated his commitment to the protection of liberty of conscience in the introduction he wrote for *The Form of Government and Discipline of the Presbyterian Church in the United States of America,* which the other committee he chaired presented to the synod, and the synod unanimously approved. Speaking for the Presbyterian church, Witherspoon proclaimed at the outset of the introduction that "God alone is Lord of the conscience." He and the church did not "even wish to see any religious constitution aided by the civil power," and he acknowledged that every Christian denomination has the authority to constitute itself as it pleases. Errors in ecclesiastical structure or even doctrine "do not infringe upon the liberty, or the rights of others." Such a theory of religious liberty was more easily fashioned in America, which, unlike most European countries, lacked an established church, and where religious pluralism was already a reality.[35]

At the same time, however, Witherspoon reaffirmed the Presbyterian idea of internal church discipline. Christ, Witherspoon attested, "hath appointed officers . . . to exercise discipline, for the preservation both of truth and duty: and, it is incumbent upon these officers . . . to censure, or cast out, the erroneous and scandalous." Witherspoon cautioned that such "ecclesiastical discipline must be purely moral and spiritual in its objects, and not attended with any civil effects." If church authority were exercised properly it preempted any need for interference by the civil authority.[36]

As an officer of both the church and the state, Witherspoon left a remarkable legacy for the church and the nation. His experience in the Church of Scotland and his interpretation of scripture shaped his views on the separation of church and state. Witherspoon believed that God had never intended—after the decline of the theocratic government of Israel—for the two realms to become intertwined as one. Church and state should work side by side, each in its own realm, to protect liberty of conscience and to encourage Christian piety. Witherspoon held that these two obligations were inseparably linked; the abandonment of one automatically resulted in the abandonment of the other. The church must produce virtuous Christian citizens and leaders, Christians must take an active role in the affairs of government, and the state must protect and encourage Christian piety, remaining careful not to impose its authority on the freedom of Christian denominations to exercise their proper authority. Witherspoon believed that his understanding of the proper separation of church and state provided the only environment in which American republicanism could survive.

Jefferson Un-Locked:
The Rousseauan Moment in American Political Thought

RICHARD K. MATTHEWS AND ELRIC M. KLINE

Locke's little book on government is perfect *as far as it goes.*
—Thomas Jefferson, May 30, 1790 (italics added)

Scholarship on Thomas Jefferson continues to abound and there appears little chance of that abating. Merrill Peterson's landmark *The Jeffersonian Image in the American Mind* (1960) offers a plausible explanation for this trend. As we approach two centuries after Jefferson's well-timed death on the Fourth of July 1826, there still exists "some mysterious attraction that causes men in every generation to interpolate Jefferson in their living worlds."[1] Recent scholarship confirms this observation: the "war on terrorism" motivated (re)examinations of Jefferson's thoughts and deeds relative to the Barbary Pirates of North Africa—the United States' initial encounter with Islamic powers; the political rise of the Religious Right sent some scholars to (re)explore his thoughts and deeds concerning the relationship between church and state; and America's historical struggle with, and denial of, racism dispatched others to (re)scrutinize his complicated, often hypocritical, and occasionally sublime thoughts (if not deeds) on race.[2]

Of course, given his Olympian status in the "American mind," critics of Jefferson continue to try to reduce him to more mortal proportions. Leonard Levy's splendid *Jefferson and Civil Liberties: The Darker Side* (1963) explores the disconnect between Jefferson's thoughts (when out of power) and his deeds (when in power) on issues of minority rights and freedom of the press.[3] More recently, Conor Cruise O'Brien attempts to topple Jefferson from his pedestal in presenting him as a racist who should be expelled from the American pantheon.[4] Then there is Joseph Ellis's widely read, albeit profoundly problematic, *American Sphinx: The Character of Thomas Jefferson* (1994). A gifted storyteller, Ellis presents us with a colorful character assassination of Jefferson, whom he charges with a penchant for "ideological promiscuity" that helps to make Jefferson "the Great Sphinx of American history."[5]

This essay will swim against these currents in Jefferson studies by presenting an exercise in comparative political thought. Although it would be difficult to find a scholar who does not see the genuinely radical dimensions to Jefferson's political philosophy, it remains doubtful that Americans appreciate just how divergent his thinking was from that of the other founders. To help sharpen this perspective, Jefferson's philosophic ideas will be compared to those of his French contemporary Jean-Jacques Rousseau. This comparison may prove to be fertile ground. In his enormously influential *The Machiavellian Moment* (1975), while analyzing Jefferson's celebrated passages on the virtues of a pastoral life, J. G. A. Pocock insightfully notes that "Jefferson is placing himself, and America, at a Rousseauan moment; man can avoid neither becoming civilized nor being corrupted by the process; but the language further reveals that the process is political and the moment Machiavellian."[6] The Jefferson-Rousseau comparison strikes a resonating chord to the extent that Rousseau sits as uncomfortably with his liberal European brethren as Jefferson does with his liberal Republican cofounders.

We do not argue that either thinker had the slightest direct impact on the other; rather, we explore what political ideas they held in common—and what ideas they did not.[7] Given Jefferson's divergence from the American mainstream, it may well be that his experiences in revolutionary France exposed him to both the political realities of socioeconomic corruption as well as the radical philosophic ideas that were in the air. Jefferson looked at Europe in general, and France in particular, as an object lesson in corruption, and he hoped to steer America clear of that nightmarish future.

To be clear, we intend to present a logical and a conceptual, but not necessarily historical, relationship between the two theorists. While there is no doubt Jefferson was familiar with some of Rousseau's writings, nowhere does he explicitly acknowledge him as an important philosopher, as he does John Locke. Nevertheless, we intend to show that the two defend, if sometimes from different vantages, much the same territory on the theoretical field. The second caveat is that we propose neither to undermine Jefferson's originality by painting him as merely the "American Rousseau," nor to deny the obvious—if misunderstood—Lockean influence on his thought.[8] Surely, Jefferson presents a unique and creative, as well as decidedly American, response to the problems of democracy and history. It would be a severe injustice to free his theory from one conceptual box only to trap him in another.

To accomplish these tasks we will first look rather extensively at the differing conceptualizations of the idea of property in Locke, Jefferson, and Rousseau. Property establishes a foundational point around which all three construct their political theories; it demonstrates the overlooked, albeit enormous, differences between Locke and Jefferson; and it begins to establish the connection between Jefferson and Rousseau. Following that discussion, we will compare the three theorists' ideas on human nature, morality, reason, and, finally, politics and citizenship.

There is no doubt that Jefferson was deeply influenced by John Locke. While secretary of state, Jefferson hosted a famous dinner with Vice President John Adams and Secretary of the Treasury Alexander Hamilton in attendance. While they dined, Jefferson identified three portraits on his wall as those of "Bacon, Newton, and Locke"—explaining that they made up his "trinity of the three greatest men the world had ever produced."[9] Locke initially gained esteem in England, in her colonies, and throughout Europe as the author of *An Essay Concerning Human Understanding* (1689); only later did his *Second Treatise of Government* (1689) earn repute in the United States as Americans found in it a compelling justification for revolution and limited government.[10] Nevertheless, it was Locke's radical epistemology in *An Essay*—that humans are born as "white paper" and can come to know everything in the world through the interplay of reason and experience—that created the materialist and environmentalist base for most of the emerging political theories of the era.[11]

Jefferson's unforgettable opening to the Declaration of Independence contains not only his most celebrated sentence but also a brief summary of the evolution of liberal thought:

> We hold these truths to be self-evident: that all men are created equal;
> that they are endowed by their Creator with certain inalienable rights;
> that among these are life, liberty, and the pursuit of happiness; that to
> secure these rights, governments are instituted among men, deriving

their just powers from the consent of the governed; that whenever any form of government becomes destructive of these ends, it is the right of the people to alter or to abolish it.[12]

Modern concepts of equality, individual autonomy, natural rights, limited government, and revolution had slowly evolved in Western thought over an extended period of years that can be traced at least as far back as Thomas Hobbes. However, when Jefferson inserts the phrase "pursuit of happiness," he raises the historic bar to the new minimum standard that legitimate government must reach. His words accomplish two significant tasks. First, by substituting "the pursuit of happiness" for "estate" (or "property") in Locke's triad of "life, liberty and estate," Jefferson acknowledges his debt to Locke even as he begins his transcendence. Second, the substitution also suggests that Jefferson believed Locke went astray in basing his political theory on property rather than on the "pursuit of happiness," which in *An Essay* Locke calls "the highest perfection of intellectual nature" and "the necessary foundation of our liberty"—language that disappears entirely in his explicitly political *Second Treatise*.[13]

Locke's stunning attempt to legitimize bourgeois property can be found in chapter 5 of the *Second Treatise*. He begins his sweeping justification of the essential prerequisites for a modern, class-divided market society by asserting that "whether we consider natural *reason* . . . or *revelation*," it is "very clear," that God "*has given the earth to the children of men; given* it to mankind in common." Next he states, with a degree of sarcasm, the philosophic problem he will easily resolve: "But this being supposed, it seems to some a very great difficulty, how anyone should ever come to have a *property* in any thing." This problem, if more than a straw man, would indeed constitute an obvious threat to any type of economic development. In light of this, Locke claims that he "shall endeavor to show, how men might come to have a property in several parts of that which God gave to mankind in common, and that without any expressed compact of all the commoners."[14]

This argument's simple beginning fails to capture adequately what Locke is ultimately up to. He presents a brilliant rationalization for the "natural" evolution of human society, beginning from biblical time when the earth was God's communal gift to humanity, to the natural individual right to the exclusive possession of property, through the invention of money, to the natural right of unlimited accumulation, culminating in the consensual—and divinely ordained—establishment of modern class-divided England. His case deftly employs both God's rational intentions for the earth and its inhabitants as well as humanity's (tacit) consent to the natural right to unlimited property accumulation (provided the spoilage prohibition is not violated) and to a class-divided market society. Through the invention and use of money, "it is plain," Locke writes, that humans "have agreed to a disproportionate and unequal *possession of the earth,* they having, by a tacit and voluntary consent, found out a way how a man may fairly possess more land than he himself can use the product of. . . . This partage of things in an inequality of private possession, men have made practicable out of the bounds of society, and without compact."[15] It is of critical significance for Locke's politics that the consensual use of money appears outside the bounds of the social contract, thereby placing the preservation of class-divided property among the natural rights for the protection of which humans institute government. In the course of his argument, Locke also introduces the labor theory of value, coupled with the trickle-down theory of common benefits, to demonstrate the overall rationality of this divine plan.

A political activist for most of his life, Jefferson rarely had time to systematize his thoughts on political theory. Still, in his scattered writings there exists a critical response to Locke's theory of property. While nowhere as biting or sophisticated as Rousseau's critique of the Lockean position, it is nonetheless devastating. In *Summary View of the Rights of British Americans* (1774), written two years prior to the Declaration of Independence, Jefferson rejects the notion of a natural right to property. Seeking to set the historical record straight for the king, Parliament, and some of his fellow patriots on the question of who holds a valid property right to British America, Jefferson begins by asserting a natural right to emigration and from there moves to establish that "America was conquered, and her settlements made and firmly established at the expense of individuals, and not of the British public."[16] While the king maintained that the colonies were his land holdings, with the relationship between the crown and the laborer being feudal in nature, Jefferson asserted otherwise. Since expatriation and free trade constituted natural rights, the colonists automatically possessed the right to establish their own positive laws regarding property.

> From the nature and purpose of civil institutions, all the lands within the limits which any particular society has circumscribed around itself, are assumed by that society, and subject to their allotment only. This

may be done by themselves assembled collectively, or by their legislature to whom they may have delegated sovereign authority: and, if
they are allotted in neither of these ways, each individual of the society
may appropriate to himself such lands as he finds vacant, and occu-
pancy will give him title.[17]

As Jefferson's list of natural rights slowly expanded over the course of his
life, he remained constant in his view of private property as a political construct playing a crucial if supportive role in allowing humans to achieve their
natural rights. "It is agreed by those who have seriously considered the subject," wrote Jefferson in 1813, "that no individual has, of natural right, a separate property in an acre of land, for instance."[18] Jefferson viewed property as a
positive right that was essential to "life, liberty, and the pursuit of happiness":
this triad comprised his summum bonum, not the accumulation of things. In
order to understand fully Jefferson's concept of property it is necessary to trace
his earlier thoughts on natural right, property, and politics.

Jefferson's implicit transcendence of Locke's theory of property can be seen
in a revealing 1785 letter written from Paris to the Reverend James Madison,
in which he describes his experience while walking with a "poor woman"
who worked as a "day-labourer." Jefferson found the conditions of "the
labouring poor" appalling, and he observes that "the most numerous of all
the classes" are "the poor who cannot find work." Moved by the plight of this
woman, Jefferson ponders a simple but potentially dangerous question: "What
could be the reason that so many should be permitted to beg who are willing
to work, in a country where there is a very considerable proportion of uncultivated lands?" He then acknowledges that he is "conscious that an equal division of property is impracticable," but not that it would violate natural right.
Indeed, he simply cautions that substantive equality is not feasible given "the
natural affections of the human mind." Nevertheless, he argues that because
"this enormous inequality produces so much misery to the bulk of mankind,
legislators cannot invent too many devices for subdividing property."[19]

Jefferson's initial suggestions to blunt the effects of inequality are simply
palliative measures. Ultimately, he had to confront the critical problem of land
scarcity caused by enclosure, the natural (Lockean) right to unlimited accumulation, and the dynamics of a market society. Locke's justification for exclusive property rights also recognizes this fundamental issue, but it is quickly
pushed to the background. On several occasions in chapter 5 of the *Second*

Treatise, Locke repeats that the legitimacy of exclusive and unlimited property accumulation assumed that the proviso—"at least where there is enough, and as good left in common for others"—was fully operative.[20] At Locke's moment in history, this was a reasonable assumption. Based on his European experiences, Jefferson knew, however, that given the inevitable dynamic of a possessive market society, Locke's "enough and as good" proviso would become a genuine problem that America would have to face. Employing natural rights language as his base, Jefferson reasoned that "whenever there is any country, uncultivated lands and unemployed poor, it is clear that the laws of property have been so far extended as to violate natural right." Since, contra Locke, Jefferson thought of property as a positive right, the "violate[d] natural right" was to "life, liberty, and the pursuit of happiness." He continues his argument echoing Locke: "The earth is given as a common stock for man to labour and live on." Like Locke, Jefferson links ownership with labor, but he reaches very un-Lockean conclusions. "If for the encouragement of industry we allow it to be appropriated," Jefferson reasons, "we must take care that other employment be furnished to those excluded from the appropriation. If we do not the fundamental right to labour the earth returns to the unemployed."[21] While Locke could legitimately respond that those "excluded" could go to America, Jefferson could not.[22] In this letter, Jefferson shies from expressing the logical conclusion that, under such conditions, "every man who cannot find employment . . . should be at liberty to cultivate" uncultivated land. He instead suggests that "it is not too soon to provide by every possible means" to ensure that every person shall have at least "a little portion of land."[23]

Later in life, Jefferson again turned to the relationship among property, equality, and economic freedom. In one of the many letters he exchanged with John Adams, Jefferson explains the fortunate advantage America has over Europe:

> Before the establishment of the American States, nothing was known to history but the man of the old world, crowded within limits either small or overcharged, and steeped in the vices which that situation generates. A government adapted to such men would be one thing; but a very different one, that for the man of these States. Here every one may have land to labor for himself, if he chooses; or, preferring the exercise of any other industry, may exact for it such compensation as not only to afford a comfortable subsistence, but wherewith to provide

for a cessation from labor in old age. Every one, by his property, or by his satisfactory situation, is interested in the support of law and order. And such men may safely and advantageously reserve to themselves a wholesome control over their public affairs.[24]

Since Americans "have land to labor," they can "exact for it such compensation as . . . to provide for a cessation from labor in old age."[25] As Jefferson appreciated from firsthand experience, as long as America remained a one-class society, the exploitative wage-slavery and dehumanizing class inequality of Europe would not inevitably develop. In America day-laborers could reject any wage offers they felt were unfair, since they always had the option of returning to their land to sustain themselves.[26]

While Jefferson differs from mainstream English liberalism on a natural individual right to property, he concurs on the English conception of constitutions. Few Americans appreciate the uniqueness of the Constitution and the historic significance of its supremacy clause, the nondemocratic amendment process, and the creation of an inherently conservative political system that structurally privileges the past over the present. Jefferson, to the contrary, never seemed to embrace the notion that a society could create a fundamental law that stood superior to other laws. As early as *Notes on the State of Virginia* (1781), Jefferson gives a brief history lesson in legal reasoning: "*Constitutio, constitutum, statutum, lex,* are convertible terms. . . . The term *constitution* has many other significations in physics and in politics; but in jurisprudence, whenever it is applied to any act of the legislature, it invariably means a statute, law, or ordinance, which is the present case." Here and elsewhere, Jefferson notes that a degree of mysticism surrounds the very word *constitution* and that this fallacy needs to be subjected to criticism: "To get rid of the magic supposed to be in the word *constitution,* let us translate it into its definition as given by those who think it above the power of the law; and let us suppose the convention instead of saying, 'We, the ordinary legislature, establish a *constitution,*' had said 'We, the ordinary legislature, establish an act *above the power of the ordinary legislature.*' Does not this expose the absurdity of the attempt?"[27]

By 1789, no doubt influenced by the revolutionary air of France, Jefferson extended his earlier thoughts to reach radical conclusions on constitutions, natural rights, and property in a letter to James Madison. Indeed, he considered his discoveries so fundamental that he elected to carry the letter back to the states in order to ensure that Madison would read it. The letter contains three significant ideas: 1) property is a social construct and instrumental to other ends; 2) each generation has a *natural* right to the earth and to start the world anew; and 3) permanent revolution is essential to the maintenance of a virtuous political life. The latter two notions were revolutionary contributions to political theory.

"The question whether one generation of men has a right to bind another," writes Jefferson, "seems never to have been started either on this or our side of the water." Caught up in discussions "on the elementary principles of society" taking place among intellectuals in prerevolutionary France, Jefferson proclaims yet another "self-evident" truth: "'*that the earth belongs in usufruct to the living*': that the dead have neither powers nor rights over it." He begins his speculations by asserting that there is no individual "natural right" to property; rather, property is "a law of society," a political construct that humans create for pragmatic reasons.[28] Jefferson then explains how neither individuals nor societies can legitimately control the earth beyond their lifespans. If a generation had absolute control of land beyond its lifetime, it too could violate the basic notion of usufruct. This constitutes yet an additional dimension to Jefferson's reinterpretation of Locke and has potentially enormous ecological ramifications.[29] As usual, Jefferson begins by accepting Locke's notion that the earth was given to humans to use, not to waste.[30] While Locke seems content to let this part of the argument rest, Jefferson pushes it to its radical extreme by emphasizing the concept of usufruct. Although both individuals and generations have a natural right to the fruits of the earth, they are also under an obligation to pass their individual and collective lands on to subsequent generations in *at least as good* a condition as they originally received it—the very essence of the concept of usufruct.[31]

The crippling effects of public debt are the immediate concern of Jefferson's letter. His own never-ending (and ultimately futile) confrontation with bankruptcy undoubtedly helped fuel his fire on this issue. After explicitly dealing with issues of generational debt, he concludes that if one generation contracts debts that it cannot repay during its lifetime, the "question of reimbursement" for the succeeding generation becomes "a question of generosity and not of right."[32] Jefferson presses the logic of his argument beyond questions of property and debt to declare "that no society can make a perpetual constitution or even a perpetual law. The earth belongs always to the living generation." In a passage that must have sent the hypochondriacal Madison running for his smelling salts, Jefferson boldly asserts: "Every constitution then, and every law, naturally expires at the end of 19 years. If it is to be enforced longer, it is an act of force, and not of right."[33] To summarize, Jefferson believes in a natural, *generational* right to property, but not a natural, *individual* right to property.[34] A crucial political construct, property should be designed to assist humans in the enjoyment of their natural rights to "life, liberty, and the pursuit of happiness." From Jefferson's radical bourgeois perspective, the maintenance of a one-class society comprises the sine qua non of a democratic community.

Where Locke's narrative celebrates exclusionary property rights as part of God's plan, Jean-Jacques Rousseau paints a less rosy picture. "The first person who, having fenced off a plot of ground, and took it into his head to say this *is mine* and found people simple enough to believe him," writes Rousseau, "was the true founder of civil society." During an age where mythical founders represented the functional equivalent of earthly gods, Rousseau suggestively wonders "what crimes, wars, murders, what miseries and horrors would the human race have been spared by someone who, uprooting the stakes or filling in the ditch, had shouted to his fellowmen: Beware of listening to this imposter; you are lost if you forget that the fruits belong to all and the earth to no one!"[35] Like Jefferson (but unlike Locke), Rousseau begins with the assumption that in the state of nature the "fruits of the earth" belong to all and it is unnatural to think that in the state of nature the earth itself could belong to anyone. The watershed event that marks humanity's fall into civil society begins with the creation of exclusionary property rights. Rousseau acquiesces to reality, recognizing the impossibility of returning to an earlier stage in human history, and he laments "that it is very likely things already came to a point where they could not remain as they were." Therefore, he elects to trace this "idea of property" back to its genesis in order to understand how it developed and culminated in "this last stage of the state of nature."[36]

In the state of nature, argues Rousseau, prior to the invention of bourgeois property rights and the creation of a state to protect these rights, there occurred random, sporadic outbursts of violence, but these were the exception rather than the norm. With the creation of property and civil society, the generally peaceful existence of humanity without government came to a close; constant, systematic, and all-pervasive competition between, and exploitation of, individuals by one another began. As Rousseau explains, "From the moment one man needed the help of another, as soon as they observed that it was useful for a single person to have provisions for two, equality disappeared, property was introduced, labor became necessary; and vast forests were changed into smiling fields which had to be watered with the sweat of men, and in which slavery and misery were soon seen to germinate and grow with the crops."[37]

The occasional and short-lived violence of premodern society was freely exchanged for an economic situation where "smiling fields" were now created by the sweat, slavery, and misery of humans. As economic inequality and class divisions further developed between those who owned and those who did not, a general condition of war ensued. Pressed by necessity, the rich devised a clever scheme to deceive the rest of the people into establishing a government principally designed to protect their property. In Rousseau's view, "Destitute of valid reasons to justify himself . . . the rich, pressed by necessity, finally conceived the most deliberate project that ever entered the human mind." The project was the creation of government based on a *social contract* designed to protect the rich from the poor under the deceptive promise of achieving justice for all. Presented with the contract, Rousseau imagines that "all ran to meet their claims, thinking they secured their freedom."[38] The modern state, then, is constructed out of a fraudulent contract. As such, it must be overthrown in order to establish a legitimate community.

This fraudulent contract is precisely the one Locke intended to justify. Famously defending private property as a natural right anterior to the creation of the state, Locke imagines that humans institute political society strictly to secure their material estates. Indeed, "government has no other end but the preservation of property."[39] The argument, which begins with the compelling assertion that individuals acquire property by mixing their labor with the raw fruits of the earth, employs an assumed "tacit consent" on the part of all individuals to the use of money in order to extend this same right to exclusionary land privileges and unlimited accumulation. As C. S. Macpherson notes in his introduction to the *Second Treatise,* Locke's reasoning relies on an ambiguity in his conception of human nature: humans are, it seems, reasonable enough to establish money, contracts, and other exchanges in the state of nature, but too belligerent to live by these rules without a government to enforce them. This ambiguity carries over into the assumption of tacit consent, undermining Locke's conclusions grounding land rights and property accumulation in natural, rather than positive, law.[40] The argument, powerful as it appears, involves a bit of clever sophistry in conflating property as such with simple possession. This maneuver does not slip past Rousseau, who distinguishes between "possession which is merely the effect of force or the right of the first occupant, and property which can only be founded on a positive title."[41] For Rousseau, as for Jefferson, property (in any meaningful sense of the word) exists only where positive law establishes, defines, and protects it. Thus, property depends on the political association; as such, it remains fundamentally responsible to the general will: "The state, in relation to its members, is master of all their goods by the social contract, which, within the State, is the basis of all rights."[42]

It must be stressed that neither Jefferson nor Rousseau uses the positive constitution of property to justify public tyranny over private possessions or any strict doctrine of communal ownership. On the contrary, private possession—and landholding in particular—remains of critical significance to their shared theories of individual liberty and republican virtue. While they can discover no natural right to private property, they understand that societies invent such rights as conducive to individuals in their pursuit of happiness. Indeed, both seem to regard the social contract as an empty promise if it cannot ensure access for *every* person to such property as he needs to pursue his own ends. In this sense, Jefferson and Rousseau may be appropriately contrasted to Locke in the following terms: Lockean government defends certain rights *of property,* or of the men who already control it, while Jeffersonian and Rousseauan theory stipulates a right *to property* for all legitimate participants in the social contract. Thus conceived as a positive, practical right, private property essentially amounts to a protected sphere of independence in the context of a nonhierarchical producing and sharing of wealth in a one-class market economy. Jefferson affirms a right of every (adult male) citizen to fifty acres of land to which he can resort for subsistence farming, thereby reducing his dependence on wage labor and mitigating the worst excesses of market exploitation. In a similar vein, Rousseau concludes that "laws are always useful to those who possess something and harmful to those who have nothing: Whence it follows that the social state is advantageous for men only insofar as all have something and none too much of anything."[43]

Both theorists emphasize an ideal of relative equality in wealth that reflects and reinforces the fundamental political and social equality among free and independent citizens. Conducive to this end, and in accordance with the natural rights of each generation, Jefferson and Rousseau conclude that all property reverts to social ownership upon the death of its possessor. When

Jefferson writes that "the earth belongs to the living," he echoes Rousseau, for whom "the right of property does not, by its nature, extend beyond the life of the proprietor, and the moment a man is dead, his goods no longer belong to him. To prescribe to him the conditions under which he may dispose of them is, therefore, at bottom, not so much seemingly to abridge the right of property, as to expand it in fact."[44] Again, while the argument replaces Locke's natural right with a positive one, the intent is to reconcile individual claims within and across generations. Indeed, writing in the context of expanding market forces that threaten to swallow up the possibility of economic independence for a great many who do not own property, Jefferson and Rousseau purchase man's "natural" right to property only to return it to him in fact. They understand the legitimate social contract to be one in which all have a stake in a society that protects all from economic exploitation. Rousseau writes that "it is therefore one of the most important functions of government to prevent extreme inequality of fortunes; not by taking away wealth from its possessors, but by depriving all men of means to accumulate it; not by building hospitals for the poor, but by securing the citizens from becoming poor."[45] Like Jefferson, Rousseau expresses distaste for direct redistribution, preferring to guarantee to citizens the economic means by which individual initiative can generate wealth—or at least prevent destitution and dependence.

In contrast, Locke opposes such minimal government influence in economic relations. Indeed, property for Locke is all but inviolable, even when life itself is forfeit. "Though I may kill a thief that sets on me in the highway," he writes, "yet I may not (which seems less) take away his money and let him go: this would be robbery on my side."[46] Likewise, the government that rightly sends men to die on the battlefield may not touch their private possessions. Locke attempts to ground this extreme position in a supposed natural right of children to their father's inheritance: "because the miscarriages of the father are no faults of the children . . . the father, by his miscarriages and violence, can forfeit his own life, but involves not his children in his guilt or destruction. His goods, which nature, that willeth the preservation of all mankind as much as is possible, hath made to belong to the children to keep them from perishing, do still continue to belong to his children."[47] This amounts, however, to nothing more than an argument of expediency whereby children are preserved, independent of the general society, by their patrimony. On this point Jefferson and Rousseau would most certainly agree—but they were also well aware that in many societies, most pointedly among the natives of North America, children were a collective responsibility and that arrangements other than individual inheritance could preserve them in case of the death of a parent. Thus, inheritance is not a natural right, but rather a positive right expedient in a market society. Locke misses the point because he assumes that humans are by nature too atomistic and self-interested to provide for the weak (e.g., children) in any other way.[48]

These theories of private property—natural right for Locke, positive right and practical institution for Jefferson and Rousseau—are at the core of vastly different approaches to politics and citizenship. For Locke, legitimate government and the rule of law protects vested property and maintains public order. The form of government is a secondary concern for him. While on its face the social contract relies on universal consent, the requirement amounts to little in practice; the contracting majority may institute any government perceived as expedient to the preservation of property, bounded only by the limitations set out in the *Second Treatise*, Section 142. To the extent that Locke appears to favor representative government, he explicitly restricts the electorate to male property holders: the property-less remain subjects to a government in which they are not real citizens. Though he struggles with his disappointment at history's varied experience with democracy, Rousseau never escapes the implications of his own conclusion that the sovereign people cannot alienate its fundamental right to self-determination. Convinced that democracy must flourish on a small scale or not at all, Rousseau gives paradigmatic status to the city-republic in which virtuous citizens subordinate property to the rigorous demands of freedom. This image appeals to Jefferson as well. Still, Jefferson's ambitions for democratic government are far broader in scope than Rousseau's: he conceives a scheme of representative and divided government that promises to hold a nation on the scale of the United States responsible to republican virtue.

<hr/>

To fully understand the importance of property for these theorists' ideas about politics and citizenship, we must first examine how each grounds his philosophic perspective in a particular understanding of human nature. Locke addresses the problem of human nature explicitly (and at length) in *An Essay*, deriving conclusions that he later takes for granted in the "state of nature" of the *Second Treatise*. More than half a century later, Rousseau replied to Locke (and all previous state-of-nature theorists) with his own rendition of human beginnings in his *Second Discourse*. Although Jefferson rarely engaged in such prolonged philosophic explorations, he returned again and again to consider questions of human nature throughout his extensive written work.

Jefferson expressly admired Locke, for *An Essay* especially—and rightly so.[49] For him, Locke's clear reasoning and careful analysis, standing on the groundwork of Hobbes's empiricism, penetrated the mysticism that clouded medieval thought to set down the more rigorous epistemological foundations of Enlightenment philosophy. In the first book, Locke establishes that no "innate principles" persist in the human mind, which he describes as "white paper" upon which experience records sense impressions and ideas. It is up to reason to combine these first simple ideas into complex abstract principles.

For Locke, this applies to moral principles as well, so that "moral principles require reasoning and discourse, and some exercise of the mind, to discover the certainty of their truth."[50] By "moral principles," Locke means formal assertions with which a person might concur or dissent. He does allow that people are born with "principles of actions" that, he writes, "are lodged in men's appetites"—drives, in other words, which direct each individual to seek pleasure and avoid pain. Of these appetites Locke concludes, "These are so far from being innate moral principles, that if they were left to their full swing they would carry men to the overturning of all morality."[51]

Independently, Jefferson and Rousseau discover a similar shortcoming in Locke's conception of morality. Recognizing the same selfish "principles of action" as Locke, they also understand that natural inclinations are more complex than simply an attraction to pleasure and an aversion to pain. Each posits a contrary principle, a sort of innate moral intuition not only anterior to reason, but also seemingly hostile to it: what Jefferson calls the "moral sense" and Rousseau "commiseration" or natural *pité*. For Rousseau, *pité* is "a natural repugnance to see any sensitive being perish or suffer."[52] "The moral sense, or conscience," writes Jefferson, "is as much a part of man as his leg or arm."[53] Strikingly, their point of departure for this critique of Locke is essentially the same: that human society cannot depend on reason alone, and if people required reason to become sociable they might never have left the state of nature. Instead, the moral (social) sentiment must be planted much more deeply in human nature. As Jefferson concludes, "Because nature hath implanted in our breasts a love of others, a sense of duty to them, a moral instinct . . . The Creator would indeed have been a bungling artist had he intended man for a social animal without planting in him social dispositions."[54] Rousseau summarizes the argument in a stinging assault on abstract moral philosophy:

So that all the definitions of these wise men, otherwise in perpetual contradiction to one another, agree only in this, that it is impossible to understand the law of nature and consequently to obey it without being a great reasoner and a profound metaphysician: which means precisely that men must have used, for the establishment of society, enlightenment which only develops with great difficulty and in very few people in the midst of society itself.[55]

Locke assumed that even the most undeveloped intellect could access the reason requisite to the most basic morality needed for survival. For him, the state of nature "has a law of nature to govern it . . . and reason, which is that law, teaches all mankind, who will but consult it", implying ready access to moral reason.[56] Still, the qualifying phrase "who will but consult it" suggests—even in the state of nature—Locke's class bias: that there are some men, property holders, who are reasonable (and "will consult it"), and others, those without property, who are not fully reasonable (and will not consult it). Based on this ambiguity in human nature, Locke constructs a theory of legitimate government that includes the property-less in a social contract of which they cannot be full (rational) citizens.[57] Jefferson and Rousseau are after a more robust and inclusive form of legitimacy and an explanation that covers political behavior in all societies—including those with common property, like those of the American natives.

Jefferson and Rousseau found, as a matter of experience, that the habits of reason often tend to contradict inclinations of conscience or commiseration. While never diminishing the importance of reason for its ability to demystify the natural world, both worry that reason often leads to disastrous results when (incorrectly) applied to moral decision-making. Most memorably, in an imaginative dialogue between his "Head" and his "Heart" (actually a letter of seduction to Maria Cosway), Jefferson finds in calculative reason a self-centered and, ironically, potentially dangerous risk-manager. Acting on the principle that "the art of life is the art of avoiding pain," reason acts contrary to the everyday social inclinations of his Heart: to live by his Head would mean avoiding friendships, which rarely last, and forsaking loves that leave him vulnerable to disappointment and betrayal.[58] Not only would the rational man avoid helping his fellows in need, but reason might have forestalled the American Revolution itself: "If our country, when pressed with wrongs at the point of the bayonet, had been governed by its heads instead of its hearts, where should we have been now? Hanging on a gallows as high as Haman's."[59] Likewise, Rousseau finds that the rational habit of drawing distinctions can overcome natural *pité* by convincing people to restrict its application. He reflects on *pité* as a kind of empathy: "Commiseration will be all the more energetic as the observing animal identifies himself more intimately with the suffering animal. Now it is evident that this identification must have been infinitely closer in the state of nature than in the state of reasoning. Reason engenders vanity and reflection fortifies it; reason turns man back upon himself, it separates him from all that bothers and afflicts him."[60]

To make the point more concrete, he considers the moral activity of a man of reason. "His fellow-man can be murdered with impunity right under his window; he has only to put his hands over his ears and argue with himself a bit to prevent nature, which revolts within him, from identifying with the man who is being assassinated." Rousseau ironically compares him to "savage man," who "does not have this admirable talent." Thus, "for want of wisdom and reason he is always seen heedlessly yielding to the first sentiment of humanity." Finally, Rousseau concludes that the moral sentiment is not lost on the modern world; rather, turning Locke's elitism on its head, Rousseau remarks, "In riots or street fights the populace assembles, the prudent man moves away; it is the rabble, the marketwoman, who separate the combatants and prevent honest people from murdering each other."[61]

The moral sense for Jefferson and natural *pité* for Rousseau are on a physiological par with the inclination toward pleasure that Locke acknowledges in *An Essay.* Neither requires "ideas" or "rules" that would be vulnerable to Locke's critique of "innate principles"—indeed, quite the contrary, since for Jefferson and Rousseau *thinking* the rule is the first cause of its decay. In this way they meet Locke's critical challenge to theorists of innate morality:

> Concerning innate [practical] principles, I desire these men to say, whether they can, or cannot, by education and custom, be blurred and blotted out: if they cannot, we must find them in all mankind alike, and they must be clear in everybody: and if they may suffer variation from adventitious notions, we must then find them clearest and most perspicuous, nearest the fountain, in children and illiterate people, who have received least impression from foreign opinions.[62]

Jefferson and Rousseau are in agreement: The moral sense, although innate, does not appear in everyone—and it may deteriorate from non-, or ill, use. Jefferson draws an analogy to the physical senses: "The want or imperfection of the moral sense in some men, like the want or imperfection of the senses of sight and hearing in others, is no proof that it is a general characteristic of the species."[63] Economic and social changes can also endanger the moral sense more generally. Rousseau laments that "our souls have been corrupted in proportion to the advancement of our arts and sciences toward perfection."[64] The usually quintessential Enlightenment figure, Jefferson strikes a less pessimistic note, but he concedes in 1815 his "fear, from the experience of the last twenty-two years, that morals do not of necessity advance hand-in-hand with the sciences."[65]

Expanding on this position, Rousseau defines two contrary principles in human nature that, taken together, generate a play of forces that compels the individual (and the species) to develop all the faculties of the mind. The first is an instinct for self-preservation, a healthy love of self comparable to the desire for pleasure in Locke's *An Essay*. For Locke, the only given is an individual's biological drive to satisfy its wants—which, in society, means the defense of "life, liberty, and estate." Like Hobbes before him, Locke follows this assumption to arrive at a fundamentally antagonistic conception of human interaction. In spite of these unpromising foundations, Hobbes and Locke both construct an impressive justification for the social contract in terms of mutual self-interest—a clear advance in political theory insofar as it establishes certain minimal grounds for sociability among even the most hostile antagonists. Nevertheless, such "pure" contracts breathe but little life into political obligation; they cannot guide the individual much beyond immediate self-interest.[66] Rousseau completes Locke's psychology by adding to the self-preservative instinct the outward-moving, socially oriented sense of *pité*. Jefferson draws the same essential distinction: "Self-love, is no part of morality. Indeed, it is exactly its counterpart."[67]

This innate sociability cements the foundation for a more robust theory of political obligation. For Locke, humans enter society for essentially private reasons. To avoid the "inconveniences" of open competition, "which disorder men's properties in the state of nature, men unite into societies, that they may have the united strength of the whole society to secure and defend their properties."[68] Yet for Jefferson as for Rousseau, "nature hath implanted in our breasts a love of others, a sense of duty to them, a moral instinct, in short, which prompts us irresistibly to feel and to succor their distresses."[69] Strikingly, Locke's rational justification of the social contract relies on exchanges of *force* to unite the "strength of the whole society" in the defense of private estates. Jefferson suggests (somewhat cryptically) that without a moral sense distinguishable from self-interest, all relations devolve into similar negotiations of force. "I believe," he writes, "that morality, compassion, generosity, are innate elements of the human constitution; that there exists a right independent of force."[70] Where Locke is satisfied to demonstrate the necessity (or prudence) of political society, for Jefferson mutual need is a less-than-satisfying justification for political obligations. Rousseau, in agreement, clarifies the stakes of their departure from the simple contract theory: "To yield to force is an act of necessity, not of will; at most it is an act of prudence. In what sense can it become a duty?"[71]

For Jefferson and Rousseau, humans are inherently social—yet both famously valorize the most independent and solitary of men. Rousseau, in the *Second Discourse,* romantically depicts the noble savage, alone in the state of nature, enjoying freedoms and virtues long abandoned by civilized men. Jefferson, also influenced by contact with Native Americans, described them in no less glowing terms. Having seen the empirical reality of society without Leviathan, Jefferson writes, "I am convinced that those societies (as the Indians) which live without government enjoy in their general mass an infinitely greater degree of happiness than those who live under European governments."[72] Among his fellow citizens, Jefferson finds his exemplar of virtue in the common farmer who supports himself independently on the fruits of his labor. "The cultivators of the earth," he notes, "are the most virtuous citizens."[73] Rousseau agrees: "It is in the rustic clothes of the farmer and not beneath the gilt of a courtier that strength and vigor of the body will be found. Ornamentation is no less foreign to virtue, which is the strength and vigor of the soul."[74]

Ironically, this common admiration for the most solitary individuals stems directly from Jefferson's and Rousseau's understanding of innate sociability. The moral sense or commiseration is an inclination to regard others as ends rather than means—as moral equals whose happiness should be treated as intrinsically good: we want others to be happy (too). Jefferson and Rousseau suffer no illusions, however, about the vulnerability of the moral sense to adverse circumstance and improper education. Thus Jefferson and Rousseau envision a republic that raises virtuous citizens who mutually regard one another as ends; and for such a society economic dependence (even interdependence) can be problematic. Being simply dependent is, intrinsically, a relation to others as means. Where dependence is part of an interdependent relationship between equal subjects, however, the relationship is between ends. Thus, the republican ideal is an association of self-sufficient and virtuous citizens suited to a society of equals in which they engage in voluntary social intercourse—for its own sake. In his "Letter to the Republic of Geneva," Rousseau describes such a society as a republic "where, each being adequate to his job, no one would have been constrained to commit to others the functions with which he was charged; a state where, all the individuals knowing one another . . . that sweet habit of seeing and knowing one another turned love of the fatherland into *love of the citizens rather than love of the soil*."[75] Thus is economic independence and equality related to the habit of treating others as an end rather than merely a means.

Jefferson confirms the relationship. "Corruption of morals," for him, "is the mark set on those who, not looking up to heaven, to their own soil and industry, as does the husbandman, for their subsistence, depend for it on the casualties and caprice of customers." Jefferson's moral argument complements and extends his political-economic doctrine that farmable land must remain available to laborers to ensure their freedom from exploitation. Moreover, he suggests that entrepreneurs and merchants, hardly victims of the marketplace, nevertheless suffer a form of moral degeneration as a result of their interactions with patrons: "Dependence begets subservience and venality, suffocates the germ of virtue, and prepares fit tools for the designs of ambition." From this he concludes, in accord with his political economy, that a republican society should never lose its ties to agricultural production: "Generally speaking, the proportion which the aggregate of the other classes of citizens bears in any state to that of its husbandmen is the proportion of its unsound to its healthy parts, and is a good enough barometer whereby to measure its degree of corruption."[76]

The corruption of morals concerns both theorists—although Jefferson, a perennial optimist, remains very much at odds with Rousseau about future human development.[77] This concern distinguishes them both from Locke, however, for just as much as Locke regards the human individual in a state of isolation, he regards human nature itself as static across time. The "white paper" of each human mind is the same; the same senses write experience onto each identical mind; and the same impulse to pleasure directs the individual's activities toward gain and competition. Because, moreover, Locke believes that moral knowledge is a matter for the understanding—for reason—he conceives a static morality that "is as *capable of real certainty, as mathematics*."[78] This view accords with his conviction that man's relationship to nature is universal and divinely ordained: "God, by commanding to subdue, gave authority so far to appropriate."[79] Man, made in God's image, is now what he has always been and what he will always be.

Rousseau, rejecting this view, begins the *Second Discourse* by posing a rhetorical question. "And how will man manage to see himself as nature formed him, through all the changes that the sequence of time and things must have produced in his original constitution, and to separate what he gets from his own stock from what circumstances and his progress have added to or changed in his primitive state?"[80] Since Jefferson and Rousseau regard the individual as inherently and immediately implicated in social reality, speculation on the mind of the infant is moot. Instead, they concern themselves with the state of the moral sentiments in general, and with whether economic, political, and social relations tend to develop or pervert them. This "nature" is flexible. It responds—sometimes rapidly—to environmental, cultural, and technological change.

Rousseau and Jefferson view humans as developmental beings. Rousseau's understanding is tied to what he calls "the faculty of self-perfection." Self-perfection, he argues, "resides among us as much in the species as in the individual." It is what enables us "*to perfect*" all of our other talents and abilities. This faculty sounds like a wonderful capacity that is almost too good to be true, and it is often misinterpreted to mean that Rousseau thinks humans can, in fact, become perfect. But that is not the case. Rousseau captures this capacity's bittersweet essence: "An animal is at the end of a few months what it will be all of its life: and a species is at the end of a thousand years what it was the first year of that thousand. Why is man alone subject to becoming imbecile?"[81] Specifically, Rousseau sees that all of our uniquely human characteristics, talents, and abilities can develop positively to make us more human; it is also possible that these same features may deteriorate to make us alienated creatures, less than fully human. Always far more optimistic than Rousseau, Jefferson thinks that it is humanity's developmental nature that permits it to advance to unknown heights. He metaphorically explains the crucial dialectic between human ontology and positive laws in a celebrated letter to Samuel Kercheval: "But I know also, that laws and institutions must go hand in hand with the progress of the human mind. As that becomes more developed, more enlightened, as new discoveries are made, new truths disclosed, . . . institutions must advance also, and keep pace with the times. We might as well require a man to wear still the coat that fitted him when a boy, as civilized society to remain ever under the regimen of their barbarous ancestors."[82]

For Rousseau, technological and economic "advancement" seems bound to increase luxury and idleness for those who can afford them, and economic subservience for those who cannot. Jefferson recognizes the same danger, but—fascinated with and inspired by humans' scientific achievements and the nearly unlimited future of an as yet underpopulated, underdeveloped America—he remains optimistic that civilization can become both virtuous and truly modern. For both thinkers, it is in politics alone that human beings become genuine agents of their own change; in politics, they can shape the world that shapes them in turn, transforming "human nature" from a limitation into a *possibility.* Thus, politics, for Jefferson and Rousseau, regains a dignity that can be traced back to Aristotle's *zoon politikon* but is lost on Locke.[83] For Locke, political associations exist merely to produce a workable compromise in the field of economic competition. Politics carves out a negative space for competing and mutually canceling individual liberties: freedom from violence and coercion; protection of life, liberty, and property. For Jefferson and Rousseau, politics can achieve these things and more, since the end of human development is not a given but open and indeterminate. Taking on positive value as an end in itself, political engagement becomes not just a responsibility but a fundamental right. Indeed, participation becomes the very definition of "liberty" and what it means to be fully human.

The American founders discovered in Locke's *Second Treatise* a compelling and relevant justification for the colonies' separation from Great Britain. Locke's influence on the disputes leading to the war cannot be overstated. Certainly they must have heard "no taxation without representation" in Locke's compelling outline of "the *bounds* which the trust . . . have *set to the legislative power,*" most notably the third prohibition, which states that the legislative power "must *not raise taxes* on the *property of the people without the consent of the people,* given by themselves, or their deputies."[84] Nevertheless, to read back into Locke's text too much of the revolutionary spirit is to enter contentious terrain. While the American Revolution may have been in part instigated by economic interests reminiscent of those motivating the *Second Treatise,* American patriots were also animated by a republican love of liberty that flourished throughout the colonies as it had not in Britain. In fact, Locke's social contract demands very little of legitimate government: "The great and *chief end,* therefore of men's uniting into common-wealths, and putting themselves under government, *is the preservation of their property.*"[85] Given the political conditions of England at the time Locke wrote, it is understandable that he takes greater interest in enumerating both the responsibilities of government to its subjects and the excesses associated with government abuse than in considering the appropriate form of political engagement for citizens. Indeed, he implicitly approves of the sort of *disengaged* citizen who raises his voice only when government has abused its prerogatives, as evident in his theory of "tacit consent," which holds, in short, that a citizen consents to the existing government merely by the fact of his residence in the country and his participation in its *economic* life. While Locke decries absolute monarchy and favors a form of limited representative government (for propertied electors), his critique boils down to simple pragmatism: a government that represents vested property is all the less likely to infringe on property rights.

Neither Jefferson nor Rousseau is satisfied with a society in which some few rule while the majority of people have no say in political decisions. Rousseau distinguishes between "subjects" and "citizens," sharpening the distinction between a Lockean government of limited representation and a truly democratic republic:

> Subjects praise public tranquility, Citizens individual freedom; one prefers security of possessions, and the other that of persons; one wants the best Government to be the most severe, the other maintains that it is the mildest; this one wants crimes to be punished, and that one wants them prevented; one thinks it is a fine thing to be feared by neighbors, the other prefers to be ignored by them; one is satisfied when money circulates, the other demands that the people have bread.[86]

In the *Social Contract,* Rousseau contributes the revolutionary argument that sovereignty resides exclusively in the public considered as a collective body of legislative equals; that sovereignty is inalienable; that therefore no representative body (nor any special class of individuals) can ever possess true sovereignty. The people cannot hand away their sovereignty by contract any more than they can write a constitutional law beyond the possibility of repeal. "The legislative power belongs to the people, and can belong only to it."[87]

The radical democratic implications of Rousseau's argument may easily be lost in the fact that he regards his version of the social contract as a fragile

155

and highly contingent historical possibility.[88] Following Montesquieu, Rousseau also believes governmental forms must vary with climate and economic conditions; genuine democratic government simply is not viable over large territories or where there are extremes in resource wealth. Even so, it must be stressed that where direct democracy cannot flourish due to historical or material circumstance, Rousseau holds that the legitimacy of *any* government requires frequent conventions of the sovereign people to affirm the form, substance, and leadership of the current regime. Moreover, precisely because democracy depends on the scale of association, Rousseau declares his preference for "a society of a size limited by the extent of human faculties—that is, limited by the possibility of being well governed—and where each being adequate to his job, no one would have been constrained to commit to others the functions with which he was charged."[89] If the city remains appropriately limited in size, both robust democracy and the ancients' conceptions of civic justice are possible.

For Rousseau, as for Jefferson, periodic conventions of the sovereign people inject explicit and literal meaning into the concept of consent. Indeed, both theorists address a philosophic audience for whom the critical measure of political legitimacy is the consent of the governed, in no small part because Locke himself famously addressed the problem in these terms. For Locke, however, *explicit* consent plays a limited, largely theoretical role greatly overshadowed by the position of "tacit consent" in his practical and theoretical framework. In the first place, the class divisions of market society presuppose the tacit agreement among men in the state of nature to use money for purposes of exchange. Locke continues to recount, as a historical matter, how early patriarchal monarchies developed from the "tacit and almost natural consent" of children to their "*father's authority and government*."[90] Explicit consent appears for Locke only once, when men in the state of nature choose to incorporate themselves under governments for their mutual security and the protection of property: "Men being, as has been said, by nature free, equal, and independent, no one can be put out of this estate and subjected to the political power of another without his own consent." Yet this beginning is also the end of explicit consent. After consenting to putting "on the *bonds of civil society*," the individual transfers his power to act to "the majority [who] have a right to act to conclude the rest."[91]

Without so much as considering any need to reconvene the sovereign, Locke then sets out to answer a question of political obligation for the generations of subjects who do not participate in the original compact. "What," he asks "shall be understood to be a *sufficient declaration* of a man's *consent,* to *make him subject* to the laws of any government." After granting the obvious point that "no body doubts but an expressed consent . . . makes him a perfect member of that society," Locke acknowledges that "the difficulty is, what ought to be looked upon as a *tacit consent,* and how far it binds—i.e., how far any one shall be looked on to have consented, and thereby submitted to any government, where he has made no expressions of it at all." Having arrived at the crux of the matter, Locke declares

> that every man, that hath any possessions, or enjoyment, of any part of the dominions of any government doth hereby give his *tacit consent,* and is as far forth obliged to obedience to the laws of that government, during such enjoyment, as any one under it; whether this his posses- sion be of land, to him and his heirs for ever, or a lodging only for a week; or whether it be barely traveling freely on the highway; and, in effect, it reaches as far as the very being of any one within the territo- ries of that government.[92]

Thus, complete political obligation extends by way of tacit consent to all descendants of the original parties to the contract (as well as immigrants and visitors) who participate in the *economic* life of the nation, regardless of the form of government originally instituted.

The subject by tacit consent does, for Locke, retain a freedom that the member by explicit consent does not. He may "quit the said possession" of all his assets, being then "at liberty to go and incorporate himself into any other commonwealth, or agree with others to begin a new one, *in vacuis locis,* in any part of the world, they can find free and unpossessed." But he who "by actual agreement, and any *express* declaration, [has] given his *consent* to be of any common-weal, is perpetually and indispensably obliged to be, and remain unalterably a subject to it, and can never be again in the liberty of the state of nature; unless by any calamity, the government he was under comes to be dissolved."[93] This gives the concept of explicit consent a curious place in Locke's thought. The subject by tacit consent appears to be bound by all the laws of the government under which he makes his living, but as a noncitizen has no right to voice his concerns about them—he may either remain subject, or leave. This subject may be said to be in, but not of, civil society. By mak- ing his consent explicit, however, he succeeds only in making his obligation more complete. Clearly, since Locke guarantees representation to property holders alone, such obligations entail political benefits only for the propertied elite, the real *citizens* of his commonwealth. His theory of tacit consent is, to this extent, irrelevant to citizenship; rather, it answers the critical question of why the masses of unpropertied noncitizens should be obliged by the laws of the contract.

For Jefferson and Rousseau, tacit consent in this Lockean sense is no consent at all. Both maintain that legitimate government depends on frequent conventions of the sovereign people, and that all subjects are also citizens with the right and duty to participate in public affairs. They differ, however, on the question of *generational consent* to laws drafted in the past, in answer to which Rousseau introduces his own theory of tacit consent: "Yesterday's law does not obligate today, but tacit consent is presumed from silence." Here he refers not to the consent and obligation of the individual citizen, but to the force of laws that the sovereign has not explicitly repealed. Writing that "the Sovereign is assumed to be constantly confirming the laws which it does not abrogate when it can do so," Rousseau implies that the sovereign need not reconsider every law of the past at each of its conventions.[94] Indeed, it should not, if such constant reconsideration should be purchased at the price of well-formed moral traditions ingrained in the citizens' hearts. While the people must necessarily assemble to express their consent or revoke it, political legitimacy requires only that they affirm or disconfirm the form and membership of the existing regime, not that they also discuss the wisdom of other matters of law.[95] The revolutionary implications of the sovereign's responsibility are evident; yet in Rousseau's doctrine of tacit consent, so is his cultural conservatism.

With respect to the individual who may, perhaps, not always attend the sovereign convention or other political meetings, Rousseau expressly rejects Locke's assertion that "mere residence" satisfies as an indicator of consent. Rather, individual consent "should always be understood with regard to a free State; for elsewhere family, goods, the lack of asylum, necessity, violence, may keep an inhabitant in the country in spite of himself, and then his mere residence no longer implies his consent to the contract or to its violation."[96] This acknowledgment no doubt serves as an additional pressure restricting the scale of political association for Rousseau, because where citizens live too far from the capital it must be disingenuous to claim that they consent to its activities.

Jefferson agrees with Rousseau's conception of sovereignty, writing that "[the people] are in truth the only legitimate proprietors of the soil and government." He carries this understanding, however, to an even more radically revolutionary conclusion than Rousseau's.[97] In the first place, while he too believed that, according to the lessons of history, democratic government depends on the moral development of the population, nowhere does he express Rousseau's misgivings about the political potential of some climates or expansive geographic extent.[98] Indeed, he dreamt of a democratic republic on the great scale of the United States—locally rooted, but of continental proportions. Furthermore, he rejected Rousseau's doctrine of tacit consent, maintaining instead that every law expires with the generation that enacted it. Every generation, he held, is born with the right to create the world anew.

It is true, as contemporary conservatives persistently remind us, that Jefferson detested the notion of a large, intrusive government; that this entailed a similar distaste for politics, however, is false. Political engagement, for Jefferson, was a fundamental right only superficially separable from "liberty"— his ideal was *maximum* politics, minimal government. Political participation would occur at the local level—his ward republics—so that every individual could take part. Representation at higher levels, moreover, would employ directed delegates—not independent trustees—to transmit the public will from the base of the democratic pyramid to the top. The whole system was designed, in fact, to transfer the republican virtue of small scale, so significant for Rousseau, as nearly as possible to governmental units at every level of a confederate national government. This conceptualization of the problem of space is present in Rousseau's work as well. In his usually ignored *Considerations on the Government of Poland* (1772), he outlines "a confederation of thirty-three small States, [that] would combine the force of Great Monarchies with the freedom of small Republics." The representatives, moreover, would "adhere exactly to their instructions, and to render a strict account of their conduct in the Diet to their constituents."[99]

Jefferson was fond of drafting model constitutions that represent more clearly how he thought a democratic government should function. After the all-important Bill of Rights, he emphasizes participation as the most important issue of democratic government.[100] In one early draft of a model constitution for Virginia, Jefferson cleverly tightens the practical unity between his political economy and republican politics. Appearing at one point to limit suffrage to males owning one-quarter acre of land in town or twenty-five acres in the country, he later decrees in the same document that every person who had never owned fifty acres of land would be entitled to an appropriation in that amount. Holding fast to the republican assumption that political participants should possess sufficient land to be free from immediate private concerns, Jefferson democratizes this principle by regarding land as instrumental in securing economic and political freedom. In effect, he subverts the doctrine that only property holders can be trusted with the vote, and thus transforms it into the dictum that all citizens are entitled to property, for that alone can provide a base for economic and political freedom.

As significant as he considered equal and universal suffrage (at least for white men), suffrage by itself does not a democracy make. Ambitious for a national polity, he still longed for the local, face-to-face politics preferred by Rousseau. To this end, Jefferson—unique among the founders and framers— envisioned an open public space in which citizens could actively participate in the politics of all levels of government. Like Rousseau, Jefferson regarded politics as an ennobling activity in which everyone has a right—as well as a duty—to participate.[101] In hopes of creating an arena for this activity, a public space for citizen participation, Jefferson makes the case for ward republics.

"Divide the counties into wards of such size as that every citizen can attend . . . and act in person," Jefferson suggested. The wards, called by Jefferson "the wisest invention ever devised by the wit of man for the perfect exercise of self-government," should control all local matters, including education, policing, and law. They also formed the democratic base for a four-tier governmental pyramid: the national government, at the peak, is "entrusted with the defense of the nation, and its foreign and federal relations"; at the next level, the state governments are concerned with "the civil rights, laws, policy and administration of what concerns the state generally"; then "the local concerns of the counties"; and ultimately the base, composed of ward republics, "direct[s] the interests within itself."[102]

Sovereignty rests in the people. In Jefferson's system this is no less true of the national than of the local governments. At the local level, voters elect every official directly, but each higher division of the pyramid functions like a mini-republic dependent on the subordinate level for its authority. Guidance and direction ascends from the base through representatives instructed to mirror the express will of the local communities.

> The elementary republics of the wards, the county republics, the state republics, and the republic of the Union, would form a graduation of authorities, standing each on the basis of law, holding everyone its

delegated share of powers, and constituting truly a system of fundamental balances and checks for the government. Where every man is
a sharer in the direction of his ward-republic, or of some of the higher
ones, and feels that he is a participator in the government of affairs, not
merely at an election one day in the year, but every day; when there
shall not be a man in the state who will not be a member of some one
of the councils, great or small, he will let the heart be torn out of his
body sooner than his power be wrested from him by a Caesar or a
Bonaparte.[103]

Like Rousseau, Jefferson does not believe that mere periodic elections can
maintain republican virtue—or even keep representatives answerable to the
represented. Yet he does not accept Rousseau's pronouncement against the
possibility of democracy in a large republic. Instead, by division and subdivi-
sion "until it ends in the administration of everyman's farm by himself," Jefferson hopes to preserve republican independence and universal engagement
as the mainspring for a vast democratic society. "Every day," Jefferson writes,
the citizen must act as a "participator in the government of affairs."[104] Thus,
the system of ward republics circumvented Rousseau's rejection of England's
representative government, but was similar to his design for Poland in that it
managed to embrace the spirit of ancient Greek politics and citizenship, with
man as the *zoon politikon*, but without the limitations of a city's scale.

This may relate to Jefferson's optimism regarding the potential of human
perfectibility. Rousseau, perennially concerned that every scientific or technological advance chipped away at the moral armor of a virtuous republic,
ultimately retreats to a culturally conservative (if politically radical) com-
munitarian ideal. His model republic is self-sufficient, isolationist, and bound
to long traditions that bolster its moral and political fortitude; his aim is not
advancement, but conservation. Jefferson, however, marvels at the achievements of humankind. His imagination is enthralled at the bare conception of
the heights that civilization might yet attain. To the extent that he worries
about the future dangers of overpopulation and wage labor in the cities—the
deleterious effects of which he has seen all too clearly in Europe—he remains
convinced that these problems are soluble by ingenuity and a kind of permanent revolution whereby the next generation begins to exercise its usufruct
of the earth and politics. Creative schemes such as the ward republics and the
economic safety valve of free land can be implemented to balance intellectual

and technological progress with the necessities of a democratic republic, but in the end generational revolutions are what make progress possible.

Critical to Jefferson's theory is the centrality of politics in everyday life. This amounts to a return to the natural order of things. Only *if* men (mistakenly) take property as a natural right—to which politics remains subordinate—can *homo civicus* become subservient to the solitary existence of *homo oeconomicus*. The solution, then, treats property as instrumental to human ends—ends expressed and implemented through a system of democratic politics. So long as this right to public expression and decision-making persists (preserved in the public space provided by the ward republics), human society can advance with every generation's opportunity to remake its political world.[105]

Jefferson and his contemporaries had been given a "fresh start" in the revolutionary experience, an experience that Jefferson felt obligated to pass on to succeeding generations. By way of the small ward republics, he argued that citizens in effect had a natural right to political participation not only in the regular process of government but in the constitutional congresses and conventions like those of the 1770s and 1780s. It remained essential to his conception of democracy that each generation should have the opportunity to "depute representatives to a convention, and to make their Constitution what they believe will be the best for themselves." In this way, "the voice of the whole people would be thus fairly, fully, and peacefully expressed, discussed, and decided by the common reason of the society."[106] Anything less than this level of participation would fall short of true democracy, either by promoting the rule of a detached elite who (at best) represent their own perception of the people's interest, or by allowing the rule of the dead from beyond the grave. Each generation has a fundamental right to begin the world anew since "every constitution then, and every law, naturally expires at the end of nineteen years. If it be enforced longer, it is an act of force, and not of right."[107]

Jefferson's proposals to maintain a spirit of revolution—the "spirit of 1776," as he put it—resemble Rousseau's institution of permanently recurring conventions of the sovereign body. Manifesting the democratic sovereign's inalienable right to constitute the administration of government according to the general will, "there must be fixed and periodic assemblies which nothing can abolish or prorogue, so that on the appointed day the people is legitimately summoned by law, without need of any further formal convocation."[108] The revolutionary character of these assemblies can hardly be overstated, for here "all jurisdiction of the Government ceases, the executive power is suspended, and the person of the last Citizen is as sacred and inviolable as the first Magistrate, because where the Represented is, there no longer is a Representative."[109]

Still, Rousseau seems to lack Jefferson's enthusiasm for revolution, which the latter appears to have found refreshing and intellectually stimulating.[110] Rousseau's theory strains between the revolutionary implications of his conception of sovereignty and his aversion to cultural innovation, so that some of his most radical conclusions stand out from the elegant rhetoric of the *Social Contract* (1762) for their sterility rather than their verve. The sovereign assembly, he writes, "ought always to open with two motions which it should be impossible ever to omit, and which ought to be voted on separately." The first of these amounts to a form of revolution by ballot, the motion being "*whether it please the Sovereign to retain the present form of Government.*" Yet the revolutionary potential of this vote is obscured, perhaps intentionally, by the second one that comes on its heels: "*whether it please the People to leave its administration to those who are currently charged with it.*"[111] Rousseau gives the impression that he expects the mode of administration and therefore the political constitution of the state to change infrequently, if at all. The potentially revolutionary first motion of the assembly, therefore, functions more as a check on tyranny than as a promise of perpetual rebirth.

Jefferson, by contrast, thought of generational revolution as a natural right on a par with the individual's right to daily political participation. Furthermore, he believed that the spirit of revolution is intrinsic to a democratic society. Permanent revolution, through which Jefferson imagined the love of liberty and the joy of creation would remain indefinitely a part of the American spirit, became a central principle to his conception of a vital, democratic community. Jefferson genuinely and unabashedly enjoyed his opportunities for political innovation—he had participated in more than his share of sovereign assemblies. In fact, regardless of whether he was familiar with the French thinker's work, Jefferson had developed in theory and extended in practice a conception of democratic sovereignty strikingly similar to Rousseau's. He succeeded, perhaps, in even some theoretical improvement, insofar as his conclusions remain true to their shared intellectual foundations but unrestrained by Rousseau's cautious cultural conservatism.

Louis Hartz famously observed that "Locke dominates American political thought, as no thinker anywhere dominates the political thought of a nation."[112] Regardless of what scholars now think of Hartz's sweeping theory of the unfolding of American liberalism, Hartz's characterization has been unreflectively applied to Jefferson. While Rousseau has always, and appropriately, been seen as a challenger to and critic of Locke, Jefferson has not. And yet the political theories of Jefferson and Rousseau have a great deal in common. To be sure, Rousseau quite consciously has Locke (and Hobbes among others) in his sight when he turns his imaginative eye on his competitors. Jefferson, pressed by more immediate political concerns, has neither the time nor the inclination for similar philosophic discourse; rather, without directly attacking Locke's political theory, he transcends it. And this transcendence occurs because (like Rousseau) Jefferson has a fundamentally different concept of humanity in mind as he constructs his radical democratic theory. Rousseau's pessimism about the enormous challenges of healing the social and political ills of a corrupt and class-divided Europe is understandable. A cautious radical, Rousseau thinks it is easier to change than to change back, and that humans may not have realized what they have lost along the way. Rousseau's wariness stands in contrast to Jefferson's optimism about the possibilities he envisions for keeping his republic free from the political and cultural decay he witnessed in France. It is as if Rousseau wants to undo the Fall, Jefferson to maintain Paradise.

J. G. A. Pocock may be on to something when he claims that in Jefferson's vision America confronts its Rousseauan moment.[113] Prior to his ascent to the highest public office, Jefferson fantasized that America could keep European corruption at bay. His theory explicitly rejects the assumption of "European political oeconomists" that "every state should endeavor to manufacture for itself." Blessed with abundant free land, America enjoyed a qualitatively different economic base than Europe, where "the lands are either cultivated, or locked up against the cultivator." The consequences of this political choice are straightforward: "Manufacture must therefore be resorted to of necessity not of choice." But it is not simply economic dependence that disturbs Jefferson; it is also the collateral damage that results from manufacturing as a way of life. When confronted with the political options of "dependence"—the "subservience and venality" that comes with manufacturing or the "genuine virtue" of "those who labour the earth . . . the chosen people of God"—Jefferson assuredly, albeit naïvely, responds, "let our workshops remain in Europe."[114] Try as he might to avoid it, Jefferson ultimately concludes that a direct confrontation with Europe is unavoidable and tragic. He alters his original pastoral vision to plant the manufacturer alongside the farmer in what Leo Marx aptly calls "the 'middle landscape" ideal."[115] Nevertheless, after he was retired from public life Jefferson found little consolation in the fact that "our enemy has indeed the consolation of Satan on removing our first parents from Paradise: from a peaceable and agricultural nation, he makes us a military and manufacturing one."[116]

During the presidency of James Madison, Jefferson's vision begins quietly to vanish from American politics. His elegant prose concerning self-evident truths and the pursuit of happiness are reserved for national celebrations like those held on the Fourth of July. The future did not belong to Jefferson. It belonged to his departed adversary Alexander Hamilton. By the time of his unfortunate demise, Hamilton's ideas had started to capture the American imagination. They helped establish the political and economic foundations for a republican empire that would eventually become the envy of the world. And yet, as American citizens face the enormous difficulties of creating a globalized, class-divided, liberal-democratic world, perhaps a Jefferson who has been "un-Locked" can provide the ideas and ideals that will allow this generation to reassert his claim "that the earth belongs in usufruct to the living."

Problematic Virtues:
Jefferson and Hamilton on Education
for Vigilant Citizens and Responsible Statesmen

KARL WALLING

We Americans live in a time of war. Much as has been the case ever since the American War for Independence, Americans continue to disagree on how much wartime power they can safely grant the national government. Some call for strengthening the powers of the national government to confront the necessities of our current war against terrorists fighting under the banner of fundamentalist Islam and against insurgents seeking to prevent the establishment of a somewhat more representative and law-governed regime in Iraq. Others worry about sacrificing ends to means. They fear that delegating too much power to the national government will cost Americans vital liberties that may never be recovered.

In one sense, our current debate is entirely new. Our highly technological, globalized world has complicated already difficult issues such as how to handle illegal combatants in American custody; how to gather intelligence about terrorists at home and abroad; the legitimacy of military tribunals; and the many other problems modern states must confront when addressing threats from transnational terrorists motivated by fanatical ideology. In another sense, the form of our current debates is nothing new. The party in opposition accuses the party in power of abusing its authority, whereas the party in power accuses the party in opposition of sacrificing the national interest to political partisanship and demagoguery based on a strict and self-destructive interpretation of the American Constitution. One party preaches the virtue of vigilance to prevent undue concentrations of power, whereas the other preaches the virtue of responsibility, so that the means chosen to defend liberty do not prove a cure worse than the tyranny they are meant to prevent.

The classic form of this debate took root more than two hundred years ago when Thomas Jefferson and Alexander Hamilton became leaders of different parties, the Federalists and the Republicans. Each party sought to educate Americans in the kinds of political virtues required to make American liberty durable. The challenges Americans face today in waging war effectively while also remaining free will not be solved automatically by recovering these different views of the proper education of citizens and statesmen. We are unlikely to understand ourselves, and what we are fighting for, both domestically and abroad, however, without some effort to understand both Jefferson's education for vigilant citizens and its best critique-cum-antidote: Hamilton's education for responsible statesmen in *The Federalist* (1787–1788).[1]

As the young author of the Declaration of Independence, Jefferson wrote of the "manly firmness" of the American people. Jefferson never ceased to be concerned with this spirit, which he considered far more important than the written, political Constitution devised in 1787. As an elder statesman in 1816, Jefferson asked, "Where . . . is our republicanism to be found? Not in our Constitution certainly, but merely in the spirit of our people. That would oblige even a despot to govern us republicanly." The great question in Jefferson's mind was how to "nurture and perpetuate" the unwritten, American moral constitution of manly vigilance.[2]

Jefferson sought his answer in the design of an educational system devised to raise up free men who would be vigilant to preserve their liberties. He believed that cultivating the habits of free minds, even in the primary schools, was the best bulwark against both political and religious despotism. As an opponent of what he sometimes called "monkish ignorance and superstition," Jefferson believed freedom required not only separating church and state, but also weakening the power of religious authorities over the hearts and minds of Americans. Hence, he would have allowed neither the Bible nor religious ministers in the classrooms of primary schools.[3] Jefferson suspected that public religious instruction of the young would be a source of corruption in a modern republic. Rather than being taught to rely on their own reason, the Virginian worried, pupils would be habituated to revere the authority of revelation. The proper reading for the young was therefore not the Bible, but the histories of ancient and modern republics, which would constitute a kind of civil religion of liberty and have its own patron saints—men like Cato, Brutus, Cicero, and Algernon Sydney. By studying the sacred texts of republican history in translation, Americans would learn to recognize despotic ambition in all its forms, whether emanating from the church or the state.[4]

Jefferson proposed that the best student from each primary school be selected for admission to a regional advanced academy. Scholarships would be available for students whose parents could not afford to pay for schooling. Jefferson described this enrollment scheme, which provided a unique combination of egalitarianism and elitism, as raking "the best geniuses from the rubbish." The artificial aristocracy based on wealth, power, and birth would have to compete with the natural aristocracy of genius, merit, and talent. Confident that the natural aristocrats would outperform their rivals, Jefferson believed that the result would be the progress of the entire society.

The curriculum of the academies would supply additional tools of intellectual and economic self-reliance. Learning classical languages would enable talented pupils to "unmask" traditional authorities based on what John Adams once referred to as the conspiracy of canon and feudal law. These authorities disguised their "usurpations" in the "supposed superlative wisdom" of ancestors, fathers, priests, and even antiquity itself. By doing so, they gave the dead control over the living. Jefferson considered this control a form of sacrilege against freedom, because, he believed, "the earth belongs . . . to the living," who cannot legitimately be deprived of their birthright to frame their own destiny. Learning practical sciences such as mathematics, navigation, geography, and surveying would supply the foundations of technological advancement, the means by which human beings conquer nature, render themselves free from want, and shape their future. Especially if they owned and worked their own land, such practical-minded, inventive citizens would depend on no one for their subsistence and would thereby be free to resist authority when justified in doing so.[5]

The finishing school of the new aristocracy would be a university. Jefferson originally contemplated reforming the old religious College of William and Mary, but he later decided to found a purely secular institution, the University of Virginia. There he banned divinity from the curriculum, and with it the possibility that reason would defer to revelation. It was far better for liberty for students to study all the modern social and natural sciences, which promoted the ever-vigilant exercise of the freedom of the mind. Free minds would produce free men.[6]

Despite Jefferson's careful design to produce a natural aristocracy of free-minded men, he placed little trust even in a properly educated, natural aristocracy. Jefferson worried that if the aristocrats had nothing to fear from ignorant and deferential citizens they would soon become despotic. Hence the vigilance of the citizenry-at-large was even more important to the flourishing of freedom than the education of elites. After learning of Shays's Rebellion, Jefferson admonished a fellow aristocrat that we should "cherish therefore the spirit of our people, and keep alive their attention. . . . If once they become inattentive to the public affairs, you and I, and Congress, and the Assemblies, and judges and governors shall all become wolves." Thus, Jefferson said he would rather give up the university than the primary schools. As Paul Rahe has suggested, Jefferson believed that the best defense against aristocratic wolves in power is citizens who have been taught to refuse to be sheep.[7]

Jefferson also stressed the importance of informal educational institutions. Giving citizens a taste for self-government—through ward government, for example—would render them suspicious of more centralized governments. In 1788, as the nation debated ratification of the Constitution, Jefferson suggested to his best friend, James Madison, that it was not enough to pit ambition against ambition in a written, political constitution. The people, and their leaders, needed "principles upon which to found their opposition." A bill of rights, Jefferson argued, would write vigilance, understood as suspicion or jealousy of power, into the hearts or moral constitution of the American people. Twelve years later, in the Kentucky Resolutions, Jefferson invoked the principles of the First, Fifth, and Tenth Amendments against the Alien and Sedition Acts. In so doing, he turned the Constitution of 1787 and its appended Bill of Rights into something old and sacred, a secular political Bible whose political Ten Commandments would be written into the moral constitution of the American people so that they would become permanently jealous of power. "Free government," Jefferson thundered, "is founded in jealousy of power. . . . It is jealousy, not confidence, which prescribes limited constitutions." For Jefferson it was the limited constitution understood as a vehicle for mobilizing popular jealousy of power rather than as a mere parchment barrier to the abuse of power that would keep the people free.[8]

Jefferson's appeal to jealousy, however, seemed to some a strange foundation for freedom. Jealousy was traditionally considered a vice, not a virtue. Jealousy destroyed Othello and Desdemona. It seemed more the stuff of tragedy than a foundation of durable liberty. Consider Alexander Hamilton's first essay in *The Federalist*. "Jealousy," Hamilton cautioned, "is the usual concomitant of violent love." While Hamilton could acknowledge that this vice often arose from something good—"the noble enthusiasm for liberty"—he believed that extremism in the defense of liberty was no virtue. Jealousy infects the love of liberty with "a spirit of narrow and illiberal distrust." This distrust leads us to forget that the "vigor of government is essential to the security of liberty" and thus to deny government the means necessary to secure our liberty.[9] Whereas Jefferson sought through a system of schooling to inculcate the modern virtue of jealous vigilance in ordinary citizens, Hamilton sought by instructing the people in constitutional thinking to moderate their vice of jealousy in order to make room for the modern virtue of responsible states-manship.[10]

The first listing under "responsibility" in the *Oxford English Dictionary* is from *Federalist* 63, which suggests both the modernity and originally American character of this political virtue. Both Federalists and Anti-Federalists used the term quite frequently; the earliest usage in Hamilton's writings is in a letter he wrote in 1780.[11] The Anti-Federalists who opposed the Constitution of 1787 tended to understand responsibility in terms of responsiveness to constituents. For them, the most responsible institutions were those closest to the people: the state legislatures or an annually elected Congress.[12] The Federalists, however, tended to use responsibility in the sense of devotion to one's work or duty. Responsible statesmen are obliged to obey the Roman maxim to preserve the republic from harm, no matter what the price.[13] The problem is that when jealousy leads republicans to demand an overly respon-sive government, this passion may make it difficult for government to fulfill its fundamental duties toward those whom it is entrusted to serve.

The Articles of Confederation, which were drafted in the middle of the War for Independence, are a good example of what Hamilton viewed as overly responsive government. To avoid any abuse of power, the Articles did not even provide for an executive or judiciary; they limited Congress to expressly delegated powers; they subjected congressmen to one year terms and rotation; and they left the execution of congressional resolutions up to the states. As General George Washington's principal military aide during the Revolutionary War, Hamilton understood well the crippling effects of the Articles' republican jealousy of power on the effort to secure American inde-pendence. In Hamilton's view, the Articles made it too easy for elected leaders to escape responsibility for making tough decisions. Whenever Washington warned that the army was starving, freezing, ill-clad, ill-equipped, plagued by desertion, or about to suffer defeat, congressmen could plausibly say that this was not their fault, but the fault of the Articles, or of the states, which often refused to fulfill their responsibility to execute congressional requisitions for money, men, and munitions. Americans could not secure their liberty, however, unless they could win the war.[14]

The result of Hamilton's wartime frustration with an irresponsible Congress was *The Federalist,* his own political primer for a free American people. Hamilton organized this enormous project, selected his coauthors, designed the structure of the book, and wrote most of the essays. As an advocate of the proposed Constitution, he sought—so far as was as possible in a free government—to eliminate excuses for political irresponsibility and to enable the firm exercise of political judgment. The necessary and proper clause of the Constitution would allow the national government to assume the responsibility of governing, even if there were no expressly delegated powers authorizing such responsibility. Far from enabling legislative tyranny, however, Hamilton insisted that power is exercised most responsibly if the executive and judiciary are independent of the legislature and the populist breezes that sometime blow it to extremes. What was needed was a system that would allow for political deliberation and judgment, for checks on the effects of political passion or self-interested behavior, and above all for vigor and energy in carrying out every responsibility assigned to the national government under the Constitution. Hamilton therefore insisted that judges and executives be selected by channels separate from the legislature and that there be lengthy terms for these positions as well as for senators. Arguing that abrogation of responsibility was more easily detected and addressed when one man bore personal responsibility for the execution of government, he also called for unity in the executive.[15]

Hamilton's constitutional defense of responsibility risked a different kind of extremism than Jefferson's efforts to inculcate vigilance. The problem with responsible statesmen is that they may assume responsibility for running everything. The more successful a government is at providing for the public good, the more the people may be willing to let it do so without its even asking their opinion. Responsibility, therefore, could be dangerous to vigilance, just as jealousy could be dangerous to responsibility. Pushed to an extreme, Hamiltonian responsibility itself might become a vice tending toward the "soft despotism" of the administrative state foreseen by Tocqueville and sometimes practiced by presidents who pretend to serve Jeffersonian ends by Hamiltonian means.[16]

The tension between Jeffersonian vigilance and Hamiltonian responsibility in a free nation was one of the central issues in the ratification debates, but it would be an oversimplification to say that Jefferson rejected the need for responsibility and Hamilton the requirement of vigilance. In *Federalist* 8, for example, Hamilton claimed that war is the greatest threat to the spirit of vigilant citizens. War, Thucydides said, is a "harsh teacher," because it reveals to us just how prone citizens are to sacrifice liberty to self-preservation. Echoing this concern, Hamilton observed that to be "more safe" in time of war citizens gradually become willing to be "less free." To avoid that danger, Hamilton called for the kind of energetic government that could unite Americans and keep war far away from American soil through the projection of naval power. With a firm union and a strong navy, Americans would not need a large army, and citizens consequently would not be "habituated" to submit to the military. Rather, Americans would view the military in a "spirit of jealous acquiescence in a necessary evil" and would "stand ready to resist it" if it appeared to be a danger to their rights. By supplying the national government the means required to take responsibility for American national security, Hamilton sought to prevent Americans from acquiring habits of mind and a spirit inimical to free government. Free government, Hamilton held, is founded not in jealousy, but in confidence, understood as security from foreign and domestic violence. The guarantee of such security is the fundamental objective of civil society, the only society that can produce and sustain the vigilant citizens required to prevent energy from degenerating into tyranny.[17]

Just as Hamilton acknowledged the need for vigilance, as president Jefferson was not hesitant to exercise political responsibility. In acquiring Louisiana, for example, Jefferson self-consciously violated his doctrine of jealously strict construction of the Constitution. Napoleon had made him an offer he believed no responsible statesman could refuse, so he asserted the prerogative to grab the offer while passing to Congress the responsibility of ratifying the treaty and thereby violating strict construction. In an interesting reversal of roles, citizen Hamilton defended a Federalist editor, Harry Croswell, against charges that he had seditiously libeled President Jefferson. His defense effectively put the president on trial in the court of public opinion and promoted the standard of truth as a defense in seditious libel cases. Hamilton also pleaded that ordinary citizens, not judges, be permitted to determine both the law and the facts in such cases, thus outflanking one of his favorite political institutions, the judiciary, with—of all things—an appeal to local government. Without these means of allowing vigilant citizens to control arrogant wolves in power, Hamilton proclaimed, "you must forever remain ignorant of what your rulers do. I never can think this ought to be. . . . My soul has ever abhorred the thought that a free man may not speak the truth."[18]

Despite this sometime reversal of roles, occasioned largely by political circumstances, Jefferson generally served as a primary spokesperson for vigilance and Hamilton for responsibility. From a theoretical perspective, the tension between Hamiltonian responsibility and Jeffersonian vigilance reflects two necessary sides of modern liberal thought, as exemplified above all in the work of John Locke. On the one hand, Locke's best defense against rebellion by the king against the constitution was vigilance among the citizens. In particular, Locke sought to inculcate vigilance against acts of prerogative—that is, executive acts without legal authority, and sometimes even contrary to law, that may be justified in the name of the public good. Even when justified, such acts of prerogative, Locke held, were dangerous for the precedents they set, including the willingness of the people to accept them. On the other hand, Locke understood that the law cannot anticipate all political problems, that sometimes political responsibility requires sacrificing at least the letter of a constitution to the higher law of societal preservation. Who shall judge whether a statesman has acted responsibly in exceeding his written authority? Locke's answer was that the people shall be judge, but to judge well they need good judgment. Locke's dilemma thus persists in the American understanding that there is a time for Jeffersonian vigilance and a time for Hamiltonian responsibility.[19]

The quarrel between Hamilton and Jefferson was between virtue and virtue, not virtue and vice. Alas, when pushed to extremes, each of these political virtues becomes a vice. Our two major parties are descendants of the great quarrel between Hamilton and Jefferson, and even today each combines a bit of both statesmen. Party competition teaches both parties to practice vigilance in opposition and responsibility in power. Thus, without ever intending it, the most important contributions of Hamilton and Jefferson to American political education may have been our party system, which is our means of inculcating their virtues and moderating their vices.

In our present circumstances, recognizing that you can have too much of a good thing may be the key to political sanity. The problem with today's heirs to Jefferson, worried about the fate of privacy and civil liberties under the Patriot Act, for example, is not that their vigilance is bad, but that their jealousy is potentially dangerous if it prevents the collection and sharing of useful intelligence about enemies who mean our country incalculable harm. The problem with today's heirs to Hamilton, more fearful of acting too late than too early to prevent another 9/11, is not that their sense of responsibility is mistaken, but rather that it may lead them to forget that the means by which Americans have traditionally secured their liberty, including requirements for warrants prior to searches, are indeed ends in themselves. Hence, one might well conclude that to avoid destroying what they are trying to save, the Jeffersonians need to open up to the virtue of responsibility and the Hamiltonians to vigilance.

Partisan conflict is necessary to achieve a balance between responsibility and vigilance, but it is also one of the most brutal and wasteful means of obtaining it. In practice, we are unlikely to transcend the political extremism born of the current war until the shoe is on the other foot, with the old party of opposition assuming the responsibilities of power and the old party of power assuming the customary role of vigilant watchdog. In the meantime, sober citizens and statesmen would do best not to follow Jefferson and Hamilton in their mutual demonization. We are more likely to achieve lasting and valuable results by beginning from a position that respects the genuine political virtues being defended by each party. The nature of political partisanship makes such mutual respect exceedingly difficult and often unlikely, especially in time of war, but it is the worthy ideal towards which the alternative political educations in statesmanship and citizenship proposed by Hamilton and Jefferson consistently point us.

John Adams, John Taylor of Caroline, and the Debate about Republican Government

ADAM L. TATE

"Mankind do not love to read any thing upon any theory of government," complained John Adams to Virginia republican theorist John Taylor of Caroline in 1814.[1] Such was the condition, he lamented, of America's republican society. Although Adams had expended much effort developing a political theory of the American founding, his published works had been largely either misunderstood or forgotten. In 1813, however, John Taylor had sent Adams a copy of his lengthy *Inquiry into the Principles and Policy of the Government of the United States* (1814), an attack on Adams's *Defence of the Constitutions of Government of the United States of America* (1787–1788). In September 1813, John Adams wrote to Thomas Jefferson that he had received a package "without Post Mark, without Letter, without name date or place." Adams remarked that the package contained "a printed Copy of Eighty or Ninety Pages" of the first chapter of the *Inquiry*, titled "Aristocracy." He told Jefferson that the writing led him to consider one man as its author, John Taylor. Taylor later sent Adams the rest of the *Inquiry*, confirming his authorship of the work. By March 1814, Adams began a remarkable correspondence with Taylor to clear up what he saw as Taylor's misunderstandings of his thought. This correspondence sheds light on fundamental tensions in American political theory.[2]

Adams and Taylor were kindred spirits in many ways: both were obsessed with the republican experiment in the United States, both believed that the legacy of the American Revolution had suffered greatly by the early nineteenth century, and both thought and wrote extensively about government and history. Moreover, both brought their unique intellectual and cultural makeup to the debate, Adams the secularized Yankee Puritan, and Taylor the enlightened Virginia slaveholder.

Many scholars have commented on the Adams-Taylor correspondence, focusing mostly on Adams's contributions. A few historians have paid attention to the arguments Taylor made in the *Inquiry* against Adams's political ideas in order to place the correspondence in context.[3] More, however, can be gleaned from the rich exchange of ideas between Adams and Taylor and the context of their careers than the scholarly literature has yet revealed. At the bottom of the Adams-Taylor discussions about the nature of aristocracies and the differences between a mixed regime and the separation of powers lay a broader question of the proper relationship between government and society. Whereas Adams believed government and society to be linked, Taylor sought to keep them separate as a necessary condition for liberty.

The Adams-Taylor debate echoed discussions among American republicans in the 1780s and must be interpreted in light of these earlier concerns. Furthermore, by the time of their correspondence, both men were effectively political outsiders. Adams's retirement, the renewal of his correspondence with Jefferson, and his ardent desire to defend his reputation shaped his discussion with Taylor. Taylor had likewise reached the end of his active political engagement. After a promising beginning to his political career as a pamphleteer for the Jeffersonian opposition, Taylor had been attacked by many Republicans for his association with the Tertium Quids, a movement of anti-administration Republicans who believed Jefferson and Madison had betrayed their principles. As such, both men entered the debate with strong intellectual commitments as well as with heavy political and personal baggage they perhaps sought to lighten.

During the Revolution, all American patriots wanted a republican form of government, but agreement about what that government should look like and how much power it should possess was difficult to achieve. Americans split into two broad ideological camps between 1776 and 1786, dubbed by historian Forrest McDonald as "nationalists" and "republicans."[4] At the heart of the debate between these two contingents was the important question: "Did human beings find freedom in order, or order in freedom?"[5]

The nationalists tended to argue that human beings were too selfish and corrupt to establish a just order in society. An outside force, preferably government, had to establish order to prevent corrupt people from killing each other amid a state of anarchy. People needed strong government. As George Washington, an ardent nationalist, wrote to John Jay in 1786: "Experience has taught us, that men will not adopt and carry into execution measures the best calculated for their own good, without the intervention of a coercive power. I do not conceive we can exist long as a nation without having lodged some where a power, which will pervade the whole Union in as energetic a manner, as the authority of the State Governments extends over the several States."[6] Government established liberty by creating order. While nationalists such as Alexander Hamilton recognized that even government officials tended toward corruption, they doubted that relying on popular virtue would prevent tyranny. Hamilton and others thus believed that a stronger national constitution could serve as a means of tying the interests of individuals to serving the public order.[7]

Republicans agreed with the nationalists concerning the human propensity to abuse power, but they believed that human beings, if left to themselves, would create systems of order to protect their lives, liberty, and property. As Thomas Jefferson put it in the Declaration of Independence, "That to secure these rights, Governments are instituted among Men, deriving their just powers from the consent of the governed."[8] Men independently formed systems of order beneficial to themselves, Republicans believed. They did not need an order imposed on them. Implicit in this view was a distrust of strong central government. As the arch-republican Richard Henry Lee of Virginia put it, "I think Sir that the first maxim of a man who loves liberty should be, never to grant to Rulers an atom of power that is not most clearly & indispensably necessary for the safety and well being of Society."[9] Republicans placed their hopes for liberty in smaller, local governments and supported the Articles of Confederation because of its explicit recognition that "each state retains its sovereignty, freedom and independence, and every Power, Jurisdiction and right, which is not by this confederation expressly delegated to the United States, in Congress assembled."[10]

The rancor of the political debate was exacerbated by the fact that nationalists and republicans suspected each other of subverting liberty at a time when liberty was most in need of succor. Nationalists believed that republicans were silly ideologues whose political prescriptions were at best naïvely foolish or at worst subversive. Sometimes they portrayed the republicans as self-interested politicians who used political rhetoric to protect their local interests at the expense of the national common good. Republicans, nationalists charged, hampered good government and failed to see that state governments abused power and threatened liberty just as much as more centralized governments did. In republican rhetoric, on the other hand, nationalists were secret monarchists who were not comfortable with government by consent. Nationalists, republicans charged, had distorted the problems of the Confederation in order to gain power and control others. To republicans, the constitutional reforms nationalists proposed would make liberty less secure by increasing the opportunities for corrupt men to exercise power over others.

In the context of this basic political division, Taylor was a republican and Adams a nationalist. Taylor believed that American political thinkers wisely had sought to limit government by constitutionally dividing power. Such an arrangement was necessary because men were tempted to use power to satisfy their "ambition and cupidity." As he wrote to James Monroe in 1798, "Is it not unreasonable, not to say unnatural, to expect that men, thus exposed to temptations which have almost universally proved irresistible, should heroically resist them, and confine their endeavors to the pure object of public good?" For a republican like Taylor, human beings could not be trusted with consolidated power. Constitutional structures must keep power confined and dispersed so that human beings could enjoy liberty.[11] Adams, too, distrusted consolidated power and human nature's ability to handle power justly, but Adams was more confident that wise politicians could create a constitutional structure that balanced the different orders in society and thus preserved free government. A balanced constitutional structure would allow men to pursue their own interests in ways that did not damage the republic. Adams did not, however, support the Jeffersonian doctrine of states' rights. He wrote that "imperium in imperio is a solecism, a contradiction in terms." The United States was "not a confederation of independent Republicks" but a "monarchical republic."[12] Thus, while both Taylor and Adams perceived the weaknesses in human nature and the tendency of men to abuse power, they adopted different solutions to the problem of the fragility of republics and came to stand on different sides of the American ideological divide.

John Adams contributed mightily to American independence as a writer, activist, congressman, and diplomat, but his most important—and controversial—writings appeared between 1787 and 1791. He solidified his reputation as a serious political theorist with the publication of his sprawling three-volume work, *A Defence of the Constitutions of Government of the United States of America.* Events both in Europe and in the United States prompted him to pen the treatise, but almost from its publication Adams believed his work to have been misunderstood and misinterpreted.

Adams wrote the *Defence* partially as an answer to those French philosophes who criticized the new state constitutions in the United States. The French reformer Turgot wrote a letter, published in 1784, attacking the new constitutions for aping English forms and refraining from centralizing government into one legislative center. Turgot and other philosophes had preferred the 1776 Pennsylvania constitution, publicized in France by Benjamin Franklin, for its unicameral legislature. Adams believed that their criticisms were naïve, uninformed, and wrongheaded. He also wrote the *Defence* in response to news of Shays's Rebellion in Massachusetts. He began writing in October 1786 and published the first volume in January 1787. Volume two followed in the summer of 1787, and the third appeared in December 1787. The major theme of the *Defence* was that factions and parties, inevitable features in all polities, could either be controlled "by a monarchy and standing army or by a balance in the constitution." Adams maintained, "Where the people have a voice and there is no balance, there will be everlasting fluctuations, revolutions, and horrors, until a standing army with a general at its head commands the peace, or the necessity of an equilibrium is made to appear to all and is adopted by all."[13] He believed that an equilibrium must be found among the one, the few, and the many. A strong executive would balance the aristocratic few and the democratic many within the legislative branch. Adams published his works, as C. Bradley Thompson has noted, for the "education of the lawgiver," hoping that those who would design constitutions in the future would pay close attention to the idea of balance. He used the history of dozens of republics in the *Defence* to uncover the truth about human nature, society, and the proper way for free people to handle power.[14]

Adams published his *Discourses on Davila,* what he termed "the fourth volume of the *Defence,*" as a series of newspaper essays in the *Gazette of the United States* in 1790 and 1791.[15] John Patrick Diggins has called the *Discourses* a treatise in "social psychology," an apt description for a work that explored the reasons why aristocracies inevitably formed in all human societies.[16] Adams wrote the book in response to the meeting of the French Constituent Assembly in 1789 and to the new partisan bickering that was erupting in America.

The *Discourses* is a running commentary on Enrico Caterino Davila's *History of the Civil Wars of France*. Adams was viciously criticized by Americans who believed that he desired in imitation of Great Britain a hereditary aristocracy for the United States. He wanted no such thing, but his sometimes murky writing left him open to such attacks. For the rest of his life, Adams would have to defend himself against charges that he had forsaken republicanism for monarchy. The Jeffersonian opposition successfully pinned such an image on Adams during his presidential administration, allowing Jefferson to capture the presidency in his "Revolution of 1800."[17]

When Adams retired to Quincy in 1801 following his tumultuous presidency, he initially did not give much thought to the *Defence* and *Discourses on Davila*. Instead, he spent his retirement working on his farm and enjoying his family. He kept up with politics mostly through a few close correspondents and through his son, John Quincy, who had begun his political career. In 1806, however, Adams's friend Mercy Otis Warren jostled him back to the realm of political theory. Adams bristled at the attack made upon him in Warren's *History of the Rise, Progress, and Termination of the American Revolution*. Warren claimed that Adams had lost his republicanism while serving as a diplomat in England. She wrote that "unfortunately for himself and his country, he became so enamoured with the British constitution, and the government, manners, and laws of the nation, that a partiality for monarchy appeared, which was inconsistent with his former professions of republicanism." Her comments were preceded by a disclaimer that Adams surely despised: "Mr. Adams was undoubtedly a statesman of penetration and ability; but his prejudices and his passions were sometimes too strong for his sagacity and judgment."[18] A furious Adams wrote several indignant letters to Warren challenging her to prove her claims against him. Warren eventually broke off the correspondence. Historian John Ferling believes that the Warren episode convinced Adams that he needed to salvage his reputation from the slanderous attacks made against him. Adams afterwards published weekly newspaper essays for three years in the *Boston Patriot*. In these essays he defended his career.[19]

After he and Jefferson resumed their correspondence in January 1812, Adams engaged in a wide-ranging defense of his political thought. Ferling remarks that "Jefferson became the means whereby Adams's self-dignity could be restored."[20] Adams acknowledged his aggressive self-defense in a July 15, 1813, letter to Jefferson: "Never mind it, my dear Sir, if I write four Letters to your one; your one is worth more than my four."[21] By renewing the old debates of the 1780s, Adams sought to cement in Jefferson's mind his contributions to American political theory and to settle old scores. He used as evidence to support his positions the historical example of the French Revolution, which had ended, as Adams had predicted it would, in tyranny. By 1814, when he began his debate with John Taylor, who like Warren accused him of harboring monarchical tendencies, Adams had been engaged actively in defending his career, reputation, and thought for eight years. Despite the fact that Adams was no longer active in politics, he brought to the discussion an urgency and intensity that Taylor undoubtedly admired.

John Taylor of Caroline supported the Republican opposition in the 1790s as a pamphleteer and harsh critic of the Hamiltonian financial plan. Having served in the American Revolution and in the Virginia legislature, he knew much about politics and readily adopted a states' rights interpretation of the Constitution. Taylor encountered John Adams's *Defence* early in the 1790s and criticized it harshly in his correspondence. In a 1796 letter to Daniel Carroll Brent, Taylor recounted a conversation he had had with Adams in 1794. The men discussed the possibility of France adopting "a democratic republican government." Adams apparently insisted that the "ignorance, vices and corruptions of Europe" prevented such a government from being established successfully. The conversation drifted to the political system of the United States and whether or not the country could retain its republican system. Taylor pointed out that "the greater degree of virtue existing here, from the circumstances of our being a young country would . . . enable us to go on some time longer as a popular government." Adams's rejoinder, Taylor recounted, was "that he expected or wished, to live to hear Mr. Giles & myself acknowledge, that no government could long exist, or that no people could be happy, without an hereditary first magistrate, and an hereditary senate, or a senate for life." To Taylor, such an opinion was political heresy.[22]

Taylor's republican opinions extended to his political activities. In 1798 and 1799, Taylor worked with Thomas Jefferson and James Madison to oppose the Alien and Sedition Acts. He introduced Madison's Virginia Resolutions in the Virginia legislature and defended them vigorously. He argued in public and private that Federalist rule revealed that too many Americans misunderstood the principles of republican government. For example, he told James Monroe that the opposition leadership was "not entirely right in directing your efforts toward a change of men, rather than a change of principles." A "change of men," he continued, "might operate temporary public benefits, but they would certainly be transient and constitutional error will still ultimately prevail." Working to unseat the Federalists, however, "has its merit, as a little sunshine is better than none." Repeating the same points to Jefferson a few months later, Taylor asked: "Did the British people ever gain by a change in ministry? . . . A southern aristocracy oppressing the northern states, would be as detestable as a northern domineering over the southern states." Taylor did not question the patriotism of the Federalists nor did he demonize them. He attributed their errors to their ideas, not to their personal motivations. This equanimable perspective would allow him to engage Adams in 1814 on an intellectual rather than on a personal level, and it would make possible a sober discussion of political principles.[23]

After the "Revolution of 1800," Taylor defended the Jefferson administration but eventually drifted from the mainstream of the party. He played a role in advising Republican congressional leaders on how to attack the Federalist judiciary. In 1803, he served one year as a United States senator. He also penned a constitutional defense of the Louisiana Purchase in response to Federalist opposition. While not going so far as to support publicly John Randolph's attacks on the administration, Taylor's sympathies lay with that Tertium Quid. In 1808, Taylor backed the effort in Virginia to nominate James Monroe as the Republican presidential candidate. Taylor and other Old Republicans had come to see James Madison as a dangerous politician who would lead the country further away from republican principles. After a contentious battle in Virginia, Madison's supporters triumphed and made him the Republican candidate in the presidential election. Madison's contingent then took their revenge on those who had supported Monroe's candidacy. Thomas Ritchie, editor of the *Richmond Enquirer,* attacked John Taylor in a series of published letters in February 1809. Much of the attack was personal in nature and included a characterization of Taylor's pamphlets in the 1790s as "confused perplexities."[24] Taylor offered a vigorous rebuttal to Ritchie's attacks, but he now found himself, along with John Randolph, as a political pariah among mainstream Virginia Republicans.

Marginalized, Taylor turned to publishing the *Inquiry* in order to explain his principles. He wrote to Monroe in November 1809, "My book! Yes, I have written one, so blotted and interlined by keeping onwards ten years in fits and starts." He noted that the book was "an answer to John Adams's book, and an antidote against sliding into the English policy," a road he feared the Republicans were now traveling. Taylor remarked: "That both the Adams's are monarchists, I never doubted. Whether monarchists, like pagans, can be converted by benefices, is a problem the solution of which I always feared Mr. Madison would attempt." He told Monroe that he had hoped to send the *Inquiry* to Jefferson before it went to press, but "there I am wrecked," due to Jefferson receiving false information about Taylor's loyalty.[25] Jefferson's recent hostility to Taylor was real. When Adams informed Jefferson in 1813 that he had received the *Inquiry* in the mail, Jefferson noted that if indeed Taylor was the author, Adams would know by the "quaint, mystical and hyperbolical ideas, involved in affected, new-fangled and pedantic terms, which stamp his writings." Jefferson told Adams again in 1814 that Taylor's work contained "flimsy theories."[26] When Taylor described the *Inquiry* in his introduction to the book as "letters from the dead," he was describing his moribund status as a Virginia Republican.

Adams and Taylor, then, engaged in their correspondence as men with little political influence. They had been left behind by the course of party politics and changing political ideas. In this way, at least, they were kindred spirits. Neither man truly believed that his arguments might have practical application anytime soon. Each, however, offered his position as the true description of the American polity and the only solution to the problems of republican government.

During the years 1814 and 1815, Adams sent thirty-two letters to Taylor concerning political theory. Scholars have long admired these letters for presenting a concise, direct explanation of Adams's thoughts on aristocracy and constitutionalism. After receiving Taylor's *Inquiry* in 1813, Adams had reread his *Discourses on Davila* and sent Taylor a copy of the work.[27] Adams stressed in his letters to Taylor the main argument of the *Discourses* that aristocracies inevitably formed in all societies. Adams had already discussed the concept of aristocracy at length in his correspondence with Jefferson in September and November of 1813, after reading Taylor's chapter "Aristocracy." Thus, Taylor's *Inquiry* influenced Adams's letters to Jefferson during this time. As with his correspondence with Jefferson, Adams sent many more letters to Taylor than he received, and the combative tone of Adams's letters to the two Virginia Republicans reveals that he was trying to settle old scores against the two men who had vigorously opposed his presidential administration. Taylor notified Adams that he supposed that the steady stream of letters were "intended as a resource for correcting the errors" of the *Inquiry* for future editions, and thus he would not respond.[28] The correspondence can therefore be seen in part as primarily a conversation among texts—the *Inquiry,* the *Defence,* and the *Discourses*—and as a lecture from Adams rather than as a conversation between two people. Nevertheless, the only parts of the *Inquiry* Adams acknowledged having read were the introduction and the first chapter. In fact, in a later letter to Taylor, Adams admitted that he had set the *Inquiry* aside and could not get back to reading it.[29] Thus, in referring to Adams's side of the argument with Taylor, the historian must assume that Adams had not read or intellectually engaged the *Inquiry* as a whole.

At the root of Adams's disagreement with Taylor lay the Enlightenment concept of nature. The sociologist Robert Nisbet noted that eighteenth-century philosophers tried "to demonstrate the provisions in nature—the nature of man and the nature of society—by which civilization had developed from primitive origins to its existing stage" so that they could direct the progress of society. These philosophers argued that in order to comprehend the natural order, one first had to "cut through the morass of customs, superstitions, traditions, and prescriptive laws" to get to the "*pristine condition* of a thing." Nature lay hidden by human institutions but could be uncovered through the use of reason. At this juncture, the philosopher appealed to natural history. The history of a thing referred to "the actual, minutely recorded unfolding of something in time." Natural history referred to "the history that we conceive as flowing from" a thing's "very nature, when not deflected or otherwise interfered with." Natural history was didactic history, in which one developed a view of nature through a combination of philosophic reasoning and reflection on the actual past. For enlightened intellectuals of the eighteenth century, it followed that the knowledge and restoration of nature was a desired end that would better the human condition. Ultimately, Adams and Taylor came to different conclusions about the nature of society, and this drove them to diverging political principles.[30]

Adams set out to explore the nature of man and society in his political writings. He wished to comprehend the extent to which political thought and practice "were founded on nature, or created by fancy." Adams told Taylor that his maxim was to "study government as you do astronomy, by facts, observations, and experiments; not by the dogmas of lying priests or knavish politicians."[31] To do this, Adams selected numerous historical examples in order to test his theories and view of nature. History served as the "facts of nature . . . the material reality that the political scientist must take as the object of his study." Influenced by Machiavelli, Adams believed that the political theorist had to understand man as he is, not as he should be. Thus, uncovering human nature as it expressed itself historically became the critical task of the political thinker. Adams sought to do this through a combination of introspection and the observance of human behavior, both in the present and in history. He told Taylor that the history of various nations and peoples, both ancient and modern, were "all among my authorities."[32]

Adams viewed human beings as weak but not as inherently wicked or depraved. He told Taylor that "men are free, moral, and accountable agents" and share "moral equality." Men, according to Adams, were primarily creatures of passion. He described man as "that gaping, timid animal" who "dares not read or think." Men found themselves surrounded by the "prejudices, passions, habits, associations, and interests of his fellow-creatures." Passion, not reason, formed the basis of human society. Adams held that because men were social by nature, the passions of each individual influenced the lives of others. He wrote in *Discourses on Davila:* "As nature intended them [men] for society, she has furnished them with passions, appetites, and propensities, as well as a variety of faculties, calculated both for their individual enjoyment, and to render them useful to each other in their social connections. There is none among them more essential or remarkable, than the *passion for distinction.*"[33]

The passion for distinction was not necessarily bad. Adams believed that "nature . . . has kindly added to benevolence, the desire of reputation, in order to make us good members of society." As men pursued good reputations, they confronted the laws of nature that rewarded "selfish activities" with "life and health" and punished "negligence and indolence" with "want, disease, and death." Nature itself directed men to channel their passions for good. Adams remarked in the *Defence* that "human nature is querulous and discontented wherever it appears." By constantly grasping for distinctions, human passions were never at a state of rest. This may be the natural condition of man, but it presented real dangers because it subjected others to the restless ambition of weak men. Men needed the restraint of government in order to enjoy liberty and peace. Nature, Adams believed, taught this lesson.[34]

Adams used his conception of human nature to demonstrate to Taylor the inevitability of aristocracy. Invoking the Enlightenment concept of nature,

Adams told Taylor, "Inequalities are part of the natural history of man." This point is critical to understanding Adams's view of aristocracy. He acknowledged Taylor's distinction between a "natural aristocracy" ("those superiorities of influence in society which grow out of the constitution of human nature") and an "artificial aristocracy" ("those inequalities of weight and superiorities of influence which are created and established by civil laws"), but he insisted that an aristocracy simply meant "all those men" who could command "more than an average of votes." For Adams, the natural history of man revealed that aristocracies, however defined, were ubiquitous. He put it even more bluntly to Taylor:

> Once for all, I give you notice, that whenever I use the word *aristocrat*, I mean a citizen who can command or govern two votes or more in society, whether by his virtues, his talents, his learning, his loquacity, his taciturnity, his frankness, his reserve, his face, figure, eloquence, grace, air, attitude, movements, wealth, birth, art, address, intrigue, good fellowship, drunkenness, debauchery, fraud, perjury, violence, treachery, pyrrhonism, deism, or atheism; for by every one of these instruments have votes been obtained and will be obtained.

Aristocracy would exist, Adams explained, "independent of all . . . artificial regulations, as really and as efficaciously as with them." Aristocracy was simply natural; that is, it flowed from human nature.[35]

Adams attempted to convince Taylor that the inevitability of aristocracy inextricably linked society and government. He maintained that "birth is naturally and necessarily and inevitably so connected and blended with property, fame, power, education . . . &c. that it is often impossible . . . to separate them." Thus, if two sons were born with equal abilities, one to Thomas Jefferson and the other to a common man, "which will meet with most favor in the world?" Adams believed that the answer was clear. He pointed out that Taylor's own marriage to the daughter of the prominent North Carolina politician John Penn and his status as a planter made him an aristocrat in Virginia. Adams noted that "birth confers no right on one more than another" but "unavoidably produces more influence in society." Thus, "the imagination . . . of a government . . . in which every man and every woman shall have an equal weight in society, is a chimera." Taylor must become a "downright leveler" if his system of equality was to work, for he would have to undo what nature had established. Even then, Adams noted, a perfectly equal society would last but a moment, as aristocracies would again form quickly. Nature, Adams assured Taylor, showed that social distinctions, formed on any basis, influenced the political order. For Adams, history proved that "those nations had been the happiest" that instituted a properly balanced government to control the passions of men. Society and government could not be separated. Nature had brought them together.[36]

For his part, Taylor remained skeptical of the use of the concept of nature when applied to politics. He understood that by claiming something was natural, a politician could impose an obligation on those he ruled. Adams had admitted as much by quoting a dictum of Pope's in his seventeenth letter to Taylor: "First follow Nature, and your judgment frame / By her just standard, which is still the same." If nature established a certain form of political rule, then the good politician must establish that form. Thus, Taylor began the *Inquiry* by distinguishing between the "moral" and the "natural" causes of human action. He used "moral" to mean "human agencies, arising from the mind's power of abstraction." He reduced "nature" to the physical world, "the direct and immediate effect of matter, independent of abstraction." Taylor charged that Federalists like Adams believe "that man can ascertain his own moral capacity" and then deduce "consequences from this postulate, and erects thereon schemes of government—right, say they, because natural." Taylor asserted that "those who affirm the doctrine, have never been able to agree upon this natural form of government," a major difficulty if indeed nature recommends a certain form. Human nature "has been perpetually escaping from all forms," he charged. Government was not natural but rather was "capable of unascertained modification and improvement from moral causes." Taylor attempted to shatter Adams's certainty that his preferred political forms were objectively best. He argued that Adams used "natural" to denote recurring human choices. Taylor thus charged that Adams's thought relied on the concept of fate. For Adams, men have always performed certain actions, and therefore they naturally must repeat those same actions. Taylor called this Adams's "political predestination." He insisted that "whenever it is impossible to prove a principle, which is necessary to support a system, a reference to an inevitable power, calling it God or nature, is preferable to reasoning: because every such principle is more likely to be exploded, than established by reasoning." The appeal to nature was the tyrant's way of escaping reason.[37]

Taylor and Adams held similar views of human nature, but Taylor was more optimistic that human beings could use knowledge to devise new political arrangements. Taylor thought that human nature was not completely depraved but that it was composed of good and evil qualities contending for domination. History revealed that human beings often succumbed to weakness.[38] Man's physical nature was "always the same," but man's moral nature could progress. That is, knowledge of good and evil could cause men to reshape their social institutions according to good principles. In looking at history, Taylor noted the great progress that had been made from states ruled by "Kings, nobles" and "priests" to the United States, with its founding principles of self-government and the division of power. Moral progress was not inevitable, however. Taylor did not perceive history as a linear progression from slavery to freedom. While he believed that some progress was indeed possible, men were always tempted to substitute passion for reason and to accept temporary gratification in place of the public good. In some sense, moral progress was based on "a suppression of personal appetites, for the sake of advancing the public good."[39] Passionate men would not always make the correct moral choices.

Taylor's view of nature revealed itself in his understanding of aristocracy. Unlike Adams, who saw aristocracies as natural, Taylor charged that "aristocracies, both ancient and modern, have been variable and artificial; that they have all proceeded from moral, not from natural causes; and that they are evitable and not inevitable." He pointed to several historical causes of aristocracy: "superior knowledge and ability, virtue, landed wealth, and paper wealth." All, he contended, can be "created, destroyed and modified by human power," which disproves that they are "natural and inevitable" causes of aristocracy. Taylor argued that the expansion of knowledge, thanks in large part to the printing press, demystified and democratized knowledge. Virtue likewise fluctuated in the population, thus making it impossible to select the most virtuous members of a society and privilege them with a special place in government. Virtue was too easily lost for society to profit by such a permanent political arrangement. "Until knowledge and virtue shall become genealogical," he commented, "they cannot be the causes of inheritable aristocracy; and its existence, without the aid of superior knowledge and virtue, is a positive refutation of the idea, that nature creates aristocracy with these tools." In similar fashion, Taylor maintained that the power of landed wealth can easily be lessened by alienation, and paper wealth by "inhibitions upon monopoly and incorporation." In fact, he asserted that the democratization of knowledge allowed reformers to assail the forms of wealth that buttressed aristocracies.

Taylor trusted reason and reform. He realized that what men make, they can unmake. Taylor used reason to examine the underlying structures of government and society in order to bring them into conformity with good, rational, moral principles.[40]

Whereas Adams used history to unveil nature, Taylor explored history to expose the artificial characteristics of political and social institutions. He thought that there had been three stages of aristocracy in Western history. The "aristocracy of the first age," that of the classical world, had been "created and supported by superstition." Progress of human knowledge had been sufficient to put to rest the superstitions that led people to view certain others as a privileged order set apart by the gods. The "aristocracy of the second age," that of the medieval world, had been formed through warfare and the feudal system. The second aristocracy, like the first, had been hereditary and perpetuated fraudulent ideas. The feudal aristocracy "starved commerce" because it "tended to discourage industry, by which commerce is supplied." The result was a general poverty and almost continuous warfare. The feudal aristocracy did exhibit the virtues of "generosity, honour and bravery," which were useful in "softening barbarism into civilization," but feudalism destroyed property rights, a necessary component of a free society.[41]

The rise of commerce dispersed the feudal aristocracy. The French Revolution, noted Taylor, had finished off the old order in France, while Walpole's financial revolution had doomed the lingering British feudal aristocracy. To explain why aristocracy had not disappeared, Taylor posited that a new fraud, not based on religious myth or war but on "paper and patronage," had created "the aristocracy of the third or present age." The aristocracy of paper and patronage was, by far, the worst aristocracy in history. Unlike previous aristocracies, the aristocracy of paper and patronage corrupted whole nations by allying with governments and oppressing the people. Taylor concluded that history revealed the artificial character of aristocracies. A careful thinker could examine the historical record to discover the specific reasons an aristocracy arose. There was nothing mysterious about the process. "A monopoly by a few," he summarized, "of renown, talents or wealth, may be reproduced, by superstition, conquest or fraud," but not by nature.[42]

Adams believed that society and government could not be separated, but Taylor's views of aristocracy convinced him otherwise. Taylor feared that the aristocracy of paper and patronage was the most dangerous aristocratic form because it cloaked itself in patriotism and the language of property rights while being kept in existence by government privilege. In other words, governments created the new aristocracy that ravaged modern societies. In England, he argued, the "English peerage" became "the creature of patronage, and the subject of paper." "The claims it once possessed to superior knowledge, virtue, wealth and independence," Taylor noted, "have long since immolated at the shrines of printing, alienation and executive power." The English government, not nature, created the aristocracy of paper and patronage, thus both destroying the aristocracy of the second age and threatening the newly won liberty at the same time.[43]

Taylor believed that the English enmeshing of government and society perpetuated this fraud, but the United States offered a better arrangement, one that instilled hope of reform. In the preface to the *Inquiry* he charged, "By the British policy, the nation and the government is considered as one, and the passive obedience denied to the king conceded to the government, whence it alters its form and its principles, without any other concurrence than that of its parts; whereas, by ours, the nation and the government are considered as distinct, and a claim of passive obedience by the latter, would of course be equivalent to the same claim by a British king." Under the British model, one must obey government because it is a function of social authority. Under the American model, government is separate from social authority and commands only limited obedience and respect. For Taylor, the American model allowed the people more control over government and offered recourse when government tried to meddle in social affairs by establishing aristocracies. The British had no such arrangement and thus fell into political corruption. Taylor could not understand why Adams wanted to re-create in the United States the British system, a system that he perceived to be virtually impossible for the people to reform. The government had to be kept separate from society as much as possible.[44]

Adams disagreed with Taylor's criticisms of the concept of nature. Taylor had noted that men had not been able to agree on a natural form of government and thus he doubted one existed. Adams responded: "If mankind have not 'agreed upon any form of government,' does it follow that there is no natural form of government? and that all forms are equally natural? It might as well be contended that all are equally good, and that the constitution of the Ottoman Empire is as natural, as free, and as good, as that of the United States." Adams rightly criticized Taylor's error of logic. In his later letters to Taylor, Adams changed his use of the concept of nature. In his twenty-seventh letter, he commented:

> You seem to admit that "aristocracy is created by wealth," but you seem to think it is "artificially," not "naturally," so created. But if superior genius, birth, strength, and activity, naturally obtain superior wealth, and if superior wealth has naturally influence in society, where is the impropriety in calling the influence of wealth "natural"? I am not, however, bigoted to the epithet *natural;* and you may substitute the epithet "actual" in the place of it, if you think it worth while.

By substituting the word "actual" for the word "natural," Adams better revealed his thinking. He retreated from the Enlightenment view of nature as the "pristine condition of a thing." For Adams, history revealed that aristocracies were central to the ways men have actually lived. He admitted to Taylor that many aristocracies were artificial in nature, but he thought the distinction largely irrelevant. Human beings, despite their powers of reason, were generally weak. History showed as much. The wise statesman had to take man as he actually is rather than as he should be. Adams thought that Taylor's logic showed the same flawed thinking of the French revolutionaries, who thought that they could reform and perfect human societies and governments through reason without any acknowledgment that man is both a creature of history and a creature of his volition. Human nature would not change. Men had always formed aristocracies and always would. The actual recurrence of aristocracies did not make aristocracies morally good, but it did inform the wise statesman that a prudent system of government had better account for the existence of aristocracies, which would inevitably develop in his regime no matter how enlightened or progressive it might be. Adams, therefore, told Taylor that the most important question was that of forming constitutions.[45]

After spending a score of pages refuting Adams's view of nature, Taylor indicated that he too thought that constitutionalism was the primary question dividing him from Adams. He noted that while they both "assign political power to the mass of virtue, talents and wealth in a nation," Adams "contends for an aristocracy from a supposition that it must possess this mass, and be the only organ of its will." Taylor maintained that he acknowledged the "sovereignty of these qualities," denied "their residence in a minority compressible into an aristocracy," and contended "for a different organ." The debate concerning the concept of nature was significant to their disagreement, but the greater difference between the men concerned the relationship of government to society. How these nuances played out in their diverging political understandings can be made even clearer by analyzing their discussion in the context of the American revolutionary debate over the mixed regime and the separation of powers.[46]

The idea of the mixed regime is a classical notion traced back to Herodotus and Plato. It was given its greatest explication in Aristotle's *Politics* and in the writings of Polybius. The theory of the mixed regime held that there were "three simple forms of government: monarchy, aristocracy, and democracy." Because each form would degenerate over time, the best regime mixed elements of the three in order to secure a balance.[47] According to this theory of politics, society is divided into different interests, and those interests must be represented and balanced in government to secure justice. Social representation is "a barrier against oppression by one class of another."[48] In such a situation, government and society are intimately linked. Social groups are recognized by government and given official sanction. Politics then becomes the appropriate theater in which to work out social problems. Theories of the mixed regime experienced a resurgence in the Renaissance revival of republicanism and played a role in the development of Anglo-American republican thinking.

The idea of the separation of powers is a modern alternative to the mixed regime. Associated most closely with Montesquieu, the doctrine of the separation of powers became in colonial America a weapon with which to attack colonial royal governments and the British constitution. The separation of powers "divides the functions of government among the parts of government and restricts each of them to the exercise of its appropriate function."[49] Under the theory of the separation of powers, social groups are not given representation in government. Instead, the theory attempts to limit the impact of government on society by reducing the scope of politics. Politics does not become the arena in which to solve social problems but simply a way to exercise the designated functions of government. These functions could be defined specifically in a written constitution. Proponents of the separation of powers presume society to be heterogeneous. Democracy and representation therefore become the ways in which individuals participate in a limited political realm.[50] The clear difference between the theory of the mixed regime and that of the separation of powers is in each's understanding of the relationship of government to society.

After the American Revolution, the theory of the separation of powers and the idea of mixed government were often combined in writing constitutions. As Forrest and Ellen McDonald note concerning the United States Constitution, "The truth is that the Constitution is ambiguous in regard to the relationship between the various branches of government, and the resolution of the ambiguity was left to be worked out by experience."[51] During the 1790s, the Jeffersonian Opposition seized upon the doctrine of the separation of powers and used it as a weapon against the Hamiltonian Federalists, who they accused of creating a mixed regime similar to the British form of ministerial government. Two poles of opinion formed. First, there were those who wanted a strict separation of powers and who did not want to compromise with a system of checks and balances. Second, there were those who accepted some separation of powers but only if they "were combined with checks and balances comparable to those of the British system."[52] M. J. C. Vile has argued that John Taylor represented the extreme of those who wanted the separation of powers, while the political writings of John Adams became "the ideal stalking-horse for those who wished to attack the elements of the theory of mixed and balanced government to be found in the Constitution."[53] While the Adams-Taylor dialogue addressed forms of government and constitutional theory, the relationship between government and society is the most divisive issue in the correspondence. Because Adams and Taylor saw that relationship so differently, it became impossible for them to agree on politics.

In his letters to Taylor, Adams clarified his arguments in the *Defence* regarding the separation of powers and the idea of balance. Adams defended the classification of social divisions into the one, the few, and the many as natural to politics. He told Taylor that "imagination cannot conceive of any government besides those of the one, the few, or the many, of such as are compounded of them, whether complicated with the idea of a balance or not."[54] The theory of mixed government, with its focus on representing social interests, rested on this classification. In the *Discourses,* Adams wrote, "The controversy between the rich and the poor, the laborious and the idle, the learned and the ignorant, distinctions as old as the creation, and as extensive as the globe, distinctions which no art of policy, no degree of virtue or philosophy can ever wholly destroy, will continue, and rivalries will spring out of them." These natural social groups "will be represented in the legislature, and must be balanced, or one will oppress the other."[55]

In light of the need to reconcile these social divisions, Adams explained to Taylor the meaning of the *Defence.* He outlined six major points of his work, focusing on his suspicion of the French desire to centralize the authority of the people into a national legislature. He argued that "the people of Massachusetts, New York, and Maryland were not to blame for instituting governor, councils, (or senates) and houses of representatives" and were "not reprehensible for endeavoring to balance those different powers." He told Taylor that "an equilibrium of those 'different powers' was indispensably necessary to guard and defend the rights, liberties, and happiness of the people against the deleterious, contagious, and pestilential effects of those passions of vanity, pride, ambition, envy, revenge, lust, and cruelty, which domineer more or less in every government that has no BALANCE or an imperfect BALANCE." Assuring Taylor of his patriotism, he maintained that his plan was "not an affected imitation of the English government, so much as an attachment to their old colonial forms, in every one of which there had been three branches" of government. In other words, Adams pointed out that he combined the separation of powers with theories of mixed government. He insisted that the *Defence* had demonstrated through the use of history that "those nations had been the happiest who had separated the legislative from the executive power, the judicial from both, and divided the legislative power itself into three branches, thereby producing a balance between the legislative and executive authority, a balance between the branches of the legislature, and a salutary check upon all these power in the judicial," as had been done in some of the state constitutions. He concluded that he "had nothing to do with despotisms or simple monarchies, unless it were incidentally, and by way of illustration." Adams stressed that he was no monarchist, nor was he trying to establish the English system in America, as Taylor charged.[56]

In his replies to Taylor and in the *Discourses,* Adams demonstrated his reliance on mixed government theory by identifying the instability of simple governments and the necessity of balance in government. He told Taylor that he believed that it was his "duty to show that democracy was as unsteady, equally envious, ambitious, avaricious, vain, proud, cruel, and bloody, as aristocracy or monarchy." The French, and by implication Taylor, had been blinded by their faith in democracy, had ignored nature, and had forgotten the lessons of history. In the *Discourses,* Adams noted that it was "a sacred truth, and as demonstrable as any proposition whatever, that a sovereignty in a single assembly must necessarily, and will certainly be exercised by a majority, as tyrannically as any sovereignty was ever exercised by kings or nobles."[57]

Simple democracy would undoubtedly fail. If a "balance of passions and interests is not scientifically concerted, the present struggle in Europe will be little beneficial to mankind, and produce nothing but another thousand years of feudal fanaticism, under new and strange names."[58] He reminded Taylor that democracies were only practical in extremely small territories, not in large nations like the United States or France. Representative democracy, he insisted, would also need balance, because representation would produce an aristocracy among those in government. There was no escaping nature. He mentioned to Taylor that democracy was no more "pernicious, on the whole, than any" of the other forms of government. But Taylor needed to understand that "absolute power intoxicated alike despots, monarchs, aristocrats, and democrats, and Jacobins, and *sans culottes*."[59] Thus, a reliance on representative democracy in the context of a separation of powers would not protect liberty. As he concluded in the *Discourses:* "The nation which will not adopt an equilibrium of power must adopt a despotism. There is no other alternative. Rivalries must be controlled, or they will throw all things into confusion; and there is nothing but despotism or a balance of power which can control them."[60] Taylor, Adams concluded, must accept the basic premises of mixed government or concede to despotism.

Adams blended the separation of powers with mixed government theory in ingenious ways, but he retained the underlying premise of mixed government theory, the premise that Taylor rejected—that society should be closely tied to government. The clearest demonstration of this lies in Adams's proposal for a "language of signs." Adams acknowledged in the *Discourses* that men shared an overwhelming "passion for distinction" that could have both positive and negative effects. "The desire of the esteem of others," he insisted, "is as real a want of nature as hunger; and the neglect and contempt of the world as severe a pain as the gout or stone." Nature provided this desire but all men did not have the same opportunity to satisfy it. This fact presented problems. It is why "the government is intended to set bounds to passions which nature has not limited; and to assist reason, conscience, justice, and truth, in controlling interests, which, without it, would be as unjust as uncontrollable." "In short," Adams added, "the science of government" could be reduced to "the knowledge of the means of actively conducting, controlling, and regulating the emulation and ambition of the citizens." The government could do this, Adams proposed, by establishing honors and titles, a language of signs, to entice men to use their passions constructively. Republican citizens would be able to compete for distinction without destroying the social order. Government would become the arena for human excellence. The state, in such a system, would harmonize disruptive passions by binding the interests of the people to certain activities. It would impose a certain order by fixing the boundaries and rewards for passionate behavior. Such a system would need a strong (and virtuous) executive to establish and referee the "game." Adams believed that competition for distinction would do more than a fear of coercion to produce virtue in citizens.[61]

Such a solution mortified devout republicans like Taylor, who viewed such social manipulation by government as anathema to free societies. Taylor's critiques of Adams's mixed government theories focused on the ways in which governments had abused and would abuse their relationships to society. Taylor began his *Inquiry* by attacking what he called Adams's "numerical analysis" of the one, the few, and the many. Adams constructed his political system "with fragments torn from monarchy, aristocracy, and democracy," what Taylor termed "rude" and "savage political fabricks." Taylor insisted that American states' constitutions had rejected the representation of social orders, however, and had opted instead for government by moral principles. By moral, he meant "human agencies, arising from the mind's power of abstraction." In other words, Americans had developed new structures of government to preserve freedom and thereby eschewed the British policy of a "balance of orders" that implied a "sovereignty of orders of men." The United States was not rooted in "orders, clans or casts, natural or factitious." Taylor considered the good moral principles used to construct the American constitutional order to be "honesty, self-government, justice and knowledge." He noted that "the numerical analysis cannot . . . enable us to foresee the character of a government, because it has no reference to moral causes or effects, good or evil." He admitted that "an absolute monarch, guided by good moral qualities, may produce national happiness," but he stipulated that this would happen only because of the king's adherence to good moral principles, not because of monarchy itself or because of the particular balance of the three orders in his government. Such cases were rare in any event, given man's propensity to abuse power.[62]

Taylor concluded that by "substituting" for mixed government a government "bottomed upon good or evil moral principles, human happiness will less frequently fluctuate with the characters of individuals." Adams's system of mixed government was not evil, like the aristocracy of paper and patronage, but outmoded.[63] Americans, by embracing the separation of powers and the separation of government from society, had made obsolete the numerical analysis central to theories of mixed government. He hoped that Americans would reject Adams's ideas and not interpret their constitutional order as a form of mixed government but rather as made of sturdier stuff.

Taylor especially feared mixed government, with its "balance of orders," because it threatened to corrupt republican government and destroy the equality of citizens. He explained his opposition to Adams's system succinctly in a 1796 letter to Daniel Carroll Brent: "His idea supposes a catalogue of distinct and independent rights to belong to each of his three orders, and that the rights of one are constantly in danger of being usurped by one or two of this capricious triumvirate; by contending for an equality among orders, he oversets all equality among men." The balance Adams sought was a balance of orders, each enjoying special rights in government. This "inevitably destroys an equality among men," Taylor charged.[64] As he put it in the *Inquiry,* "Our policy divides power, and unites the nation in one interest; Mr. Adams's divides a nation into several interests and unites power."[65] Taylor feared that if social groups were granted rights qua social groups, politics would devolve into a vicious scramble among the privileged groups for power and the expansion of their rights. Government would then become the primary sphere for social activity, as privileged groups would be compelled to fight to maintain their privileges. If a certain social order failed to participate in government, its power could be extinguished by its rivals. The first chapter of the *Inquiry* detailed this very process as it unfolded in the history of the West. Kings, priests, and aristocrats for centuries had fought to control governments and distribute the wealth of the people to themselves. Adams's political structure would repeat the errors of the past by importing to America this dominance of the political realm and giving representation to social orders in the legislature. The separation of state and society, however, would prevent such a nightmare.

The primary political tension for Taylor was not found in the contention of social orders but rather in the ascendance of government power itself over society. Taylor asserted that the separation of powers limited the scope of government in the United States. Separating the executive, legislative, and judicial powers helped to prevent dangerous government consolidation. Representative democracy allowed citizens to exercise their political rights equally. In addition, federalism, which for Taylor meant the division of power between the national and state governments, further ensured that liberty would be protected by decentralizing power. Finally, written constitutions, interpreted strictly and according to the principles by which the constitutions were constructed, prevented the usurpation of power. Such constitutional arrangements recognized the primacy of society over government. Taylor believed that by separating government and society, and by limiting government, individuals could enjoy and pursue the activities they valued. In fact, for Taylor this was precisely why liberty should be cherished. He expressed the republican faith that people, if unopposed by excessive government power, would create a stable, prosperous social order without centralized direction. Men could pursue happiness confident that those wielding political power would not rob them of their lives, liberty, or property.

⚜

In the final analysis, Adams and Taylor did not so much fail to understand the intricacies of each other's arguments as they rejected the basic assumptions of each other's political visions and their understandings of the uses of history. Adams, the nationalist, believed that weak men needed a strong government to bring social order and compel citizens through their interests to preserve the republic. Taylor, the republican, insisted that individuals could form their own social order as long as government protected their rights and otherwise left them alone. Perhaps what infuriated Adams most about Taylor's writings was the latter's belief that Americans had discovered new principles of government and could escape the fates of earlier republics. Adams perceived this to be the folly of the French philosophes, who believed that reason could remove the burden of history. He told Taylor: "America has made no discoveries of principles of government that have not been long known."[66] Americans were not magically immune from nature or history. Taylor's folly, according to Adams, was that he was an ideologue who mistook his ideas for reality.

Taylor, on the other hand, thought Adams to be too erudite for his own good. Adams's explorations of past republics had trapped him in the outmoded forms and mistaken principles of the past, blinding him to the prospect of human advancement. Adams needed to open his eyes and see the new governments, new principles, and new societies that Americans had formed since the Revolution. For Adams and the nationalist strain of American political theory, politics was the art of balancing power and administering government in ways that could check the antisocial tendencies in human nature. For Taylor and the republican strain of American political theory, politics became the art of restraining government and keeping it out of social affairs. Neither Adams nor Taylor doubted the other's sincerity or patriotism, but both believed that the political views of the other threatened the nation's liberty.

Adams's and Taylor's differing views on the relationship of state and society divided them politically, yet they remained cordial and respectful to one another after their spirited exchange of 1814. Taylor wrote Adams a brief letter in 1819 upon publication of William Wirt's celebratory biography of Patrick Henry. He told Adams that Henry "had certainly some merit as a revolutionary patriot" but was not as influential as "many other gentlemen, among whom I cordially and conscientiously class yourself, as an offering to justice, and in some degree (should this letter reach future times) to supply your forebearance to vindicate your own claim." Taylor noted that he was not a distinguished commentator on the revolutionary period, but he maintained that his participation in those events might lend credence to his recognition of Adams's contributions to independence. Adams, who had constantly celebrated the importance of fame and glory to human strivings, must have smiled while reading the letter. He responded to Taylor that he had been friends with Henry and "would not strip the laurels from other men to decorate his brows."[67] Clearly, Adams accepted Taylor's compliment.

In April 1824, a few weeks before Taylor's death, he sat down to write Adams a "farewell letter," which reads like a deathbed confession. His motivation, he wrote, was "to make an humble addition to the multitude of testimonials which exist of your patriotism and integrity, from one who has been a spectator of political scenes, from a period some years anterior to the revolutionary war." He noted that young John Adams had "braved the British lion, when his teeth and claws were highly dangerous." He mentioned that Adams's "efforts in speaking and writing were a thousandfold more efficacious than those of many individuals of great celebrity." Then Taylor commented on the politics of the 1790s and the vicious party battles that ensued during Adams's presidency. Taylor acknowledged that "party spirit was highly inflamed" in the late 1790s and carried "men into unpremeditated excesses." Adams, he claimed, had "soared above" party "prejudices" and "saved your country from a ruinous war with France." Despite his patriotism, Adams had gained nothing but hatred from many Federalists, and Taylor mentioned that he had recently reread the campaign pamphlet attacking Adams that was produced in 1800 by Alexander Hamilton. Even though he admitted having been pleased with the pamphlet in 1800, he insisted that now it "seems to me to be the most malicious, foolish, and inexcusable composition, which was ever produced by a tolerable mind." Apparently, Taylor's conciliatory spirit did not extend to the long-dead Alexander Hamilton.[68]

Adams's last letter to Taylor typified the dignity of their exchanges. He began by thanking Taylor for sending him another book (probably Taylor's *New Views on the Constitution* (1823)). He mentioned that Taylor had attacked his *Defence* in the book and had again misunderstood the argument. Adams then insisted that he had never supported consolidated government or a hereditary aristocracy. He concluded the letter, writing, "Again I thank you for your present, and wish you may contribute to preserve the present Constitution."[69] The end of their interesting correspondence reveals a great deal about the passing of the revolutionary generation in American intellectual life. Both Adams and Taylor vigorously defended their ideas of republican government to the end of their lives. Neither yielded an inch. Yet both men perceived that they belonged to a dying generation, a generation of honorable men who took ideas and the search for truth seriously. Both men appreciated their tasks as conservators of the American constitutional order, despite seeing that order differently. Adams and Taylor, like other American patriots, disagreed on important points and worked against each other politically, but in the end they saw themselves as intellectual kin. Their habits of intellect as well as their dialogue about the relationship of government to society has lasting relevance as Americans continue today to debate the proper scope and power of government in their constitutional order.

"Content with Being":
Nineteenth-Century Southern Attitudes toward Economic Development

J. Crawford King

A Bostonian would go in search of his fortune to the bottom of Hell;
a Virginian would not go across the road to seek it.
> —Louis Auguste Felix, Baron de Beaujour, *Sketch of the United States* (1814)

Even today, after a century and more of debate, historians remain divided regarding one of the most fundamental questions of American history: whether the American South of the nineteenth century was a place whose culture and values differed fundamentally from those of the North. That the natives of Chicago, Illinois, and Montgomery, Alabama, had more in common with each other than with, say, a native of Borneo or Switzerland, most historians would agree. Most would also concede that a single nation can encompass citizens with distinct cultural differences. Few would hesitate to identify the Catalan and the Andalusian as Spanish, or the Prussian and the Bavarian as German. Yet scholars still struggle to account for the chasm of cultural difference that, even now, renders the Chicagoan distinct from the Montgomerian.

Innumerable studies have examined the differences between the inhabitants of the "Old South" and the North. These differences fascinated Alexis de Tocqueville, who in *Democracy in America* (1835) describes his interest in understanding more fully American regional variation and its causes: "I am no longer comparing the Anglo-Americans with foreign nations; I am contrasting them with each other and endeavoring to discover why they are so unlike."[1] Surprisingly, few studies since Tocqueville have focused on attitudes toward business and economic life, attitudes that highlight some of the key distinctions between northern and southern culture. These differences, I will argue, were a product of culture more than of any material or institutional factor. Between the nineteenth-century North and South, one finds sharply divergent assumptions about a number of key economic and business concepts—for example, in attitudes towards business management practices, including the importance of contracts and other legal documents; in assumptions concerning the relative value of labor and of leisure; and in attitudes towards entrepreneurship, the acquisition of material possessions, and even the importance of literacy. Antebellum travelers and commentators have left a wealth of examples that reveal the profound disparity between northerners' drive for and southerners' resistance to economic development.

The antebellum South remained predominantly rural, in contrast to the North's increasing urbanization. Of course, many sparsely settled wilderness areas remained in the North, and the South's urban areas had expanded in size and influence by the end of the antebellum period. But, generally, while in the North social values were set by burghers, the tone of southern society was set by its rural dwellers. The dominance of rural leaders in the South is not surprising, given that, in 1820 only seven southern settlements were of sufficient size to be considered cities. Five of these were in close proximity, being located in Virginia, the District of Columbia, and Maryland, and just four out of every one hundred people lived in them. The larger southern cities had grown since the Revolution, but far more modestly than had the cities of the North. Whereas the economy of the South depended almost entirely on agriculture, the economy of the North became increasingly diversified, as commerce and industry flourished. New York, Philadelphia, and Boston soon outstripped southern towns in size, productivity, and economic prosperity.[2]

The contrast between North and South in the number, size, and importance of towns in the years 1825–26 was readily apparent to European visitors and to Americans alike. A German traveler noted the contrast to the South in his journey through Ohio, Pennsylvania, and New York by describing the enterprising urban areas he passed. A Hungarian traveling in Massachusetts declared that "we passed by populous villages and towns, cultivated fields, meadows, and orchards. Everywhere we saw unmistakable evidence of industry." Unlike southerners, even the rural people of New England saw themselves as part of a small community, as townspeople. The impact on the lives of New Englanders of this identification of the self as a member of a town cannot be overemphasized. "We children felt at once that we belonged to the town, as we did to our father or mother," reminisced a New England girl. While this sense of belonging lent the individual a sense of both security and importance, it could also be unduly constraining and intrusive. One observer, in comparing the typical New England town with the Virginia plantation, thought the town the more restrictive of the two, in the control it wielded over society and economic activity; the town "extended itself . . . into all the small doings of daily life."[3]

Travelers southward often commented on the lack of cities. James Fenimore Cooper observed in the 1830s that there were "fewer villages to the south than to the north," noting the paucity of towns of any size: "Baltimore, the largest city in the slaveholding states, contains, perhaps, about half as many inhabitants as Philadelphia; and New Orleans, and Charleston, and Richmond, the only other three towns of any magnitude, are not all together as large as Boston." Landscape architect Frederick Law Olmsted, who designed New York City's Central Park to offer city dwellers a tranquil respite from the urban din, seems to have found the relentlessly rural southern landscape unsettling. Olmsted considered the lower Mississippi Valley a "great wilderness" where "a few men have crept like ants into a pantry." One northern visitor to the South noted that "unlike the free States, the wealth of the South lies almost entirely in the country; towns . . . being made up of artisans and traders." Another Yankee found that the churches and post offices scattered across the isolated Virginia countryside afforded "a mode of life which differs entirely from that prevailing in the Northern States, and indeed any other part of the world."

The noted critic of southern ways Hinton R. Helper concluded in 1857 that his fellow southerners "have never entertained a proper opinion of the importance of home cities,"[4] an observation consistent with the impressions of others who traveled through the South. Tourists who sailed the popular Alabama steamboat route from Montgomery to Mobile often commented on the lack of any real urban centers along the river's meandering route. What Alabamians thought a "considerable place"—for example, the small city of Claiborne, Alabama—was dismissed by northerner Thomas Hamilton as "a petty village." Hamilton found Alabama towns "without appearance of business" and lacking any "stirring spirit of improvement." One English visitor similarly considered Selma and Cahaba not cities, but mere villages. Another Englishman, voyaging down the Alabama, noted wearily: "We passed 500 miles of this most monotonous scene, without observing a decent house on its bank." Even a southerner described Montgomery, Alabama's capital city, as a humdrum provincial town, which, though the "Cradle of the Confederacy," stood "lacking of what the world expects of a city."[5]

Not only settling but also social characteristics marked the difference between northerners and southerners, and these characteristics gradually hardened into stereotypes. "Yankees"—a term used to refer both to New Englanders and to any non-southerner—were considered hard-working, practical, enterprising, shrewd, and greedy, in contrast to southerners, who were depicted as easy-going, indolent, contented, and aristocratic in attitude. Indeed, the "laborious, economical New Englander" was often considered the antithesis of the "highminded, luxurious native of the South."[6]

Yankee characteristics were sometimes pictured as worthy and admirable. Typical of visitors' comments were those of Frenchman Michel Chevalier, who lauded the "industrious, and sober, frugal" New Englanders for their "extraordinary mechanical genius; they are patient, attentive [sic], and inventive; they must succeed in manufactures." Other travelers praised New Englanders' thrift and perseverance. One reported that the Yankee's "mind is always at work, engaged seriously on something useful or profitable." Another marveled at Yankee versatility and persistence: "Let your genuine Yankee find one path impractical, and he turns directly into another, in pursuing which he never permits his energies to be crippled by futile lamentations over past disappointments." Chevalier heartedly agreed with the New Englander who asserted that "our people can turn their hand almost to anything from whipping the universe to stuffing a mosquito." Another Frenchman, the Marquis de Chastellux, reported that the New England "doctrine teaches equality and enjoins work and industry."[7]

On the other hand, for Daniel R. Hundley, an observer of antebellum southern social hierarchy, "Yankee" was a "term of reproach. It signified a shrewd, sharp, chaffering, oily-tongued, soft-sawdering, inquisitive, money-making, money-saving, and money-worshipping individual." Olmsted reported that many southerners saw northerners in general, and New Englanders in particular, as displaying the prevailing traits of "penuriousness, disingenuousness, knavish cunning, cant, cowardice, and hypocrisy." By the time of the nineteenth-century Yankees also acquired a reputation for being know-it-all elitists. Joseph G. Baldwin, an Alabama jurist and humorist, for example, reminisced about a Connecticut schoolmistress who "was a bundle of prejudices—stiff, literal, positive, inquisitive, inquisitorial, and biliously pious"—traits Baldwin ascribed to her birthplace as well as her vocation.[8]

More than one commentator saw the Yankee type embodied in one of two historical figures: Benjamin Franklin and P. T. Barnum. A Charleston writer observed that northerners "bear . . . the impress of Franklin. The philosopher of thrift has done so much to stamp upon his countrymen the principles of his own frugality, and where the seeds of his philosophy have fallen upon flinty ground, they have made the miser more avaricious, and the churl more niggardly." Jefferson Davis saw Franklin as the "incarnation of the New England character—hard, calculating, angular, unable to conceive any higher object than the accumulation of money." Davis charged that the "hard, grasping, money-grubbing, pitiless and domineering spirit of the New England Puritan found in Franklin a true exponent." Less harsh were the references to the master showman, Barnum. Dr. Thomas Low Nichols saw northerners as "ingenious, enterprising, persevering, self-confident," traits exemplified by Barnum, the model Yankee. Twentieth-century historian Oscar Handlin sees P. T. Barnum as the perfect embodiment of the typical Yankee, "the shrewd trader who would swap anything and profit in the process."[9]

Yankees were almost always considered greedy and dishonest. Anglican cleric and traveler Andrew Burnaby praised Pennsylvanians' frugality and industry, yet he observed that they "concern themselves but little, except in getting money." He had an even lower opinion of Rhode Islanders, who, he asserted, "live almost entirely by unfair and illicit trading." Another English visitor remarked, "I must admit that a total want of conscience in laying on high prices, sharpness, and illiberality in matters of business are the common characteristics of the New Englanders." Stories about clever but crooked New Englanders were commonplace in the accounts of visitors to that region. The English farmer William Faux described an ingenious Yankee scheme to defraud unsuspecting Charlestonians, in which two friends posed as owner and slave. The "owner" sold his friend, who had been painted black, as a slave for $800. Three days later, his natural hue restored, the "slave" rejoined his friend as a free man. "Knavery damns the North," Faux observed, "and Slavery the South." Even those Yankees who were not dishonest were considered cold-hearted and exploitative. Swedish traveler Carl David Arfwedson related the story of a northerner who, hearing of an outbreak of cholera in New

Orleans, quickly chartered a ship and loaded it with coffins in order to turn a quick profit. Mary Boykin Chesnut believed that northerners even expected to turn a profit from the Civil War: "Yankees do not undertake anything that does not pay."[10]

Included in the Yankee economic stereotype was the view of the Yankee as a fraudulent peddler of wooden nutmegs and similarly worthless stuff. Oscar Handlin asserts that "an army of peddlers, shopkeepers, drummers, toolmakers, and mechanics, was the social reality behind the stereotype." "For have not Yankees," asked two young ladies, "from time immemorial . . . been renowned as peddlers? How is it that they possess such talent in this particular branch? It cannot have been acquired; no it must have been inherited." An English traveler in backwoods Tennessee wrote of the ubiquity of "Yankee clock pedlars," who duped naïve, uneducated southerners into buying worthless merchandise: "The whole country was flooded with itinerant hawkers. Through the mountain passes of Buncombe County there flowed a stream of peddlers' carts, wagons, carry-alls, and arks, which inundated the land." One southerner asked Charles F. Hoffman if there were any gentlemen in the North. When Hoffman assured him that there were some, he replied, "Well, you see, stranger, I thought they were all peddlers." Some southern states, apparently fed up with the depredations of Yankee peddlers, passed laws restricting their enterprise, imposing fines and setting up legal procedures designed to hinder them.[11] In 1835, South Carolina placed a prohibitive tax on peddlers. One legislative act prohibited peddlers from entering the state at all. By the late antebellum period, Alabama had increased a peddler's license fees to $750 for each wagon, $500 for peddlers on horseback, and $300 for peddlers on foot; the license was good not for the state, but only for a single county.[12]

⚜

Travelers reported problems doing business with southerners, who were reputed to be slipshod in their business practices. The southerner was "greatly disinclined to exact and careful reasoning," complained Olmsted. Business and legal transactions were completed on a personal, rather than on a business, basis, with little attention to the construction or enforcement of contracts. One befuddled northerner confided that "contracts are made so privately and quickly that it is difficult for a Yankee to find out whether any business is done at all." Southerners were considered cavalier with even their most important legal papers. George W. Bagby describes the filing system of a typical Virginia gentleman: "The whole character of the man is fully told only when you come to his 'secretary.' There you will find his bonds, accounts, receipts, and even his will, jabbed into pigeon-holes, or lying about loose in the midst of a museum of powder-horns, shot-gourds, turkey-yelpers, flints, screws, popcorn, old horseshoes and watermelon seed." Deeds, titles, and public records were not regarded as essential documents that should be secured in a strongbox, but more like souvenirs. Many a southerner was derelict in filing and keeping track of his records. A critic charged that "the loose manner in which the public records are kept, whether they refer to titles of land, or private contracts, is a great annoyance." He was informed by the courthouse recorder that "deeds are not always recorded, here, as they are at the North." English traveler Mrs. Basil Hall, while on her "aristocratic journey," for example, described "Crackers" as those who settled where they wished, including on others' property. Should the rightful owner appear, they would attempt to strike a bargain allowing them to stay, or else they would just move on.[13]

Southerners' nonchalance extended beyond legal documents to the practice of law itself. Joseph G. Baldwin, for example, received his license to practice law from a circuit judge who did not ask him a single question; Baldwin simply requested admission to the bar, and it was granted. Southern judges felt less constrained than their northern brethren by the need to rely on authorities, statutes, or precedents. One Missouri judge explained one of his singularly idiosyncratic rulings in this way: "The court knows well enough what its' abaywt, it ain't a-going to do no sich thing as read all them law books by no manner of means, and it's no use to carry on so, for the court decides all the pynts agin you." Perhaps Baldwin captures best the workings of a southern court: "Nothing was settled, chaos had come once again, or rather, had never gone away. Order . . . seemed unwilling to remain where there was no other law to keep it company." He went on to note that most of the county officials were ignorant, and that the electorate was largely indifferent to their qualifications for the bench: "If they were 'good fellows' and *wanted* the office, that is, were too poor and lazy to support themselves in any other way, that was enough." Baldwin concluded that if anything were accomplished, it was usually done incorrectly. "The iron rules of British law were . . . too cold and unfeeling for the hot blood of the Sunny South," Baldwin theorizes. "They were denounced accordingly, and practically scouted from Mississippi judicature."[14]

One virulent critic of southern business practices was Maine physician Charles G. Parsons, who declared, "Businessmen are guilty of practices, without losing reputation or credit, which in the free States would prove their ruin." Neither the "lawless Cracker" nor the man of means could be depended upon to uphold a written contract. For example, a respected Georgia county commissioner agreed to sell Parsons lumber. When Parsons saw a previous contract between the lumberman and another for less than he had agreed to pay, he insisted that the county commissioner honor the contract the commissioner had already made. Instead, the lumberman sold the lumber to still another buyer, and for even more than the sum to which Parsons had agreed. In another deal, Parsons engaged to buy a quantity of corn, only to discover afterwards that the corn grower had already sold it. Parsons attributed this failure to honor contracts not to dishonesty but to focusing more on leisure than on the details of business. Artisans would disappear from their work when the opportunity arose to attend a cock-fight, a fox hunt, or a parade. Agreements with business acquaintances would be abridged for personal reasons. When, for example, a hotel keeper failed to have available the carriage he had agreed to have waiting for Parsons at a specific date and time, the hotel keeper explained, "Well, father sent for my carriage yesterday, and I had to let him have it."[15]

What Parsons failed to see, or perhaps did not want to see, was that frequently, when a southerner violated a written contract, he did so because he simply did not consider paper documents binding. If he were offered a better deal than that in hand, it seemed only reasonable to accept the better offer. He could usually be counted on to keep his word, unless, of course, something came up of higher priority. It seems likely that the hotel keeper intended to have a carriage, team, and driver ready for Parsons, but when his father had need of his property, he could hardly put a stranger's request ahead of his own father's needs. Any southerner would have understood.

While southerners may have been less precise in their business practices than northerners, on the positive side they also seemed to lack the grasping desire for piling up wealth they associated with the North. Southerners agreed with Tocqueville's observation that Yankees were "taught from infancy . . . to place wealth above all the pleasures of the intellect or the heart." The erudite Frenchman considered northerners to be obsessed with "those material cares which are disdained by the white population of the South. . . . Property is the sole aim of exertion," he concluded. Southerners' attitudes toward wealth tended to be aristocratic, and northerners' interests in wealth distinctly bourgeois. There were, of course, exceptions, such as the "Cotton Snob" and the "Southern Yankee," described memorably by Daniel R. Hundley: "The Southern Yankee loves money for its own sake—the Cotton Snob loves it because it supplies him with cigars, and brandy, and fine clothes, and fine horses, yea, and fine women, too."[16] Yet, though there were doubtless avaricious southerners, wealth was not generally be-all and end-all. Many a southerner was content to take it easy and allow the rich landscape to provide for him. Southerners typically valued intangibles—resiliency of spirit, the appreciation of beauty, exuberant joy in and devotion to friends and family—far more than the mere accumulation of riches, "where moth and rust doth corrupt." An Appalachian woman eloquently began her reminiscence: "If you are the kind of folks who honor money and prestige, then I have very little to leave you. . . . But I hope by writing this book, I can pass on to you the heritage my father left me." Another memoir attests to southerners' perception of money as significant not in and of itself, but only as a means to an end: "We are a primary people. We do not understand shares and stocks, the use of money to make money. . . . Again and again we come back to the central focus of all our economic fear—to the impersonal life, to the mechanical that kills you."[17]

In the South, wealth alone did not automatically confer social prestige, as was often the case in the North. Society, in the antebellum South, allowed for easy vertical mobility, but elevation was not contingent upon wealth. "There is no part of the world where great wealth confers so little rank, or is attended with so few advantages over a moderate competency," remarked an English wayfarer of the South. Traveler and academic Frederick Hall observed, "Most of the gentlemen are *born gentlemen.* . . . From their cradles they despise money, because they are not in the habit of seeing those with whom they associate actively engaged in the pursuit of it." Another English tourist related an interchange between a fellow passenger and a Kentucky mechanic in a coach. One of the travelers remarked that if a man had money and dressed well "he may go where he will, and be received as a gentleman; ay, though he may be a gambler, a rogue, or a swindler." "But he would not be a gentleman," the Kentuckian disagreed. "No sir; nor will I ever allow that money only makes the gentleman: it is the principle, sir, and the inner feeling, and the mind—and no fine clothes can ever make it; and no rough ones unmake it, that's a fact," he continued. "And, sir, there's many a better gentleman following the plow in these parts, than there is among the richer classes: I mean those poor men who're contented with their lot, and work hard and try no mean shifts and methods to get on and up in the world." Hundley concluded that, though southern mechanics often prospered and were respected, they would not be "admitted to a social equality with the Southern elite." Similarly, the cream of Charleston society consisted mostly of planters, not merchants. These planters "considered merchandize as belonging to a rank decidedly below their own; consequently there existed a strongly marked line of distinction between them and merchants." Anne Newport Royall, observing Huntsville society, noted that "the merchants, in other states, hold the farmers in vassalage—but, here, the merchant is held in subjection by the planter."[18]

Few southerners concerned themselves with maximizing their profits. They were not a business-minded people and did not apply their energies to such ends. One traveler remarked how little attention the proprietor of an Arkansas stable paid to his business affairs—he was as apt to be off turkey hunting or taking refreshment at the saloon as he was to be at the stable, tending to business. The tourist concluded, "In traveling in the South, you become astonished at the little attention men pay to their business. The idea appears to be very prevalent, that if a business is once started, it must take care of itself." Another astute observer found that the southerner "generally dislikes the routine of business" and that "prudent and careful businessmen" were the exception. For this reason, and because of southerners' tendency toward "reckless expenditure," the observer concluded that the southern states would fail to prosper as they should. Olmsted's experiences seem consistent with this view. For example, on visiting a Texas forge and finding the smith absent, he was told by a neighbor, "Well, mechanics don't work steady here, as they do at the north." On a steamboat in North Carolina that had landed to pick up wood, Olmsted noticed, tacked to a tree, a scrap of paper bearing this inscription: "Notic [sic] to all persons takin wood from this landing pleas to leav a ticket payable to the subscriber at $1.75 a cord as heretofore, Amos Sikes."[19]

In the eyes of many, southerners were not good managers of their businesses or their personal affairs. For the most part, they did not seek to save, invest, and reinvest, choosing instead simply to get along as best they could and to enjoy life. "We are all spendthrifts," complained southern critic Hinton R. Helper. "Some of us should become financiers" and take on the "habits of enterprise and industry," he urged. Traveler Carlton H. Rogers, in an account of his southern journey, described a southerner unlikely to heed Helper's advice. When he asked this "genuine specimen of the 'Georgia cracker'" whether his shingle business was profitable, the "cracker" replied, "Wal, not particularly so, but I kinder manage to get enough grub for the old woman and children, and tha's all we orter expect in this ere world." Olmsted similarly encountered a simple Alabamian who told him, "Now, I never calculate to save anything . . . and I mean to enjoy what I earn as fast as it comes." A more successful son of Alabama, James Mallory, recorded his reflections on the "badly managed" railroad in which he was involved, complaining that the masses in the South will . . . leave it to a few liberal and wealthy men to carry them through." German traveler Jonathan David Schoepf similarly regarded southerners as "people, disposed to idleness and good living," who would "commonly buy more of the merchants, and in advance, than their labor amounts to."[20]

Bad management practices were commonplace, even in the South's most successful business sector, the running of plantations and farms. The tidy and orderly farms seen everywhere in the North were uncommon in the South. "Throughout this southern tour, few things had afforded me a greater fund of amusement than the singularly haphazard and disorderly way of living observable on the farms and plantations," declared Charles Joseph Latrobe, first lieutenant-governor of what became Australia and avid travel writer. A fellow traveler Olmsted met in Louisiana offered a theory as to why southern planters would always be in debt. They would buy Negroes and other property "without making any calculation of the reasonable prospects of their being able to pay their debts." Chesnut revealed that it had been her husband's law practice that had kept his plantation afloat: "Now it is running him in debt. We are bad managers. Our people have never earned their own bread." Though the *Virginia Farmer's Register* lifted an article from the *Portland Advertiser* urging southerners to manage their farms better and to board school teachers, feeding them what could not be sold, southerners rejected such advice and wanted nothing to do with the many progressive farm journals that came and went.[21]

One group of southerners did, however, tend to business, manage their concerns well, and prosper—northerners who had migrated south. New Yorker John Peters, who came to Vicksburg to seek his fortune, was concerned that northerners who moved south would "fall in with Southern Habbits," but generally speaking, this appears not to have been the case. One New Englander unequivocally declared: "The enterprising men are mostly from the North." Hundley scathingly disparaged those Yankees who came south to swindle southerners and transform young men into "Southern Yankees." Hundley nonetheless noted that the South's most successful businessmen were either transplanted Yankees or Yankee-trained southerners. Miss Mendell and Miss Hosmer, travelers from New York, praise Petersburg, Virginia, as a city more alive than Richmond, thanks to Petersburg's successful mills, which were run by northerners. Artist and explorer Charles Lanman likewise described the cotton and paper mills in Tuscaloosa, Alabama, as flourishing "in the hands of Yankees," and Mrs. Anne Newport Royall, indefatigable Alabama traveler, lamented shrilly how Yankees were in control of Charleston's business. Olmsted also remarked on the prosperity of southern businesses run by northerners. He observed that the merchants in the markets of Norfolk were almost all from New Jersey, and he praised the Savannah and Macon Railroad, noting that it was built and managed by northern men. "I am told that most of the mechanics and . . . successful merchants and tradesmen of Savannah came originally from the North, or are the sons of Northern men," Olmsted reported. Both Olmsted and Charles Lanman praised the Battle House hotel in Mobile as being unusually good, noting that it was run by a Bostonian. Lanman concluded that, "like most of the better hotels in the South, [it] is kept by a Yankee." Michel Chevalier contended that, no matter where one went, if mention were made of a successful merchant, he would turn out to be a Yankee, and that "if you pass a plantation in the South in better order than the others, with finer avenues, with the Negroes' cabins better arranged and more comfortable, you will be told, 'Oh! that is a Yankee's; he is a *smart man!*'"[22]

The differences in business practices discussed above may, perhaps, have arisen from a fundamental difference between northerners' and southerners' beliefs regarding the meaning and value of work. Northerners found both spiritual and material value in work, and thus felt driven to acquire and to improve. Southerners, on the other hand, tended not to find such internal reward in work, and thus felt considerably less driven toward acquisition and improvement. The English officer Basil Hall summed it up well when he wrote: "In the more northern parts of the country, we had been every where much struck with the air of bustle, and all sorts of industry—men riding about, chopping down forests, building up houses, ploughing, planting, and reaping—but here in Carolina all mankind appeared comparatively idle. The whites, generally speaking, consider it discreditable to work, and the blacks, as a matter of course, work as little as they can. The free population prefer hunting, and occupy themselves also very much with the machinery of electioneering." Years later, Olmsted would say much the same thing: "The Southerner has no pleasure in labor except with reference to a result. He enjoys life itself. He is content with being," unlike the typical northerner, who, according to Olmsted, "finds happiness in doing. Rest, in itself, is irksome and offensive to him."

Olmsted maintained that the differing attitude toward labor was the real "grand distinction" between northerner and southerner.[23] Certainly, the idea of the virtue of labor and the sinfulness of sloth was deeply ingrained in Yankees. They found it difficult to escape the omnipresent Puritan admonition, "God sent you not into this world as into a Play-house, but a Work-house." Yankee Thomas Shepard cautioned his son to "abhor . . . one hour of idleness as you would be ashamed of one hour of drunkenness." A Lowell mill girl recalled a childhood "penetrated through every fiber of thought with the idea that idleness is a disgrace. It was taught with the alphabet and the spelling-book; it was enforced by precept and example, at home and abroad; and it is to be confessed that it sometimes haunted the childish imagination almost mercilessly." The northern preacher Henry Ward Beecher contended that man's destiny was to labor; it was a part of his nature. "The indolent mind is not empty, but full of vermin," he preached in 1844. A Yankee doctor decided that no one could be completely healthy if raised in idleness. The "Superiour intellectual character" of New Englanders was due, he said, to "their early habits of industry." The noted editor Horace Greeley was a living symbol of the moral and spiritual value of labor: "As an humble farmer's son, upon the granite hills of New England," said the reformer, "I became early inured to constant toil and learned not merely to confront labor, but to respect it,—to reorganize its stern afflictions as one of the greatest blessings which Heaven sends." Northerners' agreed with the sentiment expressed in a short story by Sarah Hale that the "principle of being useful, [is something] which every republican ought to cherish."[24]

Yankees certainly practiced what they preached in regard to labor. Reared from early childhood to work diligently, they continued as adults to uphold the Yankee work ethic, and they expected others to do the same. An English traveler noted that there were "no idle hands" in Massachusetts, and that "none are seen eating the bread of idleness." A southern sojourner commented that "useful labor is nowhere disdained in New England, by any class of society." Another southerner remarked how textile workers in Connecticut commonly labored for twelve or more hours a day, "trooping to their prisons." Rich or poor, northerners worked, and in contrast to the South "the thoroughly idle gentleman was a rarity" in the North. One traveler in the Northwest observed "no signs of quiet enjoyment of life as it passes, but one of a haste to get rich. Here are no idlers." Another, speaking of a demanding Yankee overseer, remarked, "These Yankees are great workers themselves, and hard masters to other people."[25]

Northerners exemplified the work ethic not just in devotion to their occupation, but in their everyday toils within and without the home. Everyone in New England not regularly employed, such as girls, boys, and single women, was expected to spin. Indeed, the whole family could find work in the woolen industry. At night, family members gathered around the fire engaged in some aspect of woolen manufacture. A society formed in Boston to promote "Industry and Frugality" encouraged young spinsters to come and spin on the Common. And there is a report of a postman from Pennsylvania who knitted stockings and mittens as he rode along his route. New Englanders seemed truly engaged in "constant employment of every moment of the waking hours."[26]

One Yankee family's record personifies the work ethic. Henry V. Poor grew up on the frontier of Maine. As a boy, he recognized that his family needed to work in order to survive, and he resolved to work, gain wealth, and achieve. Indeed, Poor would become "a type of economic man." He inherited from his ancestors "uncommon energy" and rarely slowed; indeed, he seemed to work *all* the time. Poor felt truly alive and most energized when working and making money; he found work "exhilarating," and it made him feel "strong and virile." He took great pride in continuing to work even as he grew old. He had little interest in leisure, preferring to show the world "what a Yankee can do." His overwhelming interest in work and in material gain unfortunately resulted in the neglect of his family. In 1863, his wife, Mary, wrote wistfully to him, "What a Foe to Love is Business."[27]

Southerners, it seems, had no such foe of love. A New Jersey visitor to South Carolina was disturbed by the sloth of the inhabitants, who were afflicted by "this monster . . . by the name of Laziness." "'Take no thought of the morrow,' appears to be the motto of very much of the southern population," concluded Episcopal bishop of Minnesota Henry Benjamin Whipple. The bishop found that southern energies "either lie dormant in idleness and luxury or receive a wrong direction and are expended in visionary projects or in reckless expenditures for useless luxuries and foolish dissipation." Andrew Burnaby similarly found the "spirit of enterprise" to be singularly lacking among Virginians, describing them as "content if they can but live from day to day." Many years after Burnaby's visit, a traveler in western Virginia and the Carolinas observed a decided lack of "agricultural industry" among farmers, who, he reported, refused to build houses because doing so would involve work. Olmsted noted that in Virginia, "Nothing which can be postponed or overlooked . . . gets attended to." Another tourist noticed southerners so indolent that they would work a couple of days to earn enough to buy necessities, then would stop working until their money was gone. The experience of the German paleontologist Albert C. Koch was not atypical. The workmen Koch hired to help him dig for fossils left after two days. The workers with whom Koch replaced the first group also quickly departed. The scientist had to enlist the labor of a third group of workmen before the job was completed.[28]

When observers compared the work habits of North and South, almost always the hard-working North was praised and the lazy South ridiculed. Tocqueville, who ascribed the cause to slavery, saw such a differentiation between the Kentuckian and the Ohioan. The Kentuckian scorned labor, and "as he lives in idle independence he covets wealth much less than pleasure and excitement." The Ohioan, on the other hand, regarded material gain as his primary aim, was "tormented by the desire of wealth," and worked diligently to attain his goal. Alexander Mackay, an English barrister, judged that "the inertness of the South affords to this day a painful contrast to the cheerful activity of the North." Northerners worked hard and respected labor, whereas "for all truly industrial purposes, the energies of the white race in the South might be as well utterly extinguished." While the northerner developed self-reliance, "the Southerner . . . bred in the lap of ease and luxury, becomes impatient of enterprise, and recoils from exertion." Mackay concluded that in the North, "activity takes the place of refinement," while in the South, "refinement takes the place of activity." Southern women shared southern men's inertia. Naturalist and writer of children's books Catherine Hopley noted "the weary, listless manner of the Southern ladies, who were lounging about." She remembered how northern ladies were "ever busy with their books or pencils."[29]

Northerners, exasperated by southern laziness, sometimes commented on how a task would be better and more quickly accomplished in the North. Bishop Whipple was irked by the superfluous number of servants at a southern boarding house, in which there was a servant for every household member—a household whose work, had it been in the North, would have been completed by a couple of servants. "Such is the sloth and luxury of the mass of whites in the south," grumbled Whipple. Olmsted tells how a New Jersey farmer estimated that, while one Virginia farmhand harvested a quarter-acre of wheat a day, a single farmhand in New York would harvest two acres. Olmsted also recounts how Yankees of modest means who went South with little except know-how and the habit of hard work had made bloom the failed farms deserted by southerners. "There is," Olmsted suspected, "something in men as well as in climate."[30]

Southerners were devoted to leisure, northerners to toil; but there is some question whether Yankees found as much contentment in their work as did southerners in their leisure. Olmsted believed that "the people of the Northern states, as a whole, probably enjoy life less than any other civilized people." An Austrian who lived in Boston for ten years disagreed: "There is, probably, no people on earth with whom business constitutes pleasure, and industry amusement, in an equal degree. . . . Active occupation is not only the principal source of their happiness . . . but they are absolutely wretched without it, and . . . know but the *horrors* of idleness." Tocqueville observed that in the North, "a wealthy man thinks that he owes it to public opinion to devote his leisure to some kind of industrial or commercial pursuit or to public business. He would think himself in bad repute if he employed his life solely in living."[31]

Southerners and northerners also differed regarding building improvements and what Frederick Hall termed the "commercial spirit." The northerner, always busy and enterprising, was driven to buy and sell and to improve on what the Almighty had provided. He was "ingenious in devising, and indefatigable in executing any plan." Where there was a stream, he would construct not only a bridge but a mill dam as well. Southerners, on the other hand, were unlikely to get caught up in the building of bridges or digging of canals. They preferred to ford the stream, this being easier in the short run.[32]

Travelers often commented on the enterprising and industrious spirit of northerners. An Englishman found those working on Wall Street to be "intensely absorbed in business": "'For sale' seems to be the national motto. . . . Everything a [Northern] man possesses is voluntarily subjected to the law of interchange." Carl Arfwedson also found Yankees to be so immersed in business that, he joked, they would transport the frozen water of Boston to the

East Indies if doing so would turn a profit. An English tourist was impressed by the self-reliance of a Yankee family whom he met in central Indiana. All the boys were "self-taught shoemakers, butchers, wheelwrights, carpenters, and what not."[33] This transmission of optimism and industry from one generation to the next was typical of Yankee families. Henry V. Poor, for example, believed firmly in "social amelioration 'through technological progress.'" He saw railroads as an answer to the South's backwardness and looked upon them "as the principal agent, the prime mover in advancing the great interests of humanity." The Brown family of Rhode Island had a similar view. A merchant family involved in worldwide trade, manufacturing, and land speculation, they believed in "private enterprise in the public interest" and always strove to make a profit. Both the Poor and the Brown families worked not just energetically but thoughtfully so as to advance, steadily and deliberately, toward betterment and greater riches.[34]

This enterprising drive toward betterment seemed to be lacking in the South. One northerner expressed surprise that, in South Carolina, "there are not . . . many corporations. . . . In New England a man may put a hundred dollars in a bridge, a turnpike, a railroad, a bank, an insurance company, or a mill-dam, and thus blend his private advantage with the public good." Charles G. Parsons was a keen observer of southerners' comparative lack of interest in improving material conditions: "There are no bridges over the large rivers in Georgia, except where the railroads cross. There are numerous rivers, streams, and creeks in the state, but not sufficient energy and enterprise to bridge them." He complained: "Large trees, fall down across stage roads in the slave States, and lie there for weeks, or perhaps months, because it is not the *custom* to remove them. In many places the mail stage will meet half a dozen in a mile, and have to drive out into the woods to pass around them." During her trips from Tuscaloosa to Jonesboro, Mary Gordon Duffee was similarly surprised how little coal haulers knew or cared about geology or mining techniques: "They simply dug coal where it was most clearly exposed and estimated its value by the good it would render them in trade" for food and "the necessary jug of liquor," she observed. Charles Lanman also decried the lack of an enterprising spirit among Tuscaloosa businessmen: "While an extensive bed of coal is known to exist within a mile of town, it is customary to order, even from Philadelphia the needed supply; and that while the county affords a beautiful quality of marble, the tombstones of the place are all imported from Italy." Similarly, the Duke of Saxe-Weimar Eisenach was stunned that, though the earth around Montgomery was excellent for brick-making, there was no kiln. "The bricks which they sell here at $10 a thousand are scandalous," he proclaimed. Throughout the South similar situations existed.[35]

The difference between northern and southern senses of enterprise was so widely noted as to become proverbial. Indeed, a traditional saying had it that "a Southerner never sells what he can eat, and a northerner never eats what he can sell." Le Chevalier Felix de Beaujour put it succinctly: "A Bostonian would go in search of his fortune to the bottom of Hell; a Virginian would not go across the road to seek it." When Philo Tower, a northern clergyman and traveler, noticed the strong current of a Columbia, South Carolina, creek, he wondered why no mill had been built to take advantage of it, only to find that a dam had in fact been built and successfully run by a Yankee. With the property now in the hands of southerners, the property had fallen to ruin. "Here," lamented Tower, "within a mile of the capital city of South Carolina, is water power more than enough to grind wheat for all the inhabitants of the city but it is allowed to run to waste. When it *was* in use, it was by Yankee enterprise, and went by the significant name of a 'Yankee dam.'" Material improvements occurred significantly more often in the North. Olmsted remarked that in the North, over a span of twenty years, numerous cities, buildings, schools, mills, churches, and railroads sprang up, and across the northern countryside houses, fences, roads, canals, and bridges were visible and the education of the inhabitants noticeably improved. "But where will the returning traveler see the accumulated cotton profits of twenty years in Mississippi?" asked Olmsted. "The total increase in wealth of the population [of Virginia] during the last twenty years shows for almost nothing. One year's improvements of a Free State exceed it all."[36]

Other travelers compared the lands lying on each side of the Ohio River. Yankee Thaddeus M. Harris noticed that "the industrious habits and neat improvements of the people on the west side of the [Ohio] river, are strikingly contrasted with those on the east. Here, in Ohio, they are intelligent, industrious, and thriving; there, on the back skirts of Virginia, ignorant, lazy, and poor." Years later Thomas Nuttall made a similar comparison, claiming that the finer dwellings along the river were built by New Englanders. John Richard Beste opined that "the youngest child in my party could not help but contrast the busy cultivation, mills and factories on the one side [of the Ohio River], with the beautiful but silent forest on the Kentucky shore."[37]

The observations cited here concerning the many differences between northern and southern attitudes towards work and material progress constitute a small but representative sample of antebellum opinion. Considered in strictly material and measurable terms, certainly the South fares the worse in these comparisons. Looking solely at objective criteria, one might expect the region to be a gloomy and joyless place. The opposite, however, seems closer to the truth. Southerners did not feel "backward" or behind the times because they lacked the "improvements" produced by the northern work ethic. They were, for the most part, a satisfied lot who did not feel the lack of that which they little valued. As Confederate officer Edmund Rhett explained to British war correspondent William Howard Russell at the start of the Civil War, "We are an agricultural people, pursuing our own system, and working out our own destiny, breeding up women and men with some other purpose than to make them vulgar, fanatical cheating Yankees." Russell heard a similar opinion from Confederate States Senator Louis T. Wigfall: "We are a peculiar people, sir! We are an agricultural people; we are a primitive but a civilized people. We have no cities—we don't want them. We have no literature—we don't need any yet. We have no press—we are glad of it. We are better without them. We want no manufactures: we desire no trading, no mechanical or manufacturing classes. As long as we have our rice, our sugar, our tobacco, and our cotton, we can command wealth to purchase all we want."[38] The observations of both native southerners and those who but passed through their untamed yet aristocratic land help us understand a little more deeply how profound, indeed, were the differences between the two antebellum Americas that constituted the United States.

The IRS as a Political Weapon: Political Patronage and Retribution during the Roosevelt Era

Burton W. Folsom Jr.

"My father," Elliott Roosevelt observed of his famous parent, "may have been the originator of the concept of employing the IRS as a weapon of political retribution." Indeed, not before the presidency of Franklin D. Roosevelt had the federal government taken so much individual income. In 1935, when Roosevelt hiked the top income tax rate to 79 percent and the top estate tax rate to 70 percent, millionaires searched for deductions and loopholes to protect their private property. During the 1930s, FDR began experimenting with the IRS, which had been placed under the Treasury Department, as a means of attacking political enemies and generating more revenue for his New Deal programs.[1]

The first person to incur Roosevelt's wrath and thereby endure a long sustained investigation by the IRS was Huey Long. As a flamboyant and clever politician—some would say demagogue—Long became governor of Louisiana in 1928 and built a successful political machine in the state. He promised free textbooks, cheap health care, and other benefits to the voters of Louisiana, and he fulfilled some of his promises by levying high corporate taxes. Long and his political cohorts also took kickbacks from oil companies, highway builders, and other service providers. Long built up a strong enough cash base to sustain his minions in office in Louisiana while he served in the U.S. Senate after his election to the office in 1930.[2]

In Washington, Long became the sharpest thorn in Roosevelt's side. Long supported the president at first, but gradually came to criticize almost all his New Deal programs as inadequate or misdirected. He castigated the Agricultural Adjustment Administration (AAA) for paying farmers not to produce crops. Of the National Recovery Act (NRA), Long said, "Every fault of socialism is found in this bill, without one of its virtues." He also ridiculed Roosevelt's New Deal administrators as charlatans and incompetents. He regularly baited Democrat Joe Robinson, the Senate majority leader, and threw roadblocks in the way of legislation favored by Roosevelt.[3]

Roosevelt, after denouncing Long as one of the two most dangerous men in the country, searched his arsenal for weapons to deploy against the Louisiana senator. At first, Roosevelt tried to check Long by denying him federal patronage. The president made Louisiana unique by appointing a director from outside the state to administer federal relief programs there. Roosevelt also sent federal patronage to Long's political enemies, led by ex-governor John Parker. The order came down from Roosevelt: "Don't put anybody in and don't help anybody that is working for Huey Long or his crowd. That is 100 percent."[4]

Long responded by having the state turn down federal funds when possible. Harold Ickes, director of the Public Works Administration (PWA), criticized Long publicly for his refusal to take about half the federal money allocated to the state for highway construction. Such refusal to accept federal funds was unprecedented, Ickes said, and would cripple economic development in Louisiana. Long simply denounced the men appointed to use such money as crooks. "Pay them my further respects up there in Washington," Long told reporters. "Tell them they can go to hell."[5]

T. Harry Williams, author of an exhaustive biography of Long, thoroughly researched the patronage dispute between Roosevelt and Long. Williams concluded that Long "was not greatly concerned about the practical effect of his loss of patronage: the number of federal jobs involved was relatively small, and the number of state jobs at his disposal was more than sufficient to enable him to sustain his power. But it was humiliating to him that his enemies should control the [federal] patronage and then boast about it. It would encourage them to continue their opposition to him."[6]

Long's solution was to go national, recruiting a widespread base of supporters, perhaps for a future presidential run himself. In February 1934, Long, in a national radio speech, announced the creation of his Share Our Wealth (SOW) clubs with the slogan "Every Man a King." He promoted a steeply progressive income tax to guarantee every family a "homestead" and a minimum annual income. Long's crusade generated 60,000 letters weekly, mostly from fans eager to start SOW clubs in their own communities. As Long encouraged national membership in his clubs, Roosevelt tested Long's potential presidential support. Postmaster General James Farley, Roosevelt's accurate pollster, estimated Long's national vote at four million, and possibly six million, votes by 1936—easily large enough to swing an election to the Republicans.[7]

Farley's estimates were confirmed when Long traveled around the nation to promote SOW clubs and explore a presidential run. The Carolinas, for example, became a testing ground for Long. "South Carolina is the strongest state for Roosevelt," Long discovered. "If I can sell myself here, I can sell myself anywhere." In March 1936, Long arrived in the Palmetto State. Governor Olin Johnston tried to ignore him, especially because Roosevelt had telephoned with a threat to cut off all federal patronage if Johnston helped the Louisiana senator. Despite Johnston's snub, Long spoke on the University of South Carolina's campus, at the capitol, and throughout the state. He attracted huge crowds, and 140,000 voters in South Carolina signed cards of support for his possible presidential bid.[8]

Long's budding national support was a major threat to the president. Roosevelt wanted a second term. If Long ran for president, he might siphon enough votes from the Democrats to elect a Republican.[9] Also, Long's ability to hold Louisiana without federal patronage could spur other rebels to challenge Roosevelt's allies, who were distributing patronage in other states. Much was at stake, and Roosevelt's team turned to the IRS to investigate Long and give the president an advantage.

In January 1934, Henry Morgenthau, Roosevelt's longtime friend, became secretary of the treasury. Three days after his Senate confirmation, Morgenthau called in Elmer Irey, head of the special intelligence division of the IRS. "Get all your agents back on the Louisiana job," Morgenthau ordered. "Start the investigation of Huey Long." Morgenthau asked Irey to report to him once a week, and Irey did so for almost a year. Irey sent dozens of agents into Louisiana; one of them even infiltrated the Long organization. In the course of the probe, Irey also spoke with Roosevelt face to face, and they worked together to get the right lawyer to prosecute Long and his cohorts.[10]

Roosevelt's (or Morgenthau's) decision to use the IRS against Long was a logical move. Long was not independently wealthy, yet he somehow had enough money to buy the loyalty of his state even though his opponents were endowed with federal funds. The Roosevelt administration logically concluded that graft and kickbacks from state contracts were keeping Long in power. Long had a dilemma. Most state officials and contractors had to pay the Long machine in order to keep their jobs and state contracts. If Long refused to report these kickbacks on his tax return, the IRS could prosecute him for tax evasion. If, however, Long did itemize this cash and reported it as income, Roosevelt could publicize Long's use of politics to extort wealth and preserve power. Those who gave the kickbacks to Long would also be publicly embarrassed.

Long naturally resented the IRS's swooping down into Louisiana. On the floor of the Senate he protested the "hordes" of agents—250 at least—that had been placed on his trail and that of his friends. "They did not try to put any covering over this thing," Long complained, insisting that federal agents openly boasted that he and his associates "were all going away." Irey not only had an agent infiltrate the Long organization, but he also learned what he could from Long's enemies. Among these were the Jahnke brothers, highway contractors whose information on Long was useful to Irey. Since the Jahnke brothers were unable to get state contracts from Long, they were near bankruptcy. Irey therefore recommended and secured for them a loan from the federal Reconstruction Finance Corporation. This kept them in business and provided them with further incentive to help the IRS catch Long.[11]

By 1935, the IRS began indicting lower-level and more vulnerable members of Long's team. State representative Joseph Fisher was successfully prosecuted for tax evasion in April 1935. Then Long was assassinated in September, and his machine fell into disarray. In October, Abraham Shushan, a Long stalwart, was acquitted of tax evasion. Others eventually settled with the IRS in civil court. Tax expert David Burnham concludes that "the cases had been dropped in return for a pledge from Long's heirs to support Roosevelt in his bid for a second term." Most of the remnants of the Long machine, led by Huey's brother Earl, did in fact cooperate with Roosevelt, and the president won almost 90 percent of Louisiana's vote in 1936—a larger percentage than he got in either neighboring Texas or Arkansas. After the election, Irey was able to secure more prosecutions for tax evasion, mail fraud, and misuse of Work Progress Administration (WPA) labor for personal use. No more would Louisiana politicians thunder against Roosevelt and the New Deal.[12]

❧

Roosevelt marveled at the efficacy of the IRS in removing political opponents. Newspaper publisher William Randolph Hearst also found himself under investigation when he began opposing Roosevelt's political programs.

Such a situation was awkward for Elliott Roosevelt, the president's son, whom Hearst had astutely hired as aviation editor for his *Los Angeles Express*. According to Elliott: "At about the same time that he [FDR] sent federal investigators into Louisiana to prove the financial shenanigans of Huey Long and company, father had the Internal Revenue Service (IRS) conduct a similar scrutiny of every corner and crevice of Hearst's empire."[13] Hearst, however, did not depend on patronage and kickbacks to make his money and extend his influence. Indeed, Hearst's books were in order.

So were those of Father Charles Coughlin, the popular radio priest from Detroit who began meeting with Huey Long in 1935 and joined him in denouncing Roosevelt. The IRS sent reports on Coughlin's finances to the president, who also put James Farley, the postmaster general, to work on Coughlin's mail. Roosevelt learned much about Coughlin's financing, but could not find the evidence needed to put him in jail. The harassment prompted Coughlin to join Long and Hearst in regularly denouncing Roosevelt. Sometimes these three critics were able to join forces to defeat Roosevelt on key political issues. The president, for example, wanted the United States to join the World Court, part of the League of Nations. He was furious when Hearst in his papers, Coughlin on the radio, and Long on the Senate floor generated enough opposition to the World Court to defeat Roosevelt's plan.[14]

Elliott Roosevelt remarked that "other men's tax returns continued to fascinate Father in the [nineteen] thirties." Boake Carter, for example, was a radio commentator who criticized Roosevelt for "meddling" in the Far East and risking a war with Japan. Roosevelt—according to his son—ordered the IRS to investigate Carter. He also asked Frances Perkins, the secretary of labor, to check Carter's status as an alien and see if he could be deported.[15]

Another target of the president was Hamilton Fish, the Republican congressman from Roosevelt's home district in New York. When Fish began to oppose Roosevelt on program after program, Roosevelt at first tried to oust Fish at the ballot box. Hyde Park was Roosevelt's territory, and he hated the idea of Fish representing the president and his neighbors in Congress. When Fish kept winning reelection, sometimes by large margins, Roosevelt brought in the men at the IRS. They alleged that Fish owed $5,000 in back taxes and demanded payment. Fish challenged this ruling in court. "The case dragged on for several years," Fish observed, "costing the government many thousands of dollars as it attempted to make me pay the money, which if I had agreed, would have besmirched my reputation." Eventually, the IRS lost its case completely. It even had to pay a tax refund to Fish of $80. In 1942, the IRS launched a multiyear audit of Fish; this also failed. Finally, during World War II, Roosevelt asked J. Edgar Hoover at the FBI to investigate Fish on a charge that he was engaging in "subversive activities." That effort also fizzled, but Roosevelt finally achieved his goal when his friends in New York gerrymandered Fish's congressional district, resulting in his loss in the 1944 elections.[16]

By the 1930s, America's city bosses, who needed federal patronage to win elections and generate operating funds, were as vulnerable to Roosevelt's tactics as Huey Long had been. How these bosses fared often depended on whether or not they had value to the president. For example, Enoch "Nucky" Johnson was the political boss of Atlantic City during the 1920s and 1930s. He made his money from bootlegging, gambling, protection, and kickbacks. Johnson's tax returns always included a large amount of income listed under a vague category called "other contributions." The gamblers and racketeers in wide-open Atlantic City liked Nucky, who provided security and stability, and they were willing to lie and even go to jail to protect him.[17]

Johnson focused on local politics, which held much more profit potential than did national politics until 1932, when a new Tax Act dramatically increased federal income-tax rates and channeled more power to Washington. He seems to have been indifferent to national politics, and during the 1930s he did little either to help or to hurt President Roosevelt. Unfortunately for Nucky, however, when he chose his political affiliation in the early 1900s he happened to select the Republican Party. When Johnson was ultimately convicted of tax fraud in 1941, Roosevelt seems to have cared little one way or another. FDR simply watched from the sidelines as the IRS audited and then convicted Johnson.[18]

Whether corrupt local bosses were actually investigated and prosecuted, however, could turn on their political relationship to the Roosevelt political machine. The story of Frank Hague, the political boss in Jersey City, had a very different plot—and a different ending. Hague, born of Irish parents, grew up in a rough Jersey City neighborhood. He was expelled from school in the sixth grade. As a teenager he worked as a blacksmith and even as a boxer. Politics was a way out of the slums for Hague. He joined the Democratic political machine and worked his way up from constable to city commissioner to mayor. By 1932, the fifty-six-year-old Hague was the undisputed boss of Jersey City. He initially backed Al Smith for president in 1932, but he quickly shifted to Roosevelt after the Democratic convention. Hague promised the swing state of New Jersey to Roosevelt and threw a spectacular parade for the candidate in Sea Girt, New Jersey, with a crowd of 100,000 attending—the largest Roosevelt saw anywhere during the entire campaign.[19]

On election day, Hague's support proved to be indispensable. Roosevelt carried New Jersey by fewer than 28,900 votes out of more than 1.6 million cast. The major urban counties all went Republican, but not Hague's Hudson County. Hague delivered that county to FDR by more than 117,000 votes, nearly a three-to-one margin.[20]

Once in the White House, Roosevelt funneled all federal patronage in New Jersey through Hague and none through the governor or the state's two United States senators. When a man from Newark wrote to the governor of New Jersey asking for a job, the governor responded, "I do not have the power to appoint to these Federal positions. They are made upon the recommendation of the local organizations to Frank Hague. . . . I would suggest that you get in touch with the mayor." Roosevelt's men James Farley and WPA director Harry Hopkins helped the mayor strengthen his hold on the state. Hopkins began the federal flow by giving Hague $500,000 per month for relief in 1933 and 1934; and in the five years after that, Hopkins directed the WPA to pour an incredible $50 million into Jersey City. Harold Ickes and the Public Works Administration gave $17 million to Hague's town—some of which Hague used to build the third largest hospital in the world. Those who could not, or would not, pay their medical bills could get them reduced or removed by seeing Hague's district political leaders. Roosevelt came to Jersey City in October 1936, right before the presidential election, to dedicate Hague's hospital and receive the boss's official blessing. On election day, Hague delivered an even larger county victory for Roosevelt—an almost four-to-one margin—and New Jersey's sixteen electoral votes again went to the president.[21]

Hague used his patronage wisely and controlled his city with an iron hand. "I am the law," Hague often boasted. Political opponents had no patronage jobs and sometimes found themselves in jail for their critical remarks. Hague openly disparaged civil liberties; his enemies labeled him the "Hudson County Hitler." One outside reporter depicted Hague as "Dictator—American Style," and another called him "King Hanky Panky." Even with the torrent of federal funds cascading into New Jersey, and rumors of corruption rampant, the IRS never made a serious investigation of Hague. Nucky Johnson, with a smaller city and only local funds to swindle, went to prison. Hague never did.[22]

The IRS had ample reason to go after Hague on WPA corruption charges alone. Harry Hopkins had piles of evidence, including sworn affidavits, that Hague was manipulating elections, politicizing the dispensing of jobs, and forcing jobholders to pay 3 percent of their salaries to the Hague machine at election time. One WPA director regularly answered his phone, "Democratic headquarters." He was not discreet, but at least he was truthful. Hopkins not only did nothing to stop Hague, but actually seemed to encourage him.[23]

Roosevelt was embarrassed by Hague and never included him in his inner circle, but Hague was needed if New Jersey was to remain in the president's column. Roosevelt was firm on that and proved it when James Farley discovered that Hague had a crony at the post office who was opening and reading all mail to and from major political opponents. Tampering with the U.S. mail was a federal offense, and some of Huey Long's henchmen went to jail for misusing the post office. Farley, in fact, came to Roosevelt for instructions on how to prosecute Hague. The president, however, stopped Farley in his tracks: "Forget prosecution. You go tell Frank to knock it off. We can't have this kind of thing going on. But keep this quiet. We need Hague's support if we want New Jersey."[24]

Historian Lyle Dorsett, who has studied the evidence carefully, reports the following example of how Hague misused federal funds: "After a plea from Hague, Harry Hopkins decided to stretch the letter of the law and use WPA funds which were earmarked for labor to buy seats and plumbing for Jersey City's new baseball stadium. Hague knew he was asking Hopkins to put his neck out, but assured him it was for a good cause inasmuch as the facility was to be named Roosevelt Stadium and the president was going to be present for the grand opening."[25]

Hague was not the only politician who needed the president's help to stay out of jail. Roosevelt used his powers to help others who were useful to him. Lyndon Johnson, for example, was a young congressman from Texas in the 1930s. He always backed Roosevelt enthusiastically—even in 1937, when others abandoned Roosevelt because of his efforts to pack the Supreme Court. Johnson, who was a candidate in a special election to Congress that year, argued that the New Deal was a seamless web and that to support Court packing was an essential test of loyalty to the president and his agenda.[26]

Roosevelt came to like Johnson, especially when Johnson proved himself capable of helping Roosevelt control Texas politics. Whenever Roosevelt needed help from Sam Rayburn, the House majority leader, Johnson acted as an intermediary. When Vice President John Nance Garner of Texas mounted a presidential campaign in 1940, Johnson secretly undermined Garner in the state and swung support to Roosevelt. In return, Roosevelt channeled much federal patronage into Texas through Johnson.

Just as the president used a mayor in New Jersey as his key political connection, so he used a junior congressman in Texas to dispense patronage. Thomas Corcoran once observed that Lyndon Johnson "got more projects, and more money for his district, than anyone else. He was the best kind of Congressman for his district that *ever* was." Those who received Johnson's patronage in turn made Johnson a millionaire and financed his political ambitions for the U.S. Senate. Brown and Root, Inc., a huge Texas contracting firm, built dams and other projects with federal dollars. They also donated heavily to Johnson's two Senate campaigns in the 1940s. Campaign contributions were not tax deductible, but Brown and Root claimed these contributions on their tax return anyway—and with such carelessness that they triggered an IRS audit. The IRS investigated Brown and Root and determined that they owed over $1.5 million in back taxes and penalties. They were also vulnerable to a jail sentence.[27] Johnson, too, became an IRS target, for failing properly to report income from his campaigns.

Political allegiances proved helpful for Johnson and his allies, however. On January 13, 1944, just as six IRS agents were winding up their eighteen-month investigation of Johnson, President Roosevelt had an emergency meeting with him. That day, the president contacted Elmer Irey and accelerated the process of halting the probe. Brown and Root settled quietly—with no publicity—for a mere $372,000 in back taxes, and Johnson was not harmed at all. He had proven himself too valuable to the president to be prosecuted.[28]

Roosevelt, however, would not protect political allies from the IRS if they were insufficiently useful. An interesting example is "Big Tom" Pendergast, the Democratic boss in Kansas City. Pendergast was an early supporter of Roosevelt for president in 1932, and on election day he helped deliver Missouri to FDR. Jackson County, Pendergast's stronghold, went for FDR by more than a two-to-one margin—which must have taken some arm-twisting, because that county had voted Republican in the previous three presidential races. In return, Roosevelt had Hopkins filter federal patronage in Missouri through Big Tom.[29]

Pendergast used his new friend in a high place to consolidate further his power in Missouri. For example, he had his own construction company and, like Hague, he used his power to gain wealth, distribute jobs, and win elections. In 1934, Pendergast's choice for U.S. Senate was a failed haberdasher named Harry Truman. After Truman won his election handily, a constituent wrote asking him for a WPA job. Truman responded: "If you will send us endorsements from the Kansas City Democratic organization, I shall be glad to do what I can for you." That response spoke volumes about where political influence in Missouri was located and which party held it. Pendergast's choice for governor in 1936 was Lloyd Stark. Big Tom coerced WPA workers all over the state to vote for Stark or lose their jobs. The same procedure was employed in Roosevelt's reelection campaign. The president carried Missouri easily, with Jackson County leading the way with a three-to-one vote margin.[30]

Pendergast's exuberant attempts to deliver a large vote for Roosevelt proved to be his undoing. After the election, some observers noticed that Pendergast's first ward had cast more ballots than it had eligible voters. And some of the precincts in the ward had unanimous voting for Roosevelt—even though some voters there swore they had voted for Landon. A police captain accused of intimidating voters responded: "I wouldn't hurt none of them women, but I consider it a patriotic duty to see that votes are cast the way the ward leader wants 'em cast. After all, I'm employed by the city." Maurice Milligan, the district attorney, prosecuted more than 200 election judges, precinct captains, and partisan clerks—all of whom had legal defenses financed by Pendergast. Seventy-eight went to jail. Governor Stark, in the meantime, became nervous and took a calculated risk. He switched sides, joined forces with Milligan, and helped bring in the FBI and the IRS to investigate Pendergast.[31]

Roosevelt no doubt appreciated the large Democratic vote mustered by Pendergast, but the bad publicity that followed gave ammunition to those who were critical of the president and his New Deal. Roosevelt therefore pondered the idea of switching his patronage to Governor Stark. When seventy-eight of Pendergast's men went to jail, and when Stark's candidate defeated Pendergast's candidate in a key 1938 statewide election, Roosevelt dropped Pendergast and gave more of Missouri's patronage to Governor Stark. Roosevelt sat back as the IRS fined and imprisoned Big Tom for tax evasion. Unlike Hague in New Jersey and Johnson in Texas, Pendergast was not indispensable to Roosevelt and thus could be thrown to the IRS dogs.[32]

By Roosevelt's second term, he was accustomed to using—or at least to con-templating using—the IRS for political help. The major crises of his second term—such as the one that surrounded the Court-packing plan—stimulated the Roosevelt administration into using the IRS even more to stymie political enemies. Burt Wheeler of Montana, who helped mobilize votes against Court packing, complained loudly to Secretary Morgenthau of rumors that the IRS had been investigating him. Morgenthau promised Wheeler freedom from a tax investigation. Morgenthau later received a memo from a colleague in the Treasury Department that reported that Thomas Corcoran had come to the Department of Justice with "a request for information concerning the income tax returns of the Justices of the Supreme Court." Morgenthau refused to allow Corcoran to have those returns, and Roosevelt apparently never insisted that his decision be overridden.[33]

Wealthy Americans were a natural target for Roosevelt and the IRS. For one thing, rich people had the money that Roosevelt needed in order to fund the WPA and other programs. His 79 percent marginal tax rate on top incomes secured some of this cash, but people with wealth quickly found tax loopholes that shielded a large portion of their incomes from the IRS. The wealthy also became a target of Roosevelt's men because they constituted a nucleus of opposition to the New Deal. Most wealthy Americans resented paying some three-fourths of their annual earnings for federal programs that they loathed, and they complained loudly. From Roosevelt's point of view, hunting down rich Americans therefore not only helped to fund his political agenda but also helped to undermine his political opponents.

Roosevelt's first target among the rich was Andrew Mellon, the Pittsburgh industrialist and banker. Mellon had helped to found Alcoa and Gulf Oil, and he was on the board of directors of about sixty companies. By the 1920s, he was reputed to be the third wealthiest man in the country, trailing only Henry Ford and John D. Rockefeller. His wealth alone made him a tempting candi-date for an IRS audit, but his political actions during the 1920s made him an irresistible target. Mellon, after all, was Morgenthau's Republican predecessor in the Treasury Department.[34]

Mellon, as secretary of the treasury under presidents Warren Harding, Calvin Coolidge, and Herbert Hoover, was widely regarded as one of the greatest men ever to hold that office. His legacy was to formulate what is today called supply-side economics, the idea of cutting taxes to stimulate investment. High income-tax rates, Mellon argued, "inevitably put pressure upon the taxpayer to withdraw his capital from productive business and invest it in tax-exempt securities. . . . The result is that the sources of taxation are drying up, wealth is failing to carry its share of the tax burden; and capital is being diverted into channels which yield neither revenue to the Government nor profit to the people."[35]

Mellon wrote a popular book, *Taxation: The People's Business,* in which he developed his ideas. "It seems difficult for some to understand," he wrote, "that high rates of taxation do not necessarily mean large revenue to the Government, and that more revenue may often be obtained by lower rates." Mellon illustrated this principle with an example from the world of business. He compared the government's setting tax rates on incomes to a businessman's setting prices on products. "If a price is fixed too high, sales drop off and with them profits." Mellon asked: "Does anyone question that Mr. Ford has made more money by reducing the price of his car [from $3,000 to $380] and increasing his sales than he would have made by maintaining a high price and a greater profit per car, but selling less cars?"[36]

Mellon, of course, recognized that there was a limit to how far the government could cut tax rates and still increase revenue. "The problem of governments," he said, "is to fix rates which will bring in a maximum amount of revenue to the Treasury and at the same time bear not too heavily on the taxpayer or on business enterprises." Mellon believed that 25 percent was about as much as rich people would pay in taxes before they rushed to various tax shelters, including foreign investments, collectibles (e.g., art or stamps), and tax-exempt bonds.[37]

Mellon had a chance to test his ideas as secretary of the treasury. He persuaded presidents Harding and Coolidge to promote a plan that eventually cut taxes on large incomes from 73 to 24 percent and on smaller incomes from 4 to 0.5 percent. These tax cuts helped spur an outpouring of economic development in sectors ranging from air conditioning to refrigerators to zippers, from Scotch tape to helicopters to talking movies. Investors took more risks when they were allowed to keep more of their gains. During Coolidge's six years in office, the unemployment rate averaged only 3.3 percent and the inflation rate a mere 1 percent—the lowest "misery index" (the sum of the unemployment and inflation rates) presided over by any president in the twentieth century.

Furthermore, Mellon was vindicated in his astonishing predictions that cutting tax rates across the board would generate more revenue. In the early

1920s, when the highest tax rate was 73 percent, the total income-tax revenue to the U.S. government was a little more than $700 million. In 1928 and 1929, when the top tax rate was slashed to 25 and then 24 percent, the total revenue topped the one-billion-dollar mark. Mellon also whittled down the size of the IRS and spearheaded very few investigations. No wonder Mellon was called by his devotees "the best secretary of treasury since Alexander Hamilton."[38]

Roosevelt's philosophy of government contrasted sharply with that of Mellon's. The president believed that the way to combat the Great Depression was through high taxation, government planning of industry, quotas on farming, and massive federal relief programs. Roosevelt believed the Great Depression was partly caused by poor investments and stock manipulations by the rich. Mellon's very presence as a popular former treasury secretary served as a constant reminder to many Americans of "the good old days" when tax rates were low, jobs were plentiful, and government was unobtrusive. In Roosevelt's first term, Mellon became the object of a massive and unrelenting IRS investigation comparable to that waged against Huey Long.

"The Roosevelt administration made me go after Andy Mellon," said Elmer Irey, but Irey believed Mellon's tax returns to have been in order. The Roosevelt administration had first tried to punish Mellon through an FBI investigation. According to Irey, "Bob Jackson [future attorney general] was made chief counsel of the Internal Revenue Department and he said to me: 'I need help on the Mellon thing. The F.B.I. Investigation was no good. You run one on him.'" When Irey hesitated, he received a phone call from his boss, Henry Morgenthau. "Irey," Morgenthau announced, "you can't be 99 2/3 percent on that job. Investigate Mellon. I order it." Irey pleaded with Morgenthau that Mellon was innocent, but Morgenthau ended the conversation by saying, "I'm directing you to go ahead, Irey." Irey reluctantly began the audit, but more than ten years later he was still upset that he had been forced to launch a futile and wasteful IRS audit of an innocent man.[39]

Since Morgenthau and Roosevelt were longtime friends, and since the two of them met privately on a regular basis, it is likely that Roosevelt directed Morgenthau to launch the tax audit of Mellon. At the very least Roosevelt must have tacitly approved it. And Morgenthau was a willing accomplice. "You can't be too tough in this trial to suit me," Morgenthau told the government's prosecutor, Robert Jackson. Morgenthau added, "I consider that Mellon is not on trial but Democracy and the privileged rich and I want to see who will win."[40]

235

Mellon won. A Pittsburgh grand jury, heavily composed of working-class laborers, ignored the class rhetoric of the New Dealers and refused to indict Mellon. Then the Board of Tax Appeals voted unanimously that Mellon "did not file a false and fraudulent return with the purpose of evading taxes." The board did find some technical errors in Mellon's returns. Mellon decided to settle for $486,000—less than one-sixth of the original indictment—and get the "political prosecution," as he called it, behind him. The Roosevelt administration lost a case it never had a chance to win, but it did send a message that lining up with the Republicans could be costly.[41]

Moses "Moe" Annenberg, who was almost as wealthy and almost as Republican as Mellon, also drew an IRS audit—one that had thirty-five agents working for two-and-a-half years to prosecute him. Unlike Mellon, who was born into Pittsburgh's elite, Annenberg was a poor German immigrant who came to America at age eight. He showed skill selling newspapers for the Hearst chain and worked his way up to be circulation manager of the entire Hearst newspaper empire. Wanting to start his own business, he looked to horse racing. An investor, not a gambler, Annenberg sold racing forms (which described the horses), wall sheets (which posted the racing results), and a wire service (which was used to obtain immediate results). He developed the largest horse-racing network in the country and made many millions of dollars from that enterprise. He also invested effectively in real estate and the stock market.[42]

Annenberg continued to maintain an interest in the newspaper business, and in Roosevelt's first term he bought the *Philadelphia Inquirer*. Annenberg infused the *Inquirer*'s editorials with his Republican philosophy and quickly built the paper into a worthy competitor to the Democrat-leaning *Philadelphia Record*. The editor of the *Record*, David Stern, was an ally of Morgenthau (and his frequent chess partner) and Roosevelt, who appreciated Stern's successful efforts to elect more Democrats in Pennsylvania. Annenberg's aggressive advertising and news reporting helped the *Inquirer* sharply increase its subscriptions and sales at the expense of Stern's *Record*. The *Inquirer*'s success meant that more Pennsylvania readers were absorbing Annenberg's pungent editorials against the New Deal in general and Roosevelt in particular. "The War Against Business Goes On" and "No Room for Fascism in a Democracy" were typical of his headlines. The content was also hard-hitting. "Never before has class hatred been elevated to the status of an unctuous virtue," wrote Annenberg in one editorial. In another editorial Annenberg argued, "Government, by swinging its mailed fist at business, has not brought lasting recovery." He continued: "Under its [government's] stern restrictions and oppressive taxes, millions of employables have failed to obtain work." Roosevelt's state of the union message in 1938, Annenberg wrote, "indicates not the slightest retreat from a program and an economic philosophy which have signally failed, in five years of drastic and costly experiments, to establish the United States on a sound recovery footing."[43]

Annenberg helped lead the Republicans to a stunning victory in the 1938 midterm elections. His handpicked candidate for governor, Arthur James, was an obscure superior court judge, but he thrashed incumbent Democrat governor George Earle. The situation for the Democrats was desperate. Much New Deal money had been poured into Pennsylvania, and yet Earle was forced to leave office—and under a cloud of suspicion for taking political kickbacks. Meanwhile, Stern's *Record* was losing money because of the *Inquirer's* success. Stern turned to the federal government for help and was able to get the Federal Trade Commission to undertake a prosecution of Annenberg for selling advertising at too-low rates.

The Roosevelt administration had a better idea: an IRS investigation of Annenberg. Unlike Mellon, who as secretary of the treasury knew tax law inside out, Annenberg was careless and paid little attention to his taxes. His accountant filled out the forms and Annenberg signed them with no questions or probing. His corporate earnings—from news, horse racing, and dozens of other interests—were complicated, and it may well have been that Annenberg was trying to hide some of his revenue. Whatever the case, after Morgenthau's massive investigation it became clear that Annenberg owed the government about $8 million. He offered to pay all back taxes and fines, whatever the amount, but the Roosevelt administration wanted back taxes *and* jail time for Annenberg. As Irey told Morgenthau: "They are not going to have the opportunity to pay the tax [and avoid prison]." When Morgenthau and Roosevelt discussed the matter over lunch on April 11, 1939, Morgenthau asked Roosevelt if he could do something for the president. "Yes," Roosevelt said, "I want Moe Annenberg for dinner." Morgenthau responded, "You're going to have him for breakfast—fried."[44]

That attitude, according to Annenberg biographer Christopher Ogden, lay behind Annenberg's ultimate $8 million fine and three-year prison sentence. "The key to the Annenberg case for Morgenthau," Ogden observes, "was not simply penalizing Moses with a fine which no matter how high, he was certain that the wealthy publisher could pay. The goal was removing Moses from the scene so that he could cause no further political trouble." With Annenberg going to jail in 1940, the *Philadelphia Inquirer* became less strident, Roosevelt had an easier time carrying Pennsylvania during his reelection campaign—and the Treasury had $8 million more to spend on New Deal programs.[45]

Annenberg's fate reflected Roosevelt's disdain for wealthy Americans who sought means of tax avoidance. Tax evasion meant breaking the law. But tax avoidance meant using legal means—"loopholes" and various tax-deductible investments—to shelter income and thereby keep more of it. Alfred P. Sloan, the president of General Motors, justified the practice of tax avoidance this way: "No conscientious citizen desires to avoid payment of his just share of the country's burden. I do not seek to avoid mine. . . . While no one should desire to avoid payment of his share . . . neither should anyone be expected to pay more than is lawfully required."[46] In other words, if a taxpayer could find legitimate tax deductions, he should take them. Roosevelt, however, tended to lump "tax evasion" and "tax avoidance" together as evils.

Alexander Forbes, a Harvard classmate and cousin of Roosevelt, went one step further than Sloan in arguing against the efficacy of Roosevelt's tax policies. He argued that some of the chief tax deductions, especially charitable giving, did more good than if the money had been used for federal programs. "Look" he wrote in a letter to Roosevelt, "at the sorry spectacle presented by rows of beneficiaries of the 'boondoggle,' leaning on their shovels by the hour at futile projects, and contrast it with the great universities, museums, and research laboratories which have come from the wise and generous giving of such as Morgan, and then consider which is the major constructive force in building a stable civilization."[47]

Roosevelt was indignant. "My dear cousin and old classmate," he responded. "That being your belief, I do not hesitate to brand you as one of the worst anarchists in the United States." Facing unbalanced budgets each year, Roosevelt instinctively sought more tax revenue. Close the loopholes, publicly name the tax avoiders, and turn loose the IRS, the president urged.[48]

By 1937, Roosevelt insisted that Morgenthau be more aggressive in his investigations of wealthy Republicans. "Henry," Roosevelt urged, "it has come time to attack, and you have got more material than anyone else in Washington to lead the attack." Roosevelt also suggested that Democratic leaders in Congress create a "subcommittee to investigate tax avoidance." Exposing tax avoiders, Roosevelt told Senator Pat Harrison of Mississippi and Congressman Robert Doughton of North Carolina, would also bring the Democrats "ten million votes.""Mr. President," Morgenthau inquired,"how did you arrive at the ten million figure?" "I don't know" Roosevelt said with a smile,"but it sounded good. . . . Everything's settled."[49] Thus, Congress established the Joint Committee on Tax Evasion and Avoidance and gave it power to hold hearings, call witnesses, and secure tax returns from the Treasury.

Ironically, one witness the committee should have called was Roosevelt himself. Roosevelt may have been the first president to use a major tax loophole to shelter personal income. For donating his books, naval prints, and other material to his own presidential library in Hyde Park, Roosevelt took a $9,900 (about $100,000 in today's currency) tax deduction. Roosevelt's decision to employ tax avoidance was, of course, completely legal—just as the IRS concluded it was legal for Andrew Mellon to deduct from his tax burden the value of the paintings he donated to start the National Gallery of Art in Washington, D.C. By taking such a deduction, however, Roosevelt was in effect seconding the sentiments of his cousin Forbes, who had argued for the public value of tax-deductible gifts to "universities, museums, and research libraries."[50]

During his twelve years in office, Roosevelt expanded executive power and manipulated the IRS for political advantage, in effect reshaping the American presidency into an imperial presidency. Roosevelt's hypocrisy was hardly surprising given his blatantly partisan use of government power. On the one hand, he turned a blind eye to the transgressions of his political allies—refusing to investigate Frank Hague for tampering with the U.S. mail and calling off the tax investigation of Congressman Lyndon Johnson. On the other hand, he ordered his men to conduct aggressive investigations of political enemies like Andrew Mellon and Moses Annenberg.

Roosevelt also used his power to reward those who helped him prosecute his enemies. Though he failed to convict Mellon, Robert Jackson found favor with the president for his efforts and was appointed first to the president's cabinet as attorney general, and then in 1941 to the U.S. Supreme Court. Roosevelt also rewarded William Campbell and Frank Murphy, who helped lead the charge against Annenberg, with appointments, the former to a federal judgeship and the latter to the Supreme Court.

In the end, the Roosevelt administration elevated political corruption to a new art, abusing the power of the IRS and other federal government agencies for political advantage. Elliott Roosevelt once referred to his father's devious and bare-knuckled political tactics as "magicians' tricks." Certainly, Roosevelt, who remained popular throughout his twelve years in office and remains revered by subsequent generations of Americans, succeeded in pulling the wool over the eyes of many.[51]

Historical Consciousness versus the Will to Ignorance

BRUCE P. FROHNEN

Conservatism is inherently bound up with, if not itself a form of, historical consciousness. The conservative follows Edmund Burke in recognizing that society is a contract among the dead, the living, and the yet unborn. Each of us in this view is born into an inheritance of institutions, beliefs, and practices that he has a duty to pass on to the next generation intact. If one can add safely to the bank and capital of the ages with which one has been entrusted, that is all to the good. But it would be a vice-ridden betrayal of one's duty to risk the principal on foolish schemes of wholesale improvement.

Because one literally inherits one's culture and indeed one's life, one is perpetually immersed in history. One's family hands down physical and character traits along with a variety of family heirlooms, great and small. One grows up with the stories behind these various inheritances, tracing them back through the generations. In the same manner, one hears the stories of one's church and one's nation—of the development of institutional arrangements, the lives of saints and heroes, and changing relationships with other institutions. If one is lucky, one even will hear the stories of one's town and neighborhood, of the other families in the area and their changing relationships, of local heroes and how they saved the town and/or helped it flourish.

History is critical to the continued coherence of our lives, and of the associations and traditions that make up much of our lives. History is not, then, a mere repository of lessons. While it may be true in some sense that one who forgets the past is condemned to repeat it, the mining of history for concrete lessons relevant to current conduct is fraught with danger. Circumstances change and one who approaches history from a purely pragmatic, goal-oriented perspective often will learn the wrong lessons, or learn lessons in the wrong way, and end up making as many or more mistakes than the historically ignorant.

History's importance, in conservative terms, goes deeper than the mere learning of practical lessons. History is the context within which one acts. It requires our attention, consciousness, and understanding, so that we may interact properly with those around us and become coherent, moral persons capable of leading coherent, moral lives.

In his memoir, *Recovering the Past,* Forrest McDonald points to the essential role historical consciousness plays in the gaining of self-knowledge and moral perspective. By "thinking historically," we come to know where we are in time as well as in space. By learning what we and those around us have been, we come to understand who we are—we preserve our sanity by orienting ourselves to our moral, temporal, and phenomenological surroundings.[1]

Most important, however, is history's role as an integral part of the moral imagination. For it is through historical consciousness that we become fully human, fully capable of judging the morality of our own actions as well as the actions of others. As McDonald puts it, historical thinking "can enable us to see things around us that would otherwise be invisible—to escape the provincialism of the present." In thinking historically, "we try to understand past events and circumstances as the participants did."[2] We gain practice in using perceptual apparatuses other than our own, in seeing issues and events from more than one perspective, in distancing ourselves from our own selfish wants-of-the-moment. We need to think historically if we are to recognize our duties and act on them, even when they go against our own wishes. We need to think historically if we are to learn about, value, and act in accordance with the traditions, institutions, beliefs, and practices within which we live.

<hr>

Conservatives recognize that a morally serious person is one who has learned to value what he has been given. To value his inheritance, a person must know it. He must know how it developed, what it requires to flourish, and what place it holds for him. Only with this grounding can one transcend the mere tribalism of those who unthinkingly value only the familiar. And only with this grounding can one avoid the false cosmopolitanism of one who knows and is fundamentally attached to nothing save the delusion of his own self-creation.

Only when one has learned the roots of attachments and relations can one place an appropriate value on them and approach in irenic fashion others' attachments to their own inheritances. The moral person, in the conservative view, is able to value other societies precisely because he values his own, and because he understands the historically rooted nature of both. Thus, Burke could defend the radically different societies of Hindu India and traditional, Catholic Ireland against radical policies initiated by his own, highly valued British Parliament. The peoples of these differing societies, Burke argued, shared a fundamental right: to be governed in accordance with their tradition-based expectations.

As important as the moral benefits of historical thinking are, however, we should not lose sight of the nature of historical consciousness itself, or of its sometimes demanding requirements. The conservative can be neither a mere subjectivist nor a determinist; he views societies neither as self-justifying expressions of individual choices nor as products of an idealized History that exerts its own powers for its own ends. Rather, the conservative recognizes that there is a universal, transcendent natural law that declares the existence of a number of permanent moral principles (best summed up in the Decalogue and the Golden Rule). Judged by these standards, all societies are flawed, and some are unacceptable. But the conservative remains attached to any tolerable society because it is the product of its people's attempt, over time, to apply permanent universal standards to changing circumstances.

Reason and character being flawed, societies, as the historical instantiation of natural law, also will be flawed. They will not be improved, however, through hubristic attempts at wholesale reform. Such attempts are ahistorical. They ignore the fact that men are attached to their given way of life for good reason—because its customs allow them to interact peacefully by establishing reasonable expectations, because the stories of their lives are bound up with the stories of their communities, and because social bonds, once severed, are not easily reestablished.

Burke attacked the French revolutionary Jacobins for attempting to reconstitute society along rationalist lines because society simply cannot be constructed or reconstructed out of whole cloth. To begin with, we are attached to one another not through contracts or rational calculations, but through sympathies and common feelings rooted in daily interaction. Moreover, any society is dependent for its survival upon what Burke termed the "unsuspecting confidence" of the people.[3] If the bulk of a society's members do not accept, without hesitation, the intrinsic morality of its fundamental arrangements, that society will fall into anarchy.

Unsuspecting confidence is not merely passive. Despite the fact that conservatives are often caricatured as simply ignoring potential problems with their way of life, the conservative can conserve only through extensive reflection on the nature of his society, such that he can harmonize its internal conflicts and seek reasonable reforms consistent with its primary traditions. As Burke pointed out, "A state without the means of some change is without the means of its conservation."[4] He praised the British for basing such reforms as had been necessary over their history in a filial understanding of their constitution and the rights appropriate thereto—as an entailed inheritance.

From Magna Carta through the Restoration and the Glorious Revolution, the British eschewed rationalist theories of abstract human rights in favor of a vision of their rights and franchises as an inheritance.[5] Indeed, English charters, from Magna Carta through the English Bill of Rights, consistently took the form of declarations of preexisting rights necessary not as creative forces establishing new practices in accordance with abstract theory, but rather as corrections of dangerous trends in royal conduct that were undermining historical practices. Rights, and practices relevant to those rights, did develop and change over time through these means, but they did so incrementally and consistent with the people's overall understanding of how public life works. Those royal powers which were limited or eliminated generally were those which had been most abused or abused in ways most prejudicial to preexisting rights.[6] In this way, continuity by and large was maintained in Britain. And where, as with the English Civil War, continuity was broken, it was reestablished with relative ease and firmness.

Even if the continuity of a society's traditions is broken, one must look to history for its reestablishment. Thus, Burke lamented that the French king had acceded to the calling of a novel general assembly just prior to the revolution. This innovation, on Burke's view, helped bring about that revolution. Burdened with a majority unaware of or hostile to its duty to maintain a civil social order and the conservation of fundamental civil-social arrangements (about which it knew little or nothing), the general assembly ended up overturning French society itself. It would have been better for the king to call back into being the ancient French Estates General—assemblies rooted in centuries of practice, though long left in disuse. Such a move would have reestablished representation and consultation in accordance with historic usage and practice, guiding opinion and conduct into established modes. The ancient Estates General would have fit and reinforced the preexisting nature of the French people, strengthening their traditions and historical rights along with their attachment to their traditional way of life.

Maintaining a coherent tradition requires intelligence and creativity as well as loyalty; merely refusing to change inevitably brings ruin. The moral imagination is therefore essential to conservation, but it is important to note that the moral imagination is historical in nature. Russell Kirk defined the moral imagination as "man's power to perceive ethical truth, abiding law, in the seeming chaos of many events." The moral imagination enables men to perceive the permanent truths immanent in changing events and circumstances. Without it "man would live merely day to day, or rather moment to moment, as dogs do." The moral imagination "is the strange faculty—inexplicable if men are assumed to have an animal nature only—of discerning greatness, justice, and order, beyond the bars of appetite and self-interest."[7]

This faculty may be strange, but it is not inherently inexplicable; it transcends mere practical reason, but is not therefore irrational. The moral imagination is "the power of ethical perception which strides beyond the barriers of private experience and events of the moment. The moral imagination aspires to the apprehending of right order in the soul and right order in the commonwealth."[8] Shaped by its proper orientation toward the perception of order, rather than by the desire to satisfy particular wants-of-the-moment, the moral imagination enables us to make sense of our surroundings in all their aspects.

Those who attempt to live only in the present are imprisoned by their selfish desires, immobilized by the swirl of events around them, trapped in each unconnected moment. In practical moral terms, they are immobilized because they have denied themselves the necessary tools of prudent action. They have cut themselves off from the store of knowledge necessary to turn instinctive acts into a pattern of coherent, rational conduct. Escape through abstraction is impossible, or rather, it leads to the creation of a second, false reality in which one's actions fit a theory but not the true nature of man or the universe. The attempt leads to moral enormities of the Jacobin type, followed by ultimate failure.

Through historical consciousness—that is, by escaping the parochialism of the present through the morally informed study of history—we can gain access to examples of right conduct that help shape our character, order our values, and orient our actions toward the common good. Having achieved order in our souls, we are then able to seek public order by searching in history and elsewhere for possible courses of action that, through a process of analogy, we can apply to our current situation. We can combine reason with experience, gaining the ability to act prudently so as to maintain the coherence of our given way of life in the face of changing circumstances.

History and literature both allow us to develop our moral imagination. As history is not merely dead facts, so literature is not mere entertainment. Both allow us to see and enter into the spirit of our civilization, and thus to inculcate the habits necessary to maintain that civilization at its best. Burke, for example, pointed to the spirit of religion and the spirit of the gentleman as the core of British civilization. Kirk emphasized the role of literature in forming the moral imagination. We should not, however, treat this as an attachment to "mere" stories. Rather, Kirk saw literature as a doorway into the spirit of our civilization, and of the human soul. Burke, too, emphasized the need to understand the spirit as a guiding force of civilization. The spirit of religion and the spirit of the gentleman, he argued, were at the core of British civilization. To the extent that the manners and habits formed through common worship and common standards of conduct were reduced to the machinations of power politics and the mere pursuit of wealth, the British people lost their ability to discern, let alone put into action, the lessons embedded in their civilization. They lost the key to moral conduct that had allowed them to turn kings into companions, subdue the fierceness of pride and power, oblige "sovereigns to submit to the soft collar of social esteem," and reduce the necessity of brute force through the introduction of settled manners.[9]

Historical consciousness, and the moral imagination of which it is a part, allows us to recognize and maintain the coherence of our way of life. It teaches us to value our civilization in ways that mere pragmatism, focused as it is on satisfying wants-of-the-moment, cannot. The genius of conservatism lies in its adherents' ability to discern the universal in the particular, and to analogize from the particulars of history and literature to face changing circumstances in a manner that respects human expectations and the demands of natural law.

We live in a decidedly unconservative age, in which to be called a rebel is to be praised, provided one does not actually subject existing power structures to any transcendent moral standard. Nevertheless, it is not helpful to our understanding of the moral nature and role of historical consciousness to simply divide the world into "conservative" and "liberal" camps rooted in particular public policy positions. Conservatism, rather, should be used in reference primarily to a form of historical consciousness that appreciates tradition and seeks to sustain the tenuous threads that knit the past to the present and both to the future.

Unfortunately, not everyone who refers to himself as a conservative today thinks historically. Some who place themselves, or who are placed by others, in the conservative camp are in fact openly hostile toward historical consciousness. Thus Michael Ledeen, a neoconservative contributing editor to *National Review,* tells Americans that "creative destruction is our middle name."[10] Ledeen and others like him take the notion of "creative destruction"—a phrase coined by Joseph Schumpeter to point out the dangerous tendency of economies set up on capitalist ideological lines to destroy preexisting attachments and structures in building new ones—to be a productive guide for common action.

Schumpeter predicted that creative destruction would undermine our culture and undermine the institutions and personal relations that bind us to one another and to the healthy pursuit of rational, life-sustaining improvements. As a result, he predicted, we would become isolated individuals who pursue leisure and security and are content to let the state provide both. Indeed, Schumpeter's point was that creative destruction would turn capitalism into socialism even as it sustained the political structures of democracy.[11] Whether from conviction or from ignorance, Ledeen rejects Schumpeter's analysis even as he appropriates his terminology. In proudly proclaiming America's "revolutionary" character, Ledeen seeks to highlight not the dangers of cultural degradation but rather what he sees as the liberating promise of rejecting history.

Ledeen is clear in his disdain for history and the preservation of tradition and in his attachment to the liberation of individuals from the ties of the past. He thus makes clear, in contradiction to contemporary public policy labels, that he is attached to the ideology of liberalism—the ideology of liberation, of "progress" from the confines of tradition to individual autonomy. As John Stuart Mill summed up the liberal position, society rightfully can interfere with the individual's "liberty of action" only when that action is used to harm others. Otherwise, "over himself, over his own body and mind, the individual is sovereign."[12] Such freedom must be maintained, not only against governmental interference, but against the potentially heavier hand of nongovernmental institutions, traditions, and the people themselves, lest the "eccentric" be kept from his socially useful calling as an intellectual and moral innovator.

Because liberalism by nature seeks to free individuals from the ties of inheritance, the liberal attitude toward history is overtly adversarial. This is why, for Ledeen, Americans are a good people precisely because they are revolutionary:

> We tear down the old order every day, from business to science, litera-
> ture, art, architecture, and cinema to politics and the law. Our enemies
> have always hated this whirlwind of energy and creativity, which men-
> aces their traditions (whatever they may be) and shames them for their
> inability to keep pace. Seeing America undo traditional societies, they
> fear us, for they do not wish to be undone. They cannot feel secure so
> long as we are there, for our very existence—our existence, not our
> policies—threatens their legitimacy. They must attack us in order to
> survive, just as we must destroy them to advance our historic mission.[13]

Ledeen's America constantly and intentionally destroys its own past so that it can create everything anew. It intentionally menaces all traditional societies—whatever their benefits—and will destroy them in advancing its "historic" mission of liberating mankind from the stifling weight of its past. It would seem that it is not only the Islamicist extremists (at whom Ledeen aims the bulk of his criticism) who should fear America, but anyone who values the traditions and ways of life in which he grew up.

It would be incorrect, however, to say that Ledeen rejects all forms of tradition. What Ledeen rejects is the conservative traditions of valuing our historical inheritance and cultivating historical consciousness. He accepts an antihistorical "Enlightenment" tradition that is rooted in the French revo-lutionary ideology rejected by Burke. As George Carey has argued, current debates over America's character and proper goals are "principally an exten-sion of the basic divisions that separated Burke from the *philosophes* of the French Revolution." These divisions were rooted in disagreements concern-ing the value of historical consciousness: "Whereas Burke could see the vital and indispensable roles of traditions for the society to become an organic 'partnership in every virtue, and all perfection,' the *philosophes* were antago-nistic towards traditions, convinced that society could be torn apart to be built anew by the use of 'reason.'"[14]

Despite its antagonism toward historical traditions, Enlightenment ratio-nalism itself has been shaped over the last two centuries into a tradition of sorts. As Carey explains, the philosophes' positions have been "differentiated and refined, their major elements now constituting well-established traditions in their own right."[15] We cannot live without tradition. By nature social beings, we join with our fellows in thought and action. Every people, over time, develops shared ways of thinking and acting. If they did not, they would not be able to cooperate or to form societies, let alone forge effective movements within society. Thus, even antihistorical thoughts and actions eventually harden into traditions with their own correlative institutions, beliefs, and practices, and with their own internally generated purposes (not to say "missions").

⟨⟩

Antihistorical thinking, no less than historical thinking, is rooted in prejudices, which in the Burkean sense means "unthinking beliefs" or ingrained habits of thought and action. In the case of Enlightenment rationalism, these prejudices have become driving principles of political movements like American progressivism. As Carey notes, progressivism is characterized by its "quest for equality," its propensity to use the government to solve all human problems, "its propensity for blaming society for the wrongs or shortcomings of individuals, and, *inter alia,* its anti-traditionalist stance in the name of freedom, progress, and tolerance," all of which are "unmistakably the outgrowth of the Enlightenment."[16]

Progressivism was the predominant twentieth-century incarnation of liberalism. It was a collection of public-policy assumptions that sought to translate liberal ideology into political reality. Progressive policy positions are fundamentally hostile toward the conservative view of the human person and the social order. They go against the conservative understanding, rooted in a Burkean reading of natural law and human nature, that each of us has a duty to lead a virtuous life whatever our circumstances, and that the fundamental institutions of society are properly beyond the right of the government to attempt to change in any wholesale fashion—or indeed, of its capacity to do so. Instead, these institutions deserve the state's protection. Rather than looking to rationalistic reform, the conservative looks to historical structures and ongoing custom to help us lead peaceful social lives and to protect the local and familial associations in which we learn to be decent human beings.

The conservative valuation of historical consciousness is rooted, like conservatism itself, in the Western understanding of human nature and the order of being. It is rooted in a deep-seated vision of what all men are like and what they naturally seek. Conservatism recognizes historical consciousness as a permanent thing, an unchanging aspect of human nature; in seeking to overcome it, then, liberalism must conquer human nature. The liberal tradition opposes our natural drive to think and act historically, to make sense of our lives and relationships by placing them in time as well as in space. The conservative's historical consciousness is not merely a preference to be rejected by the liberal, but a reality the liberal must overcome.

Liberalism rejects conservative convictions regarding the person's historically rooted nature, treating them as, in effect, deeper prejudices underlying more obvious prejudices regarding the value of tradition. Of course, liberalism also puts forward certain convictions regarding human nature and human knowledge. Liberalism's true revolution in its earlier phases was not political—for rights, liberties, and limited government have their roots in the medieval consensus, not the hermetically sealed mind of John Locke or any other philosopher.[17] The first true liberal revolution was psychological and epistemological, rooted in Locke's notion of the human mind as a tabula rasa. This conviction that our minds are blank slates on which the teacher, be he educator or legislator, can write according to his will has been carried on through the philosophes and the nineteenth-century liberals up to John Dewey and contemporary progressivist educators. As Linda Raeder has pointed out, the Mills, both James and John Stuart, were particularly enamored of the idea that a combination of salutary laws and finely tuned educative practices could produce the necessary rewards and punishments to create good men, without recourse to tradition or, especially, religion.[18]

History, the liberal argues, is not an unavoidable part of human sociability; nor is it a form of knowing. Anyone can be brought up to be a functioning social being without the need for historical consciousness or the habits traditionally formed through social interaction. Indeed, according to John Stuart Mill, any moral code, if taught from birth, will discourage vice. In Mill's view, each of us through properly calibrated rewards and punishments can be made more virtuous than we would be made through tradition and historically oriented education.[19]

In the liberal view, it is within the power of the teacher, and especially of the state, to shape our character by constructing an appropriate rewards-and-punishment regime. The result is a highly didactic vision of education and of the formation of character.[20] Yet this vision of education and character formation relies no less on habituation than does the historical. Rather, it replaces a conservative view of history—in which our common nature and especially the force of religious belief and tradition have provided us with a valuable inheritance we ought to preserve—with an alternative view of history as the weight of superstition and oppression that must be overcome through rationalistic education. Valuing an ideal of individuals as rational choice-makers rather than as members of a society who are bound to others through various relationships, liberalism seeks to educate individuals to become what it values and to tear them away from the social connections and forms of knowledge it deprecates.

John Stuart Mill had a particular hostility toward forms of habituation that he felt prevented the development of rational views. For example, he objected vigorously to public prayer and the recitation of religious creeds because they formed habits in individuals that might be contrary to their conscious views.[21] The proper place to look for the source of Mill's aversion to creeds and prayer is not in a hostility toward habits per se, but rather in his hostility toward the particular habits of mind and action formed through historically received authority, and religion in particular.

Raeder has shown the great extent of Mill's hostility toward Christianity, including his belief that Christianity throughout its history had spawned ignorance and violence and revealed itself to be utterly lacking in social utility.[22] This led Mill to seek the replacement of Christianity with a "religion of humanity" that would redirect the energies devoted to the worship of God toward service to mankind.[23] Key to this endeavor, in Mill's view, was the replacement of religious educative elites with purely intellectual ones. These new elites would strip from men the accretion of their supposedly ignorant, superstitious patrimony and replace it with the tools of rational choice-making.

In his correspondence, Mill commented on the problem he faced in seeking to free men from religious elites: "Liberalism is for making every man his own guide & sovereign master, & letting him think for himself & do exactly as he judges best for himself, giving other men leave to persuade him if they can by evidence, but forbidding him to give way to authority; and still less allowing them to constrain him more than the existence & tolerable security of every man's person and property renders indispensably necessary."[24] To eliminate the ability of the elites of his day—the vast majority of whom were rooted in religious and historical institutions and understandings—to sway individual judgment was Mill's self-chosen task. He sought to make (note, not merely "allow" but "make") every man his own sovereign. To accomplish this task, Mill sought to create a new cadre of intellectuals committed to the religion of humanity. These men and women would propagate the "true" doctrine of human nature and the good, inculcating it into the masses.[25]

By eliminating the authority of preexisting elites, Mill would not, in fact, eliminate authority. Rather, he would replace the authority of one set of elites with that of another. But Mill did not see any danger to individual judgment from the authority of his new elites because their status and authority would be rooted in rationalist, scientific knowledge. According to Mill, the public should be taught to accept the methods of science as authoritative and to accept their extension to social and humanistic realms. In this way, according to Mill, the people would be freed from religious superstition and brought to accept the liberating and public-spirited religion of humanity.[26]

Mill recommended a form of scientism in which the methods proper to the experimental sciences are applied to human relations and endeavors. The resulting scientistic method, rooted in a vision of reality according to which material facts can be disassociated from one another and recombined according to rationalistic, largely numerical formulae, rests on a rejection of all forms of contextualization—from social effects to historical development to moral judgment. Factors deemed outside the area under study are to be held constant or ignored. The area of interest is then subjected to a form of analysis in which wholes are broken down into their smallest parts—single items of data susceptible to numerically based evaluation (e.g., a "survey" of political opinions, a "scale" of authoritarian attitudes, and so on).

Scientistic methodology by its very nature is inimical to the moral imagination. This is made particularly clear by Kirk's description of the moral imagination as the "power of ethical perception which strides beyond the barriers of private experience and momentary events." Kirk was especially concerned with understanding as embodied in poetry, art, and religion. The "material" of concern to the moral imagination cannot be defined numerically. Like the soul, relationships, memories, and common understandings cannot be studied through the microscope or captured in an algorithm or regression analysis.

The correlations and analogies of prudent judgment rooted in the moral imagination cannot be supported through statistical analysis, and so count only as guesses or, worse yet, subjective values, in the scientistic universe. Indeed, questions such as "how shall we live?" which are central to the moral imagination, are irremediably outside the ken of scientism. Scientism deals with them by relegating them to the status of "value questions" to be answered solely by individuals. Ironically and chillingly, perhaps the most important, inevitable question of life, "how shall we die?" is in the process of being defined for us by scientism—as a question of the "quality of life" to be answered by experts qualified by their training to determine for us whether we any longer have value to ourselves. Thus, human dignity has no place in the decision of whether the human person is, or is not, any longer to exist. It may in fact be possible to answer questions central to our humanity in scientistic terms, but only at the cost of humanity itself.

Eric Voegelin in particular has pointed out the damaging materialism brought about by scientism's misapplication of materialist methods to human beings. As Voegelin observed, such a category mistake soon dehumanizes people, treating them as objects rather than as persons born with free will. In seeking to free people from the constraints of authority so that they may become radically sovereign choice-makers, liberalism ends up reducing them to something less than persons—to objects of state-based manipulations of rewards and punishments whose behaviorial "output" is determined by the proper calibration of inputs.[27] One is truly free, for Mill, only if one thinks purely in scientistic, materialist terms, and one may need to be forced to be free by being denied the attachments, the literature, and the other social and spiritual factors that encourage development of the moral imagination.

The world of so-called social science is a world stripped of imagination and of human dignity. Postmodernists have, of course, rejected the explicitly didactic form of scientism so favored by Mill. One hears now of the need for "stories" to teach everything from history to contemporary tort law. In a way, history has returned to academic studies in the form of subjective, often conflicting, and counterfactual "histories" of particular individuals and groups. This would seem to be, if not an improvement on liberal scientism, at least a significant change from that methodology toward one rooted in a kind of imagination. But then the postmodernists may not have moved so far beyond their liberal predecessors after all. For the typical postmodernist refuses to acknowledge the objective existence of any particular history (or methodology or reality of any kind), just as Mill sought not so much to eliminate history as to re-create it in a form that was useful for his liberal ends.

The desire to rewrite one's past to suit one's emotional needs is hardly new, and it applied no less to the Mills than to others. Indeed, both Mills re-created their own intellectual histories so as to minimize the debt they might have owed to religion. Both denied the influence of Calvinism on their upbringing in favor of the ancient Greek philosophers whose work they admired. The denial of religious influences at times reached extremes. For example, John Stuart Mill ascribed his father's aversion to material and even intellectual pleasures and his enjoyment of virtuous conduct to his supposed Greek cynicism, completely ignoring the elder Mill's long career as a Calvinist minister.[28]

Veracity was not either Mill's main goal in retelling history. Indeed, John Stuart Mill followed his father in believing that, in striving to move mankind forward to a positivist, rationalist approach to life, philosophers must often teach through misdirection.[29] The philosopher, in Mill's view, has a duty to move mankind out of the shadows of religious ignorance and into the sunlight of pure reason. This goal made it necessary to eradicate religion, if necessary through falsehoods, in order to free individuals from the last vestige of the European old regime.[30]

Because religion was the primary support for ancient traditions and the whole structure of society prior to the French Revolution, it had to be removed from man's consciousness altogether. Luckily, in Mill's view, such removal was inevitable. Mill shared Comte's view "that the necessary and inevitable movement of history was from the primitive 'theological' state of the human mind (and society) through the intermediate 'metaphysical' state toward the establishment of the final 'positivist' state." Or, as Mill restated the proposition, there is a "natural law of the spontaneous decline in religious spirit."[31] Thus, Mill's liberalism has at its very root an insistent, detailed, and ideological reading of history.

<hr />

The Enlightenment-based tradition seeks to rewrite history, including American history, as the story of revolutionary progress toward ever increasing individual liberty. It presents history in teleological form—as the story of the inevitable progress of reason and individual freedom, eventually triumphing over superstition and oppression. More or less explicit in this story is the goal (or "mission") of establishing a kind of earthly paradise in which human nature itself is fully achieved and perfected.

The conservative rejects any such teleological reading of history. He is convinced that our nature cannot be fulfilled in this life, with its inherent imperfections. We remain, so long as we live in this world, in a state of change and imperfection in which our attempts to apply permanent standards to our lives are met with partial success at best, and in which we are faced with continually changing circumstances. There is also always present the temptation to fool ourselves into believing that one last, massive change—that the application of one single, abstract principle to all men—will produce utopia, allowing us to rest and enjoy ourselves and forever be free of having to join with our fellows to deal with the inevitable flux of events in time.

If one accepts the notion that history is the story of reason's spread, one can dispense with conservative pessimism regarding reason's power, and with it conservatism's attachment to tradition. The liberal need not convince us, then, that our history is characterized by injustice and oppression, but merely that it has been marked by the ascendancy of reason and freedom. Liberals have met with great success in convincing people to reinterpret the American founding as a radical event establishing liberal, progressive values of equality, toleration, and freedom unconstrained by the dictates of virtue.[32]

Not only those on the fringes of America's Left have rewritten history in this way; those in the neoconservative camp have done likewise. Seymour Martin Lipset has presented America as the "first new nation," committed by nature to goals of equality and abstract freedom.[33] Thomas West has "vindicated" the founders from charges that they did not do enough to advance universal equality, democratic participation, and individual rights.[34] And Harry Jaffa has argued that the Constitution is fundamentally defined and summed up by its goal of securing "the blessings of liberty" promised by the Declaration of Independence's abstract statement that "all men are created equal."[35]

Ignoring or actively disparaging the traditions of belief and practice that actually produced American society, with their roots in religion, history, and custom, these authors choose to define America as an ideological construct. But even an ideological construct must come from somewhere, must have some point of departure from that which came before. Thus, such observers repeat a common story in which the "dark ages" of religion gave way to an enlightened rationalism during the eighteenth century, producing liberal individualism. Seeking to "save" our founding from the charge of illiberalism, they have reduced history itself from a form of consciousness, through which we can become fully human, moral beings, into a tool of ideology.

Such projects are merely the latest wrinkle in the development of the "Whig history" criticized by Herbert Butterfield. "Whig history" (named, ironically, after the loose party affiliation in which Burke himself served) begins with the premise that the Protestant Reformation was a deliberate movement toward advancing (an inevitable) individual liberty and religious secularization. Whig history is indeed history in one sense, in that it tells of events that happened in the past; but its ideological drive to show the inevitability of the progress of individual liberty renders it, as it renders its more modern progeny, fundamentally antihistorical. By seeking in the past only friends and enemies of "progress"; by viewing the present—or some extension of the progressive trends that produced what they value in the present—as the standard by which to judge past events and conduct; by praising and blaming according to a person or event's utility for progress—through all these methods Whig historians reject history itself as an element of the moral imagination.

Ideological history imposes a second, false reality on historical events and the traditions they help constitute. Its story is solipsistic. It is told from its own modern, liberal viewpoint, and so it cannot allow one to use perceptual apparatuses other than one's own. In the ideological or Whig account, there is only one appropriate perceptual apparatus—the one we already use. Rather than pointing us beyond our own limited horizons, it shapes those horizons in a way that determines one's own perception of one's place in space and time, eliminating the need for irenic engagement with traditions of any kind. Such history precludes moral development because it rests on the assumption that one already has developed one's moral perspective sufficiently to judge one's past—and indeed one's present and possible futures.[36] The point is to bring one's society up to the standard one has set already—to change the nature of those who have not attained the intellectual's state of understanding by subjecting them to the proper rewards and punishments.

Liberals see the society they wish to establish as one devoted to the maximization of individual choice. Even the scientistic expertise liberals value so highly is aimed, the argument goes, only at providing individuals with the facts they need in order to make informed choices and at forming a state capable of maximizing choice. But even a public order tolerant of individual and group differences must be rooted in common beliefs and experiences sufficient to form a stable, working consensus concerning at least fundamental political values. Thus, today we see debates among legal theorists as to how and to what extent the liberal state must maintain a neutral stance in regard to various visions of the good, and how that ideology of neutrality is to be sustained.[37]

Liberal neutrality is a value that must be held in common by the people if it is to be made politically and socially real—if it is in fact to shape public morality. One clear motivation for liberals' engaging in Whig history is that they must paint a portrait of the past that supports a liberal consensus. By telling a story according to which the good people of the past sought increasing rationality, equality, and individual autonomy, the bad people defended superstition, hierarchy, and tradition, and the good people triumphed (or at least set us on the right path), liberals reinforce the people's identification of liberal structures with the good and with the inevitable march of progress.

The goal is a nation like Ledeen's America, in which the people take a zealous interest in the nation's fortunes "because we feel ourselves part of a common enterprise—the advance of freedom—and we spontaneously organize ourselves to achieve that enterprise."[38] But how are we to spawn such enthusiastic communal emotions in an era of rationalistic individualism? Mill saw the answer in a religion of humanity. Rather than seeking merely increased secularization—the supposedly inevitable result of Whig history— Mill actively sought to replace Christianity with a new religion, in which we would dedicate ourselves, with all the fervor once reserved for Christ, to the advancement of human utility.[39]

One problem with Mill's solution is that it purports to be the culmination of individual autonomy, but it does not make actual people really autonomous. Mill's religion of humanity prioritizes some pleasures over others, claiming that service should make us happy, thus closing off selfish pleasures as "wrong," if not "immoral," choices. Mill, of course, was convinced that scientistic logic would lead every person (or at least every sane and decent person) to choose public service. No society can be based in true, full individual autonomy and survive; there must be significant common limits to one's freedom of action if there is to be any social order at all. Mill recognized the need for such limits, along with the fact that only religion can provide such limits.

Some observers have claimed that actual religious belief is not necessary for the recognition of moral duty and the permanent standards on which it is based. Gertrude Himmelfarb, for example, has argued that English Victorians like Matthew Arnold were able to harness their own "passionate" belief in virtue to aid them in maintaining an ethic of public service—a kind of surrogate religion of morality—despite their own loss of faith. Moreover, on Himmelfarb's reading, while Victorian virtues were not "perennial," they were "for their own time and place at least, sufficiently fixed and certain to have the practical status of 'perennial.'"[40]

Himmelfarb seems to posit among the Victorians she admires a kind of will to faith in morality that was used to replace actual faith in the existence of a realm of transcendent standards that found expression in religion. There is some basis for such a belief, rooted though it is in a fundamentally Whig view of history. Because culture comes from the cult—because the habits and institutions of a society naturally arise from common practices rooted most deeply in the religion its people shared in its beginnings—it is possible to maintain those institutions and habits formed through religious interaction even if conscious belief fades. Indeed, one fundamental basis of Whig history is the belief that, while religion may have helped forge the moral ethos of our civilization, we progressively have grown out of the supposedly superstitious beliefs of our early times, even as we have maintained and refined the morals taught earlier (and imperfectly) by religious practice and institutions.

The weakness of this argument lies in its facile assumption that people will continue to bind themselves to norms the moral status of which they no longer can explain, even to themselves. A culture severed from its roots in religion will abide for a time, perhaps a long time, as its roots decay; but it is no longer a living thing, no longer capable of renewing itself over time through the unsuspecting confidence of its members. Some few men of philosophic bent may retain their ability to exercise the moral imagination, reading natural law in the order of the universe, if not finding themselves able to accept any kind of living, personal God at its source. On the whole, though, the religious consensus having faded, the moral consensus will fade as well, as more and more people will dispense with norms and restrictions that keep them from satisfying their desires without providing anything of real meaning in return.

The will to faith, then, is not sufficient, in and of itself, for the long-term maintenance of society. Furthermore, it is ill-equipped to remake society along liberal lines. Liberalism seeks to liberate. It seeks to free the individual from the constraints of history and social mores. The whole point of Mill's valuation of the eccentric is to break the individual free from existing social norms and the institutions that enforce those norms. Mill argued that "it is only the cultivation of individuality which produces, or can produce, well-developed human beings."[41] Well-developed human beings, according to Mill, are the goal, and a well-developed human being is a creature of independent, scientific judgment not ruled by the authority of the past or constrained by social authorities.

Family connections, mass opinion, and religious authority in particular, according to Mill, must be deprived of their power to sway individual judgment; each of us must come to believe that we are independent of such connections, owing no obedience to them. But how can this be, how can we not owe obedience to the authorities that have, in fact, shaped our characters and the morals pervading our society? In part, the answer lies in Mill's belief that society, as he found it, embodied bad norms. Christianity had indeed shaped public morals, but then those morals were bad, in Mill's view, and should be discarded.

We have to inquire of Mill just how existing moral norms are to be discarded. How are we to move from the supposed mistakes of a theological or metaphysical age to the supposed wisdom of a positivist age? In one sense the question already has been answered: through the religion of humanity. But I want to stress the sense in which the question is unanswerable, for the religion of humanity is the product of Mill's admission that we are by nature religious beings. Mill's religion of humanity is necessary precisely because we are not, and cannot be, purely rational creatures whose morals are shaped by a dispassionate understanding of the requirements of utility. Rather, Mill himself recognized that we are by nature moral as well as rational beings, and that we are social by nature, dependent on the authority of people and institutions as well as on habit and custom to make sense of our lives.

This is where Mill's antihistorical project, and the antihistorical bias of liberalism in general, becomes most clear and necessary for liberalism to achieve its end. Liberalism's antihistoricism is an appeal not to reason, but to a will to ignorance. It calls on us to willfully forget our social, historically bound nature so that we can leap from one system of authority, rooted in history and religion, to another system of authority, rooted in a scientistic rationalism. To achieve our new nature we must actively forget our past and transcend or deny our historicity.

There may be some kernel of truth in this liberal vision of progress. Liberal society seems to have called forth a passionate will to ignorance among many of its members. Nietzsche, wrong here as in so many other areas, posited a will to power that could lead the special, enlightened few to overcome the herd's conceptions of good and evil. In fact, the result of such a will is simple abnormity—spiritually, morally, and intellectually impoverished action and discourse. The modern desire to universalize the will to power, to call on all of us to harness it for our own liberation, was doomed from the start because it promised a "good" (self-creation) that many value in theory but that very few value in practice, given its high demands in terms of energy and the willingness to forgo material pleasures. What the call for a universal will to power produced was a common will to ignorance. By devaluing history and denying the authoritative status of obligations to constitutive associations like family, church, and town, liberalism has encouraged people to actively forget or repudiate their pasts so as to escape the duties incurred on its account.

Moreover, scientism itself encourages an active rejection of historical consciousness and the moral imagination. History now is seen at best as a source of practical lessons, with morality at best a form of toleration dependent on an active suppression of moral judgment and the historical knowledge on which so much of it is based. Why, then, bother with history at all, particularly when the social sciences claim to provide more reliable data for the making of practical decisions? In liberal society, history is only useful as an entertainment, as a kind of morality play, whether of freedom's victory or, for postmodernists, of the soon-to-be-ended oppression of various "marginalized" groups. Such stories bind us to liberal ideology, but not to particular people.

We increasingly seek an unconnected freedom in which we have no obligatory ties because we know nothing that might have given rise to them. We owe little to our families, churches, and local associations because we ignore the role they played in shaping our character. As to the need to maintain public order, this is the full extent of our obligation—to maintain the structures that serve our interests. Duties to one's neighbor now are seen as almost nonexistent, and on grounds, fundamentally, of ignorance. We owe nothing to others save "tolerance." Toleration, as currently conceived, is rooted in intentional ignorance. We dictate the willed ignorance of people's beliefs, circumstances, and characteristics, along with ignorance of the moral implications of their conduct. We tell ourselves that the purpose of such ignorance is to prevent oppression, but if that were the goal we would simply forbid actual oppression. Instead, we dictate that no one take cognizance of the facts themselves.

In fact, moral or social knowledge is inescapable, such that ignorance of it constantly must be willed. Unfortunately for the liberal, the will to ignorance is opposed by a deeper, more fundamental drive toward social belonging. As Robert Nisbet pointed out, the quest for community is always with us. No matter how individualistic our ideology or atomistic our society, we by nature seek communion with our fellows.[42] The moral enormities of the twentieth century attest to both the power and the corruptibility of this drive, whether we choose to recognize it or not. When we seek to deny the quest for community, it springs forth in abnormal form, whether in totalitarianisms like those which characterized Soviet Russia and Nazi Germany, or in the growth of a centralized welfare/warfare state such as increasingly dominates the West, or in the lesser abnormities of cults, gangs, and other false substitutes for true community. Better to recognize the actual nature of the human person, in its manifold historical and social aspects, than to deny it and, through a will to ignorance, pervert it.

The Founding Fathers and the Economic Order[1]

Forrest McDonald

If I should ask you what kind of economic order the founding fathers contemplated when they established the constitutional order, you would doubtless reply capitalism or a market economy. If I addressed that question to a similar number of professional American historians, the answer would be the same, the difference being that most of you would add, "thank God," and most of them would add, "unfortunately."

In certain important particulars, your answer is supported by the historical record. For one thing, Americans were committed to John Locke's proposition that mankind has a God-given right to life, liberty, and property, and that legitimate governments are required to protect those rights. In the Constitutional Convention of 1787, James Madison, Gouverneur Morris, and others listed the protection of property rights as the primary reason for instituting government; the sole dissenter was James Wilson.

For a second thing, the Constitution created the largest contiguous area of free trade in the world. Neither the states nor the Congress could levy taxes on the interstate movement of goods—which the states had been theoretically able to do prior to the adoption of the Constitution. For yet another, the contract clause of Article I, Section 10—"No State shall . . . pass any . . . Law impairing the Obligation of Contracts"—was a commitment to unfettered capitalism insofar as it prohibited state legislative interference into market transactions. Mystery surrounds the contract clause: it was proposed by Rufus King (who was a delegate representing Massachusetts) late in August and was roundly rejected. Somehow the clause made its way into the finished document a couple of weeks later.

As to whether the framers *intended* to create a capitalistic order, the weightier evidence balances to the contrary. Let us start by considering what they understood by property rights. The appropriate source is Sir William Blackstone's four-volume *Commentaries on the Laws of England,* a work that James Madison said was "in every man's hand." On the second page of the second volume, subtitled "Of the Rights of Things," Blackstone defines property as "that sole and despotic dominion which one man claims and exercises over the external things of the world, in total exclusion of the right of any other individual in the universe." Splendid statement, but Sir William devotes the remaining 518 pages of the volume to qualifying and specifying exceptions to his definition.

Every state had adopted English prohibitions of "offenses against public trade," which banned usury, regulated the price of bread, and forbade such practices as "forestalling" (buying or contracting commodities on their way to market), "engrossing" (buying large quantities of commodities with intent to sell them in other markets), and "regrating" (buying and reselling products in the same market). Americans, like Englishmen, also recognized that their right to acquire and hold private property was subject to rights residing in the public. As an aggregate of individuals, the public retained rights to grazing, wood gathering, hunting, passage, and water use on privately owned lands. In its corporate or governmental capacity, the public reserved the right to restrict the use of private property and even take it from the owners in certain conditions.

These legal barriers were reinforced by ideological considerations. Granted, Americans were, by and large, a practical and not an ideological people, but they had embraced a pair of ideas that took deep roots. First was republicanism. When Americans proclaimed their commitment to republicanism as part of the reaction against George III in 1776, most did so willy-nilly without knowing what it entailed. The body of literature on the subject was large and readily found, however, and soon public figures were versed on the subject. The actuating principle of a republic was public virtue, virtue meaning manly devotion of one's self to the well-being of the public. The opposite of virtue was vice, meaning effeminacy or a love of luxury.

The very idea of economic growth that inheres in a market economy was incompatible with this primary principle of republicanism. Plato, believing that relative equality of property is essential to a republic, proposed to limit inheritances and recommended that no republic be established on the sea or on a navigable river, for that "would expose it to the dangers of commerce" and the inequalities that resulted from trade. Lycurgus, "in the most perfect model of government that was ever framed," ancient Sparta, had forbidden trade altogether. And Montesquieu, whom Americans devoutly admired, declared that if people were allowed "to dispose of property [as they] pleased," a republic would be "utterly undone." As disparate a pair of Americans as John Adams and Benjamin Franklin agreed. Adams denounced credit as responsible for "most of the Luxury & Folly which has yet infected our People" and declared that anyone who could devise a way to abolish credit forever "would deserve a Statue to his Memory." Franklin characterized commerce as "generally cheating" and wrote bitterly of its corrupting and debilitating effects.

The second ideological barrier arose from the agrarian tradition and the accompanying mystique of the land. You have heard Jefferson's quotation—isn't it on the Jefferson Monument in Washington?—"those who labor in the earth are the chosen people of God if ever He had a chosen people." That attitude was widely shared in eighteenth-century America, and so was Jefferson's comment that "the mobs of great cities add just so much to the support of pure government as sores do to the strength of the human body." These prejudices found expression in assorted ways, including the ubiquitous landed property qualifications for voting and office-holding, which insured that agricultural interests would dominate government at the expense of commercial, manufacturing, and financial interests.

Moreover, the agrarian tradition impeded economic development in an explicitly anticapitalist way. Its most vituperative and generally accepted version was that formulated by Henry St. John, First Viscount Bolingbroke, and his circle of English Tory friends. Bolingbroke had led the opposition to Sir Robert Walpole (the first "prime minister"), who guided the financial revolution during the 1720s and 1730s that transformed England into a modern capitalistic state by monetizing the public debt. Bolingbroke glorified landowners and castigated "money men," coining a litany of opposition to capitalism that warped the perspective of Americans as they imbibed it and as it infected them with a "paranoid political style."

Perhaps it appears that you can't get to the modern world from there. But notice that my original question was not what kind of economic order the founders established, but what kind of order they contemplated establishing. Had I phrased it the first way, you (and the historians) would have been right. What I have been talking about was what the framers contemplated. What they actually *did* was something quite different.

Thus far I have left two crucial considerations out of account. I have spoken of private property, but the Revolutionary War resulted in the United States's collectively owning huge amounts of *public* property, in the forms of public lands and public debts. Before the Revolution, vacant land belonged to the Crown, except in the proprietary colonies of Pennsylvania and Maryland. Now the western lands, consisting of millions of acres, belonged to Virginia, North Carolina, and Georgia in the South and to the United States government in the North. The public debts (not counting $10 million owed the king of France and various Dutch bankers) totaled $65 million. The public lands were worth far more than all private lands combined, and the public debts (owned by a large number of citizens) amounted to more than all the commercial property in the country.

The common view was that the public lands should be sold to raise the money to pay off the public debts. That course was already being followed, after a fashion. Several groups of speculators contracted with Congress or state governments to buy vast tracts payable in installments with public securities at par value—a bargain for the speculators, inasmuch as the securities could be bought on the open market for ten or fifteen cents on the dollar.

At this point the second consideration I left out comes into play, namely Alexander Hamilton. Hamilton's ruling passion was the love of fame: an obsession with achieving immortality through the grateful remembrance of posterity as the Lawgiver who, in the tradition of Lycurgus of Sparta and Solon of Athens, "transmits a system of laws and institutions to secure the peace, happiness, and liberty of future generations." No small number of Hamilton's contemporaries shared that aspiration, but they saw it in relatively narrow terms, meaning the creation of a balanced constitution that would ensure the people's safety and liberty. Hamilton sought nothing less than to make over the people themselves.

Hamilton thought that his country was kept from being a great nation, indeed kept from being a nation at all, by the inertia of a society whose pervasive attributes were provincialism and lassitude. Provincialism was reinforced by habit and by interest, but in each state and every region its main prop was an oligarchy. The distribution of wealth in America was more nearly equal and society was more nearly fluid than in the Old World, but status and substantial wealth were vested in a handful of intermarried families that were essentially closed to newcomers. Now, Hamilton had nothing against a hierarchical and deferential social order; he was the politest of men (except when it came to Aaron Burr). But he vehemently abhorred dependency and servility, for these were contrary to his idea of manhood. Moreover, he hated the narrow provincialism that the American order both nourished and fed upon; and he resented, as only an outsider can, the clannishly closed quality of the system.

The system also discouraged industry—in the sense of self-reliance and habitual or constant work and effort—by failing to reward it. Status derived not from the marketplace, where deeds and goods and virtues could be impartially valued, but from birthrights. More precisely, status rested upon personal relationships that rested upon family connections, which in turn rested upon owning land and upon the mystique that land was the source of wealth and virtue. In other words, the agrarian mentality of Thomas Jefferson was well-nigh universal in America. The work ethic prevailed only among a tiny minority. And though there was little poverty in America, there was also little industry—and lots of sloth, indifference, drunkenness, and dissipation. To Hamilton, this was anathema because of its inherent injustice and because, in his eyes, it made the nation weak and despicable.

His audacious, self-appointed mission was nothing less than to remake American society in his own image. By 1786, after reading Jacques Necker's treatise on the finances of France and Sir James Steuart's book on political economy, he conceived a means of accomplishing that revolutionary change. What distinguished the diligent few was that they measured worth and achievement in terms of money, whereas the majority disdained money and made do with a cumbersome system of personal obligations, barter, and fiat credit. To transform the established order, to make society fluid and open to merit, to make industry both rewarding and necessary, what needed to be done was to monetize the whole. For money is oblivious to class, status, color, and inherited social position; money is the ultimate, neutral, impersonal arbiter. Infused into an agrarian society, money could be the leaven, the fermenting yeast, that would stimulate growth, change, prosperity, and national strength.

The first step in the process, after the Constitution had been ratified and Hamilton became secretary of the treasury, was to devise a means of establishing public credit. Credit entails credibility, believability, trust; and the United States had none. Hamilton addressed his efforts to the ultimate source of credit, the market. Rather than attempting to pay *off* the public debts in a short time (something quite beyond the nation's capacity), he proposed to consolidate state and national debts and "fund" them, which is to say provide funds for making regular interest payments but leave the question of retiring the principal—whether soon, late, or never—to the discretion of government.

In addition, he proposed the creation of a sinking fund, consisting of surplus revenues and the proceeds of a new loan in Europe, which would be used to buy government securities on the open market. The sinking fund's key function was to engage in open-market operations aimed at bringing the prices of public securities to par. Once that was done, the investing public would be convinced that public credit had been established, and when investors believed that public credit had been established, it would ipso facto be established.

Hamilton's proposals were enacted into law. As a consequence, certificates of the public debt, heretofore a politically divisive and economically crippling national burden, were transformed into capital. Moreover, capital was created into the bargain; the market value of the paper before Hamilton took office late in 1789 had been less than $15 million; a year later it was about $45 million. And taking care of the public debts left the public lands a wholly free and clear blessing for the nation.

The next step in Hamilton's grand plan was to create a national banking system. Originally, he had wanted to monetize the public debt directly—that is, to have it circulate as money—but the terms of the congressional act made that difficult. Accordingly, Hamilton used the securities as the basis for currency rather than as currency itself, in the form of subscriptions to the capital stock of the national bank. The bank's notes would circulate equally with specie as currency. Paper was supporting paper, but this was not financial trickery, as the Jeffersonians charged. Hamilton perceived that—monetary theorists to the contrary notwithstanding—money is whatever people believe is money and will voluntarily accept as money. Underlying his thinking was the realization that the United States, as a raw and undeveloped land, was long on potential natural wealth but short on institutional wealth, meaning liquid capital. He therefore regarded as desirable any stable and orderly means of increasing the money supply, within the limits of what could be efficaciously employed in developing the natural wealth. In essence, he was creating the machinery whereby the nation could be built on credit, financing its economic development not out of savings but out of the expectation of future profits.

Hamilton built on some of the arguments Adam Smith developed in *Wealth of Nations* but rejected Smith's doctrine of noninterference in its broadest sense. He recognized—as later economic theorists befogged by Marxism failed to do—that social values and habits dictate economic activity, not the other way around. "Experience teaches," he wrote, "that men are often so much governed by what they are accustomed to see and practice, that the simplest and most obvious improvements, in the most ordinary occupations, are adopted with hesitation, reluctance, and by slow gradations." Men would resist change, he believed, so long as even "a bare support could be ensured by an adherence to ancient courses." The natural order was for social habits to dictate economic norms and for government to reflect the interplay of the two. Hamilton saw the advantage of using government to bring about economic changes that would in turn alter society.

While rejecting laissez faire, however, he was emphatic in his commitment to capitalism. Primarily that commitment was moral, not economic, for Hamilton believed that the greatest benefits of government-encouraged private enterprise were not material but spiritual, the enlargement of the scope of human freedom by expanding the opportunities for human endeavor. "Minds of the strongest and most active powers," he wrote, "fall below mediocrity and labour without effect, if confined to uncongenial pursuits. And it is thence to be inferred, that the results of human exertion may be immensely increased by diversifying its objects." In its own right, to stimulate the human mind was a distinct good. "Every new scene, which is opened to the busy nature of man to rouse and exert itself, is the addition of a new energy to the general stock of effort. The spirit of enterprise, useful and prolific as it is, must necessarily be contracted or expanded in proportion to the simplicity or variety of the occupations and productions, which are to be found in a Society."

And so we return to the original question. Did the founding generation contemplate the creation of a capitalistic, free-market economy? No, the majority did not. Had the will of the majority prevailed, had the Jeffersonians prevailed, had those committed to pure republicanism prevailed, the United States would have remained an agrarian, colonial economy destined to become a collection of banana republics. Fortunately, a handful of likeminded visionaries working through Alexander Hamilton and his office as secretary of the treasury used the freedoms of the Constitution and its protections to create a capitalistic, free-market economy and ensured that the United States would become the richest, most powerful, freest country the world has ever known.

I join you in thanking them—and I thank you.

Notes

Editors' Introduction

1. Forrest McDonald, *Recovering the Past: A Historian's Memoir* (Lawrence, KS: University of Kansas Press, 2004), 50. This work provides a good overview of McDonald's biography and bibliography in his own words.

2. Ibid., 54.

3. Ibid, 56.

4. Forrest McDonald, *We the People: The Economic Origins of the Constitution* (New Brunswick, NJ: Transaction Press, 1992), 415–16.

5. McDonald, *Recovering the Past,* 73.

6. McDonald, *We the People,* 413.

7. A bibliography of McDonald's major works is included at the end of this book.

8. Turner's Frontier Thesis, promulgated in 1893, argued that Americans were defined by the existence of the rugged, open western frontier. which molded the people who lived on it into democratic individualists and which made American culture distinct from the culture of Europe. In contrast, McDonald and McWhiney held that the great mass of Celtic peoples who migrated to the American southern frontier, retained their European folkways. Rather than being changed by their environment, these Celts preserved their way of life upon coming to America. "The New World did not create a new man," McDonald argued. "It enabled men to remain what they had been" (*Recovering the Past,* 130).

9. McDonald, *Recovering the Past,* 86–88.

10. McDonald met Ronald Reagan in 1987 in conjunction with his recognition as Jefferson lecturer, had a private dinner with Richard Nixon in 1992, and was a guest at the White House during George W. Bush's first term.

11. From a conversation with Ellen McDonald.

12. Ellen Shapiro McDonald is credited as coauthor of *Requiem: Variations on Eighteenth-*

Century Themes (Lawrence, KS: University Press of Kansas, 1988) and as coeditor of *Confederation and Constitution, 1781–1789* (New York: Harper & Row, 1968).

13. McDonald would write again about both men in numerous articles and in his books *Novus Ordo Seclorum: The Intellectual Origins of the Constitution* (Lawrence, KS: University Press of Kansas, 1985), *Requiem,* and *The American Presidency* (Lawrence, KS: University Press of Kansas, 1994).

14. McDonald, *Novus Ordo Seclorum,* 194; *Requiem,* 14.

15. See Garry Wills, *Cincinnatus: George Washington and the Enlightenment* (Garden City, NY: Doubleday, 1984); Joseph J. Ellis, *His Excellency* (New York: Random House, 2004).

16. McDonald, *Recovering the Past,* 137.

17. Ibid., 137, 139.

18. Forrest McDonald, *The Presidency of Thomas Jefferson* (Lawrence, KS: University Press of Kansas, paperback edition, 1987), 167 and chapter 7. McDonald became the author of the Jefferson volume in Kansas's presidency series only after the publisher was unable to enlist a Jefferson scholar to do the book. McDonald believes that those scholars, "Jeffersonians all, did not wish to touch the presidency because Jefferson was by no means a Jeffersonian president." See McDonald, *Recovering the Past,* 137. It should be noted, however, that in his 1994 C-SPAN interview with Brian Lamb, McDonald listed Jefferson's first four years in office as one of the most successful presidential terms in American history. (Jefferson's second term, however, McDonald characterized as one of the worst.)

19. McDonald, *Recovering the Past,* 147.

20. Forrest McDonald, *Alexander Hamilton: A Biography* (New York: Norton, 1980), 4.

21. McDonald once declared to one of us (Klugewicz) that the Federalist Party's vision was the correct prescription for the United States up to the year 1830.

22. Alexander Hamilton, *Federalist 6,* in Alexander Hamilton, John Jay, and James Madison, *The Federalist,* ed. George W. Carey and James McLellan (Indianapolis: Liberty Fund, 2001), 25. As he explained in his classes, McDonald blamed the growth of the federal government not on the Federalists, not on Abraham Lincoln, not even on FDR and the New Dealers. Rather, he blamed Lyndon Johnson's Great Society for the creation of the leviathan state.

23. McDonald, "The Founding Fathers and the Economic Order," speech before the Economic Club of Indianapolis, April 19, 2006.

24. McDonald, *Recovering the Past,* 147.

25. From personal recollection (Klugewicz).

26. McDonald, *Hamilton,* 209, xi.

27. McDonald, *Recovering the Past,* 51.

28. From personal recollection (Klugewicz).

29. Quoted in McDonald, *Recovering the Past,* 95.

30. Ibid., 145.

31. Ibid., 149.

32. See Gordon Wood, *The Creation of the American Republic* (Chapel Hill, NC: University of North Carolina Press, 1998); J. G. A. Pocock, *The Machiavellian Moment* (Princeton, NJ: Princeton University Press, 1975). Both Wood and Pocock see Americans' pursuit of virtue as the key to understanding the events of the late eighteenth century.

33. McDonald, *Novus Ordo Seclorum,* viii.

34. For example, the founders created the idea of "divided sovereignty." See McDonald, *Novus Ordo Seclorum,* 277–78.

35. For example, the *Federalist* essays are replete with examples from history that supposedly buttress the points made by the authors.

36. Forrest McDonald, *The American Presidency,* 481.

37. McDonald, *Recovering the Past,* 11.

38. Ibid.

39. Ibid., 5.

40. Ibid., 20.

41. From personal recollection (Klugewicz).

42. See the concluding paragraphs of *Recovering the Past,* 165, where McDonald excerpts "The Speech" and provides a note about its provenance and unique career. "The Speech" is available in its entirety online at http://web.archive.org/web/20061004142739/http://www.as.ua.edu/history/mcdonald.htm.

The Revolutionary Origins of American Constitutionalism
C. Bradley Thompson

1. See John Phillip Reid, *Constitutional History of the American Revolution,* abridged ed. (Madison, WI: University of Wisconsin Press, 1995). While I disagree with many particulars of Reid's case, I agree with his general argument.

2. Hillsborough quoted in Theodore Draper, *The Struggle for Power: The American Revolution* (New York: Random House, 1996), 348, 364, 262; John Adams, "Novanglus; or, A History of the Dispute with America . . ." [1774–75], in *The Revolutionary Writings of John Adams,* ed. C. Bradley Thompson (Indianapolis: Liberty Press, 2000), 188; Samuel Adams to Joseph Warren, September 24, 1774, quoted in Michael Kammen, *A Machine That Would Go of Itself: The Constitution in American Culture* (New York: Knopf, 1987), 48.

3. Quoted in Draper, *The Struggle for Power,* 262; Adams, "Novanglus," 211.

4. Quoted in John Phillip Reid, *Constitutional History of the American Revolution: The Authority to Tax* (Madison, WI: University of Wisconsin Press, 1987), 4; John Adams, "The Earl of Clarendon to William Pym" [January 27, 1766], in *Revolutionary Writings of John Adams,* ed. Thompson, 51–52; quoted in Gordon S. Wood, *The Creation of the American Republic, 1776–1787* (New York: W. W. Norton & Company, 1969), 260.

5. *Boston Evening-Post,* April 27, 1761, 1; James Otis, "Rights of the British Colonies Asserted and Proved," in *Pamphlets of the American Revolution,* ed. Bernard Bailyn (Boston: Harvard University Press, 1965), 428, 455, 470; John Adams, "The Earl of

Clarendon to William Pym" [January 27, 1766], in *The Revolutionary Writings of John Adams,* ed. Thompson, 52.

6. This question has been taken up in Bernhard Knollenberg, *Origin of the American Revolution, 1759–1766* (New York: Free Press, 1965), 148–56; Bernard Bailyn, *The Ideological Origins of the American Revolution* (Cambridge, MA: Harvard University Press, 1967), 67–70, 175–98; Wood, *The Creation of the American Republic, 1776–1787,* 259–305; Willi Paul Adams, *The First American Constitutions: Republican Ideology and the Making of the State Constitutions in the Revolutionary Era* (Chapel Hill, NC: University of North Carolina Press, 1980; reprint ed., Lanham, MD: Rowman & Littlefield, 2001), 1–24; Reid, *Constitutional History of the American Revolution* (1995), 3–25. The purpose of this chapter is to uncover the deeper philosophic issues—issues that have hitherto gone unnoticed—that divided Anglo-American views on the nature, purposes, and structures of constitutional government.

7. Henry St. John, Viscount Bolingbroke, *A Dissertation Upon Parties* (London, 1735), 108; William Paley, *The Principles of Moral and Political Philosophy* (Philadelphia, 1788), quoted in James Wilson, "Lectures on Law," Robert Green McCloskey, ed., *Works of James Wilson,* 1:310.

8. Adams, "The Earl of Clarendon to William Pym" [January 27, 1766], in *Revolutionary Writings of John Adams,* ed. Thompson, 52–53; Charles Inglis, *The True Interest of America . . . Strictures on a Pamphlet Intitled Common Sense . . .* (Philadelphia, 1776), 18.

9. Paley, *Principles of Moral and Political Philosophy,* quoted in Wilson, "Lectures on Law," McCloskey, ed., *Works of James Wilson,* 1:310; John Adams, "The Independence of the Judiciary; A Controversy Between William Brattle and John Adams" [February 8, 1773], in *Revolutionary Writings of John Adams,* ed. Thompson, 101.

10. Thomas Paine, *Rights of Man,* in *Collected Writings,* ed. Eric Foner (New York: Library of America, 1995), 467–68, 525.

11. James Wilson, "Lectures on Law," in *Works of James Wilson,* 309–10.

12. Paine, *Rights of Man,* in *Collected Writings,* ed. Foner, 574.

13. While I have been influenced generally on the question of the different transatlantic constitutions by John Phillip Reid's *Constitutional History of the American Revolution* and Jack P. Greene's *Peripheries and Center: Constitutional Development in the Extended Polities of the British Empire and the United States, 1607–1788* (Athens, GA: University of Georgia Press, 1986), I have drawn sharper distinctions than they do in order to understand a larger design on the part of American revolutionaries.

14. Martin Howard Jr., "A Letter From a Gentleman of Halifax" [1765], in *Tracts of the American Revolution,* ed. Edmund S. Morgan (Indianapolis, IN: Bobbs Merrill, 1967), 66; "Debate in the House of Commons: William Pitt versus George Grenville" [January 14, 1766], in *Colonies to Nation, 1763–1789: A Documentary History of the American Revolution,* ed. Jack P. Greene (New York: W. W. Norton & Company, 1975), 70.

15. Daniel Leonard, "Massachusettensis" [1774–75], in *The American Colonial Crisis: The Daniel Leonard–John Adams Letters to the Press, 1774–1775,* ed. Bernard Mason (New York: Harper & Row, 1972), 32.

16. Thomas Hutchinson, "A Dialogue Between an American and a European English-man" [1768], in *Perspectives in American History,* vol. 8, ed. Bernard Bailyn (1974), 382.

17. "Debate in the House of Lords: Lord Camden versus Lord Mansfield" [March 7, 1766], in *Colonies to Nation,* ed. Greene, 79; "Debate Over the Authority of Parliament: The Exchange Between Governor Thomas Hutchinson and the House of Representatives" [January 6, 26, 1773], in *Colonies to Nation,* ed. Greene, 185; Leonard, "Massachusettensis" in *The American Colonial Crisis,* ed. Mason, 39.

18. "Debate Over the Authority of Parliament: The Exchange Between Governor Thomas Hutchinson and the House of Representatives" [January 6, 26, 1773], in *Colonies to Nation,* ed. Greene, 185; Leonard, "Massachusettensis" in *The American Colonial Crisis,* ed. Mason, 33.

19. Sir William Blackstone, *Commentaries on the Laws of England* [1765], in *Colonies to Nation,* ed. Greene, 86–88.

20. Ibid., 88.

21. But James Madison in the tenth *Federalist* put his finger on the fatal flaw in English reasoning: "Enlightened statesmen," he wrote, "won't always be at the helm."

22. Thomas Whately, "The Regulations Lately Made . . ." [1765], in *Colonies to Nation,* ed. Greene, 49.

23. Hutchinson, "A Dialogue Between an American and a European Englishman" [1768], in *Perspectives in American History,* ed. Bailyn, 391, 392.

24. Ibid., 396.

25. Ibid., ed. Bailyn, 399.

26. The traditional idea that the English constitution embodied a fundamental law standing above and limiting the working institutions of government remained a respectable but decidedly minority view in England during the 1760s and '70s. The idea that the courts, for instance, could declare acts of Parliament void was very much in retreat. The prevailing English view during the years of the imperial crisis was most clearly articulated in Blackstone's *Commentaries on the Laws of England* (Philadelphia: Rees Welsh & Company, 1902), 79–80: "Acts of parliament that are impossible to be performed are of no validity: and if there arise out of them collaterally any absurd consequences, manifestly contradictory to common reason, they are, with regard to those collateral consequences, void. I lay down the rule with these restrictions; though I know it is generally laid down more largely, that acts of parliament contrary to reason are void. But if the parliament will positively enact a thing to be done which is unreasonable, I know of no power in the ordinary forms of the constitution, that is vested with authority to control it; and the examples usually alleged in support of this sense of the rule do none of them prove, that, where the main object of a statute is unreasonable, the judges are at liberty to reject it; for that were to set the judicial power above that of the legislature, which would be subversive of all government."

27. Hutchinson, "A Dialogue Between an American and a European Englishman" [1768], in *Perspectives in American History,* ed. Bailyn, 401–2,

28. On the history of the legal and moral tradition undergirding the American position, see Charles Howard McIlwain, *Constitutionalism: Ancient and Modern* (Ithaca, NY: Cornell University Press, 1940); Edwin S. Corwin, *The "Higher Law" Background of American Constitutional Law* (Ithaca, NY: Cornell University Press, 1955); J.W. Gough, *Fundamental Law in English Constitutional Thought* (Oxford, UK: Oxford University Press, 1961); David N. Mayer, "The English Radical Whig Origins of American Constitutionalism," *Washington University Law Quarterly* 70 (1992): 131–208.

29. James Otis, "The Rights of the British Colonies Asserted and Proved," in *Colonies to Nation, 1763–1789: A Documentary History of the American Revolution,* ed. Jack P. Greene (New York: W. W. Norton & Company, 1975), 28–29. Joseph Hawley's conflation of fundamental law and the English constitution in 1775 is representative of the American position. To secure man's natural rights to life, liberty, and property defined for Hawley "the fundamental, the explaining and controuling principles, which framed the constitution of Britain in its first stages, . . . and which have been her constant companions through all the mutilations and distortions she has suffered in her progress to the present rank she holds in the world" (*Boston Massachusetts Spy,* February 16, 1775, quoted in Wood, *Creation of the American Republic,* 261–62). Among the many other American statements that viewed the British constitution as protecting certain fundamental rights and privileges, see: John Joachim Zubly, *An Humble Enquiry . . .* (Charleston, 1769; reprinted in *Political Sermons of the American Founding Era, 1730–1805,* ed. Ellis Sandoz, Indianapolis, IN: Liberty Fund, 1990, 273); Moses Mather, *America's Appeal to the Impartial World . . .* (Hartford, 1775; reprinted in Sandoz, *Political Sermons of the American Founding Era, 1730–1805,* 446–47); Aequus, *Massachusetts Gazette and Boston Newsletter,* March 6, 1766 (reprinted in *American Political Writing During the Founding Era, 1760–1805,* vol. 1, ed. Charles S. Hyneman and Donald S. Lutz, Indianapolis, IN: Liberty Fund, 1983, 62–66); Britannus Americanus, "Untitled," *Boston Gazette,* March 17, 1766 (reprinted in Hyneman and Lutz, *American Political Writing,* 89–90).

30. Otis, "The Rights of the British Colonies Asserted and Proved," in *Pamphlets of the American Revolution,* 446.

31. Ibid., 448.

32. Ibid., 454. In 1756, an anonymous writer presented a common view of the relationship between fundamental law and the English constitution. Magna Carta, he wrote, "is only *declaratory* of the *principal* grounds, of the *fundamental* laws and liberties of England . . . so that it seems rather to be a collection of ancient privileges from the common law ratified by the suffrage of the people and claimed by them as their reserved rights." *Boston Gazette and Country Journal,* May 10, 1756; italics added.

33. Otis, "The Rights of the British Colonies Asserted and Proved," in *Pamphlets of the American Revolution,* 454.

34. Ibid., 449. There is no better testimony for the influence of Coke's constitutional theory on colonial thought than Thomas Hutchinson's claim in 1765 that the Americans "take advantage of a maxim they find in Lord Coke that an act of Parliament against Magna Charta or the peculiar rights of Englishmen is *ipso facto* void. This,

taken in the latitude the people are often enough disposed to take it . . . seems to have determined great part of the colonies to oppose the execution of the [Stamp Act] with force and to show their resentment to all in authority who will not join them." Thomas Hutchinson to Richard Jackson, September 12, 1765, in Bailyn, ed., *Pamphlets of the American Revolution, 1750–1776*, 413.

35. Otis was not alone in expressing a simultaneously conservative and radical view of the relationship between natural law and constitutionalism. Jonathan Mayhew, for instance, in his famous sermon on "The Snare Broken" in 1766, explained to his parishioners that it "shall be taken for granted" that man's natural rights are "declared, affirmed and secured to us, as we are British subjects, by Magna Charta; all acts contrary to which, are said to be *ipso facto* null and void." In *Political Sermons of the American Founding Era, 1730–1805*, ed. Ellis Sandoz (Indianapolis: Liberty Fund, 1990), 240.

36. Otis, "The Rights of the British Colonies Asserted and Proved," in *Pamphlets of the American Revolution*, 450.

37. From the very beginning of the imperial crisis, Otis and his compatriots searched for some kind of constitutional protection against parliamentary edict. They appealed, as did the Virginia Resolves of 1765, to England's "ancient constitution (Greene, *Colonies to Nation*, 61)." The problem, of course, was that few in Britain continued to recognize the ancient constitution. Besides, it was not clear by the common law how or even if the protections of the English constitution extended to America. As we already know, the defenders of parliamentary sovereignty certainly did *not* think so. They argued instead that the rights of Englishmen were abridged and modified when men left the realm but that they were still subject to Parliament.

38. Daniel Dulany, "Considerations on the Propriety of Imposing Taxes in the British Colonies . . ." [1765], in *Colonies to Nation*, ed. Greene, 57.

39. Moses Mather, "America's Appeal to the Impartial World," 458.

40. "N.Y. Petition to the House of Commons" [October 18, 1764], in *Colonies to Nation*, ed. Greene, 39 (italics added).

41. Daniel Dulany, "Considerations on the Propriety of Imposing Taxes in the British Colonies . . ." [1765], in *Colonies to Nation*, ed. Greene, 57.

42. Richard Bland, "An Inquiry Into the Rights of the British Colonies" [1766], in *Colonies to Nation*, ed. Greene, 90, 91, 92.

43. Dickinson, "Letters From a Farmer in Pennsylvania . . ." [1767–68], in *Colonies to Nation*, ed. Greene, 132.

44. "Massachusetts Circular Letter" [February 11, 1768], in *Colonies to Nation*, ed. Greene, 134.

45. Zubly, "An Humble Enquiry . . ." [1769], in Sandoz, 271, 273.

46. The idea of "fixity" was crucial to the Americans' understanding of a constitution.

47. [Anonymous], "Four Letters on Important Subjects," in *Colonies to Nation*, ed., Greene, 384–85, 382, 389 (emphasis added).

48. Mather, "America's Appeal to the Impartial World" (Hartford, 1775), in Sandoz, 456–57.

THE COMMON-LAW TRADITION, THE CONSTITUTION,
AND SOUTHERN JURISPRUDENCE
F. THORNTON MILLER

1. For this and following paragraphs, see William Wirt, *Sketches of the Life and Character of Patrick Henry* (1817; rev. ed., Philadelphia: Thomas Cowerthwait & Co., 1841), which was important in establishing his image.

2. See Charles S. Sydnor, *The Development of Southern Sectionalism, 1819–1848* (Baton Rouge, LA: Louisiana State University Press, 1948).

3. For this and the following paragraph see Morton J. Horwitz, *The Transformation of American Law, 1780–1860* (Cambridge, MA: Harvard University Press, 1977); R. Kent Newmyer, *Supreme Court Justice Joseph Story: Statesman of the Old Republic* (Chapel Hill, NC: University of North Carolina Press, 1985); Tony A. Freyer, "Reassessing the Impact of Eminent Domain in Early American Economic Development," *Wisconsin Law Review* 6 (1981): 1263–86; my *Juries and Judges versus the Law: Virginia's Provincial Legal Perspective, 1783–1828* (Charlottesville, VA: University of Virginia Press, 1994), 97–112.

4. In terms of the empire, I am referring to common law, not admiralty law.

5. For this and following paragraphs, see "An act to establish the judicial courts of the U.S.," known as the Judiciary Act of 1789, September 24, 1789, in Richard Peters, ed., *Statutes at Large of the United States of America* (Boston: Little, Brown and Company, 1846–54), 1:73–93; Maeva Marcus and Natalie Wexler, "The Judiciary Act of 1789: Political Compromise or Constitutional Interpretation?" in Maeva Marcus, ed., *Origins of the Federal Judiciary: Essays on the Judiciary Act of 1789* (New York: Oxford University Press, 1992), 13–39.

6. For this and following paragraphs, *Chisholm v. Georgia*, 2 Dallas 419 (1793).

7. For this and the following paragraph, *Ware v. Hylton*, 3 Dallas 199 (1796); my *Juries and Judges*, 34–46.

8. See Jack P. Greene, *Peripheries and Center: Constitutional Development in the Extended Polities of the British Empire and the United States, 1607–1788* (New York: W. W. Norton and Company, 1986).

9. For this and following paragraphs, see Forrest McDonald, *Novus Ordo Seclorum: The Intellectual Origins of the Constitution* (Lawrence, KS: University Press of Kansas, 1985).

10. Numbers 10 and 51 in Jacob E. Cooke, ed., *The Federalist* (Middletown, CT: Wesleyan University Press, 1961), 56–65 and 347–53; Madison, "Parties" and "Government of the United States," *The National Gazette,* January 23 and February 6, 1792, in Gaillard Hunt, ed., *Writings of James Madison* (New York: G. P. Putnam's Sons, 1900–1910), 6:86, 91–93.

11. For example, see St. George Tucker, ed., *Blackstone's Commentaries: With Notes of Reference to the Constitution and Laws of the United States and of the Commonwealth of Virginia* (Philadelphia: William Young Birch and Abraham Small, 1803; rpt. ed., New York: Augustus M. Kelley, 1969), vol. 1, Note D, Section 11.

12. For this and following paragraphs, see *The Virginia Report of 1799–1800, Touching the Alien and Sedition Laws.* . . . (Richmond, VA: J. W. Randolph, 1850; rpt. ed., New York: Da Capo Press, 1970).

13. This theory was used later most famously by John C. Calhoun as justification for South Carolina's nullification and later by southern secessionists.

14. Indeed, the Virginia government allowed a federal sedition trial—that of James T. Callender—to take place in the state. See James Morton Smith, *Freedom's Fetters: The Alien and Sedition Laws and American Civil Liberties* (Ithaca, NY: Cornell University Press, 1956), 334–58.

15. *Commonwealth v. Caton,* 4 Call 5 (1782).

16. *Marbury v. Madison,* 1 Cranch 137 (1803); and see Robert Lowry Clinton, *Marbury v. Madison and Judicial Review* (Lawrence, KS: University Press of Kansas, 1989).

17. *Barron v. Baltimore,* 7 Peters 243 (1833).

18. For this and following paragraphs, *Crenshaw and Crenshaw v. Slate River Company,* 6 Randolph 245 (1828).

19. See Horwitz, *Transformation of American Law;* Daniel J. Hulsebosch, "Writs to Rights: 'Navigability' and the Transformation of the Common Law in the Nineteenth Century," *Cardozo Law Review* 23 (3, 2002): 1049–1106.

20. See Gerald Gunther, *John Marshall's Defense of McCulloch v. Maryland* (Stanford, CA: Stanford University Press, 1969); my "John Marshall in Spencer Roane's Virginia: The Southern Constitutional Opposition to the Marshall Court," *John Marshall Law Review* 33 (Summer 2000): 1131–40; R. Kent Newmyer, *John Marshall and the Heroic Age of the Supreme Court* (Baton Rouge, LA: Louisiana State University Press, 2001), 322–85. In *Worcester v. Georgia* (1832), the Marshall court ruled that the Cherokee Nation constituted a sovereign power over which the laws of Georgia "can have no force." Both Andrew Jackson and the state of Georgia largely ignored the Court's decision.

21. For this and following paragraphs, see my *Juries and Judges,* 74–86.

22. *Fairfax's Devisee v. Hunter's Lessee,* 7 Cranch 602 (1813).

23. *Martin v. Hunter's Lessee,* 1 Wheaton 304 (1816); for this and following paragraphs, *Hunter v. Martin, Devisee of Fairfax,* 4 Munford 1 (1814).

24. *Chisholm;* Chase opinion in *U.S. v. Worral,* U.S. Circuit Court for the District of Pennsylvania, 2 Dallas 384 (1798).

25. John Fries was a Pennsylvania farmer who in 1799 led a group of armed citizens who were resisting enforcement of a direct tax levied on houses, land, and slaves by the United States Congress.

26. Ibid.

27. See Smith, *Freedom's Fetters.*

28. *Virginia Report.*

29. St. George Tucker, "Of the Unwritten, or Common Law of England; and Its Introduction into, and Authority within the United American States," in Tucker, *Blackstone's Commentaries,* vol. 1, Note E; and on a contrasting view of the common law, see my "Joseph Story's Uniform, Rational Law," in William D. Pederson and

Norman W. Provizer, eds., *Great Justices of the U.S. Supreme Court* (New York: Peter Lang, 1993), 49–72.

30. For this and following paragraphs, *U.S. v. Hudson and Goodwin,* 7 Cranch 32 (1812); for example, his dissent in *Craig v. Missouri,* 4 Peters 410 (1830) foreshadowed the later majority opinion in *Briscoe v. the Bank of the Commonwealth of Kentucky,* 11 Peters 257 (1837).

31. *Swift v. Tyson,* 16 Peters 1 (1842); Tony A. Freyer, *Harmony and Dissonance: The Swift and Erie Cases in American Federalism* (New York: New York University Press, 1981).

32. For this and the following paragraph, *Lane v. Vick,* 3 Howard 464 (1845).

33. Taney concurred in McKinley's dissenting opinion; in time, criticism of the *Swift* doctrine mounted and *Swift* was reversed in *Erie Railroad Co. v. Tompkins,* 304 US 64 (1938); see Freyer, *Harmony and Dissonance.*

34. *Bank of Augusta v. Earle,* 13 Peters 519 (1839).

Publius on "Liquidation" and the Meaning of the Constitution
Steven D. Ealy

1. On this point, see Willmoore Kendall and George Carey, "How to Read *The Federalist,*" in Willmoore Kendall, *Willmoore Kendall Contra Mundum,* ed. Nellie D. Kendall (New Rochelle, NY: Arlington House, 1976), 411–12. I refer to two articles coauthored by Kendall and Carey as if they were written by Kendall alone. After conversations with George Carey I am convinced that the themes I am concerned with (potentiality and the Constitution as a crossroads) are among Kendall's contributions to the jointly written pieces.

2. Kendall, *Willmoore Kendall Contra Mundum,* 411. In the background of my discussion is the controversy over "original intent" that has raged among scholars and jurists during the past couple of decades; many of the pertinent writings are collected in Jack Rakove, ed., *Interpreting the Constitution: The Debate over Original Intent* (Boston: Northeastern University Press, 1990). Justice Antonin Scalia attempts to avoid the pitfalls of "original intent" jurisprudence by speaking of the "original meaning" of laws and constitutions. See Antonin Scalia, *A Matter of Interpretation: Federal Courts and the Law* (Princeton, NJ: Princeton University Press, 1997), 16–41. Scalia states his position succinctly: "What I look for in the Constitution is precisely what I look for in a statute: the original meaning of the text, not what the original draftsmen intended" (38). While this position saves Scalia from many of the thorny issues raised by "original intent," it does not save him from the difficulties raised by Publius's concept of the "liquidation of meaning," discussed below, since Publius's position recognizes that the "original meaning" itself is somewhat unclear or uncertain.

3. Willmoore Kendall and George Carey, "The 'Intensity' Problem and Democratic Theory," in *Willmoore Kendall Contra Mundum,* 498–503.

4. "How to Read *The Federalist,*" 412. Compare Douglas Adair, "The Authorship of the Disputed Federalist Papers," in *Fame and the Founding Fathers,* ed. Trevor Colbourn

(Indianapolis: Liberty Fund, 1998), 41–42: "*The Federalist,* it should be remembered, was not a scholarly commentary on the meaning of an established Constitution; it contained special pleading designed to secure ratification for a Constitution still untested." Also see Furtwangler, 43–44, 81, 87; as he says on 85, in writing *The Federalist Papers* Madison and Hamilton "began to explain [the Constitution] to themselves."

5. According to *The Federalist Concordance,* ed. Thomas S. Engeman, Edward J. Erler, and Thomas B. Hofeller (Chicago: University of Chicago Press, 1988), 306, "liquidate" occurs twice, in *Federalist* 78 and 82, "liquidated" once, in *Federalist* 37. (The word "liquidation" occurs once in *Federalist* 22, but there it bears the traditional financial meaning and so need not concern us here.) I know of only two scholars who take notice of this expression. See Jack N. Rakove, *Original Meanings* (New York: Alfred A. Knopf, 1996), 159, and J. R. Pole, editor, *The Federalist* (Indianapolis: Hackett Publishing Company, 2005), 437 fn.

6. I will identify all references to *The Federalist Papers* both by paper number and page number. Parenthetical page references inserted into the text refer to the following edition: Alexander Hamilton, James Madison, and John Jay, *The Federalist Papers* (New York: The New American Library, 1961), with an introduction by Clinton Rossiter.

7. In Noah Webster's *American Dictionary of the English Language,* originally published in 1828, the first definition and example of the verb "liquidate" is as follows: "To clear from all obscurity. 'Time only can liquidate the meaning of all parts of a compound system.' Hamilton." See *Noah Webster's First Edition of an American Dictionary of the English Language* (rept. ed., Anaheim: Foundation for American Christian Education, 1967), vol. 2, 8. (It makes for an interesting comparison with today's rules for documentation to note the editorial license Webster took in reworking this passage from *Federalist* 82.)

8. Martin Diamond, "*The Federalist,*" in Leo Strauss and Joseph Cropsey, editors, *History of Political Philosophy* (Chicago: Rand McNally & Company, 1963), 574.

9. "Education by Poetry," in *Frost: Collected Poems, Prose, & Plays* (New York: The Library of America, 1995), 717–28.

10. So great are the problems caused by the inadequacy of language that it can defeat God Himself: "When the Almighty himself condescends to address mankind in their own language, his meaning, luminous as it must be, is rendered dim and doubtful by the cloudy medium through which it is communicated" (37:229). Not surprisingly, one commentator characterizes this discussion in *Federalist* 37 as "a skeptical digression in the middle of a rather confident book." David F. Epstein, *The Political Theory of The Federalist* (Chicago: University of Chicago Press, 1984), 117.

11. Add to this argument another consideration: "the interfering pretensions of the larger and smaller States" (37:229). In *Federalist* 10 Publius argues, "As long as the connection subsists between his reason and his self-love, his opinions and his passions will have a reciprocal influence on each other; and the former will be objects to which the latter will attach themselves" (10:79). In addition to the three primary reasons for vague definitions, self-interest must also be taken into account.

12. A brilliant little book by Albert Furtwangler, *The Authority of Publius* (Ithaca, NY: Cornell University Press, 1984), is indispensable in thinking through the question of the authority of *The Federalist Papers*. Douglas Adair first uses the phrase "split personality" in reference to Publius in "The Authorship of the Disputed Federalist Papers," originally published in 1944 and reprinted in *Fame and the Founding Fathers,* 77. For the classic statement of this argument, see Alpheus T. Mason, "The Federalist—A Split Personality," *American Historical Review* 57 (1957), 625–43.

13. See both Kendall and Carey (407–11) and Furtwangler (61) on this point.

14. *Notes of Debates in the Federal Convention of 1787 Reported by James Madison* (New York: W. W. Norton & Company, 1987), 34. Italics in original.

15. Ibid., 34.

16. Ibid., 35. The "federal Constitution" C. C. Pinckney refers to is the Articles of Confederation.

17. See *Federalist* 9 and 40.

18. *Notes of Debates,* 35. Italics in original.

19. See *Federalist* 9 on the "wholly new discoveries" of political science incorporated into the Constitution (72–73).

20. According to *Federalist* 15, this is "the great and radical vice" of the Articles (108).

21. There is some slight confusion throughout this argument between "the Constitution" and the government to be established under the proposed Constitution.

22. Remember that Publius remarks in *Federalist* 1 "that it seems to have been reserved to the people of this country, by their conduct and example, to decide the important question, whether societies of men are really capable or not of establishing good government from reflection and choice, or whether they are forever destined to depend for their political constitutions on accident and force" (1:33). Publius does point to the principle of self-preservation (43:279–80).

23. See *Federalist* 40:251. In ignoring the legal requirements set forth in the Articles, perhaps the founders were simply demonstrating the same "fine disregard" that William Webb Ellis exemplified a few decades later in a different field of endeavor. At Rugby School there is a plaque that reads as follows: "This stone commemorates the exploit of William Webb Ellis, who with a fine disregard for the rules of football as played in his time, first took the ball in his arms and ran with it, thus originating the distinctive feature of the Rugby game. A.D. 1823." (Kirk Varnedoe, *A Fine Disregard: What Makes Modern Art Modern* [New York: Abrams, 1990], 9.) One aspect of prudence, perhaps, is the ability to recognize when unorthodox or even illegal actions are legitimate and necessary.

24. See the analysis of the preamble provided by Justice Joseph Story in *A Familiar Exposition of the Constitution of the United States* (Lake Bluff, IL: Regnery, 1986; originally published in 1840), 57: "We shall treat it, not as a mere compact, or league, or confederacy, existing at the mere will of any one or more of the States, during their good pleasure; but, (as it purports on its face to be,) as a Constitution of Government, framed and adopted by the people of the United States, and obligatory upon all the

States, until it is altered, amended, or abolished by the people, in the manner pointed out in the instrument itself." Note the flow of *Federalist 40*: there is a movement from recognition that ratification required nine states to a reflection on the "absurdity" of allowing one state to control the fate of twelve, noting that the proportions were "one-sixtieth of the people of America" (Rhode Island) to "fifty nine-sixtieths of the people" (40:251) to "submission to the people" (40:253).

25. Also see *Federalist 45*: "The powers delegated by the proposed Constitution to the federal government are few and defined. Those which are to remain in the State governments are numerous and indefinite" (45:293). But note that in *Federalist 37* Publius emphasizes how difficult it is to draw a line dividing the respective spheres of authority (37:227, 229); see my discussion above.

26. As noted earlier, in *Federalist 78*, Publius states that when laws clash, "it is the province of the courts to liquidate and fix their meaning and operation" (78:468).

27. On this passage see Adair, 43, 45 fn 10. In *Federalist 33* Publius writes, "it may be affirmed with perfect confidence that the constitutional operation of the intended government would be precisely the same if these clauses were entirely obliterated as if they were repeated in every article. They are only declaratory of a truth which would have resulted by necessary and unavoidable implication from the very act of constituting a federal government and vesting it with certain specific powers" (33:202). Publius links the "necessary and proper" and the "supremacy" clauses in *Federalist 33*.

28. The decades-long Cold War and current War on Terrorism both raise the question of a final and total shift from a federal to a national government. See the work of Robert Higgs for a critique of the relationship between war and the growth of governmental power in America. Higgs's basic work is *Crisis and Leviathan: Critical Episodes in the Growth of American Government* (New York: Oxford University Press, 1987), and he updates his argument in *Resurgence of the Welfare State: The Crisis Since 9/11* (Oakland, CA: Independent Institute, 2005). For an argument for the positive relationship between domestic policy and national defense, see Harry V. Jaffa, "The Case for a Stronger National Government" (Robert A. Goldwin, ed., *A Nation of States: Essays on the American Federal System* [Chicago: Rand McNally & Company, 1963], 106–25. It is hard to overestimate the influence of the William James essay, "The Moral Equivalent of War," on American political efforts toward the perpetual mobilization of manpower in the twentieth century. See William James, *Writings 1902–1910*, Bruce Kuklick, ed. (New York: Library of America, 1987), 1281–93. For a brief discussion of James see my essay, "The Necessity of Overcoming the Prejudice of Political Philosophy as a Condition for Philanthropy," *Conversations on Philanthropy, I: Conceptual Foundations* (2004), 76–78.

29. In *Federalist 46* Publius writes "that the first and most natural attachment of the people will be to the governments of their respective States" (46:294), but he also sees the possibility of future partiality to the national government (46:295). The cause of such a change would be evidence of better administration at the national level. For an interesting discussion of the possibility of the national government winning popular attachment away from the states, see Epstein, 51–54. For an interesting illustration of

the natural attachment to the states as late as the Civil War, see Nathaniel Hawthorne, "Chiefly About War-Matters. By a Peaceable Man." In *The Centenary Edition of the Works of Nathaniel Hawthorne, Volume XXII: Miscellaneous Prose and Verse* (Columbus, OH: Ohio State University Press, 1994), 416.

30. But the relative infrequency of the use of the amendment process should be noted, as should the many crucial changes in the operations of government that have occurred through judicial decisions or administrative regulations. The question of the delegation of legislative powers to administrative agencies is of crucial importance.

31. On the "derailment" of the American tradition, see Willmoore Kendall and George Carey, *The Basic Symbols of American Politics* (Baton Rouge, LA: Louisiana State University Press, 1970). It is ironic that Kendall, who sees the Constitution as a "crossroads," should be concerned with the "derailment" of the American tradition!

32. See W. B. Allen and Gordon Lloyd, editors, *The Essential Antifederalist,* 2nd edition (Lanham, MD: Rowman and Littlefield, 2002), and Colleen A. Sheehan and Gary L. McDowell, editors, *Friends of the Constitution: Writings of the "Other" Federalists 1787–1788* (Indianapolis: Liberty Fund, 1998).

33. Furtwangler, 80.

34. "American Conservatism and the 'Prayer' Decisions," in *Willmoore Kendall Contra Mundum,* 337 (italics in original).

35. Max Farrand, ed., *The Records of the Federal Convention of 1787,* vol. 3 (New Haven, CT: Yale University Press, 1966), 435.

36. Frederick Turner, *Natural Religion* (New Brunswick, NJ: Transaction Publishers, 2006), 89.

37. Kendall, "American Conservatism and the 'Prayer' Decisions," 336. Italics in original.

38. Consider two letters written by James Madison later in his life. One, dated September 15, 1821, is a response to Thomas Ritchie, who asked to examine Madison's unpublished notes on the convention in order to understand the meaning of the Constitution. See Farrand, *Records of the Federal Convention,* vol. 3, 447–48. The second is Madison's response of February 8, 1825, to Jefferson's proposal to the University of Virginia Board of Visitors for a reading list that would inculcate the proper principles of government in students. Among the works suggested is *The Federalist.* For the resolution, see Thomas Jefferson, *Writings,* Merrill D. Peterson, ed. (New York: Library of America, 1984), 479–80, and for Madison's response see James Madison, *Writings,* Jack Rakove, ed. (New York: Library of America, 1999), 808. Also consider Madison's argument in his speech on the Jay Treaty delivered to the House of Representatives on April 6, 1796: "If we were to look therefore, for the meaning of the instrument [the Constitution], beyond the face of the instrument, we must look for it not in the general convention, which proposed, but in the state conventions, which accepted and ratified the constitution" (Madison, *Writings,* 574). What is the status of *The Federalist,* which neither "proposed" nor "accepted and ratified" the Constitution, from this perspective?

GOUVERNEUR MORRIS AND SPECULATION IN THE
AMERICAN DEBT TO FRANCE: A RECONSIDERATION
MELANIE RANDOLPH MILLER

1. *The Papers of Thomas Jefferson,* ed. Julian P. Boyd et al. (Princeton, NJ: Princeton University Press, 1952–), 24:773–74 (hereafter cited as *PTJ*).

2. This may be changing; after a gap of about thirty years in which Morris was completely ignored, there are been a number of recent introductory biographies, including my own, titled *An Incautious Man: The Life of Gouverneur Morris* (Wilmington, DE: ISI Books, 2008); Richard Brookhiser's *Gentleman Revolutionary: Gouverneur Morris—The Rake Who Wrote the Constitution* (New York: Free Press, 2003); and James Kirschke, *Gouverneur Morris: Author, Statesman, and Man of the World* (New York: Thomas Dunne Books, 2005). There is still little in the way of recent in-depth work, other than William Howard Adams's excellent scholarly biography, *Gouverneur Morris: An Independent Life* (New Haven, CT: Yale University Press, 2003), and my own detailed study of Morris's time in France, *Envoy to the Terror: Gouverneur Morris and the French Revolution* (Dulles, VA: Potomac Books, 2005).

3. Alexander DeConde, *Entangling Alliance: Politics and Diplomacy under George Washington* (Durham, NC: Duke University Press, 1958). DeConde's chapter on Morris is titled "Gouverneur Morris, Anachronism in Paris"; Frank T. Reuter, *Trials and Triumphs: George Washington's Foreign Policy* (Fort Worth, TX: Texas Christian University Press, 1983); Rufus King, *The Life and Correspondence of Rufus King,* ed., Charles R. King, 6 vols. (New York: Putnam's Sons, 1894), 1:419–21; Short to Jefferson, November 30, 1789, *PTJ,* 15:564; Editorial Notes, *PTJ,* 14:190–97, 20:175–97.

4. Max M. Mintz, *Gouverneur Morris and the American Revolution* (Norman, OK: University of Oklahoma Press, 1970), 29, 104, 113.

5. Samuel Flagg Bemis, "Payment of the French Loans to the United States, 1777–1795," *Current History* (March 1926): 825, 827. William Short's papers contain a slightly different list undated (perhaps 1792), totaling 34 million livres; E. James Ferguson, *The Power of the Purse* (Chapel Hill, NC: University of North Carolina Press, 1961), 221, 260; *PTJ,* 14:191.

6. *PTJ,* 10:405–6;14:194, 192.

7. Ibid., 20:176–78.

8. Editorial Notes, *PTJ,* 14:190–97, 20:175–97.

9. Gouverneur Morris to Washington, May 27, 1791, Mark A. Mastromarino, Jack D. Warren, Philander D. Chase, eds., *The Papers of George Washington, Presidential Series* (Charlottesville, VA: University of Virginia Press, 2000), 8:208–212 (hereafter cited as *GWP, Presidential Series*).

10. Ferguson, *Power of the Purse,* 265.

11. *PTJ,* 14:191; Gouverneur Morris to Robert Morris, Commercial Letterbook, Gouverneur Morris Papers, Library of Congress (hereafter cited as *CL*).

12. Eloise Ellery, *Brissot de Warville* (Boston: Houghton Mifflin, 1915), 71–84; Robert F. Jones, *"The King of the Alley": William Duer, Politician, Entrepreneur, and Speculator,*

285

1768–1799, Memoirs of the American Philosophical Society, vol. 202 (Philadelphia, 1992), 116; Daniel Lewis Wick, *A Conspiracy of Well-Intentioned Men: The Society of Thirty and the French Revolution* (New York: Taylor & Francis, 1987), 221.

13. *PTJ*, 11:6–9.

14. For example, the editors of the *PTJ*, 14:531n; Mintz, *Gouverneur Morris and the American Revolution,* 206.

15. King, *Life and Correspondence of Rufus King,* 1:623; Gouverneur Morris to Robert Morris, May 31, 1790, *CL*.

16. Gouverneur Morris to Robert Morris, February 19, 1789, and May 10, 1789, *CL*.

17. Willink, Van Staphorst & Hubbard to Jefferson, August 13, 1789, *PTJ*, 15:342–44.

18. Entries of September 8 and September 14, 1789, Gouverneur Morris, *A Diary of the French Revolution* ed. Beatrix Cary Davenport, 2 vols. (Boston: Houghton Mifflin, 1939) 1:208, 218 (hereafter cited as *Diary*); *PTJ*, 15:473n.

19. Entry of October 27, 1789, *Diary,* 1:272.

20. See, e.g., Jefferson to Clavière, August 16, 1792, and Jefferson to Brissot, May 8, 1793, *PTJ*, 24:300 and 25:679.

21. Short to Jefferson, January 28, 1790, *PTJ*, 16:132; Jefferson to Short, April 25, 1791, *PTJ*, 20:255.

22. John Jay to Jefferson, October 24, 1787, *PTJ*, 12:265–67; entries of September 23, 1789, and September 24, 1789, *Diary,* 1:226, 227–28.

23. Gouverneur Morris to James Swan, October 11, 1790, *CL*.

24. Entry of December 5, 1789, *Diary,* 1:324–25.

25. Entry of December 29, 1789, *Diary,* 1:350.

26. Gouverneur Morris to Hamilton, January 31, 1790, *The Papers of Alexander Hamilton,* ed. Harold C. Syrett et al., 27 vols. (New York: Columbia University Press, 1961–1979), 6:234–39 (hereafter cited as *AHP*).

27. Short to Jefferson, January 28, 1790, 16:134.

28. Entry of December 12, 1789, *Diary,* 1:331; *PTJ*, 20:179–80; Willink, Van Staphorst & Hubbard to Hamilton, January 25, 1790, *AHP*, 6:210–18. .

29. Short to Jefferson, January 30, 1790, *PTJ*, 16:134.

30. Gouverneur Morris to Ternant, March 31, 1790, *CL;* Gouverneur Morris to Hamilton, January 31, 1790, *AHP*, 6:234.

31. Gouverneur Morris to Hamilton, January 31, 1790, *AHP*, 6:234–39.

32. *PTJ*, 20:177.

33. Hamilton to Willink, Van Staphorst, and Hubbard, May 7, 1790, *AHP*, 6:409; *PTJ*, 20:195.

34. *PTJ*, 20:193.

35. *PTJ*, 20:181; entry of May 26, 1791, *Diary,* 2:192.

36. Jefferson to Short, August 26, 1790, *PTJ*, 17:434; Bemis, 828.

37. *PTJ*, 20:197.

38. Entry of November 29, 1789, *Diary,* 1: 318.

39. Short to Jefferson, November 25, 1790, cited in *AHP* 7:165; Gouverneur Morris to Washington, May 27, 1791, *GWP, Presidential Series,* 8:208–12.

40. Jacob M. Price, *France and the Chesapeake: A History of the French Tobacco Monopoly, 1674–1791, and of Its Relationship to the British and American Tobacco Trades,* 2 vols. (Ann Arbor, MI: University of Michigan Press, 1973), 2:798; Gouverneur Morris to Robert Morris, November 15, 1789, *CL;* Andrew Dickson White, *Fiat Money: Inflation in France* (New York: D. Appleton, 1959), 114. These depreciation figures are approximate because no two sources consulted gave identical figures. Jean Bouchary, *Marché des Changes de Paris à la fin du XVIIIᵉ Siècle* (Paris, 1937), 109–44; Heinrich Von Sybel, *History of the French Revolution,* 4 vols. (London, 1869), 1:282. Gouverneur Morris to Short, September 18, 1790, Jared Sparks, *The Life and Correspondence of Gouverneur Morris ,* 3 vols. (Boston: Gray & Bowen, 1832), 2:109–10. The debate about *assignats* continues, although more historians agree with Morris's criticism of them than otherwise. See: François Crouzet, *La Grande Inflation: La Monnaie en France de Louis XVI à Napoléon* (Paris, 1983); J. F. Bosher, *French Finances, 1770–1795: From Business to Bureaucracy* (Cambridge: Cambridge University Press, 1970), 264, 309–10, 275.

41. Florin Aftalion, *The French Revolution: An Economic Interpretation,* (Cambridge: Cambridge University Press, 1990), 96–97.

42. Short to Hamilton, January 26, 1792, *AHP,* 10:568.

43. Short to Jefferson, November 25, 1790, received in April 1791, *PTJ,* 20:184n; Jefferson to Short, August 26, 1790, *PTJ,* 17:434; *PTJ* 20:195; Gouverneur Morris to Washington, December 27, 1791, *GWP, Presidential Series,* 9:333; Short to Hamilton, November 22, 1791, *AHP,* 9:523.

44. Hamilton to Jefferson, April 15, 1791, *AHP,* 8:289; *PTJ,* 20:193, 203; Jefferson to Short, April 15, 1791, *PTJ,* 20:195n; *PTJ,* 20:195, citing Otto to Montmorin, May 7, 1791.

45. Short could not see how France could complain about receiving depreciated *assignats* when France was using them to pay its creditors. Hamilton to Short, September 2, 1791; Short to Hamilton, March 24, 1792, *AHP,* 9:159 and 11:179; Short to Hamilton, June 19, 1791, *AHP,* 8:489.

46. *PTJ,* 22:120n; Hamilton to Jefferson, August 31, 1791, *AHP,* 9:129.

47. *PTJ,* 20:197.

48. Hamilton noted that Short had reported in June 1791 that *assignat* depreciation was 10 percent and the drop between Paris and Amsterdam was 20 percent; Hamilton assumed that this drop *included* the *assignat* fall and that therefore the exchange rate drop alone was 10 percent, that is, 20 percent (total) minus 10 percent (*assignat*). *AHP,* 9:159. Aftalion says the *assignat* had dropped 20 percent by the summer of 1791 against specie.

49. Gouverneur Morris to George Washington, May 27, 1791, *Diary,* 2:193–94.

50. *PTJ,* 20:197.

51. Washington to Gouverneur Morris, September 12, 1791, cited in *AHP,* 9:62. Hamilton assumed that the proposal included the advantage of both depreciation of *assignats* and the rate of exchange, and he specified that the U.S. wanted to keep the latter benefit.

52. Entries of February 1 and March 12, 1790, *Diary,* 1:402, 446.

53. Swan to Jefferson, October 3, 1790, *PTJ,* 20:186–87; Swan to Knox, October 3, 1790, The Knox Papers, Gilder-Lehrman Collection, Pierpont Morgan Library (hereafter cited as Knox Papers); entries of November 8, 9, 10, 1790, *Diary,* 2:52, 53, 55; Swan to Short, December 12, 1790, *AHP,* 7: 361–62; *Diary,* 2:158.

54. Entries of November 21, November 23, and December 2, 1790, *Diary,* 2:67, 69, 77.

55. Entry of April 4, 1791, *Diary,* 2:153.

56. *PTJ,* 20:189–90.

57. Entries of April 4, 8, 9, 1791, *Diary,* 2:154, 156, 157, 158. The collection of Gouverneur Morris papers in the American Philosophical Society contains a copy of the proposal dated April 7, 1791; Smith Family Papers, Series 41, American Philosophical Society, Philadelphia; Short to Hamilton, June 3, 1791, *AHP,* 8: 421.

58. Entry of May 26, 1791, *Diary,* 2:192; Short to Knox, May 27, 1791, Knox Papers.

59. Gouverneur Morris to Washington, May 27, 1791, *GWP, Presidential Series,* 8:208–12.

60. Gouverneur Morris to Hamilton, June 28, 1791, *AHP,* 8:512; entry of January 23, 1791, *Diary,* 2:106; Swan to Knox, May 27, 1791, Knox Papers.

61. Entries of April 25, 1792, May 11, 1792, *Diary,* 2:416, 426; letter to Robert Morris, May 26, 1793, *CL.*

62. I was not able to confirm that *assignats* were to be used in the Schweitzer proposal. Short told Hamilton the project relied on the exchange, and paying in livres, with no mention of *assignats;* in a later letter he said it involved *assignats.* Short to Hamilton, December 18, 1790 and June 3, 1791, *AHP* 7:355 and 8:423. The proposal may well have been modified by the time Morris got involved. Morris pointed out to Washington that if *assignats* were abolished, and that was a real possibility, given their rampant deflation, the exchange rate would immediately turn in favor of France. *GWP, Presidential Series,* 8:208–12. Washington to Gouverneur Morris, September 12, 1791, *AHP,* 9:62.

63. *PTJ,* 20:188–89.

64. *PTJ,* 20:195; Jefferson to Short, April 25, 1791, *PTJ,* 20:255.

65. *PTJ,* 20:256n; Short to Gouverneur Morris, June 12, 1791, Columbia Papers, item 1229; entries of July 3, 10, 17, 15, and 19, 1791, *Diary,* 2:218, 211–12, 215, 222, 224.

66. Gouverneur Morris to Washington, December 27, 1791, *GWP, Presidential Series,* 9:333–37.

67. Jefferson to Gouverneur Morris, January 23, 1792, *PTJ,* 23:55–57.

68. Before they made that demand, Morris had followed through on a debt payment to the new government, arranged *before* the king fell, despite protests from a skittish Short. Jefferson and Hamilton (when they learned of the coup) decided to suspend debt payments to the new regime for some time to come. Ironically, Morris was denounced by the French for refusing to make any more payments until he obtained specific authorization. See Miller, *Envoy to the Terror,* chapters 10–13.

69. Ferguson,*Power of the Purse,* 267n; Bemis, "Payment of the French Loans," 831.

70. Gouverneur Morris to Samuel Ogden, July 12, 1792, *CL.*

LORD SELKIRK'S TOUR OF NORTH AMERICA, 1803–4
J. M. BUMSTED

1. For an account of this venture, see J. M. Bumsted, "Settlement by Chance: Lord Selkirk and Prince Edward Island," *Canadian Historical Review* 59 (1978), 171–88.

2. See J. M. Bumsted, "Another Look at the Founder: Lord Selkirk as Political Economist," in Bumsted, *Thomas Scott's Body and Other Essays on Early Manitoba History* (Winnipeg, MB: University of Manitoba Press, 2000), 37–56.

3. Published as *Lord Selkirk's Diary 1803–1804: A Journal of His Travels in British North America and the Northeastern United States,* ed. with an introduction by Patrick C. T. White (Toronto: University of Toronto Press, 1958).

4. The published version of the diary bears the heading "DIARY I/ AUGUST 5TH, 1803 TO OCTOBER 3RD, 1803, THE MARITIMES," although the first entry for the text is on August 3.

5. See Burns's oft-quoted "Lines on Meeting with Lord Daer,"

6. Selkirk, *Diary,* 45.

7. An earlier reference while on Prince Edward Island spoke of "talking my best Gaelic" to four lads from Ross-shire. Selkirk, *Diary,* 17.

8. Ibid., 49.

9. Ibid., 57.

10. For Burke, see *Dictionary of Canadian Biography,* V (Toronto and Montreal: University of Toronto Press and Les Presses de l'université Laval, 1983), 123–5.

11. Ibid., 67.

12. Ibid., 74.

13. Ibid., 271–72.

14. Ibid., 83.

15. Ibid., 85.

16. Ibid., 91.

17. J. Guillamard to Alexander Hamilton, Gower St. [London], February 22, 1803, reprinted in Harold C. Syrett et al., eds., *The Papers of Alexander Hamilton,* vol. 25 (New York: Columbia University Press, 1979), 88.

18. The Quasi War was an undeclared naval war between the United States and France that took place between 1798 and 1800. At issue was the right of American merchant ships to trade with belligerent nations. At the time, the revolutionary government of France was at war with Britain, and French warships had been seizing American vessels headed to and from British ports.

19. Selkirk, *Diary,* 92.

20. See "Another Look at the Founder," 38–39.

21. Letter is reprinted in Hamilton's collected works.

22. Selkirk, *Diary,* 128. The quotations in the next few pages are all from the *Diary.*

23. For modern analyses of the early years of American politics, consult Richard Buel Jr., *Securing the Revolution: Ideology in American Politics, 1789–1815* (Ithaca, NY: Cornell University Press, 1972); William Nisbet Chambers, *Political Parties in a New Nation: The American Experience, 1776–1809* (New York: Oxford University Press, 1966); and Joseph Charles, *The Origin of the American Party System: Three Essays* (New York: Harper and Row, 1961).

24. This argument is repeated by Manning J. Dauer, *The Adams Federalists* (Westport, CT: Johns Hopkins University Press, 1984).

25. Selkirk, *Diary,* 128.

26. Helen I. Cowan, *Charles Williamson, Genesee Promoter—Friend of Anglo-American Rapprochement* (Rochester, NY: Rochester Historical Society, 1941).

27. B. A. Parker, "Thomas Clark: His Business Relationship with Lord Selkirk," *Beaver,* outfit 310 (Autumn 1979), 50–58.

28. See Gerald Craig, *Upper Canada: The Formative Years, 1784–1841* (Toronto: McClelland and Stewart, 1963).

29. Quoted in DCB, VIII, 857.

30. Selkirk to Burn, November 19, 1803, Selkirk Papers National Archives of Canada, 14291 (hereafter cited as SPNAC).

31. Selkirk, *Diary,* 145.

32. Ibid., 153.

33. For Macdonell see *Dictionary of Canadian Biography* (Toronto and Montreal: University of Toronto Press and Les Presses de université Laval), vol. VII, 554–56.

34. General P. Hunter to Selkirk, December 24, 1803, SPNAC, 14108–110.

35. Selkirk to George Chisholm, December 22, 1803, reprinted in Hazel Mathews, *The Mark of Honour* (Toronto: University of Toronto Press, 1965), 146.

36. Instructions to William Burn, December 1803, SPNAC, 14278.

37. SPNAC, 14130.

38. Miles Macdonell to John Macdonell, April 6, 1804, reprinted in A. G. Morice, "Sidelights on the Careers of Miles Macdonell and His Brothers," *Canadian Historical Review* 10 (1929), 308–32.

39. Selkirk, *Diary,* 199.

40. Ibid., 208.

41. Ibid., 202.

42. Ibid., 217.

43. Ibid., 220.

44. Ibid., 233.

45. Ibid., 239.

46. Ibid., 258.

47. For the Hamilton-Burr feud, see Roger Kennedy, *Burr, Hamilton, and Jefferson* (New York: Oxford University Press, 2000).

48. Selkirk, *Diary,* 324.

49. Notes on agreements with employees, SPNAC, 14653–655.

50. Selkirk, *Diary,* 326.

51. Selkirk Papers, vol. 4, 105–8.

52. SPNAC, 14653–655.

53. Selkirk to General Hunter, August 30, 1804, SPNAC, 14114–119.

54. Report of Upper Canada Executive Council, September 18, 1804, SPNAC, 14121–122.

55. Selkirk to Alexander Macdonell, Halifax, November 6, 1804 (rough notes), SPNAC, 14536–537.

56. The best studies of Baldoon are A. E. D. MacKenzie, *Baldoon: Lord Selkirk's Settlement in Upper Canada* (London, ON: Phelps Pub., 1978) and F. C. Hamil and T. Jones, "Lord Selkirk's Work in Upper Canada: The Story of Baldoon," *Ontario History* 57 (1965), 1–12. Neither really asks any critical questions, much less answers them.

57. See, for example, the detailed plans for the home farm at Baldoon in SPNAC, 14628–652.

58. Selkirk, *Diary,* 351–52.

59. Ibid., 354.

60. The Earl of Selkirk, *A Letter Addressed to John Cartwright, Esq. Chairman of the Committee at the Crown and Anchor: On the Subject of Parliamentary Reform* (London, 1809), reprinted in Bumsted, ed., *The Collected Writings of Lord Selkirk 1799–1809 Volume I In the Writings and Papers of Thomas Douglas, Fifth Earl of Selkirk* (Winnipeg, MB: Manitoba Historical Society, 1984), 359–66.

John Witherspoon's Philosophy of Moral Government
James M. Albritton

1. Jeffry Hays Morrison has described the political atmosphere of the Revolution as one in which "the public interest of religion" was a priority for John Witherspoon and other founders. Those men, ranging from devout Christians like Witherspoon to Unitarian deists like Jefferson, all believed that the republic must stand on virtue and that virtue must be based in religion. Morrison and I agree that Witherspoon believed the Christian religion to be the only source of true virtue. I hope to elaborate on Morrison's findings by explicating the practical implications of Witherspoon's beliefs. Jeffrey Hays Morrison, "John Witherspoon and 'The Public Interest of Religion'" *Journal of Church and State* 41, no. 3 (1999): 559–69.

2. John Witherspoon, *A Pastoral Letter from the Synod of New-York and Philadelphia,* in *The Works of the Rev. John Witherspoon,* vol. 3, 2d ed. (Philadelphia: William W. Woodward, 1802), 9, 11.

3. John Witherspoon, "An Address to the Students of the Senior Class," in *The Works of the Rev. John Witherspoon,* vol. 3, 101, 102, 103.

4. John Witherspoon, "The Dominion of Providence over the Passions of Men," in *The Works of the Rev. John Witherspoon,* vol. 3, 17, 20, 31, 32. Robert Aitken, one of

Witherspoon's former students and a printer in Philadelphia, published the first edition in 1776, the second and third editions in 1777 (both of which were reprinted in Glasgow), the fourth edition in 1778 (which was reprinted in London), and an unknown source printed a fifth edition in London in 1779. See Varnum Lansing Collins, *President Witherspoon: A Biography,* vol. 2 (Princeton, NJ: Princeton University Press, 1925; reprint, Religion in America, ed. Edwin S. Gaustad, New York: Arno Press & The New York Times, 1969), 251, 252.

5. John Witherspoon, "Sermon Delivered at a Public Thanksgiving After Peace," in *The Works of the Rev. John Witherspoon,* vol. 3, 80. Richard Sher has claimed that *The Dominion of Providence* takes on a jeremiad form because Witherspoon called the people to salvation as the war approached. Yet the same call to salvation after the war was over demonstrates Witherspoon's overarching desire for the salvation of men. He did not necessarily desire foxhole conversions as the war approached; instead, he desired that men and women truly repent and look to God for salvation and in grateful response obey him by acting virtuously. See Richard B. Sher, "Witherspoon's *Dominion of Providence* and the Scottish Jeremiad Tradition," in *Scotland and America in the Age of the Enlightenment,* eds. Richard B. Sher and Jeffrey, R. Smitten (Edinburgh: Edinburgh University Press, 1990), 46. Jeffry H. Morrison contradicts Varnum Lansing Collins, who dates the sermon as April 19, 1783. Morrison uses internal and external evidence to establish the date of the sermon as November 28, 1782. See Jeffry H. Morrison, "The Political Thought of John Witherspoon, 1768–1794" (Ph.D. diss., Georgetown University, 2001), 272–76.

6. John Witherspoon, "Christian Magnanimity," in *The Works of the Rev. John Witherspoon,* vol. 3, 97.

7. Ibid., 87, 88.

8. Witherspoon, *Works,* vol. 3, 41.

9. Ibid., 14, 13, 15.

10. Ibid., 92–94.

11. Ibid., 44, 46.

12. Ibid., 81.

13. John Calvin, *Institutes of the Christian Religion,* The Library of Christian Classics, ed. John T. McNeill, trans. Ford Lewis Battles, nos. 20–21 (Philadelphia: The Westminster Press, 1960), 1488.

14. Calvin, *Institutes,* 1492, 1494 n21, 1519.

15. Witherspoon, *Works,* vol. 3, 12, 13.

16. Ibid., 19, 20, 37.

17. Collins, *President Witherspoon,* vol. 1, 119, 125, 133, 134.

18. Ibid., 157–159, 132, 157, 158.

19. Calvin, *Institutes,* 1490; Collins, *President Witherspoon,* vol. 1, 161, 162, 177; John Witherspoon, "Thoughts on American Liberty," in *The Works of the Rev. John Witherspoon,* vol. 4, 297–300. In his biography of Witherspoon, Collins notes that Witherspoon drafted seven resolutions for the Somerset County committee of correspondence regarding their instructions to the Continental Congress. He argues that the

New Jersey resolutions are so similar, and even identical in some cases, that Witherspoon and the Somerset County committee must have played an influential role in the meeting in New Brunswick.

20. Collins, *President Witherspoon,* vol. 1, 185–89; John Witherspoon, "On the Controversy about Independence," in *The Works of the Rev. John Witherspoon,* vol. 4, 301–4.

21. Collins, *President Witherspoon,* vol. 1, 204, 207, 209, 212, 213.

22. John Witherspoon, "Address to the Natives of Scotland Residing in America," in *The Works of the Rev. John Witherspoon,* vol. 3, 47–60. The Wilkites were the followers of John Wilkes, a rogue Member of Parliament who was an ardent supporter of England and the English constitution, but who hated the Scots and the idea of a united Britain.

23. John Witherspoon, "Aristides," in *The Works of the Rev. John Witherspoon,* vol. 4, 309–16.

24. John Witherspoon, "The Druid," in *The Works of the Rev. John Witherspoon,* vol. 4, 425–45.

25. Collins, *President Witherspoon,* vol. 1, 217–19; Collins, *President Witherspoon,* vol. 2, 3, 4; John Witherspoon, "Part of a Speech in Congress upon the Confederation," in *The Works of the Rev. John Witherspoon,* vol. 4, 347–51.

26. Collins, *President Witherspoon,* vol. 2, 18, 19, 65, 66.

27. Witherspoon, *Works,* vol. 3, 61, 83, 82.

28. *Journals of the Continental Congress, 1774–1789,* ed. Worthington C. Ford et al. (Washington, DC, 1904–37), vol. 6, 1022.

29. *JCC* 21 (1781): 1074–76; *JCC* 23 (1782): 647.

30. Witherspoon, *Works,* vol. 4, 421–23.

31. Collins, *President Witherspoon,* vol. 2, 160, 161, A. A. Hodge, *The Confession of Faith: With Questions for Theological Students and Bible Classes.* Electronic edition based on the 1992 Banner of Truth reprint. (Simpsonville, SC: Christian Classics Foundation, 1996), 21–23.

32. Calvin, *Institutes,* 1487; Hodge, *The Confession,* 21–23.

33. Calvin, *Institutes,* 1488; Hodge, *The Confession,* 21–23.

34. Hodge, *The Confession,* 21–23.

35. John Willson, *John Witherspoon and the Presbyterian Constitution,* no. 3 of *We the People,* The Hillsdale College American Heritage Series, ed. Joseph S. McNamara (Hillsdale, MI: Hillsdale College Press, 1994), 31, 32.

36. Willson, 32, 34.

JEFFERSON UN-LOCKED:
THE ROUSSEAUAN MOMENT IN AMERICAN POLITICAL THOUGHT
RICHARD K. MATTHEWS AND ELRIC M. KLINE

1. Merrill D. Petterson, *The Jeffersonian Image in the American Mind* (New York: Oxford University Press, 1960), 9.

2. Joseph Wheelan, *Jefferson's War: America's First War on Terror 1801–1805* (New York:

Carroll & Graf Publishers, 2003); Winthrop Jordan, *White Over Black* (Chapel Hill, NC: University of North Carolina Press, 1968); Annette Gordon-Reed, *Thomas Jefferson and Sally Hemmings: An American Controversy* (Charlottesville, VA: University Press of Virginia, 1998); Daniel L. Dreisbach, *Thomas Jefferson and the Wall of Separation Between Church and State* (New York: New York University Press, 2003); Lenni Brenner, *Jefferson and Madison on the Separation of Church and State* (Fort Lee, NJ: Barricade Books, 2004); Forest Church, *The Separation of Church and State: Writings on a Fundamental Freedom by America's Founders* (Boston: Beacon Press, 2004).

3. Leonard Levy, *Jefferson and Civil Liberties: The Darker Side,* (Cambridge, MA: Belknap Press of Harvard University Press, 1963).

4. Conor Cruise O'Brien, "Thomas Jefferson: Radical and Racist," *Atlantic Monthly,* October 1996. See the cover and pages 53–74. These examples confirm another of Peterson's insights: "Later generations comprehended his thoughts only in fragments, crossing and colliding with each other, until it seemed that the protean figure, if ever he had a genuine historical existence, must never be rediscovered" (9).

5. Joseph Ellis, *American Sphinx: The Character of Thomas Jefferson* (New York: Alfred A. Knopf, 1997), 7, 10. Ellis's "chief quarry" was "Jefferson's character," which he saw as deeply flawed:"Jefferson's much-touted contradictions and inconsistencies were quite real, to be sure, but his psychological agility, his capacity to play hide-and-seek within himself, was a protective device he developed to prevent his truly radical and highly romantic personal vision from colliding with reality" (xii). Ellis's own "psychological agility" and "ability to play hide-and-seek within himself" makes it reasonable to question whether Ellis's flawed portrait of Jefferson is at least in part a projection of its author.

6. J. G. A. Pocock, *The Machiavellian Moment: Florentine Political Thought and the Atlantic Republican Tradition* (Princeton, NJ: Princeton University Press, 1975), 533; see also Richard K. Matthews, *The Radical Politics of Thomas Jefferson* (Lawrence, KS: University Press of Kansas, 1986), 17, 139n16.

7. For evidence that Jefferson read some Rousseau see Albert Ellery Berg, ed., *The Writings of Thomas Jefferson,* 20 vols. (Washington, DC: Thomas Jefferson Memorial Association, 1903–4) (hereafter cited as *ME*), TJ to William Lee, January 16, 1817, 15:101, where TJ writes: "The institutions of Lycurgus, for example, would not have suited Athens, nor those of Solon, Lacedaemon. The organizations of Locke were impracticable for Carolina, and those of Rousseau and Mably for Poland."

8. See Donald S. Lutz, *A Preface to American Political Theory* (Lawrence, KS: University Press of Kansas, 1992), 136, where he ranks Locke as the third most cited European author (Montesquieu and Blackstone being first and second), and Rousseau a distant fifteenth. Cf. Paul Spurlin, *Rousseau in America: 1760–1809* (Tuscaloosa, AL: University Press of Alabama, 1969), 113, where he concludes "it is obvious that Rousseau had vogue but not influence in eighteenth-century America."

9. Merrill Peterson, ed., *Thomas Jefferson: Writings* (New York: The Library of America, 1984) (hereafter cited as *TJW*), TJ to Dr. Benjamin Rush, January 16, 1811, 1236. All references to Jefferson, where possible, are from this definitive edition.

10. Lutz, *A Preface to American Political Theory,* 126, 137; and C. B. Macpherson, ed.,

Second Treatise of Government (Indianapolis: Hackett, 1980), vii; Locke's *Second Treatise* has little to offer on specific political institutions; consequently, he is rarely cited by Americans after the Declaration of Independence.

11. Rodger Woolhouse, ed., *An Essay Concerning Human Understanding,* (New York: Penguin, 1997), II.I.2: "Let us then suppose the mind to be, as we say, white paper, void of all characters, without any ideas:—How comes it to be furnished? . . . To this I answer, in one word, from EXPERIENCE."

12. *"A Declaration of the Representatives of the United States of America, in General Congress Assembled,"* TJW, 19.

13. *An Essay* II.XXI.52. Those who would interpret Jefferson as merely transplanting Locke's theory of rights to America sometimes claim that the phrase "life, liberty, and the pursuit of happiness" can actually be attributed directly to Locke. In fact, while Locke refers to life and liberty, or life and property, on as many as twenty-six separate occasions, in none of these does he include "the pursuit of happiness" as a fundamental natural right. The relevant passages on rights in *An Essay* are II.XXVIII.9; and in the *Second Treatise* sections 4, 6, 57, 59, 65, 66, 69, 74, 85, 87, 120, 123, 131, 135, 137, 139, 171, 173, 178, 180, 182, 189, 209, 221, 222. "Happiness," in *An Essay,* appears in Book II, Chapter XXI, in the context of Locke's discussion of determinations of the will, as his term for the general end that humans pursue. See especially II. XXI.44; 48; 51; 52; 61; 63. In only one instance does "happiness" appear in proximity to "life," and this only with respect to children's debt to their parents: "So [God] has laid on the children a perpetual obligation of honouring their parents, which containing in it an inward esteem and reverence to be shewn by all outward expressions, ties up the child from any thing that may ever injure or affront, disturb or endanger, the happiness or life of those from whom he received his; and engages him in all actions of defence, relief, assistance and comfort of those, by whose means he entered into being, and has been made capable of any enjoyments of life: from this obligation no state, no freedom can absolve children" (*Second Treatise,* sec. 66). It strains credibility to insist that Jefferson lifted the notion of a fundamental right to the pursuit of happiness from this passage—indeed, Locke clearly differentiates the heavy positive obligations of children from the protective, negative duties of the state.

14. *Second Treatise,* sec. 25.

15. Ibid., sec. 50; see secs. 32, 34, 42.

16. *TJW,* "The Rights of British Americans," 106. The veracity of Jefferson's account may be doubtful, but he was writing a polemic of political significance where historical accuracy was of secondary import.

17. *TJW,* 119–20.

18. *TJW,* to Isaac McPherson, August 13, 1813, 1291; see also TJ to James Madison, September 6, 1789, 959–64.

19. *TJW,* to Reverend James Madison, October 28, 1785, 841. This easily translates into an endorsement of progressive taxation.

20. *Second Treatise,* secs. 27, 33, 34, 36.

21. *TJW,* to Reverend James Madison, October 28, 1785, 842.

22. *Second Treatise,* sec. 36.

23. *TJW,* 842. This is consistent with Jefferson's constitutional grant of fifty acres of land to every male who does not already own land and explains why he willingly flaunts the Constitution to purchase the Louisiana Territory.

24. *TJW,* to John Adams, October 28, 1813, 1309.

25. See C. B. Macpherson, *Democratic Theory: Essays In Retrieval* (Oxford: Clarendon Press, 1973), 135. In light of Jefferson's unique view of property, Macpherson identified him as advocating one of the few American alternatives to the tradition of possessive individualism. "With one's own small property," Macpherson explained, "one could not be made subservient. And small property was the great guarantee against government tyranny as well as against economic oppression. It was to secure individual liberty, and all the virtues that can flourish only with sturdy independence, that Jefferson wanted America to remain a country of small proprietors." When Jefferson's position is pushed to its logical extreme, the principle becomes much more than merely a right to property ownership. Again, Macpherson captures the crucial point: "This justification of property rests, in the last analysis, on the right to life at a more than animal level: freedom from coerced labour and arbitrary government is held to be part of what is meant by a fully human life. At the same time this justification is an assertion of the right to the means of labour; the whole point is that by working on his own land or other productive resources a man can be independent and uncoerced."

26. See *TJW,* in a fascinating letter to William Ludlow, September 6, 1824, 1497. TJ acknowledges the possibility of small, communal communities: "A society of seventy families, the number you name, may very possibly be governed as a single family, subsisting on their common industry, and holding all things in common."

27. *TJW, Notes on Virginia,* 248–49.

28. *TJW,* to James Madison, September 6, 1789, 959; Jefferson's concept of property requires guards against the earth being destroyed or damaged for future use by others. If an individual had a natural right, "he might, during his own life, eat up the *usufruct* of the lands for several generations . . . and then the lands would belong to the dead, and not to the living . . . (960)."

29. For example, see Charles Bednar, *Transforming the Dream: Ecologism and the Shaping of an Alternative American Vision* (Albany, NY: State University of New York Press, 2003); William Ophuls, *Requiem for Modern Politics: The Tragedy of the Enlightenment and The Challenge of the New Millennium* (Boulder, CO: West View Press, 1997); David W. Orr, "Political Economy and the Ecology of Childhood," *Earth Ethics* (Washington, DC: Center for the Respect for Life and Environment), Fall 2003, 31.

30. *Second Treatise,* secs. 31, 36, 38, 42.

31. Cf. Luigi Marco Berssani, "Life Liberty, and . . . : Jefferson on Property Rights," *Journal of Libertarian Studies* 18, no. 1, 31–87, for a contrasting view. A tenacious scholar, Bassani is deeply concerned with scholarly attempts that he perceives turn Jefferson into a proto-socialist, and he surprisingly claims that there are "very few textual footnotes" to support the position outlined above (32). Lacking "textual footnotes" for his own position, Bassani claims that "revisionists" "fall into the error of perspective that goes beyond simply

fitting the right of property into the wrong fields. They divide rights into two fields that do not correspond to the Jeffersonian political outlook (49)."

32. *TJW,* to James Madison, September 6, 1789, 964.

33. Ibid., 963. Jefferson never gives up on this idea. See TJ to Samuel Kercheval, July 12, 1816, 1395–1403.

34. This does not mean, of course, that there is no natural right to the fruits of one's *immediate* labor. But that right does not extend, as in Locke, to "the turfs my servant has cut. . . ." *Second Treatise,* sec. 28.

35. Jean-Jacques Rousseau, *The First and Second Discourse,* ed. Roger D. Masters (New York: St. Martin's Press: 1964), 141–42.

36. *Second Discourse,* 142.

37. Ibid., 151–52.

38. Ibid., 158–59.

39. *Second Treatise,* sec. 94; see also secs. 136, 141, 155.

40. Ibid., vii–xxi.

41. *Of the Social Contract,* in *The Social Contract and Other Later Political Writings,* ed. Victor Gourevitch (Cambridge: Cambridge University Press, 2004), 54. Unless otherwise noted, all Rousseau quotes are from this edition.

42. *Social Contract,* 54; see also 56: "the right every individual has over his own land is always subordinate to the right the community has over everyone, without which there would be neither solidarity in the social bond, nor real force in the exercise of Sovereignty."

43. *Social Contract,* 56 (footnote). See also 78, where he writes; "With regard to equality, this word [civil freedom] must not be understood to mean that degrees of power and wealth should be absolutely the same, but that, as for power, it stop short of all violence and never be exercised except by virtue of rank and the laws, and that as for wealth, no citizen be so very rich that he can buy another, and none so poor that he is compelled to sell himself." Rousseau's use of the word "citizen" clearly indicates that his concern is with wage slavery. In a footnote to this passage, he continues: "Do you, then, want to give the State stability? Bring the extremes as close together as possible; tolerate neither very rich people nor beggars. These two states, which are naturally inseparable, are equally fatal to the common good; from one come the abettors of tyranny, and from the other tyrants; it is always between these two that there is trafficking in public freedom; one buys it, the other sells it."

44. *Discourse on Political Economy,* 24.

45. Ibid., 19.

46. *Second Treatise,* sec. 182.

47. Ibid., 181; see sec. 139: "nor the *general,* that can condemn him [a soldier] to death for deserting his post, or for not obeying the most desperate orders, can yet, with all his *absolute power* of life and death, dispose of one farthing of that soldier's estate, or seize one jot of his goods."

48. See also Locke's comments on inheritance in the *First Treatise,* where he admits that his description of inheritance as a "natural" right rests on the fact (according to

Locke) that the "practice is universal." "It perhaps be answered, that common consent hath disposed of it to their children. Common practice, we see indeed, does so dispose of it; but we cannot say that it is the common consent of mankind; for that hath never been asked, nor actually given; and if common tacit consent hath established it, it would make but a positive, and not a natural right of children to inherit the goods of their parents: but where the practice is universal, it is reasonable to think the cause is natural" (sec. 88). Locke's extremism on property rights extends, meanwhile, to the point that "property . . . is for the benefit and sole advantage of the proprietor, so that *he may even destroy the thing,* that he has property in by his use of it, where need requires" (sec. 92; emphasis added). Obviously, one may "destroy" certain goods, e.g. food, by consuming it; but Locke would hardly take the trouble to mention it unless he thought the right to have a more general quality. Rousseau, most likely, would be reluctant to agree: given the grounding of property in positive law, it seems subject to the general will in such a way that whatever *use* of the thing an individual may have, he is morally bound to avoid its *abuse*—namely, any use not conducive to the common good, which would seemingly include the destruction of useful property. Here Jefferson stands out as the most truly conscious of environmental concerns, and their implications for the living generation's responsibility to the future: no one has a right to "eat up the usufruct of the lands for several generations to come," for then "the lands would belong to the dead."

49. Recall that in Jefferson's trinity Locke is placed alongside two other preeminent scientific philosophers: Bacon and Newton. It is this Locke the epistemologist, not Locke the political theorist, that Jefferson admires. See *TJW,* to John Turmbull, February 15, 1789, 939–40, where TJ explains that he considers the trio as "the greatest men that have ever lived . . . and having laid the foundation of those superstructures which have been raised in the Physical & Moral sciences."

50. *An Essay,* I.III.1; see also III.XI.16: "morality is capable of demonstration, as well as mathematics"; and IV.IV.7: "moral knowledge is as capable of real certainty, as mathematics."

51. *An Essay,* I.II.13.

52. *Second Discourse,* 95.

53. *TJW,* to Peter Carr, August 10, 1787, 901. It is highly significant that for both Jefferson and Rousseau the moral sense appears as something organic, anterior to and therefore potentially antagonistic to individualized instrumental reason. While some of Locke's British liberal successors, notably Hume and Smith, would introduce "sympathy" as a moral sentiment that takes up certain roles in human life that Jefferson or Rousseau would accord to *pité* or a moral sense, sympathy in their usage depends on an identification (grounded in rational understanding) with the interests or passions of another person. Smith's discussion of sympathy helps him to distinguish between simple selfishness and self-interest, which he assumes to seek the approval of an "impartial spectator" through the lens of sympathy: the rationally self-interested individual benefits from public approval, but only comes to understand what other people expect of him by identifying with them, projecting himself into their position(s). Suggestive

of significant limitations on human acquisitiveness, many contemporary inheritors of Smith's free-market theory would do well to review his conceptualization of sympathy. Nevertheless, Smith's (and Hume's) reliance on identification as the basis for sympathy puts them at some remove from the moral sense as found in Jefferson and Rousseau, who describe an instinctual, almost visceral response to suffering in others: a feeling that foregrounds an understanding of others as ends-in-themselves rather than as a sentiment *resulting* from instrumental relations among human beings.

54. *TJW,* to Thomas Law, June 13, 1814, 1337.

55. *Second Discourse,* 94

56. *Second Treatise,* sec. 6.

57. For an extended discussion of Locke's ambiguities on human nature, see C. B. Macpherson's introduction to the *Second Treatise.*

58. *TJW,* to Maria Cosway, October 12, 1786, 872. For a detailed discussion of this illuminating letter, see Richard K. Matthews, *If Men Were Angels: James Madison and the Heartless Empire of Reason* (Lawrence, KS: University Press of Kansas, 1995).

59. *TJW,* to Maria Cosway, October 12, 1786, 874–75. In perhaps the most telling passage of the entire dialogue, the Heart retrieved the memories of two specific episodes in Jefferson's life when he behaved immorally. The first involved a soldier who "begged" Jefferson for a ride; the second concerned a "poor woman" who asked him for "a charity." In both cases the Head, dominated by reason, had automatically calculated what would protect the self, save it from pain, and then attempted to rationalize the subsequent behavior in the name of either justice or morality. Nevertheless, the Heart would have none of it; piercing through the Head's mental gymnastics the Heart tells the Head: "In short, my friend, as far as my recollection serves me, I do not know I ever did a good thing on your suggestion, or a dirty one without it."

60. *Second Discourse,* 132. See also 161: "The bodies politic, thus remaining in the state of nature with relation to each other, soon experienced the inconveniences that had forced individuals to leave it; and among these great bodies that state became even more fatal than it had previously been among the individuals of whom they were composed. Hence arose the national wars, battles, murders, and reprisals which make nature tremble . . . and all those horrible prejudices which rank the honor of shedding human blood among the virtues. The most decent men learn to consider it one of their duties to murder their fellow-men. . . . More murders were committed on a single day of fighting . . . than were committed in the state of nature during whole centuries over the entire face of the earth."

61. *Second Discourse,* 132.

62. *An Essay,* I.III.20.

63. *TJW,* to Thomas Law, June 13, 1814, 1337–38.

64. *First Discourse,* 39.

65. *ME,* to M. Correa de Serra, June 28, 1815, 14:331.

66. See *An Essay,* II.XXVIII.5: "Good and evil . . . are nothing but pleasure or pain, or that which occasions or procures pleasure or pain to us. Moral good and evil, then, is only the conformity or disagreement of our voluntary actions to some law, whereby

good or evil is drawn on us, from the will and power of the law-maker; which good and evil, pleasure or pain, attending our observance or breach of the law by the decree of the lawmaker, is that we call reward and punishment."

67. *TJW*, to Thomas Law, June 13, 1814, 1337.

68. *Second Treatise*, sec. 136.

69. *TJW*, to Thomas Law, June 13, 1814, 1337.

70. *TJW*, to P. S. Dupont de Nemours, April 24, 1816, 1387.

71. *Social Contract*, 44.

72. *TJW*, *to* Edward Carrington, January 16, 1787, 880.

73. *ME*, *"Answers to de Meusnier Questions,"* 1786, 17:116. See also *TJW*, *Notes on Virginia*, 291: "Those who labour in the earth are the chosen people of God. . . . Corruption of morals in the mass of cultivators is a phenomenon of which no age nor nation has furnished an example."

74. *First Discourse*, 37.

75. "To the Republic of Geneva," 79; emphasis added. See also *Second Discourse*, 151–52. As he traces society's development from the state of nature to modern civilization, Rousseau comes to a period he calls "the happiest and most durable epoch" of human history. A simple society of relative equals, it occurs before the division of labor and the (inter)dependence it entails. "In a word, as long as they applied themselves only to tasks that a single person could do and to arts that did not require the cooperation of several hands, they lived free, healthy, good, and happy insofar as they could be according to their nature, and they continued to enjoy among themselves the sweetness of independent intercourse. But from the moment one man needed the help of another . . . equality disappeared . . . [and] slavery and misery were soon seen to germinate and grow with the crops." Even as Rousseau stresses the happiness of a society based in mutual independence, note his emphasis on "the sweetness of independent intercourse." He envisions neither a society of solitude nor one in which a person has no concern for fellow citizens or social cooperation. Quite the contrary, Rousseau maintains (if somewhat paradoxically) that a society in which people are not bound by self-interest to cooperate naturally tends to cultivate free association for its own sake; indeed, any other association, taken up as a means to an end rather than an end in itself, is not truly *free* association at all.

76. *TJW*, *Notes on Virginia*, 291. See also *ME*, letter to Mr. J. Lithgow, January 4, 1805, 11:55: "As yet our manufacturers are as much at their ease, as independent and moral as our agricultural inhabitants, and they will continue so as long as there are vacant lands for them to resort to; because whenever it shall be attempted by the other classes to reduce them to the minimum of subsistence, they will quit their trades and go to laboring the earth." See also Rousseau, *Considerations on the Government of Poland*, 225–26: "If you want to stay happy and free, heads, what you need are hearts and arms: they are what make up the force of a State and the prosperity of a people. Financial systems make venal souls, and as soon as all one wants is profit, one invariably profits more by being a knave than by being an honest man. Money is used in misleading and secretive ways; it is intended for one thing and used for another."

77. Rousseau's *Emile: Or, on Education,* tr. Allan Bloom (New York: Basic Books, 1979), can be seen as a relatively optimistic statement. Yet compared to Jefferson, Rousseau has serious reservations about the future of humanity.

78. *An Essay,* IV.IV.7.

79. *Second Treatise,* sec. 35. It should be noted that neither Jefferson nor Rousseau share Locke's Protestant view either of labor as humanity's divine fate or the parsimoniousness of nature.

80. *Second Discourse,* 91.

81. Ibid., 114–15.

82. *TJW,* to Samuel Kercheval, July 12, 1816, 140; see also to William Ludlow, September 6, 1824, 1497, where in even grander terms reminiscent of Hegel's *Philosophy of History* Jefferson writes: "Let a philosophic observer commence a journey from the savages of the Rocky Mountains eastwardly towards our seacoast. These he would observe in the earlier stage of association living under no law but that of nature, subsisting and covering themselves with the flesh and skins of wild beasts. He would next find those on our frontiers in the pastoral state, raising domestic animals to supply the defects of hunting. Then succeed our own semi-barbarous citizens, the pioneers of the advance of civilization, and so in his progress he would meet the gradual shades of improving man until he would reach his, as yet, most improved state in our seaport towns. This in fact, is equivalent to a survey, in time, of the progress of man from the infancy of creation to the present day. I am eighty-one years of age, born where I now live, in the first range of mountains in the interior of our country. And I have observed this march of civilization advancing from the seacoast, passing over us like a cloud of light, increasing our knowledge and improving our condition, insomuch as that we are at this time more advanced in civilization here than the seaports were when I was a boy. And where this progress will stop no one can say. Barbarism has, in the meantime, been receding before the steady step of amelioration; and will in time, I trust, disappear from the earth."

83. To trace this development, see Pocock's enormously influential *Machiavellian Moment.*

84. *Second Treatise,* sec. 142; see also sects. 138–41.

85. Ibid., sec. 124; see also sec. 94.

86. *Social Contract,* 105.

87. Ibid., 82. See also "To the Republic of Geneva," 79: "I would have wished to be born in a country where the sovereign and the people could have only one and the same interest. . . . Since that would not be possible unless the people and the sovereign were the same person, it follows that I would have wished to be born under a democratic government, wisely tempered."

88. See Asher Horowitz and Gad Horowitz, *"Everywhere They Are in Chains"* (Scarborough, ON: Nelson Canada, 1988), 48–86.

89. "Letter to the Republic of Geneva," 79.

90. *Second Treatise,* sec. 75.

91. Ibid., sec. 95.

92. Ibid., sec. 119.

93. Ibid., sec. 121.

94. *Social Contract,* 109.

95. Ibid., 120.

96. Ibid., 124fn.

97. *TJW,* to P. S. Dupont de Nemours, April 24, 1816, 1387.

98. See *ME,* to Edward Everett, March 27, 1824, 16:22. "The qualifications for self-government in society are not innate. They are the result of habit and long training." See also *TJW, Notes on the State of Virginia,* 220: "It will be said, that great societies cannot exist without government. The Savages therefore break them into small ones."

99. *Considerations on the Government of Poland,* 231, 201.

100. See Julian Boyd, ed., *The Papers of Thomas Jefferson,* 30 vols. (Princeton, NJ: Princeton University Press, 1950), 12:558. In 1788, Jefferson's hostile reaction to the new constitution was largely due to its lack of a bill of rights: "But I own that it astonishes me to find such a change wrought in the opinions of our countrymen since I left them." Noting his objections, he sadly concludes, "This is degeneracy in the principles of liberty to which I had given four centuries instead of four years."

101. This makes Jefferson the one true *civic humanist* among the founders. See J. G. A. Pocock, *Politics, Language, and Time* (New York: Atheneum, 1971), 85: "Civic humanism denotes a style of thought . . . in which it is contended that the development of the individual towards self-fulfillment is possible only when the individual acts as a citizen, that is as a conscious and autonomous participant in an autonomous decision-making political community, the polis or republic."

102. *TJW,* to Samuel Kercheval, July 12, 1816, 1399–1400.

103. *TJW,* to Joseph C. Cabell, February 2, 1816, 1380.

104. Ibid.

105. See Hannah Arendt, *On Revolution* (New York: Viking Press, 1963), 235: Jefferson "knew, however dimly, that the Revolution, while it had given freedom to the people, had failed to provide a space where this freedom could be exercised. Only the representatives of the people, not the people themselves, had an opportunity to engage in those activities of 'expressing, discussing and deciding' which in a positive sense are the activities of freedom."

106. *TJW,* to Samuel Kercheval, July 12, 1816, 1403.

107. *TJW,* to James Madison, September 6, 1789, 963.

108. *Social Contract,* 111.

109. Ibid., 112.

110. In 1787, in response to Shays's Rebellion, Jefferson produced two of his famous observations on revolution, *TJW,* to James Madison, January 30, 1787, 882: "I hold it that a little rebellion now and then is a good thing, and as necessary in the political world as storms in the physical"; and to William Smith, November 13, 1787, 911: "God forbid we should ever be 20 years without such a rebellion . . . We have had 13 states independent 11 years. There has been one rebellion. That comes to one rebellion in a century and a half for each state. What country before ever existed a century

and a half without a rebellion? . . . The tree of liberty must be refreshed from time to time with the blood of patriots and tyrants. It is its natural manure."

111. *Social Contract,* 120.

112. Louis Hartz, *The Liberal Tradition in America* (New York: Hartcourt, Brace & Co., 1955), 140.

113. See Asher Horowitz and Richard Matthews, "A 'Narcissism of the Minor Difference': What Is at Issue and What Is at Stake in the Question of Civic Humanism," *Polity,* Fall 1997, 1–27.

114. *TJW, Notes on the State of Virginia,* 290–91.

115. Leo Marx, *The Machine in the Garden* (New York: Oxford University Press, 1964), 139. Marx explains: "The ideal, in fact, is an abstract embodiment of the concept of mediation between the extremes of primitivism and what might be called 'over-civilization.'"

116. *TJW,* to William Short, November 28, 1814, 1357.

PROBLEMATIC VIRTUES: JEFFERSON AND HAMILTON ON EDUCATION FOR VIGILANT CITIZENS AND RESPONSIBLE STATESMEN
KARL WALLING

1. All citations from this classic work by Alexander Hamilton, James Madison, and John Jay will be from *The Federalist,* ed. Clinton Rossiter (New York: Mentor, 1961).

2. Jefferson to Samuel Kercheval, July 12, 1816, in *The Portable Jefferson,* ed. Merrill D. Peterson (New York: Penguin, 1985), 555–58. The best account of Jefferson's educational project is in Lorraine Smith and Thomas L. Pangle, *The Learning of Liberty: The Educational Ideas of the American Founders* (Lawrence, KS: University Press of Kansas, 1994), 106–24, 250–64.

3. See *Notes on the State of Virginia* in Peterson, and Jefferson to Roger C. Weightman, June 24, 1826, in Peterson, 193–99, 585. Jefferson did not go so far as to ban religious instruction as such, but the teachers would be forbidden to provide any religious instruction contrary to the beliefs of any sect. For all practical purposes, they would be compelled to teach (or preach?) the deism of the Declaration of Independence.

4. Peterson, 193–99.

5. Peterson, 196; and Jefferson to James Madison, September 6, 1789, in Peterson, 445.

6. *Notes,* and *Report of the Commissioners for the University of Virginia,* in Peterson, 196–98, 332–46. To liberate the mind, Jefferson felt compelled to protect the body. The Virginia philosophe stressed that traditional corporal punishments for unruly students should be forbidden at the university. Discipline could be accomplished through other means that would not risk turning vigilant watchdogs of liberty into lapdogs of authority.

7. Jefferson to George Wythe, August 13, 1786; to Edward Carrington, January 16, 1787; to James Madison, January 30, 1787, in Peterson, 398–99, 414–18; and Jefferson to Joseph Cabell, January 13, 1823, in *Early History of the University of Virginia as*

Contained in the Letters of Thomas Jefferson and Joseph C. Cabell, ed. Nathaniel F. Cabell (Richmond, 1856), 266–68. See also Paul A. Rahe, "Self-Reliance: Thomas Jefferson & the Inculcation of Modern Republican Virtue," a paper presented at a conference on Thomas Jefferson and the Education of a Citizen at the Library of Congress, May 13–15, 1993, and *Republics: Ancient and Modern* (Chapel Hill, NC: University of North Carolina Press, 1994), vol. 3, 145–83.

8. Jefferson to James Madison, March 15, 1789, and *Kentucky Resolutions of 1798,* in Peterson, 281–90, 438–40.

9. *Federalist* 1:35. The authors of *The Federalist* declaimed adamantly against this republican vice. See, for example, Madison's remarks in *Federalist* 55:346 and Hamilton's in *Federalist* 26:166–74. Consider also Madison's "melancholy reflection that liberty may be endangered by the abuses of liberty as well as by the abuses of power" (*Federalist* 63:387).

10. These are modern liberal virtues because they do not correspond directly either to the classical virtues (the courage, moderation, justice, and wisdom of Plato's *Republic*) or the Christian virtues (the faith, hope, and charity of the Bible and Christian teaching). Nor do they correspond to an altruistic love of the common good, as described by Gordon Wood in *Creation of the American Republic* (New York: W. W. Norton, 1967), 65–70, or the Arendtian *vita activa* of public personalities discussed by J. G. A. Pocock in *The Machiavellian Moment: Florentine Political Thought and the Atlantic Republican Tradition* (Princeton, NJ: Princeton University Press, 1975), 40, 56, 58, 84, 98, 333, 335, 350, 485, 539, 546, 549, 551. One is fearful of private loss of individual rights; the other seeks a kind of private gain—honor—by producing public benefits. They are qualities necessary to freedom in a republic, however, and therefore genuine civic virtues. Yet they are also *different kinds of civic virtues* in such great tension with each other that advocates of responsibility are likely to be seen as vicious by the advocates of vigilance, and vice versa. For a very insightful though somewhat excessively Madisonian account of responsibility in *The Federalist,* see Michael P. Zuckert, "The Virtuous Polity, the Accountable Polity: Liberty and Responsibility in *The Federalist,*" *Publius, the Journal of Federalism* 22, no. 1 (Winter 1992), 123–42. For the historical and theoretical foundations of the modern civic virtues of vigilance and responsibility, see the trio of essays on "The American Faces of Machiavelli" by Brad Thompson, Paul Rahe, and Karl Walling in *The Review of Politics* 57, no. 3 (Summer 1995), 299–481.

11. See Hamilton to James Duane, September 3, 1780, in *The Papers of Alexander Hamilton,* ed. Harold G. Syrett (New York: Columbia University Press, 1961), 2:405.

12. See "Centinel" 1 in *The Anti-Federalist Papers and the Constitutional Debates,* ed. Ralph Ketcham (New York: Mentor, 1986), 231.

13. See, for example, Madison's discussion of responsibility in the Senate in *Federalist* 63:382–90, and Hamilton's account of responsibility in the executive in *Federalist* 70:424–29; 71:431; and 72:434 (on the love of fame and reeligibility as inducements for the highest degree of responsibility likely in a republican statesman), and Hamilton to Duane, *Papers,* 2:401.

14. Hamilton to Duane, *Papers,* 2:401–29.

15. See *Federalist* 33:201–5; 70–71: 432–40; 78:469–72.

16. See Tocqueville's remarks on the arbitrary power democratic peoples sometimes allow public officials in *Democracy in America,* trans. George Lawrence (New York: Harper, 1969), vol. 1, 205–7, 253–54; and Franklin Delano Roosevelt's "Commonwealth Club Address" and "Call for Federal Responsibility," September 24, 1932, and October 13, 1932, in *The Annals of America,* ed. William Benton (Chicago: Britannica, 1968), vol. 15, 158–66, 185–87. Note, however, that Hamilton's defense of an energetic national government headed by an energetic executive can be read as the best defense against prerogative and the arbitrary power it risks: only a constitutionally strong executive could avoid the necessity of frequently breaking the law to preserve the republic from harm. See *Federalist* 25:167; 72:439–40, and Harvey C. Mansfield Jr., "Republicanizing the Executive," in *Taming of the Prince: The Ambivalence of Modern Executive Power* (New York: Free Press, 1989), 247–78. Moreover, Hamilton was not quite as strong an advocate of centralization as is commonly believed. Although he advocated centralization for national purposes—war, foreign affairs, commerce, and revenue—he left the police powers of health, welfare, safety, and morals up to the states. Local government, he claimed, was best for "purposes of local regulation" and, interestingly enough, "the preservation of the republican spirit." The safety of a republic, he claimed, required combining a "due dependence on the people" with a "due responsibility" for their welfare, which was perhaps the fundamental goal of his politics. *Federalist* 70:472.

17. See *Federalist* 8:66–71 and 11:84–91, and *The Landmark Thucydides,* ed. Robert B. Strassler (New York: Simon and Schuster, 1996), 3.82. Hamilton is perhaps more responsible for preserving the spirit of vigilant citizens than Jefferson. After all, the University of Virginia was the only part of Jefferson's educational program that was ever adopted, but Hamilton's strategic vision has been the cornerstone of American national security—and the free spirit it protects—for over two centuries. See, for example, Edward Meade Earle, "Adam Smith, Alexander Hamilton, Friedrich List: The Economic Foundations of Military Power" in *Makers of Modern Strategy. From Machiavelli to the Nuclear Age,* ed. Peter Paret (Princeton, NJ: Princeton Univesity Press, 1986), 217–61; and Karl Walling, *Republican Empire: Alexander Hamilton on War and Free Government* (Lawrence, KS: University Press of Kansas, 1999).

18. Jefferson to John Breckenridge, August 12, 1803, in Peterson, 497. See also Leonard Levy, *Jefferson and Civil Liberties, the Darker Side* (Cambridge, MA: Harvard University Press, 1963) and Julius Goebbel, ed., *The Law Practice of Alexander Hamilton* (New York: Columbia University Press, 1964), vol. 1, 796, 844–48.

19. See Locke's discussion of prerogative in the *Second Treatise* in *Two Treatises of Government,* ed. Peter Laslett (Cambridge: Cambridge University Press, 1988), sec. 161–66: 375–78, as well as his reliance on popular judgment in the dissolution of government, sec. 240–43.

JOHN ADAMS, JOHN TAYLOR OF CAROLINE, AND
THE DEBATE ABOUT REPUBLICAN GOVERNMENT
ADAM L. TATE

1. John Adams to John Taylor, undated, in *The Political Writings of John Adams,* ed. George W. Carey (Washington, DC: Regnery Publishing Inc., Gateway Editions, 2001), 403.

2. John Adams to Thomas Jefferson, September 15, 1813, in *The Adams-Jefferson Letters: The Complete Correspondence between Thomas Jefferson and Abigail and John Adams,* 2 volumes, ed. Lester J. Cappon (Chapel Hill, NC: University of North Carolina Press, 1959), 2:376.

3. Two historians have offered extended treatments of the Adams-Taylor discussion. Gordon Wood, *The Creation of the American Republic, 1776–1787* (Chapel Hill, NC: University of North Carolina Press, 1969), 567–92. Joseph J. Ellis, *Passionate Sage: The Character and Legacy of John Adams* (New York: W. W. Norton & Company, 1993), 145–65. Two other historians use the Adams-Taylor correspondence well in explicating the thought of Adams: C. Bradley Thompson, *John Adams and the Spirit of Liberty,* (Lawrence, KS: University Press of Kansas, 1998). Thompson is the best interpreter of Adams's political thought. Russell Kirk, *The Conservative Mind: From Burke to Eliot* (Washington, DC: Regnery Publishing, Inc., 7th Revised Edition, 1995), 71–113. See also Stanley Elkins and Eric McKitrick, *The Age of Federalism: The Early American Republic, 1788–1800* (New York: Oxford University Press, 1993), 529–37. Henry H. Simms, *Life of John Taylor: The Story of a Brilliant Leader in the Early Virginia States Rights School* (Richmond, VA: William Byrd Press, 1932), 133–44. There is also an interesting discussion of the correspondence from the perspective of the history of science in I. Bernard Cohen, *Science and the Founding Fathers: Science in the Political Thought of Jefferson, Franklin, Adams, and Madison* (New York: W. W. Norton & Co., 1995), 196–236.

4. Forrest McDonald, *E Pluribus Unum: The Formation of the American Republic, 1776–1790* (Indianapolis: Liberty Fund, 1979), 13–15, 27–35. I describe nationalists and republicans a bit differently than does McDonald. In *E Pluribus Unum,* McDonald considered Adams a republican, given both his alliance with Virginia republicans in the 1770s and his temperament. In light of Adams's views by the late 1780s on government and the relationship between freedom and order, I treat him as a nationalist. In doing so, I am neither disagreeing with McDonald nor returning to a Progressive interpretation of American ideological divisions. Instead, I am looking at the ideological divisions of the late 1780s in the specific context of the relationship between freedom and order. For two great critiques of the Progressive interpretation of the 1780s, see Richard B. Morris, *The American Revolution Reconsidered* (New York: Harper & Row Publishers, 1967), 127–62, and John M. Murrin, "1787: The Invention of American Federalism," in *Essays on Liberty and Federalism: The Shaping of the U.S. Constitution,* eds. David E. Narrett and Joyce S. Goldberg (College Station, TX: Texas A&M University Press, 1988), 20–47. Also, McDonald has provided a wonderful brief summary of his reading of Adams in a recent book review, "The Unlovable Mr. Adams," *Claremont Review of Books* 5, no. 4 (Fall 2005): 20–21.

5. Walter A. McDougall, *Freedom Just Around the Corner: A New American History, 1585–1828* (New York: Harper Collins Publishers, 2004), 281.

6. George Washington to John Jay, August 1, 1786, in *The Founders' Constitution*, vol. 1 (Indianapolis, IN: Liberty Fund, 1987), 162.

7. McDonald, *E Pluribus Unum*, 29, 32–35. McDonald, *Novus Ordo Seclorum*, 138–42.

8. Thomas Jefferson, Declaration of Independence, July 4, 1776, in *The Founders' Constitution*, vol. 1, 9.

9. Richard Henry Lee to Samuel Adams, March 14, 1785, in *The Founders' Constitution*, vol. 1, 161.

10. Article II of the Articles of Confederation, in *The Founders' Constitution*, vol. 1, 23.

11. John Taylor to James Monroe, March 25, 1798, in "Letters of John Taylor of Caroline County, Virginia," ed. William E. Dodd, *John P. Branch Historical Papers of Randolph-Macon College* 2 (1908): 269.

12. Quoted in Gordon Wood, *Creation of the American Republic*, 581. John Ferling notes that during his retirement Adams ended up as a National Republican like his son John Quincy. *John Adams: A Life*, 425. Merrill Peterson notes that when Adams saw a copy of the Philadelphia Constitution of 1787, he argued that the government under the Constitution had to be "wholly national" or else it would not work. Merrill D. Peterson, *Adams and Jefferson: A Revolutionary Dialogue* (New York: Oxford University Press, 1976), 44. Both of these examples give credence to my categorization of Adams as a "nationalist" in the context of 1780s. For Taylor as a republican, especially in his view of social order, see the perceptive article by Gillis J. Harp, "Taylor, Calhoun, and the Decline of a Theory of Political Disharmony," *Journal of the History of Ideas* 46, no. 1 (January–March 1985): 107–20.

13. Adams, *A Defence of the Constitution of Government of the United States of America* in *The Political Writings of John Adams: Representative Selections,* ed. George A. Peek Jr. (Indianapolis: Bobbs-Merrill Educational Publishing, 1954), 145. On Adams's dislike of the French and his conviction that Europe would not support American republicanism, see Edmund S. Morgan, *The Meaning of Independence: John Adams, George Washington, and Thomas Jefferson* (Charlottesville, VA: University Press of Virginia, 1976), 18–22.

14. C. Bradley Thompson, *John Adams and the Spirit of Liberty,* 106. See also Thompson's summary of Adams's political thought ("John Adams and the Science of Politics") in *John Adams and the Founding of the Republic,* ed. Richard Alan Ryerson (Boston: Massachusetts Historical Society, 2001), especially 246–50. For Adams's use of history, see H. Trevor Colbourne, *The Lamp of Experience: Whig History and the Intellectual Origins of the American Revolution* (Indianapolis: Liberty Fund, 1998; 1st edition, 1965), 104–19. Zoltan Haraszti, *John Adams and the Prophets of Progress* (Cambridge, MA: Harvard University Press, 1952), 139–64. Stephen G. Kurtz, "The Political Science of John Adams, A Guide to His Statecraft," *William and Mary Quarterly* 3rd Ser. 25, no. 4 (October 1968): 605–13. Joyce Appleby, "The New Republican Synthesis and the Changing Political Ideas of John Adams," *American Quarterly* 25, no. 5 (December 1973): 578–95.

15. John Adams, *The Works of John Adams,* 10 vols., ed. Charles Francis Adams (Boston: Little, Brown and Co., 1856): 10: 96. Haraszti, *John Adams and the Prophets of Progress,* 165–79.

16. *The Portable John Adams,* ed. John Patrick Diggins, (New York: Penguin Books, 2004), 337.

17. Background on *Discourses on Davila* can be found in Thompson, *John Adams and the Spirit of Liberty,* 107–28. Adams's presidency and his portrayal by the opposition are depicted in two recent short, accessible works: John Ferling, *Adams vs. Jefferson: The Tumultuous Election of 1800* (New York: Oxford University Press, 2004). John Patrick Diggins, *John Adams* (New York: Henry Holt and Company, 2003). Peterson, *Adams and Jefferson: A Revolutionary Dialogue,* 43, details the use the opposition made of the *Defence* and *Discourses* in the presidential campaign of 1796.

18. Mercy Otis Warren, *History of the Rise, Progress, and Termination of the American Revolution Interspersed with Biographical, Political, and Moral Observations,* 2 vols., ed. Lester H. Cohen (Indianapolis: Liberty Fund, 1989), 2:675. Warren droned on: "It may be however be charitably presumed, that by living long near the splendor of courts and courtiers, with other concurring circumstances, he might become so biassed [*sic*] in his judgment as to think that an hereditary monarchy was the best government for his native country." 2:676.

19. John Ferling, *John Adams: A Life* (New York: Henry Holt and Co., 1992), 429. Ferling discusses Adams's retirement on pages 417–44. He makes passing reference to the debate with Taylor. In David McCullough's *John Adams* (New York: Simon & Schuster, 2001), no mention is made of Adams's discussion with Taylor. But McCullough gives a solid narrative summary of Adams's retirement years on pages 568–651. Peterson briefly mentions the correspondence with Taylor and links it to Adams's correspondence with Jefferson at the time (*Adams and Jefferson: A Revolutionary Dialogue,* 115). Peter Shaw calls Adams's writings during his retirement "the tale of the outcast obsessed with injustice." He also notes, "As if in illustration of his life-long, self-defeating independence of everyone but his family and a few local friends, Adams lived in self-imposed isolation, broken occasionally by visitors interested in meeting the ex-president and patriot." (*The Character of John Adams* [Chapel Hill, NC: University of North Carolina Press, 1976], 285.) See also John R. Howe Jr., *The Changing Political Thought of John Adams* (Princeton, NJ: Princeton University Press, 1966), 217–51.

20. Ferling, *John Adams,* 432. See also Henry May, *The Enlightenment in America* (New York: Oxford University Press, 1976), 278–304.

21. John Adams to Thomas Jefferson, July 15, 1813, in *The Adams-Jefferson Letters,* 2:357.

22. John Taylor to Daniel Carroll Brent, October 9, 1796, in "Letters of John Taylor of Caroline County, Virginia," 267. Many historians have written on Taylor, but the following works should be consulted. Henry Harrison Simms, *Life of John Taylor: The Story of a Brilliant Leader in the Early Virginia States Rights School* (Richmond, VA: William Byrd Press, 1932). Andrew Nelson Lytle, "John Taylor and the Political

Economy of Agriculture," *American Review* 3 (September 1934): 432–47; (October 1934): 630–43; 4 (November 1934): 84–99. Eugene T. Mudge, *The Social Philosophy of John Taylor of Caroline: A Study in Jeffersonian Democracy* (New York: Columbia University Press, 1939). Manning J. Dauer and Hans Hammond, "John Taylor: Democrat or Aristocrat?" *Journal of Politics* 6 (November 1944): 381–403. C. William Hill Jr., "Contrasting Themes in the Political Theories of Jefferson, Calhoun, and John Taylor of Caroline," *Publius* 6 (Summer 1976): 73–91. C. William Hill Jr., *The Political Theory of John Taylor of Caroline* (Rutherford, NJ: Farleigh Dickinson University Press, 1977). Duncan MacLeod, "The Political Economy of John Taylor of Caroline," *Journal of American Studies* 14 (December 1980): 387–406. Robert E. Shalhope, *John Taylor of Caroline: Pastoral Republican* (Columbia, SC: University of South Carolina Press, 1980). M. E. Bradford, "A Virginia Cato: John Taylor of Caroline and the Agrarian Republic," in *Arator: Being a Series of Agricultural Essays, Practical and Political: In Sixty-Four Numbers,* by John Taylor (Indianapolis: Liberty Classics, 1977), 11–46. See David Mayer, ed., "Of Principles and Men: The Correspondence of John Taylor of Caroline and Wilson Cary Nicholas, 1806–1808," *Virginia Magazine of History and Biography* 96, no. 3 (July 1988): 343–56. David N. Mayer, *The Constitutional Thought of Thomas Jefferson* (Charlottesville, VA: University Press of Virginia, 1994), 135–44. James McClellan, introduction to *New Views of the Constitution of the United States,* by John Taylor (Washington, DC: Regnery Publishing Inc., 2000), xi–lxix. Joseph R. Stromberg, "Country Ideology, Republicanism, and Libertarianism: The Thought of John Taylor of Caroline," *Journal of Libertarian Studies* 6, no. 1 (Winter 1982): 35–48. Michael O'Brien, *Conjectures of Order: Intellectual Life in the American South, 1810–1860,* 2 vols. (Chapel Hill, NC: University of North Carolina Press, 2004), 2:785–99.

23. John Taylor to James Monroe, March 25, 1798, in "Letters of John Taylor of Caroline County, Virginia," 269. John Taylor to Thomas Jefferson, June 25, 1798, in "Letters of John Taylor of Caroline County, Virginia," 273. On Taylor in the 1790s, see Lance Banning, *The Jeffersonian Persuasion: Evolution of a Party Ideology* (Ithaca, NY: Cornell University Press, 1980), 192–207. Helpful concerning Taylor and the Virginia and Kentucky Resolutions is William Watkins, *Reclaiming the American Revolution* (New York: Palgrave Macmillan, 2004), esp. chapters 1–4. Watkins also covers Republicans' suspicions of John Adams. See the insightful work of Kevin R. C. Gutzman, *Virginia's American Revolution: From Dominion to Republic, 1776–1840* (Lanham, MD: Lexington Books, 2007). Gutzman superbly places Taylor in the context of Virginia.

24. Harry Ammon, "James Monroe and the Election of 1808 in Virginia" *William and Mary Quarterly* 3rd Ser. 20, no. 1 (January 1963): 55–56. Ammon, *James Monroe: The Quest for National Identity* (New York: McGraw Hill Book Co., 1971), 270–88. Simms, *Life of John Taylor,* 115–32. Norman K. Risjord, *The Old Republicans: Southern Conservatism in the Age of Jefferson* (New York: Columbia University Press, 1965), 77–79, 86–97. Richard E. Ellis, *The Jeffersonian Crisis: Courts and Politics in the Young Republic* (New York: Oxford University Press, 1971), 5–55. Richard E. Ellis, "The

Market Revolution and the Transformation of American Politics, 1801–1837," in *The Market Revolution in America: Social, Political and Religious Expressions, 1800–1880,* eds. Melvyn Stokes and Stephen Conway (Charlottesville, VA: University of Virginia Press, 1996), 149–76.

25. John Taylor to James Monroe, November 8, 1809, in "Letters of John Taylor of Caroline County, Virginia," 301–2. Ten years later, however, Jefferson would support Taylor's works on states' rights: see Merrill D. Peterson, *Thomas Jefferson and the New Nation: A Biography* (New York: Oxford University Press, 1970), 992–94.

26. Jefferson to Adams, October 28, 1813, and January 24, 1814, in *The Adams-Jefferson Letters,* 2:392, 421.

27. Haraszti, *John Adams and the Prophets of Progress,* 166.

28. Taylor to Adams, May 20, 1814, Adams Papers Microfilm (Boston: Massachusetts Historical Society), reel 418. Shaw argues that Adams "achieved a simplification without loss of passion" in his letters to Taylor. This is a solid point. *The Character of John Adams,* 301.

29. Adams to Taylor, March 12, 1819, in *Works of John Adams,* 10:375.

30. Robert Nisbet, *Social Change and History,* 140, 158. Clinton Rossiter made similar points in connection with American revolutionary theory. See his *Seedtime of the Republic: The Origin of the American Tradition of Political Liberty* (New York: Harcourt, Brace & World, Inc., 1953), 366–67.

31. Thompson, *John Adams and the Spirit of Liberty,* 127. Adams to Taylor, undated, in *The Political Writings of John Adams,* 401. See James W. Ceaser, *Nature and History in American Political Development: A Debate* (Cambridge, MA: Harvard University Press, 2006), 4–88. Ceaser defines nature as "something in the structure of reality that can be accessed through reason" and "something unchanging that can provide a standard of right" (6).

32. Thompson, *John Adams and the Spirit of Liberty,* 148, 113–19. Adams to Taylor, undated, in *The Political Writings of John Adams,* 386.

33. For a good discussion of Adams's view on human nature, see Thompson, *John Adams and the Spirit of Liberty,* chapter 8. Adams to Taylor, undated, in *The Political Writings of John Adams,* 375, 379, 402. Adams, *Discourses on Davila,* 338–39.

34. Adams, *Discourses on Davila,* 340. Adams, *Defence,* 311, 315. See also Kirk, *The Conservative Mind,* 90.

35. Adams to Taylor, undated, in *The Political Writings of John Adams,* 372–73, 378. See also Adams to Jefferson, November 15, 1813, in *The Adams-Jefferson Letters,* 2:397–402, for a similar discussion of aristocracy. Taylor's arguments were clearly on Adams's mind when he discussed the same topic with Jefferson.

36. Adams to Taylor, undated, in *The Political Writings of John Adams,* 424, 428, 426, 381, 380, 410. See also: J. R. Pole, *Political Representation in England and the Origins of the American Republic* (New York: Macmillan, St. Martin's Press, 1966), 214–23.

37. Adams to Taylor, undated, in *The Political Writings of John Adams,* 402. Taylor, *Inquiry on the Principles and Policy of the Government of the United States,* ed. Roy Franklin Nichols (New Haven, CT: Yale University Press, 1950), 35–36, 43. Taylor wrote

to Jefferson in 1798, "Indeed I am unable to discern any natural political state; not only is a political state in the antithesis to a state of nature, but as all nations and countries seem liable to revolutions in government, and even in character from artificial causes." Taylor to Jefferson, June 25, 1798, in "Letters of John Taylor of Caroline County, Virginia," 272.

38. See Taylor, *Inquiry,* 161, 365, 384. Taylor, *A Pamphlet Containing a Series of Letters Written by Colonel John Taylor of Caroline, to Thomas Ritchie, Editor of the "Enquirer" in Consequence of an Unwarrantable Attack Made by that Editor upon Colonel Taylor* (Richmond, VA: E. C. Stanard, 1809), 14. On the concept of "advancement" as opposed to the Enlightenment cult of progress, see Ceaser, *Nature and History in American Political Development,* 28. Ceaser distinguishes between thinkers who advocated an inexorable law of human progress from those who believed in human advancement. Taylor fits in here. He did not follow French Enlightenment thinkers such as Condorçet in proposing a law of progress. But he did believe in the possibility of human advancement.

39. Taylor, *Inquiry,* 38, 390, 60, 89. Paul Conkin correctly notes that Taylor's beliefs, especially about human nature, "were in the end much closer to Adams' than he ever admitted." *Prophets of Prosperity: America's First Political Economists* (Bloomington, IN: Indiana University Press, 1980), 47.

40. Taylor, *Inquiry,* 36, 41–43.

41. Ibid., 50, 57, 251, 72.

42. Ibid., 50–60 (quotations on 50–51, 55). See Harp, "Taylor, Calhoun, and the Decline of a Theory of Political Disharmony," 112–14.

43. Taylor, *Inquiry,* 53.

44. Ibid., 33. Clinton Rossiter noticed the distinction revolutionary thinkers made between state and society: "Society itself was therefore natural, and few men, if any could be said to be in it by free choice. Colonial thinkers were understandably confused in this matter, but it seems clear that the most thoughtful of them made a distinction between society and government." *Seedtime of the Republic,* 371.

45. Adams to Taylor, undated, in *The Political Writings of John Adams,* 372, 430. See Thompson, *John Adams and the Spirit of Liberty,* 168–69. See also George Carey, introduction to *The Political Writings of John Adams,* xxviii, on Adams's concerns about the false hopes Enlightenment philosophes placed in the power of reason.

46. Taylor, *Inquiry,* 58.

47. Carl J. Richard, *The Founders and the Classics* (Cambridge, MA: Harvard University Press, 1994), 124–25. Carl J. Richard, "The Classical Roots of the U.S. Congress: Mixed Government Theory," in *Inventing Congress: Origins and Establishment of the First Federal Congress,* ed. Kenneth R. Bowling and Donald R. Kennon (Athens, OH: Ohio University Press, 1999), 12–19.

48. Martin Diamond, "The Separation of Powers and the Mixed Regime," in *As Far as Republican Principles Will Admit,* ed. William A. Schambra (Washington, DC: AEI Press, 1992), 61.

49. M. J. C. Vile, *Constitutionalism and the Separation of Powers* (New York: Oxford University Press, 1967), 33.

50. Diamond, "The Separation of Powers and the Mixed Regime," 61, 64–65.

51. Forrest McDonald and Ellen Shapiro McDonald, "The Constitution and the Separation of Powers," in *Requiem: Variations on Eighteenth-Century Themes* (Lawrence, KS: University Press of Kansas, 1988), 150. See also Forrest McDonald, *Novus Ordo Seclorum*, on the incompatibility of Montesquieu's understanding of separation of powers and the checks and balances of the English system, 82–84.

52. Vile, *Constitutionalism and the Separation of Powers*, 153. See also Forrest McDonald and Ellen Shapiro McDonald, "The Constitutional Principles of Alexander Hamilton," in *Requiem*, 127–48.

53. Vile, *Constitutionalism and the Separation of Powers*, 161. This is not to say that Adams idealized the ancient republics as models for the United States. He did not. He thought their examples would allow for a more complex and accurate political science. See Thompson, *John Adams and the Spirit of Liberty*, 146–47. Paul Rahe, *Republics Ancient and Modern: Classical Republicanism and the American Revolution* (Chapel Hill, NC: University of North Carolina Press, 1992), 254.

54. Adams to Taylor, undated, in *The Political Writings of John Adams*, 388.

55. Adams, *Discourses on Davila*, 386. Adams had made a similar point in *Thoughts on Government* (1776): "The principal difficulty lies, and the greatest care should be employed, in constituting this representative assembly. It should be in miniature an exact portrait of the people at large. It should think, feel, reason, and act like them. That it may be the interest of this assembly to do strict justice at all times, it should be an equal representation, or, in other words, equal interests among the people should have equal interests in it" (*The Portable John Adams*, 235).

56. Adams to Taylor, undated, in *The Political Writings of John Adams*, 409–10.

57. Ibid., 409. Adams, *Discourses on Davila*, 360.

58. Adams, *Discourses on Davila*, 360.

59. Adams to Taylor, undated, in *The Political Writings of John Adams*, 384, 398–99. See Ellis, *Passionate Sage*, 158–59.

60. Adams, *Discourses on Davila*, 387.

61. See Thompson, "John Adams and the Science of Politics," 246–52. Adams, *Discourses on Davila*, 339, 341, 382, 355, 377, 354. Thompson demonstrates that the young Adams believed that lawgiving was the highest path to glory and fame (*John Adams and the Spirit of Liberty*, 43). I disagree with Paul Rahe's contention that Adams downgraded public life and subordinated it to the private sphere. Adams enjoyed his private life and complained about his public duties in letters to his wife (the letters Rahe uses to argue his point) precisely because he was absent from home so often. John Taylor, however, demonstrates Rahe's point here. Rahe, *Republics Ancient and Modern*, 564. Gertrude Himmelfarb, *The Roads to Modernity: The British, French, and American Enlightenments* (New York: Vintage Books, 2004), 37. Himmelfarb suggests that Scottish Enlightenment thinkers emphasized the private sphere. Taylor also demonstrates her point.

62. Taylor, *Inquiry*, 31–32, 35, 39, 62.

63. Ibid., 62. See Ellis, *Passionate Sage*, 154, for a similar point. I would qualify the idea, put forth by Gordon Wood and Joseph Ellis, that Adams was alienated from

American political thought. Perhaps his particular theories of American government were "outmoded" because of their classical emphasis, but many American thinkers believed that government should influence society. See McDonald's *Novus Ordo Seclorum* for Hamilton's view that government "could . . . redirect man's habits toward self-improvement and thus for the improvement of the society as a whole" (137). See Ellis, *Passionate Sage,* 154, 165.

64. Taylor to Daniel Carroll Brent, October 9, 1796, in "Letters of John Taylor of Caroline County, Virginia," 262.

65. Taylor, *Inquiry,* 378. Quoted in Vile, *Constitutionalism and the Separation of Powers,* 169–170.

66. Adams to Taylor, undated, in *The Political Writings of John Adams,* 398. On Adams's dislike for ideologues, see Ellis, *Passionate Sage,* 150. Ellis also charges that Adams did not really understand Taylor's *Inquiry.* I agree, but this is primarily because he did not read the entire work.

67. *Works of John Adams,* 3:58, 10:376.

68. Ibid., 10:411–12.

69. Ibid., 10:413.

"Content with Being": Nineteenth-Century Southern Attitudes toward Economic Development
J. Crawford King

1. Alexis de Tocqueville, *Democracy in America,* 2 vols. (New York: Alfred A. Knopf, 1946), vol. 1, 321. Included also is information from Grady McWhiney, "Southern Distinctiveness: The Ethnic Dimension," a paper delivered at the University of Alabama, April 15, 1983. The author gratefully acknowledges Professor McWhiney's assistance.

2. Charles S. Sydnor, *The Development of Southern Sectionalism, 1819–1848,* vol. 5 of *A History of the South,* ed. Wendell Holmes Stephenson and E. Merton Coulter, 10 vols. (Baton Rouge, LA: Louisiana State University Press, 1948–68), 19, 251; John Hope Franklin, *A Southern Odyssey: Travelers in the Antebellum North* (Baton Rouge, LA: Louisiana State University Press, 1976), 3.

3. Karl Bernhard, Duke of Saxe-Weimar Eisenach, *Travels through North America during the Years 1825 and 1826,* (Philadelphia: Carey, Lea and Carrey, 1828), vol. 2, 103–202; Sandor Boloni Farkas, *Journey in North America,* trans. and ed. Arped Kadarkay (Santa Barbara, CA: Clio Press, 1978), 111; Lucy Larcom, "Old New England," *A New England Girlhood* (Boston, 1889), 93–117, rpt. Clement Eaton, *The Leaven of Democracy: The Growth of the Democratic Spirit in the Time of Jackson* (New York: George Braziller, 1963), 103; Alice Morse Earle, *Home Life in Colonial Days* (1898; rpt.; Middle Village, NY: Jonathan David Publishers, 1975), 390–91.

4. James Fenimore Cooper, *Notions of the Americans: Picked up by a Travelling Bachelor,* 2 vols. (1828; 2nd ed., London: Henry Colbar, 1856), vol. 2, 385; Frederick Law Olmsted, *A Journey through Texas* (1857; rpt. New York: Burt Franklin, 1969), 39–41;

Eugene L. Schwaab, ed., *Travels in the Old South: Selected from Periodicals of the Times,* 2 vols. (Lexington, KY: University Press of Kentucky, 1973), vol. 2, 329; Catherine C. Hopley, *Life in the South from the Commencement of the War,* 2 vols. (1863; rpt. New York: De Capo Press, 1974), vol. 1, 73–75; Hinton Rowan Helper, *The Impending Crisis of the South: How to Meet It* (New York: Burdick, 1869), 332.

5. Thomas Hamilton, *Men and Manners in America* (Philadelphia: Carey, Lea & Blanchard, 1833), 333, 335; John Shaw, *A Ramble Through the United States, Canada, and the West Indies* (London: J. F. Hope, 1856), 214; Thomas Cooper DeLeon, *Four Years in Rebel Capitals,* ed. E. B. Long (New York: Collier , 1962), 43–44.

6. Frederick Hall, *Letters from the East and from the West* (Washington, DC: F. Taylor and W. M. Morrison, 1849), 8; Charles Fenno Hoffman, *A Winter in the West,* 2 vols. (New York: Harper, 1835), vol. 2, 244–45.

7. Michel Chevalier, *Society, Manners, and Politics in the United States,* trans. Thomas Gamaliel Bradford (Boston: Weeks, Jordan, 1839), 104, 132; Adam Hodgson, *Letters from North America,* 2 vols. (London: Robinson, 1824), vol. 2, 138; Alex. Mackay, *The Western World, or Travels in the United States in 1846–1847,* 3 vols. (1849; 2nd ed., New York: Negro University Press, 1968), vol. 1, 42, 38; Andrew Burnaby, *Travels through the Middle Settlements in North America* (London: T. Payne, 1775), 61, 80; Francois Jean, Marquis de Chastellux, *Travels in North America,* 2 vols. (Dublin: Colles, Moncrieffe, 1787), vol. 2, 436.

8. Daniel R. Hundley, *Social Relations in Our Southern States,* ed. by William J. Cooper, Jr. (1860; rev. ed., Baton Rouge, LA: Louisiana State University Press, 1979), 129–30; Frederick Law Olmsted, *The Cotton Kingdom: A Traveller's Observations on Cotton and Slavery in the American Slave States.* (1860; rpt. New York: Alfred A. Knopf, 1953), 548; Joseph G. Baldwin, *The Flush Times of Alabama and Mississippi: A Series of Sketches.*(New York: D. Appleton, 1853), 291.

9. Schwaab, *Travels Selected from Periodicals,* vol. 1, 232–34; John J. Craven, *Prison Life of Jefferson Davis* (1866; rpt. Biloxi, MS: Beauvoir, 1979), 85–86; Thomas Low Nichols, M.D., *Forty Years of American Life, 1821–1861* (1864; rpt. New York: Stackpole, 1937), 69; Oscar Handlin, "Yankees," *Harvard Encyclopedia of American Ethnic Groups,* ed. Stephen Thernstrom (Cambridge, MA: Harvard University Press, 1980), 1028.

10. Burnaby, *Travels,* 61, 89–90; Thomas Colley Grattan, *Civilized America,* 2 vols. (London: Bradbury and Evans, 1859), vol. 1, 70; William Faux, *Memorable Days in America . . .* (London: W. Simpkins and R. Marshall, 1823), 37, 106; Arfwedson, *United States,* vol. 1, 68; C. Vann Woodward, ed., *Mary Chesnut's Civil War* (New Haven, CT: Yale University Press, 1981), 410.

11. Handlin, "Yankees," 1028; Misses [Sarah] Mendell and [Charlotte] Hosmer, *Notes of Travel and Life* (New York, 1854), 228; George W. Featherstonehaugh, *Excursion through the Slave States . . .* 2 vols. (London: John Murray, 1844), vol. 2, 21; Schwaab, *Travels Selected from Periodicals,* vol. 2, 330; Hoffman, *Winter in the West,* vol. 2, 196–98, 244–45.

12. William W. Freehling, *Prelude to Civil War: The Nullification Controversy in South Carolina, 1816–1836* (New York: Harper and Row, 1965), 334; Hoffman, *Winter in*

the West, vol. 2, 244–45; Schwaab, *Travels Selected from Periodicals,* vol. 2, 330; Alabama *Acts* (1859), 8–9.

13. Olmsted, *Cotton Kingdom,* 615; Philo Tower, *Slavery Unmasked* (rpt. New York: Negro University Press, 1969), 212; George W. Bagby, *The Old Virginia Gentleman* (New York: C. Scribner's Sons, 1910), 187; Margaret (Hunter) Hall, "Mrs. Basil Hall," *The Aristocratic Journey . . . 1827–1828,* ed. Una Pope-Hennessy (New York: G. P. Putnam's Sons, 1931), 235.

14. Tocqueville, *Democracy in America,* vol. 1, 230; Baldwin, *Flush Times,* 51, 53, 56, 57, 59; see also 177–91, 324; Featherstonehaugh, *Excursions,* vol. 1, 329; Charles Grandison Parsons, *Inside View of Slavery* (Boston: J. P. Jewett and Company, 1855) has a critical chapter on "Southern Jurisprudence," 139–51.

15. Parsons, *Inside View,* 90–91, 93–95.

16. Tocqueville, *Democracy in America,* vol. 1, 410–12; Hundley, *Social Relations,* 175–76.

17. Verna Mae Slone, *What My Heart Wants to Tell* (Washington, DC: New Republic Books, 1979), xi; Ben Robertson, *Red Hills and Cotton: An Upcountry Memoir* (New York: Alfred A. Knopf, 1942), 106.

18. Jonathan Dix, *Transatlantic Tracings* (London: W. Tweedie, 1853), 230; Hall, *Letters from East and West,* 243–44; Lady Emmeline Stuart-Wortley, *Travels in the United States during 1849 and 1850* (New York: Harper and Brothers, 1851), 101; Hundley, *Social Relations,* 120–21; George Townsend Fox, *American Journals, 1831–1832, 1834, 1841, 1868* (Durham, UK: November 1834), microfilm in possession of Grady McWhiney; Anne Newport Royall, *Letters from Alabama, 1817–1822* (Tuscaloosa, AL: University of Alabama Press, 1969), 245.

19. Schwaab, *Travels Selected from Periodicals,* vol. 2, 447; Henry Benjamin Whipple, *Bishop Whipple's Southern Diary, 1843–1844,* ed. Lester B. Shippee (Minneapolis: University of Minnesota Press, 1937), 43–44; Olmsted, *Journey through Texas,* 251; Olmsted, *Cotton Kingdom,* 151.

20. Helper, *Impending Crisis,* 357; Carlton H. Rogers, *Incidents of Travels in the Southern States* (New York: R. Craighead, 1862), 260–64; Olmsted, *Cotton Kingdom,* 384; James Mallory, *Journal, 1843–1877* (original owned by Edgar A. Stewart of Selma, Alabama; microfilm copy, University of Alabama), July 15, 1856; Jonathan David Schoepf, *Travels in the Confederation,* 2 vols., trans. and ed. Alfred J. Morrison (rpt. New York: Benjamin Publishers, 1968), vol. 2, 131.

21. Charles Joseph Latrobe, *The Rambler in North America,* 2 vols. (London: R. B. Seeley and W. Burnside et al., 1836), vol. 2, 32; Olmsted, *Cotton Kingdom,* 330; Woodward, *Mary Chesnut's Civil War,* 246; "Yankee Management," *Farmers' Register* 1, no. 3 (April 1833), 167; Albert Towthey Demaree, *The American Agricultural Press, 1819–1860* (New York: Columbia University Press, 1940), 393–98; for an analysis of how hard southern farmers actually worked, see Forrest McDonald and Grady McWhiney, "The South from Self-Sufficiency to Peonage: An Interpretation," *American Historical Review* 85 (December 1980), 1095–1118.

22. "John Peters' Diary of 1838–1841," ed. Margaret L. Brown, *Mississippi Valley His-*

torical Review 21 (March 1935), 531; Henry Barnard, "A New England Visitor in the Old South," ed. Bernard C. Steiner, "The South Atlantic States in 1833 as seen by a New Englander," *Maryland Historical Magazine* 13 (December 1918), 317–28, in Eaton, *Leaven of Democracy,* 164; Hundley, *Social Relations,* 98–116; Mendell and Hosmer, *Notes of Travel,* 178; Charles Lanman, *Adventures in the Wilds of the United States and British American Provinces,* 2 vols. (Philadelphia: John W. Moore, 1856), vol. 2, 276; Mrs. Anne Royall, *Mrs. Royall's Southern Tour,* 3 vols. (Washington, 1831), vol. 2, 23; Olmsted, *Cotton Kingdom,* 120, 212, 220; Lanman, *Adventures,* vol. 2, 189; Chevalier, *Society, Manners, and Politics,* 106.

23. Captain Basil Hall, *Travels in North America,* 3 vols. (Edinburgh and London: Simpkins and Marshall, 1829), vol. 3, 48; Olmsted, *Cotton Kingdom,* 616.

24. Perry Miller, *The New England Mind: The Seventeenth Century* (Cambridge, MA: Harvard University Press, 1954), 44; Louis B. Wright, *The Cultural Life of the American Colonies, 1607–1763* (New York: Harper and Brothers, 1957), 25; Lucy Larcom, "Among Lowell Mill-Girls: A Reminiscence," *Atlantic Monthly* 48 (November 1881), 596; Daniel T. Rodgers, *The Work Ethic in Industrial America, 1850–1970* (Chicago: University of Chicago Press, 1978), 6; Henry Ward Beecher, *Seven Lectures to Young Men* (Indianapolis: Thomas B. Cutler, 1844), 21; Parsons, *Inside View,* 40; Rodgers, *Work Ethic,* 10.

25. Faux, *Days in America,* 38; John Drayton, *Letters Written during a Tour through the Northern and Eastern States of America (1794),* in Warren S. Tryon, comp. and ed., *A Mirror for Americans: Life and Manners in the United States 1790–1870 as Recorded by American Travelers,* 3 vols. (Chicago: University of Chicago Press, 1952), vol. 1, 11; Franklin, *Southern Odyssey,* 48, 84; Rodgers, *Work Ethic,* 15; J. Milton Mackie, *From Cape Code to Dixie and the Tropics* (New York: G. P. Putnam, 1864), 199; Nichols, *Forty Years,* 151.

26. Earle, *Home Life,* 180, 189, 203–4, 323.

27. James R. McGovern, *Yankee Family* (New Orleans: Polyanthos, 1975), 140–41, 6, 99–101, 79.

28. Schwaab, *Travels Selected from Periodicals,* vol. 1, 23; Shippee, *Whipple's Diary,* 60; Burnaby, *Travels,* 27–28; Olmsted, *Cotton Kingdom,* 86; Schwaab, *Travels Selected from Periodicals,* vol. 2, 394; Shaw, *A Ramble,* 221–22; Albert C. Koch, *Journey Through a Part of the United States of North America in the Years 1844 to 1846,* trans. and ed. Ernst A. Stadler (Carbondale, IL: Southern Illinois University Press, 1972), xxiv.

29. Tocqueville, *Democracy in America,* vol. 1, 364; Mackay, *Western World,* vol. 2, 143, 9; Hopley, *Life in the South,* 123.

30. Shippee, *Whipple's Diary,* 61; Olmsted, *Cotton Kingdom,* 104.

31. Olmsted, *Cotton Kingdom,* 620; Francis J. Grund, *The Americans in Their Moral, Social, and Political Relations,* 2 vols. (London: Longman, Rees et al., 1837), vol. 2, 1–2; Tocqueville, *Democracy in America,* vol. 2, 152.

32. Hall, *Letters from East and West,* 241.

33. J. Benwell, *An Englishman's Travels in America* (London: Binns and Goodwin, 1853), 15–16, 62; Arfwedson, *United States,* vol. 2, 67–68; Franklin, *Southern Odyssey,*

83; Faux, *Days in America,* 263.

34. McGovern, *Yankee Family,* 99, 79; James Blaine Hedges, *The Browns of Providence Plantations* (Providence, RI: Brown University Press, 1968), especially chapter 9, 186–216.

35. Schwaab, *Travels Selected from Periodicals,* vol. 1, 235; Parsons, *Inside View,* 96; Mary Gordon Duffee, *Sketches of Alabama . . . ,* ed. Virginia Pounds Brown and June Porter Nabers (Tuscaloosa, AL: University of Alabama Press, 1970), 12; Lanman, *Adventures,* vol. 1, 2; vol. 2, 277–78; Bernhard, *Travels through North America,* vol. 2, 31; Schwaab, *Travels Selected from Periodicals,* vol. 1, 90; Thomas Ashe, *Travels in America . . . in 1806 . . .* (London: E. M. Blant, 1808), 95; Hugh Jones, *The Present State of Virginia . . . ,* ed. Richard L. Morton (Chapel Hill, NC: University of North Carolina Press, 1956), 80–81; James Silk Buckingham, *The Slave States of America . . . ,* 2 vols. (London: Paris, Fisher, Son and Company, 1842); Burnaby, *Travels,* 15.

36. Owen S. Adams, "Traditional Proverbs and Sayings from California," *Western Folklore* 6 (January 1947), 63; Louis Auguste Felix, Baron de Beaujour, *Sketch of the United States* (London: J. Booth, 1814), 134; Tower, *Slavery Unmasked,* 168–69; Olmsted, *Cotton Kingdom,* 21–22.

37. Tocqueville, *Democracy in America,* 364; Thaddeus Mason Harris, *Journal of a Tour . . .* (Boston: Manning & Lorgin, 1805), 357; Thomas Nuttall, *A Journal of Travel into the Arkansas Territory* (Philadelphia: Thomas W. Palmer, 1821), 69; John Richard Beste, *The Wabash . . . ,* 2 vols. (London: Hearst and Blackett, 1855), vol. 1, 231–32.

38. William Howard Russell, *My Diary North and South,* 2 vols. (London: Bradbury and Evans, 1863), vol. 1, 214, 258–59.

The IRS as a Political Weapon: Political Patronage and Retribution during the Roosevelt Era
Burton W. Folsom Jr.

1. This essay is heavily drawn from the author's *New Deal or Raw Deal? How FDR's Economic Legacy Has Damaged America* (New York: Simon & Schuster, 2008), 146–67. Elliott Roosevelt, *A Rendezvous with Destiny* (New York: G. P. Putnam's Sons, 1975), 102; Roy C. Blakey and Gladys C. Blakey, *The Federal Income Tax* (London: Longmans, Green and Co., 1940); and U.S. Bureau of Census, *Historical Statistics of the United States* (Washington, DC: Government Printing Office, 1975).

2. A good study of Long is in Alan Brinkley, *Voices of Protest: Huey Long, Father Coughlin, and the Great Depression* (New York: Alfred A. Knopf, 1982).

3. T. Harry Williams, *Huey Long* (New York: Alfred A. Knopf, 1969), 635. Forrest McDonald helped raise money at the American History Research Center in Madison, Wisconsin, to help fund research for Williams's book, which won the Pulitzer Prize.

4. Williams, *Long,* 795.

5. Ibid., 639.

6. Ibid., 638.

7. Williams, *Long*, 692–706; Melvin G. Holli, *The Wizard of Washington: Emil Hurja, Franklin Roosevelt, and the Birth of Public Opinion Polling* (New York: Palgrave, 2002), 66–67.

8. Williams, *Long*, 815–16.

9. Holli, *Emil Hurja*, 66–67.

10. Elmer Irey, *The Tax Dodgers* (New York: Greenberg, 1948), 93, 97.

11. Irey, *Tax Dodgers*, 88–117; Williams, *Long*, 794.

12. Irey, 98; David Burnham, *A Law Unto Itself: Power, Politics, and the IRS* (New York: Random House, 1989), 231–36; and Edgar Eugene Robinson, *They Voted for Roosevelt: The Presidential Vote, 1932–1944* (Palo Alto, CA: Stanford University Press, 1947).

13. Roosevelt, *Rendezvous*, 102.

14. Roosevelt, *Rendezvous*, 97; Burnham, *IRS*, 235. On Coughlin, see Francis Biddle, *In Brief Authority* (Westport, CT: Greenwood Press, 1976), 238–39; and Thomas Fleming, *The New Dealers' War* (New York: Basic Books, 2001), 113–14.

15. Roosevelt, *Rendezvous*, 175; Burnham, *IRS*, 235

16. Hamilton Fish, *Memoirs of an American Patriot* (Washington, DC.: Regnery, 1991),143–44.

17. Irey, *Tax Dodgers*, 245–70.

18. Irey, *Tax Dodgers*, 269; Robinson, *They Voted for Roosevelt*, 128.

19. Lyle W. Dorsett, *Franklin D. Roosevelt and the City Bosses* (Port Washington, NY: Kennikat Press, 1977), 98–111.

20. Robinson, *They Voted for Roosevelt*, 128–29.

21. Dorsett, *City Bosses*, 102–5; Robinson, *They Voted for Roosevelt*, 128.

22. Dorsett, *City Bosses*, 98, 106.

23. Many letters and statements describing this corruption are available in the National Archives in File 610, "WPA, New Jersey, Political Coercion." Dorsett, *City Bosses*, 104.

24. Dorsett, *City Bosses*, 103.

25. Ibid., 104.

26. Johnson's background is capably presented by Robert A. Caro, *The Years of Lyndon Johnson: The Path to Power* (New York: Alfred A. Knopf, 1982).

27. Caro, *Path to Power*, 501, 742–53; Robert A. Caro, *The Years of Lyndon Johnson: Means of Ascent* (New York: Alfred A. Knopf, 1990), 15, 16, 74, 272–75, 285–86.

28. Caro, *Path to Power*, 742–53. See also Burnham, 222–23.

29. Lyle W. Dorsett, *The Pendergast Machine* (New York: Oxford University Press, 1968).

30. Dorsett, *City Bosses*, 76; Robinson, *They Voted for Roosevelt*, 118.

31. Dorsett, *City Bosses*, 70–82; Irey, 225–44.

32. Dorsett, *City Bosses*, 70–82.

33. Gary Dean Best, *Pride, Prejudice, and Politics: Roosevelt versus Recovery, 1933–1938* (Westport, CT: Praeger, 1991), 151; Morgenthau Diary, May 14, 1937, Roosevelt Presidential Library.

34. David E. Koskoff, *The Mellons* (New York: Thomas Y. Crowell, Co., 1978).

35. Andrew Mellon, *Taxation: The People's Business* (New York: Macmillan, 1924), 13; Lawrence L. Murray III, "Andrew Mellon: Secretary of the Treasury, 1921–1932: A Study in Policy" (Ph.D. dissertation, Michigan State University, 1970), 111–17.

36. Mellon, *Taxation*, 9, 16–17, 79–81, 96–97; Andrew Mellon, "Taxing Energy and Initiative," *Independent* 112 (March 29, 1924), 168.

37. Mellon, *Taxation*, 9, 51–59.

38. Benjamin G. Rader, "Federal Taxation in the 1920s: A Re-Examination," *Historian* 33 (May 1971), 415–35. I give a summary of the Mellon plan in *The Myth of the Robber Barons* (Herndon, VA: Young America's Foundation, 2003), 103–20.

39. Irey, *Tax Dodgers*, xii–xiii; and Burnham, *IRS*, 229–30.

40. John Morton Blum, *From the Morgenthau Diaries: Years of Crisis, 1928–1938* (Boston: Houghton Mifflin Co., 1959), vol. 1, 324–25.

41. Burnham, *IRS*, 229–30.

42. See Christopher Ogden, *Legacy: A Biography of Moses and Walter Annenberg* (Boston: Little, Brown and Co., 1999); and John Cooney, *The Annenbergs: The Salvaging of a Tainted Dynasty* (New York: Simon and Schuster, 1982).

43. Ogden, *Legacy*, 191.

44. Ogden, *Legacy*, 212–13. Morgenthau Diary, April 11, 1939.

45. Ogden, *Legacy*, 212, 239. Having put Annenberg in jail, Roosevelt was determined to keep him there. Francis Biddle, the president's attorney general, made sure Annenberg's appeals for parole were denied. Harold Ickes, secretary of the interior, wrote the president, "In his much smaller sphere, Annenberg has been as cruel, as ruthless and as lawless as Hitler himself." Roosevelt responded, "I think you are right about Mr. Annenberg."

46. Blum, *Morgenthau Diaries*, vol. 1, 335.

47. Roosevelt, *Rendezvous*, 174–75.

48. Blum, *Morgenthau Diaries*, vol. 1, 327–37.

49. Ibid., 327–29, 333.

50. Roosevelt, *Rendezvous*, 200–201, 174.

51. Ibid., 213.

HISTORICAL CONSCIOUSNESS VERSUS THE WILL TO IGNORANCE
BRUCE P. FROHNEN

1. Forrest McDonald, *Recovering the Past: A Historian's Memoir* (Lawrence, KS: University Press of Kansas, 2005) 10.

2. Ibid.

3. Edmund Burke, "Letter to the Sheriffs of Bristol," *Works* (London: John C. Nimmo, 1899), vol. 2, 234.

4. Burke, "Reflections on the Revolution in France," vol. 2, *Works*, 259–60.

5. Ibid., 272–73.

6. Lois G. Schwoerer, *The Declaration of Rights, 1689* (Baltimore: Johns Hopkins University Press, 1981).

7. Russell Kirk, *Enemies of the Permanent Things* (Peru, IL: Sherwood Sugden & Co., 1988), 119.

8. Russell Kirk, *Eliot and His Age* (Peru, IL: Sherwood Sugden & Co., 1984), 7–8.

9. Burke, "Reflections," 256.

10. Michael A. Ledeen, *The War Against the Terror Masters* (New York: Truman Talley, 2002), 212–13.

11. Joseph A. Schumpeter, *Capitalism, Socialism, and Democracy,* 3rd ed. (New York: Harper, 1950).

12. John Stuart Mill, "On Liberty," *Collected Works of John Stuart Mill,* ed. J. M. Robson, vol. 18 (Toronto: University of Toronto Press, 1977), 224.

13. Ledeen, *The War Against the Terror Masters,* 213. I hereby apologize to Dr. McDonald for ignoring his oft-stated prohibition against long block quotes. In my defense, I would note that, as a political scientist rather than a historian, I am accustomed to readers skipping over vast portions of my writings.

14. George W. Carey, "Traditions at War," *Modern Age* 36 (Spring 1994), 237. Citation omitted.

15. Ibid.

16. Ibid.

17. See the symposium on "Rethinking Rights," *Ave Maria Law Review* 3 (2005): 1.

18. Linda C. Raeder, *John Stuart Mill and the Religion of Humanity* (Columbia, MO: University of Missouri Press, 2002), 12–13. See especially 13, where Raeder quotes John Stuart Mill's approval of his father's doctrine of "'the formation of all human character by circumstances,' most of which are under human control."

19. Ibid., 32, 34.

20. Ibid., 34.

21. Ibid., 18–19.

22. Ibid., 28–29.

23. Ibid., 35–36. I should note, as does Raeder herself, that Raeder's thesis owes much to the work of Joseph Hamburger. See in particular his *John Stuart Mill on Liberty and Control* (Princeton, NJ: Princeton University Press, 1999).

24. Ibid., 75.

25. Ibid., 75.

26. Ibid., 78–79.

27. Eric Voegelin, *The New Science of Politics: An Introduction* (Chicago: University of Chicago Press, 1952).

28. Raeder, *John Stuart Mill and the Religion of Humanity,* 14.

29. Ibid., 49.

30. Ibid., 52.

31. Ibid., 48.

32. Ibid., 241–42.

33. Seymour M. Lipset, The *First New Nation: The United States in Historical and Comparative Perspective* (New York: Basic Books, 1963).

34. Thomas G. West, *Vindicating the Founders: Race, Sex, Class, and Justice in the Origins of America* (Lanham, MD: Rowman & Littlefield, 1997).

35. Harry V. Jaffa, *The American Founding as the Best Regime: The Bonding of Civil and Religious Liberty* (Montclair, CA: Claremont Institute for the Study of Statesmanship and Political Philosophy, 1990).

36. See Sir Herbert Butterfield, *The Whig Interpretation of History* (New York: Norton, [1931] 1965), especially pages v and 5.

37. See especially the discussion provided in Patrick Neal, "Liberalism & Neutrality" *Polity* 17, no. 4 (April 1995), 468–96.

38. Ledeen, *The War Against the Terror Masters*, xix.

39. Raeder, *John Stuart Mill and the Religion of Humanity*, 11–13.

40. Gertrude Himmelfarb, *The De-moralization of Society:From Victorian Virtues to Modern Values* (New York: A. A. Knopf, 1995) 26–28.

41. John Stuart Mill, *On Liberty*, ed. David Spitz (New York: W. W. Norton & Co., [1859] 1975), 60.

42. Robert A. Nisbet, *The Quest for Community* (New York: Oxford University Press, 1953).

THE FOUNDING FATHERS AND THE ECONOMIC ORDER
FORREST MCDONALD

1. This chapter is a transcription of Forrest McDonald's final public speech, delivered to the Economic Club of Indianapolis on April 19, 2006.

Forrest McDonald
Career Notes and Bibliography

FORREST MCDONALD, born Orange, Texas, January 7, 1927. Graduated Orange High School, 1943. Served U.S. Navy, 1945–46. Married Ellen Shapiro 1963. Five children. Nine grandchildren. Three great-grandchildren. Education: B.A., 1949; M.A., 1949; Ph.D., 1955—all University of Texas, Austin.

PROFESSIONAL EMPLOYMENT:
University of Texas, Teaching Fellow, 1950–51
State Historical Society of Wisconsin, 1953–58
Brown University, Associate Professor, 1959–64; Professor, 1964–67
Wayne State University, Professor, 1967–76
University of Alabama, Professor, 1976–87; Distinguished University
    Research Professor, 1987–02; Emeritus, 2002

VISITING PROFESSORSHIPS:
Columbia (1962); Duke (1963); New York University (1966); West Florida
    (1975); James Pinckney Harrison Professor, William and Mary (1986–87)

HONORS AND FELLOWSHIPS:
Social Science Research Council, Research Fellow, 1951–53
Master of Arts, Honorary Degree, Brown, 1962
Guggenheim Fellow, 1962–63
Volker Fund Fellowship, 1962–63

Relm Foundation Fellowship, 1965

Earhart Fellowships, 1969, 1976, 1984

American Council of Learned Societies, Research Grant, 1975

Distinguished Graduate Faculty Award, Wayne State University, 1975

George Washington Medal (Freedom's Foundation), 1980

Fraunces Tavern Book Award for *Alexander Hamilton,* 1980

Outstanding Scholar Award, University of Alabama, 1980

First Burnum Distinguished Faculty Award, University of Alabama, 1980

Mortar Board, Honorary Membership, 1982

Board of Foreign Scholarships (presidential appointment), 1985–87

Finalist, Pulitzer Prize, for *Novus Ordo Seclorum,* 1986

American Revolution Round Table Book Award, 1986

Benchmark Book Award, 1986

National Endowment for the Humanities, 16th Jefferson Lecturer in the
Humanities, 1987

American Antiquarian Society, Membership, 1988

Doctor of Humane Letters, Honorary Degree, SUNY–Geneseo, 1989

Ingersoll Prize, Richard M. Weaver Award for Scholarly Letters, 1990

Heritage Foundation, Salvatori Award for *The American Presidency,* 1994

Frederick Moody Blackmon—Sarah McCorkle Moody Outstanding Professor Award, University of Alabama, 1995

Alabama Library Association 1996 Book Award for *American Presidency*

Templeton Honor Rolls for Education in a Free Society, 1997–98: Professor;
Scholarly Book, *We the People*

Mount Vernon Society and the Organization of American Historians chose
Presidency of George Washington one of the Ten Great Books on Washington, 1998

Gerhart Niemeyer Award for Distinguished Contributions to Scholarship,
Intercollegiate Studies Institute, 2003

ADVISORY AND PROFESSIONAL SERVICES:

Rovensky Fellowship Selection Committee, 1965–88

Contributor, *National Review,* 1978–2001

Board of Editors, *Continuity,* 1980–2000

Richard M. Weaver Fellowship Selection Committee, ISI, 1980–

Encyclopedia Britannica Editorial Review Board, 1981–82

Faculty Advisor, *The Southern Historian,* 1983–89

Bicentennial of the Constitution, Claremont Advisory Board, 1983–89
Board of Editors, *Intercollegiate Review,* 1984–2002
Reader, National Graduate Fellow Program, 1985, 1986
Academic Board, National Humanities Institute, 1985–
Advisory Board, *Constitution,* 1988–94
Academic Council, National Legal Center for the Public Interest, 1988–94
Advisory Board, *Campus* Magazine, 1990–2002
Editorial Board, *Encyclopedia of the American Constitution,* 1990–92
Secretary of the Publications Committee, St. George Tucker Society, 1991–92
Advisory Council, Center for the Study of Interactive Learning, 1992–2002
President, 1988–90; Trustee, 1983–86, 1988–91, 1994–97, Philadelphia Society
Academic Sponsor, Earhart Fellowship Program, 1993–96
Selection Committee, Adair Prize Committee, 1995–96
Senior Fellow, Grady McWhiney Research Foundation, 1997–
Lady Thatcher Essay Competition Judge, Intercollegiate Studies Institute, 1997

BIOGRAPHICAL AND HISTORICAL ARTICLES ABOUT MCDONALD:
"Forrest McDonald," by Justus Doenecke, *The Dictionary of Literary Biography,* vol. 17 (Detroit: Gale Research, 1983)
"If Jefferson et al Could See Us Now," by Leslie Werner, *New York Times,* Feb. 12, 1987
"Forrest McDonald, the 1987 Jefferson Lecturer," by Linda Blanken, *Humanities,* March–April 1987
"Historian Calls for Sustained Adherence to the Framers' Precepts," by Angus Paul, *Chronicle of Higher Education,* May 6, 1987
Who's Who in America, 45th edition, 1988; 46th, 1990; 47th, 1992; 48th, 1994
Also listed in "The World Who's Who of Authors," 1975; "Dictionary of International Biography," 1976, 1979, 1982, 1985; "Directory of American Scholars," starting in the 6th ed.; "The International Authors and Writers Who's Who," starting in the 8th ed.; "Men of Achievement," 5th ed.; "Community Leaders and Noteworthy Americans," 9th, 11th eds.; "International Who's Who in Education," 1980; "International Who's Who in Community Service," 3rd ed.; "Who's Who in the South and Southwest," starting in the 17th ed.

Interview transcript in *Booknotes,* by Brian Lamb, (New York: Time Books, 1997)

"Live with TAE," by Bill Kauffman, *The American Enterprise,* October–November 2001

Books:

Let There Be Light: The Electric Utility Industry in Wisconsin (Madison, WI: American History Research Center, 1957)

We the People: The Economic Origins of the Constitution (Chicago: University of Chicago Press, 1958; new ed., New Brunswick, NJ: Transaction Press, 1992)

Insull (Chicago: University of Chicago Press, 1962; new title ed., Frederick, MD: Beard Books, 2005)

E Pluribus Unum: The Formation of the American Republic (Boston: Houghton Mifflin, 1965: new ed., Indianapolis: Liberty Press, 1979)

The Presidency of George Washington (Lawrence, KS: University Press of Kansas, 1974; paperback ed., 1985)

The Phaeton Ride: The Crisis of American Success (New York: Doubleday, 1974)

The Presidency of Thomas Jefferson (Lawrence, KS: University Press of Kansas, 1976; paperback ed., 1987)

Alexander Hamilton: A Biography (New York: Norton, 1979; paperback ed., 1980; www.questia.com media service, 2002)

Novus Ordo Seclorum: The Intellectual Origins of the Constitution (Lawrence, KS: University Press of Kansas, 1988), with Ellen Shapiro McDonald

The American Presidency: An Intellectual History (Lawrence, KS: University Press of Kansas, 1995; paperback ed., 1995)

States' Rights and the Union: Imperium in Imperio, 1776–1876 (Lawrence, KS: University Press of Kansas, 2000; paperback ed., 2000)

Recovering the Past: A Historian's Memoir (Lawrence, KS: University Press of Kansas, 2004)

Children's Books:

Enough Wise Men: The Story of Our Constitution (New York: G. P. Putnam, 1970)

The Boys Were Men: The American Navy in the Age of Fighting Sail (New York: G. P. Putnam, 1971)

TEXTBOOKS:

The Torch Is Passed: The United States in the Twentieth Century (Reading, MA: Addison-Wesley, 1969)

The Last Best Hope: A History of the United States (Reading, MA: Addison-Wesley, 1972) in one, two, or three vols., with Leslie E. Decker and Thomas P. Govan

A Constitutional History of the United States (New York: Franklin Watts, 1982; new ed., Florida: Krieger, 1986)

EDITED VOLUMES:

Empire and Nation: John Dickinson and Richard Henry Lee (Englewood Cliffs, NJ: Prentice-Hall, 1962; new ed., Indianapolis: Liberty Fund, 1999)

Confederation and Constitution, 1781–1789 (New York: Harper & Row, 1968), with Ellen Shapiro McDonald

SECONDARY AUTHORSHIP:

First Hand America, David Burner with Eugene Genovese, Elizabeth Fox-Genovese, Forrest McDonald (St. James, NY: Brandywine Press, 1990)

FOREWORD OR PREFACE TO:

Still the Law of the Land? Essays on Changing Interpretations of the Constitution, Joseph McNamara and Lissa Roche, eds. (Hillsdale, MI: Hillsdale College Press, 1987)

Charles C. Thach Jr., *The Creation of the Presidency, 1775–1789* (Indianapolis: Liberty Fund, 2007)

Burton W. Folsom Jr., *Entrepreneurs vs. the State* (Reston, VA: Young America's Foundation, 1987)

Ratifying the Constitution, Michael Allen Gillespie and Michael Lienesch, eds. (Lawrence, KS: University Press of Kansas, 1989)

The Constitution and the American Presidency, Martin L. Fausold and Alan Shank, eds. (Albany, NY: SUNY Press, 1991)

M. E. Bradford, *Original Intentions* (Athens, GA: University of Georgia Press, 1992)

F. Clifton White, *Suite 3505* (Ashland, OH: John M. Ashbrook Center, 1993)

Raoul Berger, *Government by Judiciary,* 2nd ed. (Indianapolis: Liberty Fund, 1997)

Russell Kirk, *The Roots of American Order* (Wilmington, DE: Intercollegiate Studies Institute, 2003)

Joseph Addison, *Cato and Selected Essays* (Indianapolis: Liberty Fund, 2004)

Lori J. Owens, *Original Intent and Judicial Confirmation* (Lewiston, NY: Edwin Mellen Press, 2006)

CHAPTERS IN PUBLISHED VOLUMES:

"The Fourth Phase: The Completion of the Continental Union, 1789–1792," *Fame and the Founding Fathers,* Edmund Willis, ed. (Bethlehem, PA: Moravian College, 1967)

"Charles A. Beard," *Pastmasters: Some Essays on American Historians,* Marcus Cunliffe and Robin Winks, eds. (New York: Harper & Row, 1969)

"Background Essay on the Constitutional Convention," *The American Constitution: A Simulation Exercise,* William Coplin and Leonard Stittleman, eds. (Chicago: Science Research Associates, 1969)

"The American Revolution in International and Regional Perspective," *Perspectives on the American Revolution,* James Haw, ed. (Fort Wayne, IN: Indiana University Council on the Humanities, 1975)

"The Constitution and Hamiltonian Capitalism," *How Capitalistic Was the Constitution?* Robert Goldwin and William Schambra, eds. (Washington, DC: American Enterprise Institute, 1982)

"A New Introduction," Charles A. Beard, *An Economic Interpretation of the Constitution of the United States* (New York: Free Press, 1986)

"Interpreting the Constitution: Judges versus History," *John M. Olin Lectures on the Bicentennial* (Washington, DC: Young America's Foundation, 1987)

"Prologue," Grady McWhiney, *Cracker Culture: Celtic Ways in the Old South* (Tuscaloosa, AL: University of Alabama Press, 1988)

"Economic Freedom and the Constitution: The Design of the Framers," *Public Choice and Constitutional Economics,* James Gwartney and Richard Wagner, eds. (Greenwich, CT: JAI Press, 1988)

"Forrest McDonald: Historian," Bill Moyers, *A World of Ideas: Conversations with Thoughtful Men and Women about American Life Today and the Ideas Shaping Our Future* (New York: Doubleday, 1989)

"Introduction," *Records of the Debates in the Federal Convention of 1787 as Reported by James Madison* (Birmingham, AL: Legal Classics Library, 1989)

"Cultural Continuity and the Shaping of the American South," *Geographic Perspectives in History,* Eugene Genovese and Leonard Hochberg, eds. (Oxford: Basil Blackwell, 1989)

"Washington, Cato, and Honor: A Model for Revolutionary Leadership,"

American Models of Revolutionary Leadership, Daniel J. Elazar and Ellis Katz, eds. (Lanham, MD: University Press of American, 1992)

"I Have Seen the Past and It Works," *Derailing the Constitution: The Undermining of American Federalism,* Edward B. McLean, ed. (Bryn Mawr, PA: Intercollegiate Studies Institute, 1994)

"The Bill of Rights: Unnecessary and Pernicious," *The Bill of Rights: Government Proscribed,* Peter Albert, ed. (Charlottesville, VA: University of Virginia Press, 1997)

"George Washington: Today's Indispensable Man," *Patriot Sage: George Washington and the American Political Tradition,* Gary L. Gregg II and Matthew Spalding, eds. (Wilmington, DE: ISI Books, 1999)

"Presidential Character: The Example of George Washington," in *The Presidency Then and Now,* Phillip G. Henderson, ed. (Lanham, MD: Rowman & Littlefield, 2000); earlier in *Perspectives on Political Science,* Summer 1997

"Thomas Jefferson," *Presidential Leadership: Rating the Best and the Worst in the White House,* James Taranto and Leonard Leo, eds. (New York: Dow Jones, 2004)

"Preamble," *The Heritage Guide to the United States Constitution,* Matthew Spalding and David Forte, eds. (Washington, DC: Heritage Foundation, 2005)

ARTICLES IN DICTIONARIES AND ENCYCLOPEDIAS:

"Samuel Insull," in *Dictionary of American Biography* (New York: Charles Scribner's Sons, 1958); in *Encyclopedia Britannica* (Chicago: William Benton, 1959); and in *Encyclopedia Americana* (New York: Americana Corporation, 1970)

"Floyd Leslie Carlisle, "Harvey Crowley Couch," "Matthew Scott Sloan" in *Dictionary of American Biography* (New York: Charles Scribner's Sons, 1972)

"United States History, 1763–1816," in *Encyclopedia Britannica* (Chicago: William Benton, 1974)

"John Dickinson," "Alexander Hamilton," "Samuel Insull," "J. P. Morgan," "Gouverneur Morris," "John Randolph" "Jacob Schiff," and "Roger Sherman," in *American Biographical Encyclopedia* (Phoenix: P. W. Pollock, 1974)

"Articles of Confederation," "Continental Congress," "Constitutional Convention," "Declaration of Independence," "Federalist Essays," "Federalist Party," and "Hartford Convention," in *Academic American Encyclopedia* (Princeton, NJ: Arete Publishing Company, 1980)

"Conservatism," in *Encyclopedia of American Political History* (New York: Charles Scribner's Sons, 1984)

"Irish," "Scotch-Irish," "Scots, Highland" and "Celtic South," with Grady McWhiney, in *Encyclopedia of Southern Culture* (Chapel Hill, NC: University of North Carolina Press, 1989)

"Pardon Power," "Tenth Amendment," and "Alexander Hamilton," in *The Oxford Companion to the Supreme Court of the United States* (New York: Oxford University Press, 1992)

"George Washington," "Executive Prerogative," and "Albert Gallatin," in *The Encyclopedia of the American Presidency* (New York: Simon and Schuster, 1994)

"The Cabinet," in *The Constitution and Its Amendments,* 4 vols. for junior high students (New York: Macmillan Reference, 2000)

"Alexander Hamilton," *New Dictionary of National Biography* (Oxford: Oxford University Press, 2003)

"John Dickinson," "Alexander Hamilton," and Gouverneur Morris," in *American Conservatism: An Encyclopedia* (Wilmington, DE: ISI Books, 2005)

"Alexander Hamilton," in *American National Biography* (New York: Oxford University Press, 1999)

ARTICLES:

"The Relation of the French Peasant Veterans of the American Revolution to the Fall of Feudalism in France," *Agricultural History,* October 1951; reprinted in *The Military and Society,* ed. Peter Karsten (Hamden, CT: Garland, 1998)

"The People Get a Light," *Wisconsin Magazine of History,* Spring 1954

"The Complete Historian," *Wisconsin Magazine of History,* Summer 1957

"Street Cars and Politics in Milwaukee, 1896–1901," *Wisconsin Magazine of History,* Spring 1956 and Summer 1956

"Samuel Insull and the Movement for State Utility Regulatory Commissions," *Business History Review,* Autumn 1958

"Rebuttal to 'Charles A. Beard and the Constitution: A Critical Review of Forrest McDonald's *We the People,*'" *William and Mary Quarterly,* January 1960; also in Bobbs-Merrill Reprint Series, H-141, 1963; reprinted in *The Declaration of Independence and the Constitution,* Earl Latham, ed. (Lexington, KY: D. C. Heath, 1976)

"HUAC and the Popular Majority," *Supplement* to the *Brown Daily Herald*, Providence, RI, June 2, 1961

"The Papers of Alexander Hamilton," review articles appearing in the *William and Mary Quarterly*, January 1963, January 1969, October 1974, October 1976, October 1977, April 1980

"The Anti-Federalists, 1781–1789," *Wisconsin Magazine of History*, Spring 1963; also in *Reinterpretation of the American Revolution*, Jack Greene, ed. (New York: Harper & Row, 1968), and in *American History: Recent Interpretations*, Abraham Eisenstadt, ed. (New York: Thomas Y. Crowell, 1969)

"Constitutional Aspects of American Federalism," *Canadian Historical Association Report*, June 1964

"The Antebellum Southern Herdsman: A Reinterpretation," with Grady McWhiney *Journal of Southern History*, May 1975; also in *The Southern Common People: Studies in Nineteenth-Century Social History*, Edward Magdol and Jon I. Wakelyn, eds. (Westport, CT: Greenwood, 1980)

"A Mirror for Presidents," *Commentary*, December 1976

"In Search of Southern Roots," with Grady McWhiney, *Reviews in American History*, December 1977

"A Founding Father's Library," *Literature of Liberty*, January–March 1978

"The Ethnic Factor in Alabama History: A Neglected Dimension," *Alabama Review*, October 1978

"George Washington, Symbol of Nationhood," Public Research Syndicated, February 1979; e.g., "How George Washington Sculpted the Presidency," *Quad City Times* (IA), May 1980; *Tuscaloosa News*, February 12, 1989

"A Comment," *Journal of Politics*, February 1980

"The Ethnic Origins of the American People, 1790," with Ellen Shapiro McDonald, *William and Mary Quarterly*, April 1980

"The Hostage Crisis of 1803," *Washington Post*, May 20, 1980; also under a different title, *Newsday*, May 8, 1980; and Public Research Syndicated

"The Celtic South," with Grady McWhiney, *History Today*, July 1980

"The First President and the Presidency Today," Public Research Syndicated, May 1980; e.g., February 21, 1988, *Washington Times*, *Tuscaloosa News*, and *Providence Journal*; also under title, "George Washington and Origins of the Presidency," in *The New Federalist Papers*, eds. J. Jackson Barlow, Dennis Mahoney, and John West (Lanham, MD: University Press of America, 1989)

"Understanding Alexander Hamilton," *National Review*, July 11, 1980

"The South from Self-Sufficiency to Peonage: An Interpretation," with Grady McWhiney, *American Historical Review*, December 1980

"The Rhetoric of Alexander Hamilton," *Modern Age*, March 1981; also in *Rhetoric and American Statesmanship*, Jeffrey Wallin and Glen Thurow, eds. (Durham, NC: Carolina Academic Press, 1983), and in Modern Age: *The First Twenty-Five Years*, George A. Panichas, ed. (Indianapolis: Liberty Press, 1988)

"The Unsinkable Myths," *National Review*, September 4, 1981

"Conservative Scholarship and the Problem of Myth," *Continuity*, Spring/ Fall 1982

"AHR Forum: Comparative History in Theory and Practice," with Grady McWhiney, *American Historical Review*, February 1982

"Celtic Names in the Antebellum Southern United States," with Grady McWhiney, *Names: Journal of the American Names Society*, June 1983

"How Conservatism Guided America's Founding," *Imprimis*, July 1983

"The Historical Roots of the Originating Clause," with Michael Mendle, *Modern Age*, Summer/Fall 1983

"Forum: Does America Still Exist?" *Harper's*, March 1984

"Commentary: United States Population, 1790," with Ellen Shapiro McDonald, *William and Mary Quarterly*, January 1984

"Why Yankees Can't (and Won't) Leave the South Alone," *Southern Partisan*, January 1985; also in Oran P. Smith, ed., *So Good a Cause* (Columbia, SC: The Foundation for American Education, 1993)

"Celtic Origins of Southern Herding Practices," with Grady McWhiney, *Journal of Southern History*, May 1985

"Russell Kirk: The American Cicero," *National Review*, December 31, 1985; also in *The Unbought Grace of Life: Essays in Honor of Russell Kirk* (Chicago: Open Court, 1994)

"Character in Acting," *Chronicles*, June 1987

"Capitalism and the Constitution," *The World & I*, June 1987

"Economic Freedom and the Constitution: The Design of the Framers," *Florida Policy Review*, Summer 1987

"To Secure the Blessings of Liberty: The Making of the Constitution," *The World & I*, September 1987; "Understanding the Constitution: Three Bicentennial Lectures," *Colorado College Studies*, 1988

"Supreme Court Nominees: A Look at the Precedents," *Wall Street Journal*, September 16, 1987; and in "Hearings before the Committee of the Judiciary, U.S. Senate on the Nomination of Robert H. Bork," Part 2, Serial No. J-100–64 (Washington, DC, 1989)

"The Constitution at 200: Is It Time to Change the System?" *St. Petersburg Times,* September 6, 1987, and special section, September 17, 1987

"The Middle Delegates in the Convention," *Political Science Reviewer,* Fall 1987; abstracted in *International Political Science Abstracts,* 1989

"Line-Item Veto: Older than the Constitution," *Wall Street Journal,* March 7, 1988; "The Framers' Conception of the Veto Power," in *Pork Barrels and Principles* (Washington, DC: National Legal Center for the Public Interest, 1988); and in *The Congressional Record,* May 15, 1994

"The Scarlet Letter: The Private Lives of Public Figures," a symposium, *Policy Review,* Spring 1988

"John Dickinson, Founding Father," with Ellen Shapiro McDonald, *Delaware History,* Spring/Summer 1988

"How Great Was Ronald Reagan?" a symposium, *Policy Review,* Fall 1988

"The Democratic Chimera," *The World & I,* July 1989

"A Republic, Madam, If You Can Keep It," with Ellen Shapiro McDonald, *Notre Dame Journal of Law, Ethics & Public Policy,* July 1989

"Cleaning Up the Justices' Messes," *Wall Street Journal,* July 31, 1989

"How the Fourteenth Amendment Repealed the Constitution," *Chronicles,* October 1989

"Rugged Individualism: Frederick Jackson Turner and the Frontier Thesis," *The World & I,* May 1990

"On the Study of History," *Chronicles,* February 1991

"Was the Fourteenth Amendment Constitutionally Adopted?" *Georgia Journal of Southern Legal History,* Spring/Summer 1991

"A Nation Once Again?" *National Review,* July 11, 1994

"The American Presidency: Has It Helped Us 'To Form a More Perfect Union?'" Heritage Lecture Series Pamphlet No. 498, October 1994

"Sacrifices the Founders Made for the Common Good," *American Civilization,* March 1995

"George Washington: Today's Indispensable Man," *Intercollegiate Review,* Spring 1995; also in *Tuscaloosa News,* February 19, 1995, and other newspapers across the country

"National Standards for United States History: An Idea Whose Time Should Never Come," *Continuity,* Spring 1995

"Colliding with the Past," *Reviews in American History,* March 1997

"Blues, Baptists and Bacon Grease—The Southernization of America," *San Diego Union Tribune,* April 3, 1997

"Images and Realities—The Two Sides of JFK," *San Diego Union-Tribune,* December 17, 1997

"Unmaking of the Presidency," *National Review,* March 23, 1998

"The Political Thought of Gouverneur Morris," *Continuity,* Spring 1998

"Original Unintentions: The Franchise and the Constitution, *Modern Age,* Fall 1998

"Background and History of Impeachment," Hearing before the Subcommittee on the Constitution, House of Representatives, Serial No. 63, November 9, 1998, Washington, DC, GPO, 214–18

"Clinton, the Country, and the Political Culture: A Symposium," *Commentary,* January 1999

"The Clinton Presidency: A Symposium," *Continuity,* Fall 2001

"Debt & Taxes," *Claremont Review of Books,* Winter 2003

MOVIE SCRIPT:

"Design for Liberty: The American Constitution," Liberty Fund production through Wadlow Grosvernor International, London, 1986

BOOK REVIEWS:

More than 150. Appearing in: *American Historical Review, Benchmark, Business History Review, Chronicles, Claremont Review of Books, Commentary, Detroit News, Fillson's Quarterly, Humanitas, Journal of American History, Journal of Economic History, Journal of Southern History, Maryland Historical Magazine, National Review, New England Quarterly, New York Historical Society Quarterly, New York Times Book Review, Pennsylvania Magazine of History and Biography, South Atlantic Quarterly, Southern Partisan, St. Petersburg* (FL) *Times,* (London) *Times Literary Supplement, University Bookman, Virginia Quarterly Review, Washington Times, William and Mary Quarterly, Wisconsin Magazine of History*

EXCERPTS REPRINTED FROM MCDONALD'S BOOKS CAN BE FOUND IN VARIOUS ANTHOLOGIES AND TEACHING COLLECTIONS; SEE, FOR EXAMPLE,

Leonard W. Levy, ed., *Essays on the Making of the Constitution* (New York: Oxford University Press: 1969)—"We the People"

Earl Latham, ed., *Declaration of Independence and the Constitution* (Boston: D.C. Heath, 1976)—"We the People"

Eugene D. Genovese and Forrest McDonald, *Debates on American History* (St. James, NY: Brandywine Press, 1981); pamphlet taken from *An American Portrait: A History of the United States* by David Burner and Tom West (New York: Scribner)

Taking Sides: Clashing Views on Controversial Issues in American History (Guilford, CT, Dushkin Publishing) (1987)—"We the People" (1989)—"The Presidency of Thomas Jefferson"

Journal of Business Leadership (1989)—"Insull"

Lance Banning, ed., *After the Constitution: Party Conflict in the New Republic* (Belmont, CA: Wadsworth, 1989)—"Presidency of Thomas Jefferson"

Wilcox, ed., *Readings in American History* (vol. 1, 1985)—"Alexander Hamilton"

Allen F. Davis and Harold D. Woodman, eds., *Conflict and Consensus: Early American History* (Houghton Mifflin, 1988)—"Novus Ordo Seclorum"

Bilagtortenet (World History, Institute of History of the Hungarian Academy), 1988—"Constitutional History of the United States"

Kermit Hall, ed., *Major Problems in American Constitutional History* (Belmont, CA: Wadsworth, 1992)—"Novus Ordo Seclorum"

Contributors

James M. Albritton is assistant professor of history at Huntingdon College in Montgomery, Alabama. Previously he served as dean of faculty and academics and as assistant headmaster of Trinity Presbyterian School in Montgomery. He earned his Ph.D. in 2003 at the University of Alabama at Tuscaloosa, where Forrest McDonald directed his dissertation on John Witherspoon's view of the relationship between church and state in America. Albritton also holds a master of divinity degree from Covenant Theological Seminary. He is the author of several articles and book reviews and the recipient of several awards.

J. M. Bumsted is a retired professor of history at the University of Manitoba. He received his B.A. from Tufts College and his Ph.D. from Brown University. While attending Brown he took courses with Forrest McDonald, who converted him into a research-oriented historian. Bumsted has taught at Tufts University, Simon Fraser University, and the University of Manitoba. He has published more than thirty books, mainly in Canadian history. He is a member of the Royal Society of Canada and has served as president of the Manitoba Historical Society (2006–8).

Lenore T. Ealy is president of Thinkitecture, Inc., a consultancy engaged in understanding and promoting the transformative work of philanthropy and the voluntary sector. Since 2001 she has been director of The Project for New Philanthropy Studies at DonorsTrust and is currently an affiliated senior scholar with the Mercatus Center at George Mason University. She is the founding editor of *Conversations on Philanthropy*, an occasional journal that explores the role of philanthropy in a free society, and was coeditor, with Robert C. Enlow, of *Liberty and Learning: Milton Friedman's Voucher Idea at Fifty* (2006). Ealy earned an M.A. in history from the University of Alabama, where she studied with Forrest McDonald, and took her Ph.D. in the history of moral and political thought from the Johns Hopkins University. She has held professional positions at the Milton & Rose D. Friedman Foundation, the Intercollegiate Studies Institute, and the Heritage Foundation, and is a past trustee of The Philadelphia Society.

Steven D. Ealy is a senior fellow at Liberty Fund. From 1981 to 1993 he was professor of government at Armstrong State College in Savannah, Georgia. Ealy received his Ph.D. in political science at the University of Georgia. He is the author of *Communication, Speech, and Politics: Habermas and Political Analysis* (1981). His recent work includes a number of articles on Robert Penn Warren and articles on the intellectual foundations of American philanthropy and on constitutional interpretation. He also recently coedited the Eric Voegelin–Willmoore Kendall correspondence for the *Political Science Reviewer*. He serves on the Board of Visitors for the Pepperdine University School of Public Policy, is a contributing editor of *Conversations on Philanthropy*, and is a member of the Advisory Editorial Board of *Society*.

Burton W. Folsom Jr. is Charles Kline Professor of History and Management at Hillsdale College. Folsom received his Ph.D. at the University of Pittsburgh (under Samuel P. Hays) in 1976 and has taught at the University of Pittsburgh, the University of Nebraska, Murray State University, and Northwood University. Folsom has also been a senior fellow at the Mackinac Center for Public Policy in Midland, Michigan, and historian in residence at the Center for the American Idea in Houston, Texas. His books include *Urban Capitalists* (1981), *Empire Builders* (1998), and *The Myth of the Robber Barons* (1987), which is in its fourth edition and includes a foreword by Forrest McDonald. Folsom's latest book, *New Deal or Raw Deal? How FDR's Economic Legacy Has Damaged America*, was published in 2008 by Simon & Schuster.

Bruce P. Frohnen is associate professor of law at Ohio Northern University College of Law. Among his books are *Virtue and the Promise of Conservatism: The*

Legacy of Burke and Tocqueville; The New Communitarians and the Crisis of Modern Liberalism; Rethinking Rights: Political, Historical, and Philosophical Perspectives (editor, with Kenneth L. Grasso), and *American Conservatism: An Encyclopedia* (editor, with Jeremy Beer and Jeffrey O. Nelson). His articles on topics ranging from constitutional history to city planning have appeared in such journals as the *Harvard Journal of Law & Public Policy, Modern Age,* and the *George Washington Law Review.* He is editor of the *Political Science Reviewer.*

J. Crawford King teaches at John C. Calhoun Community College in Decatur, Alabama. He is the author of "The Closing of the Southern Range: An Exploratory Study," published in the February 1982 issue of the *Journal of Southern History.* Following a temporary appointment at Samford University, he taught at the Saint James School in Montgomery, where he was also high school principal. A native of Evergreen, Alabama, he graduated Phi Beta Kappa and magna cum laude from the University of Alabama in 1976, where he also obtained his M.A. and Ph.D.

Elric M. Kline is a candidate for the Ph.D. in political science from Rutgers University. He is writing a dissertation under Drucilla Cornell and Stephen Bronner, applying critical theory to understand the ideological function of conceptions of free will and determinism. At Rutgers he teaches legal philosophy, gender and political theory, and democratic philosophy. He has also taught political economy and American politics at Lehigh University, where he earned his M.A. in 2004. He graduated Phi Beta Kappa and magna cum laude from Moravian College in 2001 with a B.A. in mathematics and philosophy.

Stephen M. Klugewicz is director of education of the National Constitution Center in Philadelphia. A native of Bowie, Maryland, he earned his M.A. and Ph.D. in American history at the University of Alabama, where Forrest McDonald directed his dissertation. His academic concentration was eighteenth- and nineteenth-century American political and intellectual history. He has served as director of education programs at the Bill of Rights Institute, executive director of the Collegiate Network, and executive director of The Robert and Marie Hansen Foundation. Klugewicz has also worked as a consultant to nonprofit organizations, and spent seven years teaching at private secondary schools. His writing—on history, politics, and classical music—has been published in various academic and popular journals. He and his wife, Kerri, have four young children: Teresa, 7; Madeleine, 5; Andrew, 3; and Isabelle, 1.

Richard K. Matthews is the NEH Distinguished Professor of Political Science and chair of the political science department at Lehigh University in Bethlehem, Pennsylvania. Professor Matthews has received several excellence-in-teaching awards, including the 1991 CASE Pennsylvania Professor of the Year award. At Lehigh he offers courses in the history of Western political thought, political ideologies, and American political thought. He is the author of *The Radical Politics of Thomas Jefferson: A Revisionist View* (1986) and *If Men Were Angels: James Madison and the Heartless Empire of Reason* (1995). He is the editor of *Virtue, Corruption, and Self-Interest: Political Values in the Eighteenth Century* (1994), and the coauthor of *The Philosophic Roots of Modern Ideology: Liberalism, Conservatism, Communism, Fascism, Islamism* (4th ed., 2010). Currently, Matthews is working on a book on the political thought of Alexander Hamilton.

Melanie Randolph Miller is the editor of the Gouverneur Morris Papers: Diaries Project, an NEH-funded project to transcribe and annotate the 1794–98 diaries of Gouverneur Morris. She has a B.S. in aeronautical engineering from the Massachusetts Institute of Technology, a J.D. from the Boalt Hall School of Law at UC–Berkeley, and a Ph.D. in American history from George Washington University. She is the author of a book about Morris's years in Paris titled *Envoy to the Terror: Gouverneur Morris and the French Revolution* (2005), and of a short life of Morris titled *An Incautious Man: The Life of Gouverneur Morris* (2008). She worked for the Federal Aviation Administration for many years and continues to consult for the agency in the area of international agreements.

F. Thornton Miller is professor of history at Missouri State University. He received his Ph.D. at the University of Alabama in 1986 and has taught at the University of Alabama, Birmingham Southern College, and Huntingdon College. He has published a monograph, *Juries and Judges Versus the Law: Virginia's Provincial Legal Perspective, 1783–1828* (1994), and is the editor of a critical edition of John Taylor's *Tyranny Unmasked* (1992). His many articles on legal and constitutional history and the history of the early American republic have appeared in such periodicals as the *Virginia Magazine of History and*

Biography and the *John Marshall Law Review,* and in such reference volumes as *Historic U.S. Court Cases* (1992, 2001), *Great Justices of the U.S. Supreme Court* (1993), *The American Presidents* (2000), and *Encyclopedia of American Civil Liberties* (2006).

Adam Tate is associate professor of history at Clayton State University in Morrow, Georgia. He is the author of *Conservatism and Southern Intellectuals, 1789–1861* (2005). He earned both his M.A. (1996) and his Ph.D. (2001) from the University of Alabama, where he studied with Forrest McDonald.

C. Bradley Thompson is the BB&T Research Professor and professor of political science at Clemson University. He is also the executive director of the Clemson Institute for the Study of Capitalism. Thompson is the author of the award-winning *John Adams and the Spirit of Liberty* (1998). He also edited *The Revolutionary Writings of John Adams* (2000) and *Antislavery Political Writings, 1833–1860: A Reader* (2004). He is currently completing two books, one titled *The Ideological Origins of American Constitutionalism* and another titled *Our Killing Schools: How America's "Ed" Schools are Destroying the Minds and Souls of Our Children.*

Karl Walling is professor in the Department of Strategy and Policy at the U.S. Naval War College. He earned his B.A. from St. John's College in Annapolis, Maryland, in 1984, and a joint Ph.D. from the Department of Political Science and the Committee on Social Thought at the University of Chicago in 1992. He has held academic appointments at Michigan State University, the University of Chicago, Carleton College, Colorado College, Ashland University, and the United States Air Force Academy, where he was voted the best professor in the social sciences in 1995. He has been a program officer at Liberty Fund, a fellow in the Program on Constitutional Government at Harvard University (1992), and a John M. Olin Fellow in History and Political Philosophy (1996). His books include *Republican Empire: Alexander Hamilton on War and Free Government* (2000) and *Strategic Logic and Political Rationality* (2002), coedited with Brad Lee. He is currently at work on a book titled *Strategy and Politics in Thucydides'* Peloponnesian War.

Index